YOU ARE A CHAMPION

YOU ARE A CHAMPION

A Memoir of Miracles and Pure Resilience in Crisis

ELLENOR P. RATCLIFF

LNOIR'S FIDELITY PUBLISHING, LLC

Houston, Texas

2020

Published by Lnoir's Fidelity Publishing, LLC.,

Lnoir's Fidelity Publishing, LLC., Registered Offices:
5900 Balcones Drive, Ste 100, Austin, Texas 78731

Copyright © Ellenor Perkins Ratcliff, 2020
All rights reserved.

Page 437 constitutes an extension of this copyright page.

Illustrated Edition, Part 1
ISBN 978-1-735-2806-1-5 (paper)
ISBN 978-1-735-2806-0-8 (e-book)

Printed in the United States of America
Cover Art by MICHAEL LAFRANCE LYNCH
Book Design & Concept by ELLENOR PERKINS RATCLIFF

No part of this publication may be reproduced or transmitted in any form or by any means, electronic or mechanical, including photocopy, recording, or any information storage and retrieval system, without permission in writing from the publisher.

Requests for permissions of this work should be submitted to the following address: Permission Department, Lnoir's Fidelity Publishing, LLC., www.LnoirsFidelityPublishing.com

DISCLAIMER

No information pertaining within this book is legal advice. The author and publisher hold no liabilities of its use. This work has been provided for educational purposes and is told in the truth of real life experience of the author and individual told stories, with individuals and organizations listed herein. I am not an attorney; the reader should contact their attorney for advice regarding their particular legal issue or to verify truth of the contents herein. Before acting on any information given within the book, you, the reader, should first seek legal advice from legal counsel in your proper jurisdiction, regarding your particular legal issue. Third-party links have been provided for the convenience of the reader. All links should be individually verified. I make no recommendations or endorse any third-party sites. The author and publisher hold no liability to the use of contents within this book.

This book is dedicated to all suffering persecution.

God has seen the oppression and God said, "Retribution is Coming."

Draw near to God.

NO LIE CAN LIVE FOREVER!

Contents

Author's Note

Introduction 1

Chapter 1: The Beginning

Strange Place 3

Trouble with GDIT!

Hidden Destiny, Come, Find Me 5

Transportation Service

Unforeseen Circumstance #1 8

Work Injury

Help! 9

Human Resource Horror& Harris Health System

Hidden Destiny, Come, Find Me 10

Chapter 2: Constructive Discharge

The Finally 16

U. S. EEOC Intake

Journey for Justice 18

U. S. EEOC Visit

Journey for Justice 21

Harris Health System

Are You Afraid of My Employer? 22

Disability Rights Texas 23

Auto Accident

Unforeseen Circumstance #2 24

Chapter 3: U. S. EEOC, The White House, Texas Department of Human Service, CMS and Department of Justice

Journey for Justice 25

Texas Department of Insurance

GDIT, Attorney & Broadspire - Workers' Compensation 26

Legal Assistance

Desperate but Hopeful 29

U. S. EEOC, The White House & Department of Justice

Journey for Justice 30

Police /Vehicle Profiling

Young Men Experience 32

U.S. EEOC

God is Merciful 33

Chapter 4: U. S. Southern District of Texas

Journey for Justice 38

God Will Encourage You

Push Baby Push! 42

Department of Justice

Response 43

The Miracle Worker

God Did It! 43

Others See Your Success

Do You Have the Faith? 44

The Pain

Green Backpack 44

Texas Workforce Commission

Journey for Justice - Unemployment Claim 46

Texas Department of Insurance

Journey for Justice - Who is OIEC? 48

Chapter 5: Harris Health System - Do You Work for the Patient or Employer?

OIEC, Workman's Comp & Harris Health 50

Harris Health System

Medical Records 55

Office Of Injured Employee Counsel

BRC Exchange 58

Chapter 6: Texas Department of Insurance

Division of Workers' Comp - Compliance & Investigation (MS-8) 61

Texas Department of Insurance

Open Records Department - Records Request 63

Centers for Medicare & Medicaid Services

Call Center Contractor 65

Federal Bureau of Investigation

Journey for Justice 66

Chapter 7: Faith & Works

What are You Doing? - March 2016 67

The Call

Intercessors 74

Can You Praise God in Advance?

Crazy Faith - April 2016 76

Do You Know Who You Are?

Walls of Injustice Come Down 81

Fasting and Prayer

Faith and Works - May 2016 91

Faith and Works

Are You Willing to Die? 92

Fasting and Prayer

Faith and Works - July 2016 92

Fasting and Prayer

Faith and Works - October 2016 97

Chapter 8: Baytown Police Misconduct - Auto Accident

Unforeseen Circumstance #3 99

Elderly Assistance

Help! 101

Baytown Police, Allstate & Who Did I Hire to Represent Me?

Unforeseen Circumstance #4 102

Den of Robbers

Revelation 106

Leaders Bring Nations To Ruin

Home of Worship 108

Make The Pain Stop

My Heart Bleeds 109

Keep Fighting 110

United Nations Human Rights Council

Complaint of Human Rights Violation 111

Chapter 9: School Assault by Students & Bully Teacher

Unforeseen Circumstance #5 114

Honest Error V's Medical Malpractice

Unforeseen Circumstance #6 116

Do Doctors Report Their Errors or Conceal Their Errors?

Medical Malpractice 117

Chapter 10: Breach of Contract

Unforeseen Circumstance #7 118

Assault by Crown Eagle Realty 120

Harris County Constable Precinct 5

Press Charges/Fraud/Investigation 121

Harris County District Attorney

Refusal 122

Crown Eagle Realty

Cashed My Check - Retaliatory Eviction 123

Chapter 11: Oppressed & Traumatized

Where Can I Get Healed? 126

Navy Veteran, Help!

State Bar of Texas 127

State Bar of Texas, Who Are You Really?

I See You! 130

Chapter 12: You Are Important to God!

Shareholders of Injustice 133

God Answers! 133

What Are You Doing Here?

Thriving & Surviving 134

Death and Resurrection

You Will Never Be Seen The Same Again! 135

Friends Through Adversity

Thank You! 136

Social Media Injustice Protest, September 2015 - January 2017

Facebook 137

Document Section 170

Confession 435

Acknowledgements 436

Permissions 437

Timeline of Events in Chronological Order

Corruption, Collusion & Cover-Up 438

Events Outside of My Journey for Justice 449

AUTHOR'S NOTE

Dear Reader, *You are a champion because God said it to be so, and therefore in God, we win!* Regardless of how it looks, remember what God showed you, and stand on God's Word. It's the only thing that will sustain you in trying times. Always remember the fight was given to those who endured to the end, and not the weak or the strong. I speak blessings to you in your life experiences. *Endure until the end and God will make you prosperous in Him.*

To Jurors All Over The World: God said, "My people perish for the lack of knowledge." In the court of law, before you consent to deliberations, I ask you to consider the law of God, and consider the actions against plaintiffs of any accidents, before giving a verdict not to award damages for injuries. Did you know insurance companies motivated people in power to create a law, which lawyers can't mention the word insurance company in court? These companies have colluded and refused to give the plaintiffs rightful compensation. Funds have been purposely held while plaintiffs' lives become unraveled, in an effort to make plaintiffs settle for pennies.

Insurance companies have taken advantage of citizens all over the United States, because of the lack of their knowledge. Some even label jurors to be ignorant when it comes to the effects of accidents. Which accidents cause individuals and families to be torn monetarily, mentally, and physically by losing time, pain, and anguish. Some of them have lost everything while injured and fighting for protection under the law and have not been rightly awarded monetary damages which is an insult to injury. Judge righteously! Many families have been seen as litigious when in truth, the family has stood for their right as injured plaintiffs but are made to be the villains. Rewrite the law and give every plaintiff what is right in the eyes of God. It's time we stop these insurance companies from taking advantage of plaintiffs who have been injured and are then faced with an insult to injury. Remember, your family, friends, neighbors, and associates that you care about when adjudicating. Remember to give in the same measure you would expect given unto you, your family and friends. God loves justice!

My Life Change! My life has changed spiritually and mentally for the greatest good of God. When you have endured and have shown yourself worthy, you will not remain the same, you will be increased. God is not going to do everything for you; there are some steps you will have to work on for yourself. While dealing with many physical and mental challenges, and trying to overcome, my daughter introduced me to several products in September 2019. My life has totally changed in the physical! I'm no longer the tired and drained individual I was due to my medical conditions, which are later expressed in this book. For authentication purposes, I have chosen not to allow editing of emails, letters and Facebook posts within this book.

Introduction

They conspired against me. During this whole ordeal with my employer and seeking justice, I *protested* on Facebook and Instagram. As I was protesting, Facebook would delete my post about God and my injustice experience, as well as disable the hashtag for General Dynamics Information Technology, the EEOC and political parties. I noticed after Facebook bought Instagram, Instagram started making the same moves and I couldn't hashtag General Dynamics Information Technology.

Through dealing with this entire experience of oppression, I'm fighting in court for restitution in cases that have come along during this journey, as well as trying to survive and thrive. With everything, I had already experienced with my employer, I was involved in a slip and fall incident, vehicular accidents, assault, and undergone surgery and physical therapy. *It has been extremely challenging, mentally, and physically, but I can't give up.* If you are fighting for what's right, I believe in you! Please know it will work out for your good. Ask God to come by his spirit and fight for you, read (Deuteronomy 20:4). Ask God for guidance. We must learn how to stand on the Word of God again.

Photograph by M.A.C. Photography
Edited by: Ellenor P Ratcliff

How did I find myself in such a deep, desperate and repulsive condition? The people watched and walk pass my suffering as if our ancestors died in vain. Who could I run to, for I was drowning in red, white, and blue? He said, "Do you trust me?" I had no clue what God meant, but I said yes and gave my best. As I lifted my hand and caught my breath, I screamed for help. Is this last cry for help in vain? No one came. How could I escape? I felt my breath escaping my lungs, I felt a hand rubbing my back; he was calling me back. My lungs began to fill with air, I can breathe. I know just who it was, that saved me from dying on that day. For I was given hope for tomorrow, hope even in my sorrow.

I was drowning, but the master took my hand and guided me in ways I never experienced in the land. All through the hurt, and the pain, a broken heart, after believing those I supported, especially politically would come to my rescue, but like many others, I was fooled. I was so angry, and it blinded my mission. I needed healing, and I needed it quickly. I must get back to my Father's business.

Fighting these giants, is there any hope for such a tragic situation? God lifts me, guides me, and sends messengers from near and far to help me in this journey, all glory to God. God has given me dreams and visions to lead me on the way. Protecting my spirit and space was key to my journey. I had to give up some places, people, and things because there was something much more important at hand. I'm thankful to God. He didn't forget me, but chose me, to lift Him on high in ways, undoubtedly He, would be glorified. God's dreams, my destiny, what will this turn out to be. All praises to the King, Lord, God, Jehovah, ruler over everything. He is my King, the creator, the driver of my dreams.

Chapter 1: The Beginning

After several unforeseen events (accident and death) and nearly becoming homeless again. This single mother prayed and asked God to open the door, to be gainfully employed. God gave me a dream, I was sitting behind a cubical at a desk with a phone headset on my head. As I began searching for work, I visited the Workforce Solutions office and received help to aid me in finding a job. It was not going so well, and I decided to lie on my resume and job application. I added my childcare business to my resume as if I only managed the business. I asked an associate if she would be my job reference and say the childcare was hers.

I was dumbing down my accomplishments. I assumed it would give me a better chance at becoming employed. So I thought! My experience of applying at McDonald's and other places to support my children didn't quite pan out, because I was "overqualified" and I didn't want to hear that again. Well, little did I know the associate was not in agreement, and she could have told me no. I completed a couple of job applications with a Workforce Solutions counselor and was getting results. I left all my information the same on my resume. I was called in for an interview at a church and a couple of other places. I visited the church and was completing my application.

While sitting there in the seat writing, I felt a push. I knew it was for me to tell the truth regarding my childcare business, which I referenced on the job application. I told the interviewer the business was mine. Well, I was taken on a tour to view the campus, and when the manager opened the door to where my office would be, it was not what God showed me in my dream. Although the interview went well, I forgot what I asked the associate to say, and what was written on the application that was in the manager's possession. I was at the bus stop when I received a call; it was the manager from the church, she stated, "Everything looked great on your background, but there was an issue."

The interviewer mentioned one thing I didn't really think about, she stated, "The reference you gave said the childcare was not her business." I reminded the manager, I did tell you in the interview that the business was mine and the manager said she wouldn't be able to hire me. God had a greater plan! Due to my accomplishments, I explained to the manager, my experience made it difficult to find work. The manager stated she worked in the corporate world before. The fact remains, she hadn't experienced what I had experienced, and as a result of that conclusion, it was pointless to go on. I waited and called my associate, I asked her, "Why didn't you tell me you were uncomfortable with saying the business was yours?" I don't remember what she said, and it no longer mattered.

I thought about the other job applications I entered, and how she may have possibly done the same thing. I changed my resume to reflect the proper information, which was the Owner/Director. This taught me not to lie, and it never works out for me. I went back to the Workforce Solutions office, and told the worker what I did, and that I didn't tell the truth on my resume or application, and that I didn't get the job. "For I know the plans I have for you," declares the LORD, "plans to prosper you and not to harm you, plans to give you hope and a future." (Jeremiah 25:11)

OMG! I can't tell you how real this scripture has been in my life. Many of us push to be a part of something, to earn income when God is taking us to a higher dimension in him. Settling will keep you counting pennies. I decree and declare that you will no longer count pennies but move in the ways of God and become prosperous, in the mighty name of Jesus, Amen.

Resource and Information: God is our source, and we must understand that we all have a destiny in God. For it is better for the plans of God to be fulfilled because God will make you prosperous.

Well, things were now looking up, I received another job lead from the Workforce counselor, and I was given the information for employer General Dynamics Information Technology. I was scheduled for an interview. The company came to the Workforce Solutions office. All the correct employment information was written on the application and my resume, I then submitted the completed application to GDIT HR Department. A friend to my family drove me to the location for a second interview. The interview went well and I aced it. I loved what I was going to be doing. My job was to help the American people enroll in the Affordable Care Act. I felt good, and it was promising.

On September 5, 2013, at 7:58 a.m., I received an email from General Dynamics Information Technology, thanking me for my interest in a career opportunity. On September 5, 2013, at 2:38 p.m., I received an email from the employer regarding an offer. On September 5, 2013, at 3:37 p.m., I received an email from the employer, giving me five days to complete the remaining employment process and a letter (refer to **Exhibit 1 & 2**) that sealed the deal for employment with Vangent, Inc., a General Dynamics company to start working September 23, 2013. Upon completing the offer, I received another email on September 6, 2013, at 11:14 a.m., with details regarding training to officially start working for Vangent/GDIT on September 9, 2013.

I was to arrive at 7 a.m., for training, Monday through Friday. I didn't know what I was going to do about my children. I never left them at home so early, and I was worried about how I would get the children to school. I would wake at 3:30 a.m., in the morning, make sure my children's arrangements were taken care of then I could leave for work. I stood outside alone at 4:30 a.m., in the morning. My first bus arrived for 4:49 a.m. I arrived at the second stop, then transferred to the last bus stop, to arrive for work at the scheduled time of 7 a.m. and was always on time. I hired a bus service to pick up my children and take them to two different schools.

Well, as the journey begins, I was totally in the dark about what I was about to experience. There were so many user names and passwords, as well as scripted lines to become familiar with. My experience in the corporate world, to owning my own business, prepared me for everything I was about to experience, at least that's what I thought. Before working at GDIT, I never experienced employees allowed to spray perfume, and cologne freely on the job. I have always been the kind of person who takes pride in her work. It was always easy for me to adapt to any work environment. My job performance exceed satisfactory-level performance.

There was nothing I could not do. I was a go-getter. I wasn't letting any challenge get in my way. My best foot was always put forward. When I didn't know how to do something, I asked or studied to learn more. To remain in good standing with the Workforce Solutions office, I emailed the counselor on September 7, 2013, at 1:03 p.m., regarding the new hire orientation with GDIT (refer to **Exhibit 3**). This was an obligation to maintain SNAP (food stamps) benefits, with the Texas Department of Human Services. A "verification of hours," was received from the Workforce Solutions office for my employer to complete (refer to **Exhibit 4**). As the employees became familiar with training and job responsibilities, there was only one problem, it was freezing in the training room, and we were required to get permission to bring coats.

While in training, every employee received a document that read, "VANGENT - Dress Code Standards - For Employees in Call Center Locations, Revised 2-1-12," at the top of the document someone wrote in all uppercase letters, "NO CELL PHONES ALLOWED IN BUILDING!" *We were informed people were fired for having their cell phones on their person.* One day during training, we were taken down-stairs for a briefing. In this briefing, every employee was given the "Benefits Guidebook 2013, the Employee Acknowledgment Form, Helpful Contact Information, GSA 14-Day Benefits Statement of Understanding, Direct Deposit information, Tax Form Instructions and VANGENT - HUMAN RESOURCES GUIDELINE #H301 - ATTENDANCE GUIDELINE (5 pages), and General Dynamics Information Technology - Dress Code Standards - For HCSD Employees in Call Center Locations, Revised 6-12-2013 (Version 2)."

In the guidebook, it mentions, "Workers' Compensation. The Plan may disclose your health information as necessary to comply with applicable workers' compensation or similar laws." The dress code standard document with "NO CELL PHONES ALLOWED IN BUILDING!" VANGENT and General Dynamics Information Technology also addressed "business casual attire" to support "GDIT HR Policy-305."

The policy spoke regarding, what was acceptable or unacceptable attire. And how Vangent/GDIT HCSD expected, "all employees to maintain personal hygiene that does not impede their ability to perform assigned duties, or negatively have an effect on others in the workplace. **Overly strong or offensive odors** or scents such as perfume and cologne, unclean attire, or body odor will not be allowed in the workplace. This dress code is intended to clarify expectations for the minimum standard for dress in the workplace."

Looking back at these policies really made me wonder. How could a company receive federal funding through the contract and violate employees at such great lengths? In the training, I remember the speaker going over all the policies and procedures.

Resource and Information: Learn the policies and procedures of the company you are working for. Don't leave yourself open to failure because you failed to educate yourself. Often times you can protect yourself by learning everything about your employer. If the employer is government-funded, learn the procedures for filing complaints with the government entity your employer is regulated under. If you believe you have been discriminated against by an employer, who does business with the federal government, contact the Office Of Federal Contract Compliance Programs (OFCCP) by utilizing the following link to file a complaint https://www.dol.gov/ofccp/regs/compliance/pdf/pdf start.htm. The (OFCCP) organization covers the U.S.A. Any victim of employment discrimination can get assistance from anyone or an organization to file a complaint against the employer doing business with the federal government, otherwise, your discrimination complaint should be filed with Texas Workforce Commission, Civil Rights Division first, to ensure you are protected on the state level. U.S. EEOC was "established to protect you on the federal level." If you live in another state, contact the regulation's office regarding your protection on the state level.

Transportation Services   **Unforeseen Circumstance #1**

My job is secured, and now I can provide a good living for my children. There was one thing left to do. I needed a safe and secured way of travel for my children to and from school. Children were always dropped off at the apartment by a yellow school bus. I waited downstairs to inquire about transportation services one day. I selected to allow the company to pick up my children. Everything was going well until my child informed me an older girl was bullying her on the private transportation bus. I was informed there would be an assistant present at all times. When I first secured the transportation service, the driver had an assistant for the safety of the children. The bus held 44 to 48 students. I questioned the driver regarding the bullying of my child. I also wanted to know where was the assistant, as promised.

The driver assured me the assistant was only out for the day but would be on the bus from then on. Well, I thought things were better, but everything turned for the worst! My child was still bullied by this older middle or high school age student on the bus. My child brought a knife on the bus to protect herself. The bus made it to school, and a student yelled, "She has a knife!" My children were taken to the office, and I was called regarding the situation. Because the transportation service was private and not an HISD bus, my child wasn't charged.

It was only by the grace of God; my baby was not charged. This situation could have landed my child in juvenile detention, a place in which my baby did not belong. All of these challenges took place due to bus driver negligence. Older children should be separated from the younger children, to ensure the younger children, were protected while in transit. After that situation, I never used another private bus service. I was able to get my children in childcare and didn't have to worry about any bullying.

Resource and Information: If you are located in Texas, and have an issue with a private bus service, contact the Texas Department of Public Safety. You can utilize the following link to select your region https://www.dps.texas.gov/schoolbus/. You will be provided with the phone number, the fax number, mailing address, and a list of counties your region serves. If you live elsewhere, contact your state transportation agency. Find out what regulations are placed on private transportation services, who transport children. Investigate the transportation service. Ensure the company you want to use has gone through the proper channels to get certified. If the company hasn't obtained the proper certification, don't use the service. It's better to be safe than sorry. Don't risk your child(ren) life or safety.

A young man in his twenties came to me regarding a work-related injury and informed me that his job sent him to the doctor. After hitting his head, he was sent back to work too soon, at the Home Department store. The young man was dizzy and was placed back on regular duty. He made another visit to the doctor and was still sent back to work. After all the issues, I told him to ask the doctor certain questions and to find out why she was sending him back to work with all the symptoms of a concussion.

The young man ultimately stops working for this store, which sold products for building and gardening. I'm not sure if he pursued workman's comp or not. But one thing I know for sure is that this young man was not in a safe environment, and it strongly seems as though the doctor was working for the employer and not the health and safety of the injured employee. The young man also told me about others who were visiting this same doctor's office and how people were getting screwed over.

As I have personally had my own experience as an injured employee, I have learned that I have a right to see any doctor of my choosing and that I don't have to accept the doctor my employer wants to send me too. I've learned how to protect my own interest, by advocating for myself because many of these employers don't care about their employees and will do anything not to be held accountable.

Resource and Information: If you are injured on the job in Texas, contact the Texas Department of Insurance – Division of Workers Compensation (DWC). Utilize the following link to file a claim https://www.tdi.texas.gov/wc/employee/index.html. You report your injury, do not wait for your employer to report your injury. The employer can lie and state you didn't report to them within 30 days and have your claim denied. If you are conscious and able, report your injury the same day. If not, report your injury as soon as possible.

Continued from page 7: Answering incoming calls to assist the American people was great. I was signing people up for health coverage through the Affordable Care Act (Obama Care). My job was always done with pride, and I love helping others. One day, two gentlemen walked through the call center. I vaguely remember the man who interviewed me, but I believe, one of those men walking, was him. The man stated, "If anyone needs help with anything, go to the HR Department."

On the first occurrence of issues with my job, I approached the Human Resource Department staff, Z. Bosie. When we spoke, I told the HR staff member, CSR's were spraying perfume at the lockers, and her response was, "We can't stop CSR's from wearing perfume." I'm not sure if I approached Z. Bosie first or if I sent an email first, but one thing was for sure, Z. Bosie never responded to my emails. On October 3, 2013, I made an urgent visit (refer to **Exhibit 5**) to the doctor at or around 1:45 p.m., I was having difficulty with my breathing and the doctor stated my breathing was restricted. As I was having this difficult time at work, I initially thought it was because of the vents I was setting under at my cubicle.

When I returned to work on October 4th, I sent an email notice to my supervisor and gave my doctor excuse (refer to **Exhibit 6**) by hand, as well as emailed (refer to **Exhibit 7**) Z. Bosie, HR Generalist at 6:03 p.m.

The email says, Dear Z. Bosie, On yesterday I missed work due to my Asthma. I made a visit to the doctor's office and was told my breathing is restricted... I'm really uncomfortable. In training, I asked if the temperature could be elevated, on several occasions. Candy instructed us to bring a coat. I'm fine with bringing a coat... I'm contacting you to ask for a reasonable accommodation. Is there an area that people such as myself who suffer from Asthma can sit?...

On October 10th, I emailed my supervisor, A. Clem regarding breathing issues I was having. Not only was I having trouble at work, but also on the verge of losing my childcare assistance from Workforce Solutions. Workforce Solutions gave me a form (WS Verification of Hours Form (REV 3/11/11) for my employer to complete. HR Generalist, Z. Bosie gave me the most difficult time getting the verification form completed. The company didn't want any paper on the call center floor, but how else was I going to get this verification completed, after all, it was not my job, but my duty to make sure the form was completed, to maintain my childcare assistance.

On October 11, 2013, at 9:16 a.m., I sent a notice by email (refer to **Exhibit 8**) to the Workforce Solutions counselor handling my case and informed her of my difficulty and childcare issues.

The email says, Good Morning, Ms. Peters, My name is Ellenor Perkins and my Social is ***.**.****. The office in my area is the hobby office, they are closed. Several times I have emailed, J Heart and J Glade. J Glade did respond last week and told me to contact the Astrodome office. However, I emailed Joy my check stub prior to Jean telling me to contact your office. I visited the hobby office before they closed. I was told by Joy that my childcare would revert to a fee and that fee would be based on a percentage. I need my childcare ASAP. I was just dropped and nothing else was done. I work for GDIT and it's a hassle. They don't sign any verifications and I can't access the GDIT site outside of work. I was instructed by someone at your office to submit verification of work hours although company won't verify and to submit my check stubs. I need a caseworker who will respond. If u can email me the name and email address for a worker, I would appreciate it. I must leave home for 7:00 am on Metro in order to make it for work, 9:30. It's not possible at this time for me to visit the Workforce Office. I'm off work at 6:00 pm. Thank you for your assistance.

On October 17th, I made an urgent visit (refer to **Exhibit 9 & 10**) to the doctor at 8:15 a.m., for breathing issues. On October 21st, I had a follow-up appointment for October 3rd visit. While dealing with issues on the job, I was having issues at my apartment complex. Broadway Square Apartments were not properly maintained. I called and complained about the air conditioner not properly working, mold on vents and other maintenance issues. I visited the office and complained in person and the maintenance man came to my apartment repaired the air conditioner and cleaned the vents. Maintenance took forever to repair the air conditioner. Later I visited the office and staff stated it was only dirt on the vents. On October 24th, I had a follow-up for an urgent visit from October 17th and returned to work. On October 28, 2013, I emailed my supervisor at 10:47 a.m. and informed him that I will be out all day for October 31, 2013, and I also emailed at 11:21 a.m., regarding my doctor appointment for asthma on November 1, 2013.

October 29th, at 3:24 p.m., I emailed (refer to **Exhibit 11**) Z. Bosie, HR Generalist regarding CSR's spraying perfume, the email says, Hello, on yesterday, a co-worker came back to their desk after smoking. This person was loaded with perfume; this person was not seated on either side of me. I was sitting at my desk and I begin having an asthma attack (my breathing became restricted). I did not make a scene, but I medicated myself. There is a growing problem with co-workers wearing fragrances that you can smell twenty feet away. I understand people want to smell nice; however, it should not be at the expense of others health. The fragrances are worn very heavy. Many people are not taking into consideration that there are some who suffer from Asthma and allergies. I'm not the only one who has spoken about this issue. Can you please address these issues? I also have a follow up appointment for my asthma on November 1, 2013, due to mold exposure in my apartment at the beginning of this month and due to difficulty, I'm facing on the call center floor. Thank you.

On October 30th, I emailed Z. Bosie at 11:39 a.m., regarding HR Policy; November 8th, at 10:56 a.m., Z. Bosie received a forwarded email from October 30, 2013, at 11:39 a.m., November 8th, my supervisor and I had a verbal communication. November 8, 2013, at 12:25 p.m., I emailed (refer to **Exhibit 12**) my supervisor A. Clem and sent a carbon copy to his manager, W. Reimer regarding Medical Condition, Can you move me for now?

The email says, Good Morning, I would like to know, if there is possibly any virtual positions are available (working from home)? I was diagnosed with asthma some time ago. I enjoy working here at GDIT, however, the perfume, smoke and etc., that I smell are becoming unbearable. My breathing becomes restricted and I began to have a difficult time (this is one of the reasons I have missed days from work). I don't want to resign, that's my reason for asking, if there is a position I can work from home. Please inform me if there is a way I can transfer to another position, where I'm not exposed to smoke/perfume. I'm aware that I must contact my supervisor and the Human Resources Recruiting Representative, regarding my interest in a new position in accordance with GDIT's in staff Transfers and Promotions Policy #406.

After visiting the doctor, I was informed, just because something may cause someone to have shortness of breath or asthma symptoms, doesn't mean they initially have asthma. It must be a period of exposure and testing.

November 8, 2013, at 12:28 p.m., I emailed (refer to **Exhibit 13**) my supervisor A. Clem. The email says, Z. Bosie did not respond to the email. I understand if there is nothing GDIT can do, I do need a response one way or the other. Thanks."

I also forwarded the same email to "Z. Bosie. At 12:45 p.m., I received an email (refer to **Exhibit 14**) from my supervisor A. Clem which he also sent a carbon copy to W. Reimer in response to the email I sent at 12:25 p.m.

The email says, "Ellenor, I do not think that virtual will be possible, but let me get with Beal and see if there is anything that can be done here. I saw your other emails as well. I know it ties directly in to this. So we will see what we can do to accommodate." At 12:48 p.m., I told supervisor, Thanks. At 3:31 p.m., I sent my supervisor A. Clem another email (refer to **Exhibit 15**), regarding not feeling well. The email says, Someone has sprayed on more perfume. I begin feeling good the first part of the day. I'm not feeling well and I don't want it to get worst. Can I leave?

I left the job early. At 3:32 p.m., I received an email (refer to **Exhibit 16**) from my supervisor A. Clem. The email reads, "Yes and we will just need to adjust your time card accordingly on Wednesday. And I will get with Beal first thing Monday for you. I'm sorry it's been so rough up here for you definitely do not want you to feel so out of sorts at work and I really want to see what can be done for you." I replied and said, Thanks.

November 12, 2013, at 6:03 p.m., I received a forwarded email (refer to **Exhibit 17**) from W. Reimer, my supervisors' boss. The email says, "L. Bair, is virtual workplace a possibility? Just asking. Thx. November 13th, at 7:38 a.m., I received a forwarded email (refer to **Exhibit 18**) from L. Bair to W. Reimer and a forwarded email from W. Reimer to A. Clem at 10:01 a.m. The email says, "No, Sorry."

November 18, 2013, at 9:51 a.m., I received an email (refer to **Exhibit 19**) from my supervisor, A. Clem. The email says, "Just wanted to let you know we tried to see what could be done as far as virtual. If things continue on please let us know and we will see if there is another area you might be able to be moved to?" On this day I verbally told my supervisor, I may have to resign.

There wasn't much progress dealing with the situation at work. I was given verbal warnings, and low scores, for not coming back from breaks on time, due to having to medicate myself after exposure. There were so many points against me. I was suffering from smelling the fragrances after it had been sprayed on the call center floor. Since my employer exhibited poor behavior towards my medical condition and my suffering, I start keeping a mental record of everything that was happening as it unfolded; I had to go back and look at the emails that were sent to my supervisor and human resource department and would write it down on my breaks or when I had an asthma attack.

My children and I left Broadway Square Apartments in October after the ill-treatment received. Several attempts were made to get another apartment elsewhere, but it fell through, my children and I shortly stayed with someone else, and then we went to live in The Salvation Army Shelter.

On November 19, 2013, I began feeling ill downstairs at work, due to someone smoking near the building. I departed at 9:40 a.m., for the clinic. After visiting my doctor at Harris Health System, I was given a note (refer to **Exhibit 20**).

On November 21st, I provided my doctor statement for my medical condition. On November 22nd, I informed my supervisor A. Clem that I will leave early to visit the shelter, and I had to do the same thing on November 25th, but this time, I sent the email to S. Johnson and informed her that I was leaving at 2:00 p.m. There was a conflict with my working hours and The Salvation Army programs. My son caught the stomach flu, and I had to leave work at 4:00 p.m., on December 3, 2013. December 16th, at 2:01 p.m., I emailed the supervisor and informed him I was having issues with the shelter and had to leave work at 2:30 p.m. December 18th, I informed the supervisor, I had a doctor appointment at 1:38 p.m.

On December 19th, at 1:21 p.m., I saw my doctor at Harris Health System, for my asthma symptoms, and was given a notice (refer to **Exhibit 21**) to return to work on December 20th. My supervisor gave me verbal warnings, and I responded to his verbal warnings on December 20th. On December 27th, at 12:37 p.m., I told S. Johnson I was feeling ill.

December 30th, I purchased (refer to **Exhibit 22**) more masks from Walgreens at 7:21 a.m., and on that same day, I forgot to log into my work phone at 3:38 p.m. On December 31, 2013, I made an urgent visit (refer to **Exhibit 23**) to Harris Health System and saw Dr. R. Ramage. My lungs were in bad condition, which caused me to have shortness of breath, and whizzing; my doctor made me stay off work for a whole week.

January 6, 2014, I had a follow-up with Dr. E. Simpson and had an x-ray of my chest before I could be released to return to work. After the examination, the doctor released me, and I returned to work on January 7th of 2014. After that experience, I contacted Z. Bosie again on January 7th, at 12:25 p.m., regarding issues on the call center floor (CSR's spraying perfume). An email was sent to my supervisor A. Clem to inform him I was taking a break at 12:00 p.m. – 12:15 p.m., and that I logged in at 12:18 p.m., after talking with the Human Resource Department.

February 6th, I missed work, and I didn't make it to the doctor because I was having trouble breathing. It felt like someone was sitting on my chest. I tried to recover the best I could. I made an urgent visit to Harris Health System on February 7th, when Dr. R. Ramage discussed with me my x-ray results from January 6th, and after my examination sent me home. There was a follow-up with the doctor for February 10th, at 8:17 a.m. After my examination, I was released (refer to **Exhibit 25**) to return to work on February 10th. I wanted my note to be backdated to February 6th, since that was the original date I took sick, but I was told, "Administration does not allow it since you didn't actually visit the clinic on the 6th." I told the staff I couldn't make it because I was very ill.

February 13, 2014, I visited Harris Health System at 8 a.m., to see a specialist in the Pulmonary Department, and was evaluated for the possibility of asthma.

Supervisory staff at my job asked me, "How long does it take for you to recover after an asthma attack?" While I was visiting the Pulmonary Clinic, I asked Dr. N. Hanania to give me a note and I stated the exact question HR asked me. The note is supposed to tell my job, how long it takes for me to recover after having an attack.

The doctor would not give me a note explaining the duration on time, instead, he gave me another note (refer to **Exhibit 26**).

Upon returning to work, I gave the certification from the specialist doctor to Z. Bosie, HR Generalist.

Resource and Information: You have a right to be protected by your employer under federal and state laws. As a patient of Harris Health System, you have a right to services by your physician. If you have not received proper treatment, you can file a complaint directly with the Texas Department of State Health Services. The complaint must be sent to the Health Facility Compliance Group (MC 1979), Texas Department of State Health Services, P.O. Box 149347, Austin, Texas 78714-9347. You can also fax your complaint to 512-834-6653 or call the Complaint Hotline number at 1-888-973-0022 and file a complaint by phone.

Chapter 2: Constructive Discharge   **The Finally**

On February 17, 2014, my supervisor A. Clem walked me to the new area. I was introduced to my new supervisor. I wore my mask, as usual. As we walked through an area in the call center the perfume was very strong, It was, if the perfume was freshly applied. This was the area I would pass through daily and my cubicle would be in the area as well. I remember talking to the lady sitting beside me. I was contemplating what I should do. I needed my job but risking death from an attack was no longer an option. I really had to make a sound decision for my children and myself. The company continuously showed me they didn't care about me. I should have quit that job long ago, but I needed the money.

After thinking about what I had been through, I emailed the new supervisor, W. Reimer, and A. Clem, informing them of my resignation. Z. Bosie also received an email from me on February 17, 2014.

The email says, <u>Ellenor Perkins Po Box 321168 Houston, Texas 77221; General Dynamics 5959 Corporate Drive, Houston, Texas 77036. February 17, 2014; Dear Z. Bosie, Human Resources Department: Effective today, I will resign. I have done my very best under the circumstances. I have spoken with you on numerous occasions in regard to CSR's spraying perfume on the call center floor. I have not seen one email addressing this issue, it is not being enforced. When we met as a group in the large conference room, this was addressed in September, once. The dress code has been enforced on a number of occasions. My condition has worsened instead of getting better. An email was sent to Roy, Reimer and Clem, they are all aware; I have spoken to A. Clem, my superior on numerous occasions as well. I asked for accommodations and was told it was nothing GDIT could do. Bosie, I stated on numerous occasions, I understand your company can't stop CSR's from wearing perfume. However, they should have not been allowed to spray it on the call center floor. There are other CSR's who have witnessed this action as well. They should not have to suffer with this issue either. The last notice from doctor that I delivered to you shows, I haven't been diagnosed with Asthma as of yet, so there is clearly something wrong. This is why I must resign. I have done everything within my power to cope with the issue (wearing a mask throughout the call center, which raised alarm and staying in my seat much as possible, I was smelling the perfume although I wore a mask) and my health is declining because of the exposure. This is why I couldn't give you a report of the duration of time it would take for me to return to my desk after being exposed and medicating myself. I know I was penalized because of this, but it was completely out of my hand. I was given verbal warnings and that was not fare, since</u>

<u>GDIT never sent out a notice for employees not to spray perfume on the call center floor. I stopped taking my breaks downstairs so I wouldn't be exposed to smoke as well. GDIT would not accommodate me and this is the end result. I truly wished it could have been a different outcome. Again, there was no resolve. Disappointedly.</u>

I was having such a difficult time at Vangent/GDIT. Wearing the mask did not lessen the exposure as much because now, I'm still exposed to perfume/cologne being sprayed, as well as feeling as if I was suffocating. I was retaliated against while still working at the company. The HR department knew I was having trouble with my breathing. There were certain times an employee must be on the phone enrolling the American people for health insurance, but I couldn't adequately do my job. When I would experience exposure, causing me to have an asthma attack, I would medicate in the breakroom and try to recover, then return to the same condition on the call center floor. Because it took me a little while to recover at times, I was coached and given points which were ways that lead to termination under Vangent/GDIT policy.

On many occasions, I asked the company to enforce company policy; Vangent/GDIT refused to enforce company policy, and I was constructively discharged on February 17, 2014.

My record of perceived disability was aggravated daily. Vangent/GDIT did not care about the conditions on the call center floor, which caused my asthma attacks.

On February 20, 2014, at 4:29 p.m., I saved a note (refer to **Exhibit 27**) to myself, regarding the wording of the email that was sent to GDIT supervisors, and Human Resource Department on February 17, 2014. On March 3, 2014, a formal resignation (refer to **Exhibit 28 & 29**) was sent certified mail **(7013 0600 0002 4184 4828)** to General Dynamics Information Technology located at 5959 Corporate Dr, Houston, Texas 77036.

Resource and Information: I know many of you may need your job to provide financially, but please don't sacrifice your health and life, especially if you have children. When a company has a lack of ethics, take action as soon as possible. If you sustain an injury, contact the Texas Department of Insurance – Division of Workers Compensation (DWC), utilize the following link to file a complaint https://www.tdi.texas.gov/wc/employee/index.html. Also, contact Occupational Safety and Health Administration (OSHA). Utilize the following link to report safety and health concerns you notice https://www.osha.gov/. Exposure to any chemical that causes breathing issues should be reported. Chemicals are chemicals.

As the day's past, I began researching the process of pursuing justice because I know I was violated. On March 10, 2014, I printed (refer to **Exhibit 30**) from the EEOC website, "How To File A Charge of Employment Discrimination." When you visit the EEOC online, to file a charge, there is a shortlist of questions you are asked. The site will direct you to the Intake Questionnaire page and thank you for using the EEOC Assessment System.

On March 17, 2014, the U.S. Equal Employment Opportunity Commission Intake Questionnaire (4 pages) was completed (refer to **Exhibit 32 - 35**), and I organized all my evidence (refer to **Exhibit 36 - 41**) supporting my claim.

My evidence included 16 pages of pure facts. On the fourth question, I completed my claim for employment discrimination for disability, and stated, GDIT would not enforce policy. View attachment 1, Exhibit a., b., and c. **Attachment 1** is titled, <u>Continued Answer to Question 4</u>; and says, <u>This information is from handouts CSR's received from GDIT/Vangent in September of 2013. Please review attachment, Exhibit A and B. *"Revised 2-1-12, VANGENT expects all employees to maintain personal hygiene that does not impede their ability to perform assigned duties, or negatively have an effect on others in the workplace. Overly strong or offensive odors or scents such as perfumes and cologne, unclean attire, or body odor will not be allowed in the workplace." "Revised 6-12-2013 (Version 2), "GDIT HCSD expects all employees to maintain personal hygiene that does not impede their ability to perform assigned duties, or negatively have an effect on others in the workplace. Overly strong or offensive odors or scents such as perfumes and cologne, unclean attire, or body odor will not be allowed in the workplace."*</u> The documents have been quoted.

The original documents were submitted to the EEOC as evidence. Also, submitted to the EEOC was the formal resignation letter, the doctor's excuse from November 19, 2013, and the certification from February 13, 2014. The fifth question asked, "What happened that was discriminatory?" I explained how I was ignored on October 4, 2013, at 6:03 p.m. after sending emails. The notice was regarding restricted breathing, asking for reasonable accommodation. Z. Bosie, HR Generalist also received an email on October 10, 2013, regarding notice of breathing issues. I gave my supervisor's name and said view Attachment 2. **Attachment 2** is regarding the emails sent prior, due to the exposure. Question six asked, "How the actions were discriminatory?" I explained under GDIT, HSCD Dress Code Standards it states, *"Overly strong or offensive odors or scents such as perfumes and cologne, unclean attire, or body odor will not be allowed in the* *workplace."* The above statement has not been enforced by GDIT.

On many occasions, I asked for assistance, regarding CSR's spraying perfume on the call center floor. I then asked if there was a virtual position and told the EEOC to view attachment 3. **Attachment 3** is titled, <u>Continued Answer to Question 6;</u> and it says, <u>Human Resources Department didn't respond to my emails, basically ignoring me. My supervisor attempted to help me, but without instructions from human resources, our team was not addressed regarding the issue, nor was any other team addressed. This is why I believe I was discriminated against. There was never an email or verbal communication, asking CSR's not to wear or spray overly offensive scents (perfume and etc.) on the call center floor</u> and I included emails of communication. Question seven asked what were the reasons given for the acts of discrimination. I explained what I was told, *"We can't stop CSR's from wearing perfume."* <u>Z. Bosie, HR Generalist There was also another HR person in her office as well; she was a female of color. My supervisor apologized for CSR's spraying perfume, but never spoke with the team regarding the issue."</u> Question eight asked who had similar experience or the same treatment. I gave the names of staff and what action each staff witnessed.

One staff stated, "It was too strong." Question nine asked if I have a disability. I said, yes. Question ten asked what my disability is and what the disability prevents or limits me from doing. I answered, allergic, asthma and when exposed to allergens (perfume) it prevents me from breathing, working and other duties. Question eleven asked what medications I take, and I listed each one. Question twelve asked did I ask my employer for changes or assistance to perform on my job and I said, yes. It said, "If "YES", when did you ask?" I listed the first day October 4, 2013, then it said, "How did you ask?" I said, in writing and email. It then says, "Who did you ask?" I said, Z. Bosie, HR Generalist. I was asked to describe the changes or assistance I asked for. I said, I asked for reasonable accommodation due to restricted breathing.

Then finally the form asked, how did my employer responded to my request. I said, she did not respond to the email. Other times I was told verbally, *"We can't stop CSR's from wearing perfume."* I told the EEOC view doctor statements for November 19, 2013, February 13, 2014, and view all communication between me and GDIT. **Attachment. 4** is titled, <u>Continued Answer to Question 12;</u> and I included emails of communication. Question thirteen asked if there were witnesses to the alleged discriminatory incidents and what would the witness tell EEOC. I gave the names of staff, then stated one staff would say. "I never received an email asking CSR's not to wear or spray overly strong or offensive odors or scents such as perfumes and cologne." I also included A. Clem and stated that he would say, "I never received direction from HR to inform

CSR's not to wear or spray overly strong or offensive odors or scents such as perfumes and cologne. There was never an email or verbal communication sent to CSR's or Supervisors."

I added most of the people on my team as witnesses, as well as those who set near me, who were still working at GDIT when I constructively discharged, which U.S. EEOC never questioned, per witnesses. All the Associate Specialist, Customer Service staff that I also listed as witnesses were P. John, O. Wheel, M. Black, S. Dee, K. Aunn, L. Sign, J. Cut, John, D. Kole, and Mrs. Eve. The others listed are supervisors, mangers or HR staff who were listed as witness A. Clem, S. Johnson, W. Reimer, Rian, Z. Bosie and anyone employed before December 2013 can also testify to not receiving an email or verbal communication enforcing the dress code on overly strong or offensive odors.

I told EEOC to view attachment 5, which also states, "All witness can attest that CSR received a single document, which stated *"NO CELL PHONES ALLOWED."* This was because CSR's would have phones on their person and that was against the rules. In fact, many employees were fired for such actions. There was an HR briefing in September 2013. In this briefing CSR's received two packets, the first packet contained information regarding: Helpful Contact Information, Employee Acknowledgement Form, GSA 14- Day Benefits Statement of Understanding and Dress Code Standards. The second packet contained: Human Resources Guideline #H301- Attendance Guidelines; this packet has five pages. CSR's received no verbal, electronic or written communication for wearing, *"Overly strong or offensive odors or scents such as perfumes and cologne,"* prior to February 17, 2014. CSR's can attest to the fact that former CSR's were fired for violating dress code standards (wearing clothing too short or too tight) and having cell phones in restricted area (call center floor). Secure floor policy and dress code were enforced on a consistent basis through email and verbalization from supervisor. CSR's completed mandatory training, time sheet, testing and etc., based on information sent through email and Ethernet. CSR's often received emails on a daily, weekly or annual basis. Again, there was no email sent addressing CSR's not to spray or wear overly offensive or strong scents.

U.S. EEOC Visit

On March 20, 2014, I visited the EEOC, which was at that time located on 1201 Louisiana Street, 6th Floor, and approached the window. After submitting my EEOC Intake Questionnaire and supporting documentation (evidence) to the clerk at the window, I was asked to have a seat, and someone would assist me. A bald European man walked out into the waiting area. I felt this evilness about him, as he introduced himself. His spirit was so dark. I can't recall, ever feeling that way in my adult life before meeting him. *My spirit was alarmed.* We walked to his office, and I was questioned. I gave details of the exact encounters with my employer. J. Crosbie typed information on the computer and asked me to verify it. J. Crosbie did not say what I stated. In fact, J. Crosbie typed a portion of my statement, into his own words, and I was alarmed, but I said, okay. I signed, he signed, and then he left to get the charge notarized.

My charge of discrimination was officially filed (refer to **Exhibit 42 & 43**) with the U.S. Equal Employment Opportunity Commission, under charge # 460-2014-01770. On March 25th, I viewed OSHA information online and copied information to have for future reference. On the website it mentions, *"You have the right to a safe workplace…,"* and how the "Occupational Safety and Health Act of 1970 (OSH Act) was passed to prevent workers from being killed or seriously harmed at work." There are also details on how to file a complaint to request an on-site OSHA inspection. After reading the information, I made contact by phone for help, due to the exposure I experienced; I didn't want another employee to have the same experience, but I didn't get any assistance.

On March 27, 2014, I sent a letter (refer to **Exhibit 44**) to EEOC regarding the permanent closure of GDIT Houston location at 5959 Corporate Dr. On March 27, 2014, J. Crosbie introduced himself on the EEOC Houston District Office letterhead (refer to **Exhibit 45 & 46**), and his business card was attached. J. Crosbie was the Federal Investigator who was over my case, and he never informed me of my rights under ADA and ADAAA. In fact, J. Crosbie never investigated my case. I made contact with some of the witnesses. Some told me there was no contact from J. Crosbie or EEOC. To the individual reading my book, sometimes we don't know what to ask God for, but God is expecting you to expect something from him. Here is your first chance to ask God for anything you need if you have never asked before. God can do all things; I've seen it for myself.

Harris Health System   **Are you afraid of my employer?**

On April 24, 2014, I visited Harris Health System to see the specialist in the Pulmonary Department again. I don't remember what this doctor said because I felt he was a horrible doctor. All I remember is from the notice given (refer to **Exhibit 47**), I was finally given an official diagnosis of Asthma and Allergic Rhinitis. I couldn't understand, why he would write at the end of the notice, "This letter was given to her upon request." I know I was poor financially at the time and I know the doctor didn't care about my suffering. All he cared about was covering his protocol in a way that I didn't understand.

I had private doctors before, never in twenty years of going to the doctor on my own as a grown woman, had a doctor ever written, "This letter was given to her upon request." There was something deeper to this madness. I believe maybe he had friends who own the company, worried that my employer would retaliate or maybe he was a shareholder of Vangent/GDIT. All I know is, it didn't make any logical sense. Are you afraid of my employer? If you fear my employer, you fear the wrong one. You should fear my father, the one whom can destroy your soul.

On June 26th, I was scheduled to return to the pulmonary clinic at 8:30 a.m., but I was not going back to that horror of a place. On July 1st, I was scheduled to return to the Smith Clinic for CT scan. I was not working, I was sick, desperate and trying to get help from medical staff prior to the specialty appointments I attended. I couldn't trust the system with my care anymore. My children's benefits were in jeopardy because some doctors think they know every darn thing.

During the difficult time of attempting to get my form completed, I visited the Valbona clinic to pick up my form (H1836), regarding my disability and was taken to administration after learning my form was still not completed.

As I sit there I heard this woman crying because she was having a similar issue, and I thought to myself, *people should not have to endure such treatment,* these doctors act as if we are lying about the issues we are experiencing medically. What happened to the oath doctors took to service the people? Have these facilities become another corrupt breeding ground to deny patients of their rights?

On July 28, 2014, Dr. Juneja finally completed my forms (refer to **Exhibit 48**) for Texas Health and Human Services Commission regarding my disability, after I raised hell. I needed the form to maintain benefits for my children. On August 14, 2014, at 10:20 a.m., I was scheduled to visit Dr. Juneja.

Resource and Information: To file a complaint against a physician who chooses to neglect your medical need, contact Texas Medical Board by utilizing the following link to file a complaint http://www.tmb.state.tx.us/page/place-a-complaint. You can submit a complaint online or print and mail the complaint form to Investigations Department MC-263, P.O. Box 2018, Austin, Texas 78768-2018. If you live in another state, contact the Federation Of State Medical Boards by utilizing the following link to locate your states Medial Board to file a complaint https://www.fsmb.org/contact-a-state-medical-board/.

Disability Rights Texas

November 2014, I contacted Disability Rights Texas for help by email, through their system and a case was opened. June 22, 2015, at 8:45 a.m., I received an email from Disability Rights Texas including an attachment responding to my initial plea for help. The document attached was dated for May 29, 2015 and has 29 pages. June 22, 2015, at 2:35 p.m., I emailed (refer to **Exhibit 49**) Disability Rights Texas, requesting information. At 2:54 p.m., I received an email from Disability Rights Texas regarding my complaint, and I responded at 3 p.m. and sent Disability Rights Texas an email (refer to **Exhibit 50**) regarding the correct spelling of my name after a verbal conversation.

My second unforeseen circumstance while on this journey for justice was on February 15, 2015, when we were rear-ended by a driver. While asleep in the passenger seat, I remember waking up in a panic. I made sure to tell the driver get a photocopy of the driver's license, as well as the insurance card. We contacted the police, but the driver refused to stay at the scene of the accident. He drove off, claiming he needed to get his sick child to the doctor. At least we did get the proper documentation. We gave the information to the officer and everything was recorded.

EMS arrived and took me to the hospital. Before leaving the scene, I remember this paramedic, he had the nerve to say nothing was wrong with me, as if he was Superman with x-ray vision. He pissed me off, and I ignored his ignorance because he really didn't have a clue. The EMS ride was the worst ever. I did better traveling in my own vehicle. We found out the guy insurance was expired, which caused me to file against my own insurance.

I really didn't want to file against my insurance. After all, we didn't cause the accident, but I had no choice. It turned out I had some serious injuries, and every time I fell asleep in a vehicle, I would wake up in a panic. It took an extremely long time for me to get through the stress of that accident.

Resource and Information: If you are conscious, but dizzy, after an accident, don't get out of your car until you know you can safely move. Ask anyone who comes to your aid to get the driver's license, insurance card, license plate number, vehicle identification number (VIN), telephone number of the person, and vehicle that hit you and all involved. Also, ask someone to take pictures with your phone if you have one or ask the person to please take pictures on their phone and send the pictures to your email. If you are having issues that cannot be resolved with the auto insurance carrier, contact Texas Department of Insurance by utilizing the following link to submit a complaint https://www.tdi.texas.gov/consumer/auto-insurance-complaint.html.

Chapter 3: U.S. EEOC, White House, HHS, CMS and DOJ **Journey for Justice**

Continued from page 21: I made contact and left messages for J. Crosbie on many occasions, but J. Crosbie never made contact. J. Crosbie only responded on March 26th, 2015, a year and six days later. On March 26, 2015, which is 373 days, I finally received a determination on the charge I filed with the EEOC March 20, 2014, by mail (refer to **Exhibit 51 - 53**). M. S. Ebel, EEOC Acting District Director stated, "... Based upon its investigation, the EEOC is unable to conclude that the information obtained establishes violations of the statues..."

And this was my first denial for justice to be served. After a year he finally called me back, I asked J. Crosbie, "Why did the EEOC choose not to charge Vangent/GDIT?" J. Crosbie stated, "GDIT was not obligated to enforce the fragrance policy and gave reasonable accommodations." I knew immediately that J. Crosbie a federal investigator, was not upholding the *Vision* and *Mission* of the EEOC and violated the oath to serve under the Constitution. My case was closed, after I presented sound evidence. I believe M. S. Ebel and J. Crosbie were paid off to dismiss my case. April 9, 2015, at 8:15 a.m., I saved a note (refer to **Exhibit 54**) to myself regarding state regulations.

On April 10, 2015, I wrote for reconsideration (refer to **Exhibit 55 - 58**) which is called, "Notarized Substantial Weight Review," and I submitted to U. S. Equal Employment Opportunity Commission located at 1201 Louisiana Street, 6th Floor, Houston, Texas 77002. While writing the reconsideration letter to the EEOC, I also submitted a copy of the "Notarized Substantial Weight Review," on April 10, 2015, by certified mail **(7011 0470 0003 5828 4862)** to HHS, Attention: Sylvia Matthews Burwell located at 200 Independence Ave., SW Washington, DC 20201 (refer to **Exhibit 59**). A copy of the "Notarized Substantial Weight Review," was submitted on April 10, 2015, by certified mail **(7011 0470 0003 5828 4879)** to The White House, Attention: President Obama located at 1600 Pennsylvania Ave, NW Washington, DC 20500 (refer to **Exhibit 60**). A copy of the "Notarized Substantial Weight Review," was submitted on April 10, 2015, by certified mail **(7011 0470 0003 5828 4855)** to CMS, Attention: Andrew Slavitt located at 7500 Security Blvd, Baltimore, MD 21244 (refer to **Exhibit 61**).

April 10, 2015, at 8:45 p.m., I heard, "On this day, April 10, 2015, I decree and declare that anyone who plans to harm my family or friends will be cursed. The plans you make to harm us will be carried out into your own lives. You will be cursed and that of your children."

On April 29, 2015, I was denied due process a second time (refer to **Exhibit 62 - 64**). M. S. Ebel denied me stating, "The EEOC has no obligation to reconsider the final findings we have issued on a charge. EEOC Directors, therefore, may decline to review a request to reconsider an

EEOC final findings unless the Charging Party presents substantial new and relevant evidence, or a persuasive argument that the EEOC's prior decision was contrary to law or the facts." Remember the overwhelming supporting evidence that you have viewed in this book, yet M. S. Ebel denied me. Vangent/GDIT was contracted with CMS, so I contacted CMS by phone for accountability.

TDI **GDIT, Attorney & Broadspire – Workers' Compensation**

On May 7, 2015, I contacted an attorney for assistance with workers' compensation benefits, and received an email on May 11, 2015, at 5:47 p.m., from the attorney's office regarding an appointment. On May 11, 2015, I contacted the Texas Department of Insurance with guidance from the attorney, regarding insurance coverage for Vangent/ GDIT. After researching, I finally made to the correct insurance company on May 14, 2015. On May 14, 2015, I hired an attorney to represent me against General Dynamics Information Technology for workers' compensation benefits (refer to **Exhibit 65**).

After providing the attorney office with my records, I was contacted May 20, 2015, at 12:39 p.m., and was informed to pick up my original documents. During the meeting with the attorney, I forgot to ask one question regarding the fee for representation, I sent an email (refer to **Exhibit 66**) on May 20, 2015, at 5:02 p.m. On May 26, 2015, at 5:25 p.m., I contacted (refer to **Exhibit 67**) my attorney regarding contact made with GDIT. June 2, 2015, at 2:24 p.m., I contacted (refer to **Exhibit 68**) my attorney again regarding the fee for representation.

GDIT Human Resource Department contacted me June 2, 2015, at 4:56 p.m., by email (refer to **Exhibit 69**) regarding my web inquiry for workman's comp. June 3, 2015, at 4:49 p.m., I emailed (refer to **Exhibit 70**) GDIT Human Resource Department and CC my attorney. GDIT Human Resource Manager contacted (refer to **Exhibit 71**) me June 4, 2015, at 3:54 p.m., with a response regarding worker's compensation claim. June 4, 2015, at 4:08 p.m., I contacted my attorney and forwarded the email (refer to **Exhibit 72**) received from GDIT.

June 5, 2015, at 5:28 p.m., I contacted (refer to **Exhibit 73**) GDIT HR Department and sent a carbon copy to my attorney regarding Broadspire conversation. GDIT HR Department contacted (refer to **Exhibit 74**) me June 8, 2015, at 10:50 a.m., regarding a partner submission for my claim. June 9, 2015, at 8:51 a.m., I contacted (refer to **Exhibit 75**) my attorney regarding the conversation GDIT HR Department and I had regarding my claim.

On June 9, 2015, Broadspire, A Crawford Company received notice of my on the job injury. I must tell you, the devil can't stand for you to fight, and stand for righteousness, so the devil will use anyone (a vessel) willing.

When I first called to speak with D. Fields, she became upset with me and I heard it in her voice, however, I asked myself, Why is she mad at me? I'm only calling regarding my claim. I found out that Vangent/GDIT never reported my injury to Division of Workers Compensation nor did the employer report my injuries to their insurance carrier, Broadspire. June 10, 2015, at 11:07 a.m., I contacted (refer to **Exhibit 76**) GDIT HR Department for a follow-up regarding the June 8, 2015, conversation. June 10, 2015, at 3 p.m., I forwarded the conversation between GDIT HR Department and I to my attorney.

June 10, 2015, at 3:35 p.m., GDIT HR Department contacted me regarding my claim number. June 10, 2015, at 6:56 p.m., I contacted (refer to **Exhibit 77**) my attorney and forwarded the email GDIT HR Department sent me. June 24, 2015, at 7:36 a.m., I emailed (refer to **Exhibit 78**) my attorney regarding the doctors who treated my condition. On June 24, 2015, I completed Broadspire forms, I received a total of six documents but will only provide a few documents (refer to **Exhibit 81/ 84**).

On June 25, 2015, I faxed the claim to D. Fields of Broadspire and submitted 9 pages of facts. Broadspire received an email (refer to **Exhibit 86**) from me June 26, 2015, at 11:25 a.m., with two attachments (GDIT policy and resignation letter). June 26, 2015, at 12:51 p.m., I contacted my attorney and forwarded the email (refer to **Exhibit 87**) I sent to Broadspire.

On July 9, 2015, Broadspire, A Crawford Company contacted (refer to **Exhibit 88 & 89**) me regarding my job injury claim, and I was denied due to the fraudulent activity of Vangent/GDIT. Vangent/ GDIT's HR Department told Broadspire I never reported any injury on the job to HR per Ms. Fields, insurance adjuster. July 16, 2015, at 6:54 p.m., I contacted (refer to **Exhibit 90**) my attorney for a follow-up since I had not heard from him in two weeks and to deliver additional information. July 17, 2015, at 1:03 p.m., I emailed (refer to **Exhibit 91**) Broadspire regarding the treatment I received and the denial. July 17, 2015, at 1:06 p.m., I contacted (refer to **Exhibit 92**) my attorney and forwarded the email I sent to Broadspire.

Vangent/ GDIT lied. All the medical excuses I gave on more than several occasions as well as the email communication while working at Vangent/GDIT proves the company lied. If I had not presented any doctors' excuse, informed the company that I was sick and listing the cause, I would have been fired. July 22, 2015, at 2:03 p.m., I contacted (refer to **Exhibit 93**) my attorney regarding the notice I received from Broadspire. July 22, 2015, at 2:30 p.m., I contacted (refer to **Exhibit 94**) my attorney regarding one of the witnesses. Broadspire contacted (refer to **Exhibit 95**) my attorney and I on July 23, 2015, at 1:24 p.m., regarding sending out a copy of the denial. Broadspire contacted (refer to **Exhibit 96**) me on July 23, 2015, at 1:25 p.m. and asked me to confirm my address. July 23, 2015, at 3:18 p.m., I contacted (refer to **Exhibit 97**) Broadspire and noted the denial was received.

Due to all the lies told by Z. Bosie I contacted (refer to **Exhibit 98**) my Attorney July 29, 2015, at 7:18 a.m., to have Z. Bosie statement discredited.

On August 21, 2015, the attorney in which I had so much hope in presented (refer to **Exhibit 99 & 100**) a "Withdrawal of Representation" regarding the workers' compensation claim submitted to Broadspire at the negligent and corruptible behavior of Vangent/GDIT and gave me some instructions. Thank you for the instructions! This was truly devastating, and I knew this attorney would help me get justice but here I am, denied yet again.

Contact was made with a firm in Florida for help and on August 26, 2015, the law firm sent a letter (refer to **Exhibit 101**) of rejection. So here I stand, totally dismayed after my attorney drops me and another attorney denies my plea for help. Did I say I was devastated? On this day, I wrote a poem called, "Justice, Where Art Thee?" JUSTICE, WHERE ART THEE? Where is this land of Liberty? Freedom and Justice for all you see, yet you have still forsaken me.

I submitted an inquiry to Lawyers.com in hope of receiving legal help. September 1, 2015, at 8:28 p.m., I received a response from Lawyers.com in regard to my inquiry, and also received a transcript of the inquiry on the same morning at 8:39 p.m. An attorney responded to my inquiry and contacted (refer to **Exhibit 102**) me September 1, 2015, at 11:15 p.m., regarding my "Civil Rights Matter." After communicating with the attorney's office by phone I was asked to submit documents for review and I sent an email (refer to **Exhibit 103**) on September 4, 2015, at 12:30 p.m., with the following documents attached, The dress code standard document with "NO CELL PHONES ALLOWED IN BUILDING!" Vangent, Dr statement for November 19, 2013, doctor letter of certification for February 13, 2014, and doctor statement for April 24, 2014. September 4, 2015, at 2:31 p.m., I emailed (refer to **Exhibit 104**) the attorney's secretary and attached, EEOC Intake Questionnaire 4 pages; Additional Information; Attachment 3 to question 6 on Intake Questionnaire 1 page; Resignation letter 2 pages, EEOC Right to Sue 2 pages Form 161 and Charge of Discrimination 2 pages Form 5.

On September 8, 2015, the law firm also sent a letter (refer to **Exhibit 105**) of rejection. On October 7, 2015, at 11:04 a.m., I emailed (refer to **Exhibit 106**) my prior attorney regarding another witness. On October 7, 2015, at 11:37 a.m., I received a response email from my prior attorney regarding another witness. On October 7, 2015, at 11:58 a.m., I emailed (refer to **Exhibit 107**) my prior attorney.

January 19, 2016, at 4:04 p.m., I emailed (refer to **Exhibit 108**) my old attorney regarding action. As I search for a new attorney I submitted an inquiry to Findlaw.com and received a response (refer to **Exhibit 109**) on February 27, 2018, at 4:05 p.m. and received another response from a law firm with the attached transcript.

Resource and Information: It's okay if no one will help you, ask God to lead you, open doors, as well as give you the understanding for the process you will have to go through, so you can be equipped. If you are having issues that cannot be resolved with your employer's carrier, regarding your employer's workers' comp coverage, contact Texas Department of Insurance by utilizing the following link to submit a complaint https://www.tdi.texas.gov/wc/ci/wccomplaint.html.

On July 7, 2015, Martin Ebel contacted (refer to **Exhibit 110 &111**) me regarding the letter I mailed to President Obama, asking for action. Martin Ebel stated, "This is in response to your April 10, 2015, inquiry to President Obama concerning the charge of employment discrimination… You were not accorded a substantial weight review, because that process only occurs where a Fair Employment Practices Agency (FEPA) (such as, for example, the Texas Workforce Commission) has made a determination on a charge that was DUAL FILED with BOTH a FEPA and the EEOC. Your charge was not filed with a FEPA, but rather was filed directly with the EEOC, so a substantial weight review is not possible."

Once denied by the EEOC again, after writing to the President for action on April 10, 2015, I took it a step further, and sent the entire file with evidence, that was submitted to the EEOC on March 20, 2014. When I wrote (refer to **Exhibit 112 - 114**) to the President of the United States on August 6, 2015, via certified mail **(7015 0640 0006 5089 8715)** located at 1600 Pennsylvania Ave, NW Washington, DC 20500, for justice to be served, there was no response. On September 1, 2015, I contacted (refer to **Exhibit 115, pages 113 & 114 are the same pages submitted to President**) U.S. Attorney General Loretta E. Lynch via certified mail **(7015 0920 0002 0409 1466)** located at 950 Pennsylvania Ave, NW Washington, DC 20530-0001.

The Attorney General also received the exact documents submitted to President Obama on August 6, 2015, and EEOC on March 20, 2014. There was no response from Department of Justice. On September 11, 2015, contact (refer to **Exhibit 118 & 119**) was made to L. P. Marlin, Assistant General Counsel for Vangent/ GDIT via certified mail **(7015 0920 0002 0409 41473)** located at 3211 Jermantown Road, Fairfax, VA 22030, regarding a settlement.

September 14, 2015, I contacted (refer to **Exhibit 120**) *President Barack Obama for the 3rd time*, via certified mail **(7011 0470 0003 5834 9387)** located at 1600 Pennsylvania Ave, NW Washington, DC 20500 and *U.S. Attorney General Loretta E. Lynch* (refer to **Exhibit 121**) via Certified Mail **(7011 0470 0003 5834 9394)** located at 950 Pennsylvania Ave, NW Washington, DC 20530-0001. Neither President Obama nor Attorney Loretta Lynch responded.

September 25, 2015, L. Marlin, Assistant General Counsel responded (refer to **Exhibit 122**), denying me JUSTICE and responded with a denial per the EEOC determination. On October 2, 2015, I printed (refer to **Exhibit 123**) from TWC website, "How to Submit an Employment Discrimination." The United Sates Equal Employment Opportunity Commission (U.S. EEOC) has a duty, a sworn duty and that Vision is, "Justice and Equality in the Workplace" and the Mission is to, "Stop and Remedy Unlawful Employment Discrimination."

As an Aboriginal (black) law-abiding woman, I knew Martin S. Ebel and Jeremy Crosbie made a conscious choice not to enforce the policy guidance of U.S. EEOC to assist an Aboriginal (black) law-abiding woman, I knew it wasn't over. The Most High God charged me long ago and commanded me to stand for righteousness. Now I had to walk totally by faith because I was denied every turn I made. It was totally up to my higher power to guide me because within my own strength it was too much to bear. Now, it was time to take this battle for justice to a new level.

Resource and Information: If you have an issue of discrimination with your employer or prior employer, please find an alternative to U.S. EEOC especially if you are a person of color. This organization is organized against blacks. If you must file with the EEOC for whatever reason, make sure you have an attorney who is truly working for you. The alternative I found for filing discrimination is with, Texas Workforce Commission, Civil Rights Division. Please file with TWC first, if at all possible, utilize the following link https://twc.texas.gov/partners/civil-rights-discrimination. Your information will be shared with EEOC under a work sharing agreement. Hopefully, you will have a better experience with protecting your rights on the state level first. As you can see my horror story with the U.S. EEOC is on the federal level and I was not protected at all.

Police/Vehicle Profiling   **Young Men Experience**

There were two Aboriginal American young men traveling to Rosenberg, Texas, for work at Frito-Lay; in a course of 3 to 4 months. The young men stated, they had been stopped over 13 times by the police. They were stopped by Hispanic, Aboriginal American and European officers. When I learned of their experience it was really alarming because we are dealing with authorities who kill by abusing their power at an alarming rate.

Officers all over this country were killing unarmed black men at an alarming rate, as if it were open season, and honestly, I was worried about all the boys and men I know who have dark skin. The young men felt as if they were targeted because of the vehicle.

Resource and Information: If you experience police misconduct, file a complaint. Send your complaint to the chief of police and send a copy to Internal Affairs. If you experience racial profiling keep a record of the days, time, officer's name and badge number. You don't have to make a big scene, stay alive! Make sure you remember what has taken place. Being afraid is natural especially when your spirit feels danger from those abusing their power. You have a right to protect yourself by remembering all the details of events, and writing them down as soon as possible, should you live through the traffic stop. Sadly, it has become a harsh reality of abuse by authorities. Maybe one day, no human will feel threatened for driving or minding their own business walking. If you are an organization that helps black, and brown people who have fallen victims to abuse of power, be proactive in the betterment of the lives of ingenious men and women.

Prayer – God always comes through. One morning I prayed to God and asked for help. As I was driving, I heard, "The enemy of my enemy is my friend." I thought nothing of it. I contacted someone, and the person didn't answer my call, so I left a message. Later we connected and in our conversation the person said to me, "The enemy of my enemy is my friend." I was shocked and told the person, I heard that in the car when I was driving. When I heard those words from the individual's mouth, I knew God sent my help. God sent my help, the source informed me that J. Crosbie never informed me of my "record of perceived disability." I wrote (refer to **Exhibit 124**) down the exact instructions, regarding submitting an amendment for the charge I filed. Then I wrote on the EEOC form, "The EEOC failed to process my complaint properly. The EEOC didn't advise me of a record of perceived disability." On November 17th, I completed (refer to **Exhibit 125 - 129**) the amendment.

On November 19, 2015, God sent me back to U.S. Equal Employment Opportunity Commission to ask for a continuance to amend the prior charge under ADAAA violations, charge no # 460-2016-00589. The Lord told me to type these words on the continuance in Red, "Every individual who puts a hand or mouth to this complaint and does nothing for the justice of this family will be cursed. My father in heaven will bring TERROR upon your house and you will lose all you treasure in Jesus' name, Amen." Also, typed in red was, "The EEOC failed to process my complaint properly. The EEOC didn't advise me of a record of perceived disability."

While I was speaking with R. Wilkerson he told me I didn't have to use legal terminology; readers, please remember God sent me help on what to write to the EEOC. God then told me when to actually visit the EEOC, so why wouldn't I use the proper terminology to get the justice I sought. After all? Legal terminology is what the EEOC recognizes and that is how the EEOC has sued other employers who violated the law regarding discrimination. I asked Wilkerson why my amendment was not notarized (refer to **Exhibit 130**), and he stated, "The charge did not need to be notarized."

As I was leaving the U.S. EEOC location on Louisiana, at the elevator, R. Wilkerson asked me was he bond by the words written in red after he "assisted" me with taking my continuance. This let me know he was worried about the consequences, yet he participated with the corruption. Also, included with this charge was an enclosure with the EEOC Form 161.

As I sit here on my bed making edits to this book God gave me a revelation; when God sent me back to the EEOC, I learned God is even merciful to my enemies. God gave all of them so many chances. Truly, God's ways are not our ways. (Isaiah 55:8-9) says, "For my thoughts are not your thoughts, neither are your ways my ways, said the LORD. For as the heavens are higher than the earth, so are my ways higher than your ways, and my thoughts than your thoughts." Since neither the president nor attorney general contacted me in private, as I had contacted both of them on numerous occasions, I was left with no choice but to ask for justice in public.

On November 20, 2015, at 9:35 a.m., I posted (refer to **Exhibit 131**) the following on my Facebook page: President Barack Obama and Attorney General L. Lynch, Good Morning. Prior communication with you and AG Lynch has been conducted in private and there has been no resolve. We are asking for every charge Jeremy Crosbie of EEOC, allegedly investigated, to be reviewed by an outside *Auditing Agency*. This agency must have no business or financial connections with the U.S. Government. Also, I'm asking for you to reinstate my charge. Jeremy Crosbie is a racist, and I was not given due process. General Dynamics Information Technology Violated ADA and ADAAA Violations. There is proof, and we will not rest until General Dynamics Information Technology, Jeremy Crosbie and Martin S. Ebel are brought to justice. Jeremy Crosbie and Martin S. Ebel have participated in public corruption and political rights violations.

We demand JUSTICE! To all listed in hashtag, please join me in this fight for justice. Some of you have received my support through voting and etc.; now I stand in the need of your support. Thank you, for your support in advance and I listed the hashtags (#EndPublicCorruptioninAmerica #EndPoliticalRightsViolations #AfricanAmericanDisabledCitizensMatter #MichaelPWilliams #MelissaHarris-Perry #JamesRucker #TriciaRose #CynthiaMcKinney #SylvesterTurner #RachelDolezal #ADA.gov #ADAAA #CornelWest #MajoraCarter #VanJones #RosaClemente #HenryLouisGatesJr. #MichaelEricDyson #RandallRobinson #CraigWatkins #AlSharpton #JesseJackson #AliceWalker #BoyceWatkins #FarhanaKhera #GabyPacheco #JuanRodriguez #FelipeMatos #CarlosRoa #NewsOne #RolandMartin #OprahWinfreyNetwork #TheAfricanHistoryNetwork #Codeblack Life #Magic102houston #Praise92 #Afro-American Newspapers #HoustonAreaUrbanLeague #NAACP #MinisterLouisFarrahkan #Fox26News #KPRC2 #CW39 #abcnews #FBI). My newest encounter on November 22, 2015, has encouraged me to fight, because they fought. Thank you! I don't believe that we meet people by accident. I truly believe that every person we meet is meant to cross our path for some reason, be it a gift or a lesson.

A demand for correction of charge was sent by email (refer to **Exhibit 132**) on November 30, 2015, at 8:52 a.m., to the EEOC District Director, R. Wilkerson.

One day I received a call from someone I wouldn't have expected. When he called, he said,

"Is this Ellenor Perkins?" I said yes and that was it. He didn't ask how he could help me or anything, nor did he give me his name. He didn't know I knew who he was, and at the time I received the call he was running for mayor. Prior to his call I voted for him, but in the second run I didn't vote for him. I was really disappointed because he could have at the least asked, "How can I help you?" On December 7, 2015, while in the midst of battle, I established two names which is part of the manifestation of my destiny.

Federal Investigator, R. Wilkerson and R. O. Irvin, District Director of U.S. EEOC sent me a notification (refer to **Exhibit 133 & 134**) on December 7, 2015. Instead of amending my initial charge #460-2014-01770, I was assigned a new charge number 460-2016-00589 and justice was again obstructed. Also, included with this dismissal was the Enclosure, EEOC Form 161, CP Enclosure and the EEOC Form 5 (11/09).

After researching online, and various places, I became upset with God after reading the cries for help on the internet. I asked God, "Why have you allowed all these people to go through this?" I was dismayed at the hundreds of people who were suffering the same injustice as I. They were literally crying out for help. God did not answer my question, made in anger.

December 10, 2015, I sent a note to myself regarding the gentleman who I contacted for help. The first note I sent was dated November 12, 2015, at 11:56 a.m., and said, Good Morning Sir, My name is Ellenor Perkins Ratcliff. Currently, I have filed a charge against the EEOC for public corruption, based upon the color of my skin. This cause is not only about me, but every individual that has faced such corruption. I'm in need of sponsors for the cause. Can you help me? I sent another note, November 13, 2015, at 11:48 a.m., the notice said, Good morning Sir, I was informed that a claim of unemployment was made Feb 20, 2014, however I didn't qualify due to income requirements.

A new claim was filed today against GDIT in regard to a hostile working environment, and I did use the term constructive discharge. At the end of the conversation, I asked key questions. Supervisor informed me, *TWC does not use constructive discharge, it uses different verbiage.* July 1, 2014, to June 30, 2015, I have no income. The issue of constructive discharge will be investigated and TWC will seek payment through, alternative base period. In the meantime I must register in three days and search for work 3 times a week. A letter will be mailed once investigation is completed. Can you call me at 1 p.m., today? I have questions regarding EEOC questionnaire that I began working on last night. Thank you, Ellenor.

I sent another note November 18, 2015, the notice said, Visited the EEOC. The person urged me to come in the morning, so my complaint could be entered right away. It was said that I may have missed the time to amend but come in anyway. I've learned that the Director has been fired. So, please pray with me that time has not lapsed and justice will be served. I sent another note, November 20, 2015. The note said, Good Morning, I visited EEOC November 19, 2015, and investigator stated, "I couldn't amend, but I was told if I still wanted to file the new charges I could, but it would not be investigated." I was told EEOC no longer has jurisdiction.

The face of EEOC has changed. There are more blacks working now. Also, there is a new Director. I was disappointed but God has led me on this path for his purpose. I will not give up. Pray for me. I don't know if you have Facebook, you can look at my information publicly without following or friend requesting. Look at it and tell me what you think. If I don't get resolve that way, a protest will be organized. Well, I started the protest process 2 months ago. Now that I know you're on my side, I feel comfortable with giving you that information. Have a Blessed day!

The Lord instructed me to contact Rayford O. Irvin and I made contact by email (refer to **Exhibit 135**) at 4:34 a.m., on December 15, 2015, regarding God sending me. December 15, 2015, at 4:50 a.m., I emailed (refer to **Exhibit 136**) the secretary of EEOC regarding my issues with the charge made and noted errors. December 15, 2015, at 4:56 a.m., I sent a note (refer to **Exhibit 137**) to myself. At 4:59 a.m., on December 15, 2015, I emailed (refer to **Exhibit 138**) Mr. Irvin and warned him. J. Saindon of EEOC responded (refer to **Exhibit 139**) to me at 10:56 a.m. on December 15, 2015, regarding my email sent at 4:34 a.m.

One day, I asked God, "How am I going to make a difference?" God did not answer me. R. O. Irvin with the EEOC denied (refer to **Exhibit 140 & 141**) my second request on December 28, 2015, after God told me to contact him on December 15th.

August 18, 2016, I contacted (refer to **Exhibit 142**) another gentleman at 10:23 p.m., and thanked him for assisting me, after providing information regarding the Judiciary Committee, and included a list of my journey to the doctor. The document said, Dear Doctor Anonymous: Thank you for providing information regarding the Judiciary Committee and it's practices. The information has been very informative. We have seen the recent flood in Louisiana, and I hope you are doing well despite the flood. My name is Ellenor and I have quite an experience with judicial injustice. It all began when my past employer violated my rights according to the Americans with Disabilities Act. A case was filed with the U.S. Equal Employment Opportunity Commission and justice was obstructed. Do you have any suggestions for me, I plan to write the House Judiciary Committee regarding a federal judge here in Houston. Below is everyone I contacted regarding my injustice.

February 28, 2017, at 6:26 a.m., I sent a note (refer to **Exhibit 143**) to myself, it was a drafted letter. I never mailed the letter to President Trump. I also sent a note (refer to **Exhibit 144**) to myself at 6:32 a.m., regarding activity for January 18, 2017.

I was so sick and tired of this process; I just wanted it all to be over. On September 4, 2018, I contacted (refer to **Exhibit 145**) President Donald Trump regarding my journey of injustice. The White House received my letter (refer to **Exhibit 146**) on September 12, 2018.

God said to me, "A time for retribution is coming." I heard this at 4:36 p.m., on September 30, 2018. The White House sent a letter (refer to **Exhibit 147 & 148**) addressed to my name on November 20, 2018.

Resource and Information: We must be careful to let God have his perfect will, and that all things are revealed. For there is a set time for every prophecy to come forth. When God was merciful to the enemies of his people, God was giving grace for the enemy to right the wrong; but like so many of them, they couldn't help themselves, and were thereby destroyed by their own deceitful hearts. If God has given your enemy grace, get out of God's way and let God work.

Chapter 4: U.S. Southern District of Texas   **Journey for Justice**

       After some research, I made calls to inquire on the process for filing a lawsuit. Once given the online information regarding the court, I downloaded the complaint form I found online and additional documents. I viewed the website and was a little optimistic. I guess it was just wishful thinking after all the denials I experienced; maybe now I would have progress. After completing the "Original Complaint" (refer to **Exhibit 149 - 151**) which was 3 pages, the "Exhibit and Witness List" (refer to **Exhibit 152 & 153**) which was 2 pages and the "Application to Proceed in District Court Without Prepaying Fees or Costs," I visited the Southern District of Texas on October 7, 2015 and submitted my lawsuit. I approached the counter and told the clerk, I need to file a lawsuit against the EEOC.

       While waiting there, a woman, the same race as I am stated to me, "You are going to sue EEOC?" I boldly said, "Yes." By this time the clerk who was providing me assistance gave me a packet (refer to **Exhibit 154 – 159, 162 & 163**) - ("Guidelines for litigants without lawyers – Sothern District of Texas, 7 pages (I have only provided 8 pages for your viewing); Appendix A - Employment Discrimination Complaint 3 pages; Appendix D - Summons In A Civil Action; Appendix E – Notice Of A Lawsuit and Request To Waive Service Of A Summons; Appendix F – Waiver Of The Service Of Summons; and AO240A - Order to Proceed Without Prepaying Fees or Costs) I needed to complete.

       In all, I submitted to federal court: Appendix B - Original Complaint (4:15-cv-03038); Exhibit and Witness List - AO187, AO187A; Application To Proceed In District Court Without Prepaying Fees or Costs – AO240 (2 pages); Appendix F – Waiver Of The Service Of Summons (U.S. Attorney Kenneth Magidson); Appendix F – Waiver Of The Service Of Summons (U.S. Attorney General Loretta E. Lynch); Appendix F – Waiver Of The Service Of Summons (U.S. Equal Employment Opportunity Commission); Motion for Court Appointed Attorneys (refer to **Exhibit 165**) ; (EEOC file includes reasonable doubt (21 pages); EEOC, How to File a Charge of Employment Discrimination (2 pages); TWC, How to Submit an Employment Discrimination Complaint, reasonable doubt (2 pages); Correspondences with United States President, Attorney General Lynch and CMS (10 pages); Medical record of perceived disability, reasonable doubt (9 pages); General Dynamics Information Technology, reasonable doubt (2 pages); Attorneys contacted (5 pages).

       I completed the additional court papers below and filed in federal court. My Southern District of Texas case number is (4:15-cv-03038). I brought a civil suit against U.S. EEOC, U.S.

Attorney General Lynch, U.S. Attorney Kenneth Magidon, Jerome Cosby, and Martin S. Ebel.

I was not aware, when you sue the EEOC, you have to also sue the Attorney General, and the U.S. Attorney. The clerk informed me that I needed to complete an "Affidavit of Financial Resources" and return it to the court. I was given a receipt (refer to **Exhibit 166**) as proof that my case was officially filed. I completed the Affidavit of Financial Resources on October 14th and returned to the federal court to submit the document.

While there, I asked questions regarding the application for not paying court fees. I also asked who would be my judge. The clerk told me my request was approved, and the judge was Lynn Hughes.

I asked for a copy (refer to **Exhibit 167**) of the court paper. When I received the copy, I saw that someone wrote, "The clerk will directly assign this case to Judge Lynn N. Hughes. They marked out civil and wrote, "Miscellaneous." I'm always researching, so I took the time to research information on Judge Lynn N Hughes.

Although there were some articles against him, I still had faith God would work it all out. Order of Conference was mailed (refer to **Exhibit 168 - 171**) to me on October 15, 2015, and it mentions, "Pretrial conference on January 11, 2016, at 11 a.m., before Judge Lynn N. Hughes, at 515 Rusk Avenue, Room 11122, Houston, Texas." On October 15, 2015, I was mailed (refer to **Exhibit 172 - 174**) a second document (Instrument 4, Instructions) from The United States District Court.

Instead of granting my motion for a court appointed attorney, I was told I could represent myself. The court had no intention of actually holding a fair trial by jury. On October 23, 2015, at 4:45 p.m., I sent a note (refer to **Exhibit 175**) to myself regarding subpoenas for witnesses. While going through the court proceedings, it's important to subpoena witnesses. On October 29, 2015, I visited the court with my completed subpoenas (refer to **Exhibit 176**), and submitted for seven (7) witnesses to be served. I will only provide one subpoena for viewing.

While at the courthouse to get the subpoenas processed, the elderly European woman who stamped my court papers for service became angry with me. And again, I must tell you, the devil can't stand for you to fight and stand for righteousness, so the devil will use anyone (vessel) willing.

November 4, 2015, I received mail (refer to **Exhibit 177 - 180**) from The United States District Court.

The judge entered two judgements, "Final Dismissal with Prejudice" and a "Opinion on Dismissal" (H-15-3038) on November 3, 2015.

Every culprit will be held accountable, for the laws have been broken, and the Lord will act. Pharaoh is evil and must be destroyed. You have acted against a child of the Most High God, and he has heard the cries of his children. You have oppressed us and denied us due process.

May my father in heaven bring TERROR upon your house; for you have together diminished the trust of God's children and the people of The United States. May the Lord judge you one hundred times the measure you have given in Jesus's name, Amen. I learned the subpoenas I submitted to The United States District Court were actually served by the U.S. Marshall.

On November 5, 2015, I Googled my name and found (refer to **Exhibit 181**) my case on Justia's website, https://dockets.justia.com/docket/texas/txsdce/4:2015mc02406/1302445. If you have time, type the link in your browser, you will be able to view the case docket. On November 17, 2015, Ogletree Deakins responded (refer to **Exhibit 182 - 193**) to my subpoenas for L. Marlin and Z. Bosie to testify and produce. One mistake I made was giving too much evidence (EEOC file includes reasonable doubt (21 pages); EEOC, How to File a Charge of Employment Discrimination (2 pages); TWC, How to Submit an Employment Discrimination Complaint, reasonable doubt (2 pages); Correspondences with United States President, Attorney General Lynch and CMS (10 pages); Medical record of perceived disability, reasonable doubt (9 pages); General Dynamics Information Technology, reasonable doubt (2 pages); Attorneys contacted (5 pages) to Judge Lynn H. Hughes.

I should have followed legal procedures, but what did I know at the time. I was ignorant to the legal process, and my ignorance lead to the judge taking advantage, and abusing his power.

While on Facebook for a short moment to make an inspirational post, July 2019, I saw an interesting post my friend shared; This post mentioned, "specialized docket", "COURTCORRUPTION?!" and said, "Everyone needs to ask if they were placed on a specialized docket."

When reading, I thought about the court papers which I had in my possession. I shared the post and wrote, My case was placed on a specialized docket, when I sued United States Equal Employment Opportunity Commission in the United States District Court. The idiots even wrote on my federal paper, "The clerk will directly assign this case to Judge Lynn H. Hughes." September 6, 2019, at 3:25 p.m., as I'm reading to make sure everything in my manuscript is lining up, something happened, I'm directed to the letter Martin S. Ebel wrote on July 7, 2015, in particular I'm looking at the part which says, "You were not accorded a substantial weight review, because that process only occurs where a Fair Employment Practices Agency (FEPA) (such as, for example, the Texas Workforce Commission) has made a determination on a charge that was <u>DUAL FILED</u> with BOTH a FEPA and the EEOC. "<u>Your charge was not filed with a FEPA, but rather</u>

was filed directly with the EEOC…"

As I sit here on September 11, 2019, at 10:12 p.m., going over the letter again dated July 7, 2015, the printout from March 10, 2014, and printout from October 2, 2015, has opened my eyes. The letter says, my charge was not filed with a FEPA. Under the work-sharing agreement of the EEOC or FEPA (Texas Workforce Commission), on printout March 10, 2014, it says "the charge also will be automatically filed with the other agency. This process, which is defined as dual filing, helps to protect charging party rights under both federal and state or local law." Now I have some questions. Who didn't dual file my charge? Why wasn't my charge dual filed? Why wasn't I protected on the state level regarding my employment discrimination?

Resource and Information: We have all heard about the judicial system especially when it comes to criminal courts, and ingenious men and women of America. Many of us know, the judicial system has been a force, weaponized, and utilized to promote the evil genocide by the European culture to enslave the black community. If you come across such a judge, you can only win by practicing spiritual warfare first. Second, ask God to give you strategy. Third, make sure you report the judge's conduct. You can file a complaint with the United States courts by utilizing the following link and completing the complaint process https://www.uscourts.gov/judges-judgeships/judicial-conduct-disability/faqs-filing-judicial-conduct-or-disability-complaint; or you can contact the State Commission on Judicial Conduct, and submit the complaint form online. Write a letter following the details at the following link or request a complaint form be mailed to you http://www.scjc.texas.gov/complaint-faq/.

On January 9, 2016, early in the morning I heard, "This is not the time." I knew exactly what God was saying to me, and Marvin Sapp's song, "Not The Time Not The Place" came to mind. I began to push my way.

I'm not doing this in my own strength, but guidance of the Holy Spirit. This is a huge task, but my father in heaven has equipped me.

February 1, 2016, I wrote a letter (refer to **Exhibit 194**) that I never sent to the EEOC, added intro to video name, video title, and selected and recorded music for my video. Contact was made to some popular music artist, but I was either ignored or told no I can't use their music, I understood.

February 9, 2016, I continued to record my video and created new signs (refer to **Exhibit 196 - 198**). February 14th, I continued to create and this day I was designing art for my t-shirt. I added a shield to the cross drawing and the color pattern. You can view my design below.

February 22nd, I continued to edit credits for the video, and added the church victims from the Charleston shooting, and details for following me on social media. I continued to work on my protest flyer.

February 26, 2016, I added Lady Justice Resource Services to Instagram (@ladyjusticeepr), and my first post was February 18, 2016. I recorded my poem, recorded the intro to my poem, selected my background for credits to stroll against, I received consent to use names for audio recording, recorded music to video, and I shared the video to all social media sites., Facebook - https://www.facebook.com/ellenor.p.ratcliff?ref=bookmarks; Twitter - https://twitter.com/LadyJusticeEPR; and Instagram – https://www.instagram.com/ladyjusticeepr/.

March 1, 2016, a friend told me, "God said, change is coming." I continued to create more signs.

Resource and Information: God is my continued source! In the events of this battle, I have truly learned, my greatest purpose is to live, move and have my being in God. I love the way God encourages me when it seems that I can't go on, and the battle is just too much for me to bare, for that is the time when God gives me his strength and pour into my soul. (Psalm 73:26) says, "My flesh and my heart may fail, but God is the strength of my heart and my portion forever." (Isaiah 40:29) says, "He gives power to the faint, and to him who has no might he increases strength. (Psalm 31:24) says, "Be strong, and let your heart take courage, all you who wait for the Lord!" (2 Thessalonians 3:3) says, "But the Lord is faithful. He will establish you and guard you against the evil one."

Department of Justice   **Response**

Department of Justice (DOJ) finally responded (refer to **Exhibit 199**) on March 4, 2016, after I contacted Attorney General Loretta Lynch by mail on September 1st, and September 14, 2015, by certified mail. DOJ responded to me six months after the fact. Reverend Martin Luther King said, "Justice too long delayed is justice denied."

I was naïve concerning justice in America, this country is evil, and all levels have participated. Many of them have accepted bribes, especially the U.S. Equal Employment Opportunity Commission. God gave me a dream about a well-known person on March 8, 2016. We must lean and depend totally on God, he works in mysterious ways.

Resource and Information: Who do you report the Department of Justice to, when the agency doesn't accurately do their job?

The Miracle Worker   **God Did It**

For my birthday on *June 1, 2016*, I posted, how good God had been to me. Thank You LORD!!! Give God the glory. Alone in my room July 2014, I stopped breathing; I felt a hand rub my back, and I was breathing fine.

No one but God has brought me through, I don't take one moment for granted. I was supposed to die, but God. He has allowed me to see 39 years of the good, bad and the ugly. I'm willing to do whatever God tells me, regardless of the critics. The LORD is my everything!!!!

Resource and Information: As I took, what I thought was my last breath, tears filled my eyes. I wanted to know, who would take care of my children. I was scared and worried about them, because this world is such a dark place. God is miraculous, and no one can tell me any different. God will step out of himself and come to your rescue. I'm a witness.

Others See Your Success   **Do You Have The Faith?**

A few weeks ago God brought to memory when my mother was alive and a great friend from Atlanta became my mentor.

One day she told me a little detail about my building, I specifically remember her speaking about the doors. At the time I was operating a residential childcare home and we thought it had something to do with children, but now I know, God was doing something bigger than I could have imagined.

Unknowingly this was the calling to my destiny. I'm sitting here October 22, 2019, at 5 in the morning adding to my book and I remember to add my experience from 2013 when a friend's associate told him, "I see her …" I said that to let you know, God has shown others parts of your future and have used various individuals to speak life into your situation.

I have witnessed some people who learn who you are, say nothing at all but they watch. Walk circumspect because you represent the Most High God. I wouldn't dare want to put a stain on his name.

The Pain   **Green Backpack**

This journey left me so broken. My heart was bleeding, and it seems like there's not a way out. I had this green Army color looking backpack. One day, I walked over to pick up the backpack, and I experienced great pain. I was looking for something that was pertaining to this journey, and it was located in my green Army color looking backpack.

I had no idea how broken I was, I touched the green backpack that contained the trouble of my experience. The pain hit me with great force, and I started crying.

After that experience I couldn't touch the backpack for months to come. When I would see it sitting over in the corner I didn't remember what God told me, all I remember was the pain I felt.

My heart was torn into two, because of everything I had gone through. No one with the power or ability would help me.

As the months passed, I asked God for healing, and to restore me. I've asked for restoration often. One day, I had to go back to that same green Army color looking backpack, but this time it was different.

No longer does the pain of the journey fill my heart, and I couldn't remember what the pain felt like. All I know is, the painful documents contained within that green backpack, no longer held me captive.

God is a healer. He mends the broken-hearted and restores the soul. To my readers, sometimes you must walk it out. It's the only way for God's destiny to be fulfilled in your life.

Continued from page 41: Since I was still pursuing justice, knowing Vangent/GDIT violated me I was not stopping, so I filed for unemployment benefits with the Texas Workforce Commission on November 8, 2015. November 16th, I was denied unemployment benefits (refer to **Exhibit 200**), and was not informed of a special qualifying due to disability. Notification was received (refer to **Exhibit 201**) on November 20, 2015, informing me of the denial from Texas Workforce Commission regarding my claim for unemployment benefits, for an alternate base period.

As I struggle to gain the reasoning behind the madness I'm experiencing, I learn little by little, there is a greater purpose, and I continue to take the proper steps to lead me to the place of my destiny. After contacting TWC in July, on August 6, 2019, Texas Workforce Commission, Open Records Department sent (refer to **Exhibit 202 - 208**) the request I had long been awaiting from the *unemployment request, 190621-008*. I thought to myself, now I have proof Vangent/GDIT lied, when I was seeking unemployment benefits from TWC.

I strongly believe Vangent/GDIT lied to U.S. Equal Employment Opportunity Commission, Broadspire a Crawford Company-New Hampshire Insurance Co., and Center for Medicare and Medicaid. The first four pages is the breakdown of charges, the "retention schedule for major program records," pages six to eight is the second report, and it mentions the following information, "Quit" and the reason was, "Health or Medical Reason," page fourteen to seventeen is a report on "fact finding statements," and pages eighteen to twenty-one is regarding the unemployment report that I received back in November 2015.

The package received is 21 pages in all. The most important details to me is stated on pages 9, 10, 11, 12 and 13. Page 9 lists the employer response deadline, and the employer separation reason. Page 10 lists my first, and last day of work for Vangent/General Dynamics Information Technology. Page 11 lists the reason for separation, and Vangent/General Dynamics Information Technology stated, "Voluntary QT/Separation," and gave my separation date of 02-17-14. Page 12 lists my employer's response for me quitting. Vangent/General Dynamics Information Technology said, I quit for personal reasons. Additional information says, "The claimant voluntarily quit for personal reasons."

At the bottom of the page, it asks the question, "Did the claimant take actions to avoid quitting?" You guessed it, Vangent/General Dynamics Information Technology said, "No." Liars! Page 13 lists a statement which says, "The claimant voluntarily quit for personal reasons.

Did he/she give a specific reason (other than personal) for resigning (marriage, domestic obligations, school classes, etc.)? No other details are available as the site is now closed."

Wow! It is three years, eight months, four weeks, and three days later, as of August 6, 2019. The truth has been revealed through evidence, Vangent/GDIT lied to Texas Workforce Commission to deny me unemployment benefits.

Resource and Information: If you need to file for unemployment, make sure to file as soon as you are laid off, fired or have to resign due to conditions on the job. Make sure that you request a copy of the investigation after your employer has responded to the claim, and a decision has been made regarding your unemployment benefits. You can contact Texas Workforce Commission, Open Records Department by utilizing the following link to file a complaint https://apps.twc.state.tx.us/OpenRecords/submitform. Records for unemployment claims are retained with TWC for 4 years and civil rights department records are retained with TWC for 3 years. Complete the 7 sections online to request unemployment records, as well as civil rights employment discrimination records, filed with U.S. EEOC or TWC. You can request a copy of an investigation filed with HUD for housing discrimination as well. If you don't live in Texas, you must contact your state regulation office, on guidance regarding obtaining public records request for unemployment, civil rights employment discrimination or housing discrimination.

While researching online, I was going through all the tabs of information provided at my fingertips. I saw information for submitting a complaint. Well, here I am again, in the fight for justice. I viewed information regarding the Office of Injured Employee Council (OIEC), and the Texas Workers' Compensation Act.

Never had I before heard of OIEC, nor was there any mention from the attorney about this organization. Maybe the workers' compensation attorney, who helped me with my claim in 2015, was not knowledgeable in regard to, the OIEC. Here I was digging deeper and researching more on December 14, 2018. I made calls to the Texas Department of Insurance – Division of Workers' Compensation. Information was sent to me regarding my claim denial, for benefits submitted to Broadspire a Crawford company. On that day I happen to call Broadspire and asked for the adjuster who originally denied my claim. I was informed, Ms. D. Fields was no longer with the company.

My call was never returned after I left a voicemail message on December 17, 2018. I called back and spoke to someone by the name of Stephanie. She laughed at me when I explained the reason for my call. After speaking with the Texas Department of Insurance in December, I was informed I would get a call. A call was received from Office of Injured Employee Counsel Intake. Information was given regarding the process, and I was given the website, www.oiec.texas.gov. The staff stated, "The office has received your referrals, and the Houston West-Field Office will be handling your complaints of Fraud.

Your case will be forwarded to an ombudsman, and Form 41 is on file. Your application was processed on 12-21-18, and a docketing team sets case development appointment for the ombudsman, you should get a call from a number starting with (512). The ombudsman is B. Vill." I was given the steps of OIEC process. 1st Step – Intake Submission, 2nd Step – Process Intake, 3rd Step – Docketing Team sets case development appointment for the ombudsman, 4th Step – You will receive a call from area code (512-804), to notify you regarding date/time of case development appointment, and you will also be notified by mail. 5th Step – There will be a 45-minute case development appointment (appointments are 45 minute). I was also informed, I would receive an email with instructions. The email (refer to **Exhibit 209**) was received December 18, 2018, at 4:41 p.m. As instructed, I completed each step. On December 20, 2018, I faxed (refer to **Exhibit 210 - 219**) the completed Intake packet to the Office of Injured Employee Counsel, with supporting documentation. The total pages faxed were 26. On that day, I received an Intake Packet in the mail from the Office of Injured Employee Counsel as well.

January 2, 2019 was my case development appointment and I spoke with the Assistant Ombudsman. January 9th, I faxed (refer to **Exhibit 220 - 224**) the OIEC an updated medical providers list, and HIPPA Authorization form, since some of the information for the doctors who treated me changed. Later I called and was informed causation letters were sent to all the medical providers on my list. These doctors "treated" or serviced me, in one way or another concerning my asthma. January 11, 2019, I received a package from OEIC, and it was the causation packet that was sent to each doctor I listed. The information had not yet been received by the OIEC. On January 30, 2019, I faxed Dr. Hus office regarding completing the packet, and I faxed Dr. Cal office regarding completing the packet. On February 1, 2019, I faxed Dr. Mus office regarding completing the packet. All doctors were contacted by phone/ fax regarding my medical records.

After contacting OIEC on February 8th, it was verified Dr. C sent in records on the 4th. On February 11, 2019, I contacted Harris Health Administration, and asked for the name of the supervisor of Vallbona Clinic, then I contacted Mr. Mat at the corporate office to make sure business was handled properly. Mr. Mat sent a notice over to Mr. Part, and asked Mr. Part to call me; the same day I contacted Dr. M. Mus office, to verify if medical records were sent and was informed, "11 pages are being faxed as we speak." Contact was made with OIEC, and it was confirmed that Dr. Cal/ S. Associates sent the documents, and it was received on the 4th.

February 13th, I contacted the supervisor of Vallbona Clinic, and he stated, "Kate should have called you." February 14, 2019, I contacted OIEC, and it was verified Dr. Husain records were received. The (OIEC) had not received my records from Harris Health System. Contact was made with the medical records on February 15th. I asked for a release. Once received, I completed and faxed Harris Health System the HIPPA form, and requested my medical records be released to OIEC.

February 18th, I contacted Harris Health for medical records, Kate asked me to fill out the HIPPA Authorization again and fax it to the number given. February 21, 2019, the Ombudsman called me, he needed the doctor who treated me to complete the document. As a result of his call, I contacted Harris Health regarding the doctor. I wanted to know why the doctor had not completed the request. I spoke with the supervisor of the clinic and informed him I still needed the documents completed. He stated, "I thought it was completed," then he stated, "I will talk to the doctor."

I contacted OIEC and was given the choice to put my case on hold or go through with the benefit review conference, and we decided to place the case on hold. I received a letter (refer to **Exhibit 225 & 226**) from Office of Injured Employee Council, dated March 19, 2019, stating my case will be on hold until causation analysis forms are completed.

Chapter 5: Harris Health - Do you work for the patient or employers?

OIEC, Workman's Comp & Harris Health

After making many calls to Harris Health System, and getting the run around, the manager finally told me, "You need to see Dr. June in order for the doctor to complete the causation paperwork." I told him, I stop coming to the clinic, because I couldn't get the help I needed. And I told him, I have a private doctor. The manager of the clinic said, "You need to get your new doctor to complete the forms." I said, "No I don't, those forms are regarding documentation on services I received from 2013-2014." The manager said, "You need to call and make an appointment."

When I called the appointment line, the appointment was too far off, for the time I needed the causation paperwork returned to OIEC. I called back and told the manager, I need you all to make the appointment because you have given me the run around, and my papers are due soon. The manager stated, "You need to call eligibility." I told him I will pay myself. How much does it cost? The manager said, "I don't think they are taking self-pay, let me find out and I will call you back." The manager of the facility called me with an appointment that was too far off.

Afterward, I called the compliance department of Harris Health, and explained my situation. I was given a sooner appointment for March 28, 2019. When I visited (refer to **Exhibit 227)** the clinic on this day, it was about nothing but games.

Although the doctor knew I was suffering at my job, she refused to complete the causation papers without seeing me, and remind you, she knew how I was suffering. And worst of all, she still refused to complete the papers after my doctor visit to the clinic. Maybe she assumed I was lying, all the times I had been to Harris Health System with restricted breathing, and maybe the pulmonary clinic was lying about my diagnosis too. Dr. June even completed my benefit papers, and added my diagnosis on July 28, 2014, which states, "Primary disabling diagnosis," the doctor wrote "Allergic Rhinitis triggering Asthma Environmental allergies," the "Secondary disabling diagnosis," the doctor wrote, "Asthma," but wouldn't say the exposure on my job was causing me to have asthma attacks. I was extremely pissed. She took me to the administrative office.

The manager told me a doctor does not have to complete a form, if it's been over a year since you were seen. I told him, "I don't care how long it was, I was treated here, and your doctors have a duty to their patients." I also told all of the staff standing around me, not to patronize me; these people think we are complete idiots. Since the doctor refused to provide the proper information regarding my medical situation, and the treatment I received while I was a patient of

Harris Health System, I contact the OIEC the earlier part of May to move forward. I received a call regarding, the preparation appointment for May 31st at 11 a.m.

A notice of a Benefit Review Conference was mailed (refer to **Exhibit 228 - 230**) to me on May 15, 2019, and I was informed my review would be on June 18, 2019. The letter was also sent to New Hampshire Insurance Co., and a copy of the letter was mailed to General Dynamics Corp, 2941 Fairview Park Dr., Falls Church, VA 22042 – 4522. A notice (refer to **Exhibit 231 & 232**) from Office of Injured Employee Council was received on May 16, 2019, regarding the preparation appointment to discuss my case on May 31, 2019, at 11 a.m. After realizing there was a conflict in my schedule, I called to reschedule the appointment for May 31st. The OIEC mailed me a second notice (refer to **Exhibit 233 & 234**) on May 17, 2019, regarding a new appointment for June 4, 2019, at 3 p.m.

June 18, 2019, I arrived for my hearing, and brought copies of the medical information, as well as the information from the attorney who helped me with my workers' comp claim. Before arriving, I imagined the opportunity to face the liars who violated me. The ombudsman greeted me, and we walked to an area where he spoke to me regarding my case. I was informed, the attorney was not able to view the email sent with all my information pertaining to the claim, and I learned, because the doctor wouldn't connect my aggravation on the job, to my difficulty with asthma attacks, it would be difficult going before the judge. The ombudsman attempted to print the exact information, which was emailed to the attorney for New Hampshire Insurance Co., but there were issues with the printer (everything happens for a reason). It was my desire to face the liars, but only the attorney arrived.

After all the questions, and information given at the hearing, I took notice that the attorney was ill prepared. I ultimately decided to reschedule the hearing. Rescheduling gave the attorney time to view the evidence, which I gave to Office of Injured Employee Council from the claim, and I would also have the opportunity to contact an attorney and get help on causation. During the meeting I was given a two-page HIPPA form and was asked if I would approve a HIPPA authorization from the attorney.

Due to my experience I was not signing anything without consulting an attorney. I was informed, the attorney can go to the judge, and order me to sign. I told the ombudsman, he would have to go to the judge. I was escorted out of the meeting area to the lobby, and then to the hallway, where the ombudsman and I talked. I asked questions regarding the name of the attorney, and gentleman who mediated. Information was given regarding connecting my daily exposure on the job to the asthma attacks, experienced on a daily basis. I felt good and left with a positive outlook.

July 3, 2019, I called and was able to contact someone regarding worker's comp assistance and was informed a doctor will be in contact. Well, the doctor did call back, and questioned me regarding my issues, and stated he didn't have a doctor to help in that area since it had been so long. I ask the doctor if he had a referral, and he stated, "You need a toxicologist."

Well, if you all don't know me by now, I started researching on a toxicologist. I remember seeing a law office in the Katy Magazine. I called and gave information regarding my issue in hope of receiving help. The clerk stated her attorney could not assist me but gave me a referral for an attorney who deals with my specific issue.

My mother always said, "Nothing beats a failure but a try." When I contacted the attorney and explained my issue, the attorney explained exactly what the ombudsman stated. I told the attorney about the mediation held by the OIEC, and the attorney stated, "A Benefit Review Conference." I said, yes. The attorney gave me additional information and informed me of what I needed to do, and to call back once I obtained that information. On that same day I contacted OIEC, and spoke with the representative, then explained I wanted to request a designated doctor from DWC. July 5, 2019, I called back and asked if the ombudsman responded. I also asked the representative to send the supervisor a carbon copy (cc), when sending the message to request for a designated doctor, and I was given the name of the supervisor. July 16th, the ombudsman called me back but I missed the call. The ombudsman left me a message. The message was, "A designated doctor is only given once the carrier accepts liability."

On July 17, 2019, I was contacted by a therapy center and was referred by an unknown person for workman's comp help. My appointment was scheduled for July 18th. July 23, 2019, I contacted the therapy center to give other medications that I didn't write down on the admission forms. At that time I was asked for the workman's comp claim number, so I gave the number under DWC: 152*****, New Hampshire Insurance Co., but I explained, the Office of Injured Employee Counsel may be handling my case and I gave the telephone number 866-393-6432. Here I am thinking my request was granted by OIEC, but I was mistaken.

After contacting the OIEC regarding information I received from the therapy center, I asked to speak with a particular person, and I was informed by OIEC that there was no such person in their organization. Due to what the representative stated to me (no such person in the organization), I asked to speak with the supervisor of the ombudsman, because maybe he scheduled the referral. The representative sent a message to the ombudsman to contact me regarding the issue at hand.

Because my mind was going a thousand miles per hour, on July 24th, I called back to the therapy center to question the referral department. I wanted to know who made the referral, and if there was a telephone number, or a name of the company the person called from. The center told me, "The only thing I see in the system is that Mr. Right is a referral source." I told her I don't know if he is my adjuster or what, and I was asked for the carrier name and claim #number. I gave the assistant the name, New Hampshire Insurance Co and claim number 1880*****-001. I asked the assistant to call me back, once she has spoken with the company.

I received information on whom the new adjuster was and the telephone number. August 15, 2019, I visited the therapy center again for re-examination under workman's comp and was scheduled to see the doctor back in a month. Harris Health System had not sent over my records as requested. The doctor told me to give it another week, and then contact to verify if Harris Health System has sent over my records. After waiting as instructed, I contacted the therapy center on August 20th, and my medical records from Harris Health System were still not in possession of the therapy center.

I completed the HIPPA form, instructing the department to release my medical records from, 2010 to 2019.

I faxed (refer to **Exhibit 235 & 236**) the form to ensure it was received and waited for a confirmation. I also sent the confirmation and fax (refer to **Exhibit 237 & 238**) to the therapy center, so they would be aware that I did complete Harris Health System HIPPA form. On August 29, 2019, I contacted Office of Injured Employee Council and ask for the ombudsman, to talk about the information I was given regarding the insurance company. The representative took my information regarding the therapy center, and the doctor I have seen on two separate occasions and whom I would see again on September 16th. I inform the OIEC representative that the clinic couldn't tell me where the referral source came from, but on July 24th, the clinic did give me the name of the insurance adjuster and telephone number. I said it was weird not knowing who the referral source was, and the representative stated, "This information will be forwarded to your ombudsman."

The ombudsman, and I were finally able to talk after a game of phone tag; we talked, and I was given information regarding the situation, and how it was not the normal course of action. I was told to be careful, because I could be stuck with the medical bills, if the insurance carrier is not the one sending me to the therapy center. The ombudsman was really concerned about me getting stuck with the medical bills and gave me some other important information. Here we are almost a month later, and time for me to see the therapy center doctor, I called September 13, 2019, to verify if my medical records had been received, since my appointment is Monday, and I was informed the medical records from Harris Health System had yet to be received.

September 16, 2019, I visited the therapy center to see the doctor. When I checked in, I received a missed call from the therapy center. I informed the front office, someone had just called me from here and the person asked, "Are you Ellenor P Ratcliff," and I said yes. The doctor made a referral and the information I gave for my employer's insurance was not working, it was kicked back. The specialist needed my employer's name, address, phone, and fax number. I told the staff, I had already given my employers carrier and all of their contact information. I was told, "Yes but the employer's information is needed." I informed the staff, that I didn't have that information with me, but I will see if I can find the information online. I brought some of the medical records, I was able to locate with detailed doctors' notes and testing, regarding my treatment during the time I was having issues with exposure on the job.

The doctor comes in and I think that everything is fine because the front office informed me about a referral, but I learned the insurance carrier was still denying me and wasn't going to pay for me to see the specialist. I told the doctor I will pay out-of-pocket if I have must. The doctor viewed my medical records and noticed some interesting things, which tied my asthma exacerbations (attacks), on the job to the exposure, I had been complaining about all the time, while working for the company. When I complained, the doctors and staff were keeping notes of what I had been saying, even when I threatened to call the news and CDC. As the doctor continued to talk, I told the doctor, I'm going to keep fighting, I've fought this long and I'm not going to stop.

I told the doctor something big is going to happen, and that I have records of the company lying regarding what took place on the job and told the doctor sometimes you have to leave enough rope for companies to hang themselves (meaning the evidence far outweighs them getting out of this lie). I asked for the referral and was scheduled back to visit the doctor for a follow-up.

When I returned to my vehicle, I was thanking God for what he was doing, and as I sat in the vehicle at 11:44 a.m., I heard the voice of the LORD say, "Trust in the LORD with all your heart, and lean not to your own understanding." This excited me, and I knew it meant for me to stop trying to figure out who sent me to the treatment center.

Harris Health System   **Medical Records**

While at home, I began to look at my medical records and was reading everything. The first record I read was dated January 6th, the record list my visit at 9 a.m., to MLK Clinic. I was tested for CBC/DIFF. Under results, it said, "Abnormal, Final result (1/6/2014 11:44 PM)" and gave the component results; the second test for UA CHEMISTRIES list my results "Final result (1/6/2014 2:22 PM)" and gave the component results; the third test for Basic Metabolic Panel list my results as, "Abnormal, Final result (1/7/2014 12:27 AM)" and gave the component results. The fourth test (refer to **Exhibit 239**) was a Chest X-ray 2 views. On January 16, 2014, at 4:45 p.m., the doctor reviewed my x-rays, and she stated, "I have reviewed your labs/exams. There are some abnormalities. Please have patient schedule an appointment to discuss these results. Thanks."

The x-ray results was compared to the results from 1-31-2013. February 13, 2014, the record list my visit at 8 a.m., to Smith Clinic for the pulmonary department when I was tested (refer to **Exhibit 240**) for IGE, Total. Under results, it said, "Abnormal, Final result (2/13/2014 4:35 p.m.)" and gave the component results. February 18, 2014, the record list my results from Smith Clinic, pulmonary department after further testing on 2-13-14 for Allergens Zone 6. Under results, it said, "Abnormal, Final result (2/18/2014 7:26 a.m.)" and gave the component results.

February 19, 2014, the record list my visit at 8 a.m., to Vallbona Clinic for breathing issues (refer to **Exhibit 241 & 242**). "Chief complaint: Breathing Problems, …1. SOB followed by Pulm- She has had EKG, CXR, PFT, TTE and methacholine challenge appts in future. <u>Pt spoke at length about call center job she started 9/2013 where "people spraying perfume" that causes her sxs, but sxs worsened after quit her job. She has written emails to HR that rule was not enforced and wants to report to CDC</u> also…She also reports fatigue. Admits to onset of these sxs when exposed to mold which is noted on pulmonary notes. <u>Pt says she was told by Pulm she doesn't have asthma</u>…"Per last pulmonary visit 6 days ago: Ms. Perkins…<u>with PMH of Allergic Rhinitis, GERD, 3 year history of asthma symptoms with SOB, chest tightness, still poorly controlled despite multiple medications.</u> Asthma: listed current medications, but <u>still having problems when exposed to triggers at work,</u> continue current regimen. <u>Counseled on avoiding triggers</u>, EKG to evaluate chest tightness given findings on CXR… Methacholine challenge given normal PFTs RTC after methacholine challenge." Medical history listed is "Allergic rhinitis no dm or ht, Mold suspected exposure, reflux, allergic and depression."

Physical exam showed "No distress. Cardiovascular: Normal rate, regular rhythm and normal heart sounds. Pulmonary/ Chest: Effort normal and breath sounds normal. No respiratory distress." Assessment/Plan said, "1. SOB (shortness of breath) – Keep appts: TTE 3/2014. PFT, Pulm FU 4/2014, give Pt phone # to call for Allergy clinic appt 2. Other malaise and fatigue – Iron profile, Vitamin B12... Keep Md appt 4/15/14." And as usual my blood pressure was excellent. April 15, 2014, the record list my visit at 10 a.m. to Vallbona Clinic for follow-up. Under doctors notes it says, "Patient is here for – Lab Follow-up, Medication Follow Up..." the records list my past medical history of, "Allergic rhinitis no dm or ht, Mold suspected exposure, reflux, allergic and depression" and "Review of Systems, Cardiovascular, Gastrointestinal, Musculoskeletal" as well as chart review.

Several objectives were listed but I want to focus on the following: "General Appearance: no apparent distress, Nasal mucosa normal and Lungs: bilateral scattered wheezing." Assessment/Plan said, "1. Obesity, unspecified 2. Allergic rhinitis" and two medications were listed "3. Medication refill 4.Extrinic asthma with exacerbation" and the doctor prescribed four medications for me to take. And my blood pressure was excellent as usual. June 24, 2014, (the record list) my visit to Vallbona Clinic for Well Woman Exam. The nurse notes mention, "Patient was engaged in plan of care and encouraged to continue to be actively involved in patient own care, therefore, improving safety..." Under doctors notes it says, "1. Well woman," and list information, 2. Says, "Med refill" and list two medications, "she wants to get outside, will change PCP as she has insurance.

Also she mentions she wants to see outside PULM but will keep CT appt today and PULM FU appt 6/25/14." The same past medical history is listed as before, and gave info regarding my well woman exam, and history of never being a smoker, and occasional user of alcohol. Assessment/Plan said, "1. Well Woman 2. Asthma – refill for outside pharmacy per Pt request" and listed two medications for me to take. "3. Allergic rhinitis – Refill for outside pharmacy per Pt request" and listed one medication for me to take. And as usual my blood pressure was excellent. July 25, 2014 (the record list), my visit to Vallbona Clinic for a lab follow-up. The nurse notes (refer to **Exhibit 243**) mention how I walked out of the other doctor's office, and said, I want to go to administration because I need the paperwork filled out and I need to see my own doctor. It says, "Patient was overheard telling someone on the phone that she is going to call a news station to make a report... Patient also had complaint about paper works that she needed filled out...Patient was informed that Dr. Juneja will be back next week...Dr. Juneja decides or does not decide to fill out the paper work. Patient did not want to hear what I had to say and walked off to the administration office." LVN notes said, "Patient left without being properly discharged.

Patient wanted a form to be filled out but Dr. A denied due to the fact that all the results are normal pertaining to condition she claims she has. Patient wanted to speak with administration, left to go to administration and therefore left with no discharge papers." Patient chief complaint is, "<u>Patient states any kind of smell/ odor like perfume, cooking makes her short of breath and so can not work</u>, needs CT sinus results…states it was done outside." The records list my past medical history of, "Allergic rhinitis no dm or ht, Mold suspected exposure, reflux, allergic and depression" and gave past medical history of never being a smoker and occasional user of alcohol. Assessment/Plan said, "1. <u>Asthma</u> 2. Heartburn 3. Seasonal allergies." And my blood pressure was excellent as usual.

August 14, 2014, record list my visit to Vallbona Clinic, The nurse notes (refer to **Exhibit 244 & 245**) mention verified allergies and list the Vitamin B12 shot I needed and received. August 17, 2014, record list my visit to Vallbona Clinic, doctor's note mentions follow-up, as well as decreased energy and said, "<u>She was given forms for food stamps few weeks ago where it was mentioned that she can work part-time given that her pulmonary status is not compromised</u>. She admits she is going to change her PCP with her insurance card. She discussed the same forms earlier which were not completed and appears <u>upset about why her first forms were not filled</u> and her last forms showed need to work…The results of these point toward upper respiratory allergies more than any asthma as underlined by the spirometry tests and <u>we have no imaging to determine how extensive her allergic sinus problems are</u>. In light of these exams and procedures <u>there is not evidence</u> of me filling disability for breathing issues…Patient is informed about this and offered medication help."

The records list my past medical history of, "Allergic rhinitis no dm or ht, Mold suspected exposure, reflux, and allergic…" as well as plan of action… Assessment/Plan said, "1. <u>Allergic rhinitis</u> - cause unspecified continue medications as prescribed 2. <u>Weakness</u> - Refills on each ensured Vitamin B12 Cyanocobalamin 1000MCG INJ in Clinic. And my blood pressure was excellent as usual.

I really want the doctor notes, from each time I left work with breathing issues, but as you can read from the notes above, my doctor at the time of me working for Vangent/GDIT, knew I was suffering. There was testing, x-rays (and well) the doctor's own notes, as well as other medical professionals. Yet, the doctor who treated me would not complete my causation papers. The moment you put someone else interest, over the health of your patient, you should be released as a physician, never to practice medicine as long as you live. September 18, 2019, I faxed (refer to **Exhibit 246**) OIEC the information on a new medical provider, for causation documents to be mailed.

September 23, 2019, I contacted the OIEC by phone to verify if the fax was received. There was confusion in the order I listed my name on the fax cover. The representative stated, "Write your claim number on each page in the future." September 25, 2019, I received mail (refer to **Exhibit 247, 248 & 251 - 257**) from Flahive, Ogden & Latson Attorney At Law, P.C. which contained 13 pages in all, and it was a request for my medical records to be sent to Discover Resource Litigation Support Services, 825 West 11th Street, Austin, TX 78701; TDI, Division of Workers' Compensation, 7551 Metro Center Drive, Suite 100, Austin, TX 78744-1609; Complex Legal Services, Inc., 3201 Cherry Ridge Dr., Ste. B-207, San Antonio, TX 78230 and to Flahive, Ogden & Latson.

The first page was the BRC Exchange Letter, the second page was who the information was sent to, the third page was the HIPPA Form of release, the fourth page was a continuance of the HIPPA release. Page one of the DWC claim says, "DWC Form-001(Employer's First Report of Injury or Illness) and gave instructions. Page two of the DWC claim says, "Instructions for Employers First Report of Injury or Illness (DWC Form-001)." Page three of the DWC claim says, "Employers First Report of Injury or Illness, DWC Form – 1 (Rev. 10/05) and gave brief instructions. Then there is a page which says, "Workers Compensation – First Report of Injury or Illness, (Form IA-1(r 1-1-02). There were two pages of instructions which were, "Employer's Instructions" and "Employer's Instructions – cont'd." Look very carefully at the dates on the claim forms.

September 25, 2019, the 13 pages I received from Flahive, Ogden & Latson Attorney At Law, P.C., was faxed (refer to **Exhibit 258**) to OIEC to ensure my ombudsman was notified of the change. Due to the different procedure of Harris Health, I didn't complete the request I received but, on September 27, 2019, I completed Harris Health System HIPPA form, and released records from 2010 to 2019, to make certain, each individual company listed on the attorney request would receive my medical records. I also completed the HIPPA request for the workman's comp doctor, who has evaluated me over the past three months for this medical issue, which was aggravated on a daily basis while working for Vangent/GDIT. I won't list the HIPPA authorizations here but the form number is 284355 and it's the same blank HIPPA authorization displayed earlier in this book.

Early in the morning on September 28th, God gave me a song. September 30th, I contacted Harris Health to verify if all the HIPPA request was received, and it was confirmed. October 7th, I visited the workman's comp doctor, the therapy center still didn't have my medical records from

Harris Health System. The doctor gave information on remedies I could use, to help my breathing when exposed, as well as preventatives and I was scheduled to come back in a month. Without my prior medical records, we are at a standstill. I contacted Harris Health and soon found out I made an error. The date was corrected on the HIPPA authorization. This whole time I thought something was going on, but it was my error that held up my medical records (for my doctor to receive them).

October 9th, I visited Harris Health System to get a copy of my medical records, and to verify information. And was informed the companies would have to pay for the medical records, and that each one would be sent an invoice, except for the treating doctor (any doctor who treats you can have access to your medical records, as long as you, the patient gives permission through HIPPA authorization).

Early in the morning on October 13th, God gave me a song. Early in the morning on October 17th, God gave me a song.

Early in the morning on October 30th, I heard in my sleep as I was waking up, "He's doing it all again." On numerous occasions, I called the medical records depart and there was no answer. On October 30th, I showed up and no one was in the medical records department. I visited the administration office, to leave a message for the medical records department. A call was received on the same day, and I was informed the regular person who handles the records was out for a week. Since I did visit the location on the 9th, I questioned if any of the companies responded to the invoice (to receive my medical records), and at that time, not one of the four companies had responded.

November 6, 2019, I visited the workman's comp doctor at the therapy center and was evaluated.

The doctor looked in the system and verified the medical records from Harris Health System was received. This was great news! Now the doctor can actually view what I had been stating for the last six years.

November 13, 2019, I visited the pulmonary specialist, referred to by the workman's comp doctor, and things went well. I will undergo new testing, in an attempt, to find out if there are any other triggers, other than smells and allergens that may be causing the allergic rhinitis/asthma. The doctor was aware of how I was treated at Harris Health System, and I told the doctor I left that place, because of the doctors not properly treating me when I was suffering.

The doctor was informed, of all the specialist I saw in the past, outside of Harris Health System, when I first started having problems years ago. I told the doctor, tomorrow I will fax over the list of specialist I saw.

Resource and Information: If you are injured on the job in Texas, and you don't believe the company is working within your best interest, contact the OIEC in addition to contacting the workman compensation division of TDI. If an attorney will not help you it's okay, contact the OIEC. You can contact the Office of Injured Employee Council by utilizing the following link https://www.oiec.texas.gov/contact/index.html. Make sure to keep all documentation in relation to your on the job injury. Make sure you keep notes of everything. If you don't live in Texas you must find out if there is an organization within your state that assists injured employees.

Chapter 6: Texas Department of Insurance

Division of Workers' Comp - Compliance & Investigation (MS-8)

A Workers' Compensation Complaint Form was completed (refer to **Exhibit 259 - 261**) on December 18, 2018, against Broadspire – New Hampshire Insurance Company and Vangent/ General Dynamics Information Technology (refer to **Exhibit 262 & 263**). Both DWC154 forms for Broadspire, and GDIT were faxed to Austin, Texas. January 8, 2019, I received notification (refer to **Exhibit 264 & 265**) from Texas Department of Insurance – Workers' Comp Division, on complaint number 241971, regarding Vangent/GDIT dated 1/7/19. January 11, 2019, I received notification (refer to **Exhibit 266 - 268**) from Texas Department of Insurance – Workers' Comp Division, on complaint number 241975, regarding Broadspire dated 1/10/19.

I was driving one day, and all of a sudden on January 23rd God gave me a vision, I pulled over and wrote it down. March 19, 2019, at 11:45 a.m., I contacted Texas Department of Insurance – Division of Workers' Comp – Compliance & Investigation (MS-8) by phone, to follow-up on problem report Id: 241971, regarding General Dynamics Information Technology complaint. I was told "There are 3 statuses: open, pending and closed. Your case is still open and has not been assigned. Once the respondent submits the documents requested, your case will be assigned."

March 19, 2019, at 11:48 a.m., I contacted Texas Department of Insurance – Division of Workers' Comp – Compliance & Investigation (MS-8) by phone, to follow up on problem report Id: 241975, regarding Broadspire a Crawford Company – New Hampshire Insurance Co. I was told "There are 3 statuses: open, pending and closed. Your case is closed, and an educational letter was mailed on January 10th. You need to go through the complaint process with the field office. The contact details are located on the letter." I didn't quite understand, so she stated, "The dispute is handled by OIEC local office."

Since I already submitted my intake application for help with the OIEC, there was nothing else I needed to do, but follow the procedures of OIEC. April 8, 2019, I contacted TDI – Division of Workers' Comp – Compliance & Investigation (MS-8) by phone, to follow-up on problem report Id: 241971, regarding General Dynamics Information Technology. I was told, "The case is open/pending and the department has 180 days to act on the case. As of 4-8-19, it is 111 days." June 4, 2019, I received notification dated May 29, 2019, from Texas Department of Insurance – Division of Workers' Comp – Compliance & Investigation (MS-8), and was informed complaint #241971, regarding General Dynamics Information Technology was closed.

Since I received a closure letter, I call Texas Department of Insurance – Division of

Workers' Comp – Compliance & Investigation (MS-8) on July 9, 2019, to follow-up on problem report Id: 241971, regarding General Dynamics Information Technology. My purpose for calling was to verify if GDIT actually sent the documents requested.

After giving my name and problem report number, I was told, "Our files are confidential." I asked, even if I filed the complaint. She said, "All I can tell you is if your file is open or closed. We sent you a letter May 29th, to the address… and the letter wasn't returned." I told her, I have the letter. I asked, "Who regulates your agency?" She stated, "The governor overseas and appoints commissioners." I said, thank you and hung up the phone.

Resource and Information: If you need to report fraud of your employer or insurance carrier, contact the Division of Workers' Compensation Fraud Unit, by utilizing the following link to file a complaint https://www.tdi.texas.gov/wc/ci/wcfraud.html. Select the link to the right, Report WC Fraud and select "print or save a printable fraud reporting form (pdf)." Make sure you document every activity (calls, fax, verbal communications and etc.) to protect yourself. I come to the realization that I completed the wrong form, for reporting fraud of my employer and their insurance carrier. I should have used form FR029, and not DWC154, to report fraud. Form DWC154 is for reporting "violations of Title 5, Subtitle A, of the Texas Labor Code or Texas Department of Insurance, Division of Workers' Compensation (DWC) rules." My error has given you a heads up. If you don't live in Texas, you must contact your state regulation office, for guidance on reporting insurance fraud by employers and insurance carriers.

Texas Department of Insurance   **Open Records Department – Records Request**

      As I was going through my huge binder full of evidence, I began to research more regarding the U.S. EEOC, and TWC dual filing system for Civil Rights Complaints. On June 20, 2019, I downloaded an open records request form. June 21, 2019, I completed TWC open records request (refer to **Exhibit 269**), I attached it with a copy of my driver's license and emailed (refer to **Exhibit 270**) it at 12:27 p.m.; then entered my social security number into the system (refer to **Exhibit 271**). The purpose of my request was for me to get the response, Vangent/GDIT gave U.S. EEOC regarding charge no #460-2014-01770, and the response, Vangent/GDIT gave TWC regarding unemployment claim id 03-20-14 and 11-08-15.

      A response was received (refer to **Exhibit 272**) from Texas Workforce Commission by email, at 2:32 p.m., on June 21, 2019, to inform me the request was received. July 21, 2019, I responded (refer to **Exhibit 273**) to the email from Texas Workforce Commission Open records at 2:40 p.m. June 25, 2019, I contacted TWC – Open Records Department. TWC – Open Records Department responded with a letter (refer to **Exhibit 274 & 275**) dated June 25, 2019, regarding Request Job#: 190621-008 for unemployment insurance claim. TWC – Open Records Department responded with a second letter (refer to **Exhibit 276 & 277**), also dated June 25, 2019, regarding Request Job#: 190621-009 for Civil Rights Division, which the EEOC was obligated by law, to share my civil rights claim under charge no #460-2014-01770, against Vangent/GDIT to protect my rights on the state level.

      July 1, 2019, TWC sent an invoice (refer to **Exhibit 278 - 280**) for the open records I requested. A liar is not consistent and will forget what was uttered prior. On Jul 23, 2019, I contacted TWC open records by phone, to follow-up on the request and was informed, it was received and my document will be placed in the mail today. Texas Workforce Commission - Open Records Department, sent a very important piece of mail (refer to **Exhibit 281 - 283**) on July 26, 2019.

      I longed to receive this document, I received my copy of request no. 190621-009. This request was for the charge the EEOC was supposed to dual file, so that I would be protected on the state level. Now I was going to have proof, from the state that Vangent/GDIT lied. I believe, my employer lied to U.S. Equal Employment Opportunity Commission, Broadspire a Crawford Company-New Hampshire Insurance Co, Center for Medicare and Medicaid, and the Texas Workforce Commission. Vangent/GDIT possibly, lied to Office of Injured Employee Counsel.

      After having hope the document would have important details, I open the document and there was no information enclosed. I needed this information, to attest, to the statements made by my prior employer Vangent/General Dynamics Information Technology. I paid for and received, a certified and official seal of the Texas Workforce Commission, informing me, no records were located as a result of the search for my charge no: 460-2014-01770, filed with the U.S. EEOC.

I was so disappointed. July 26, 2019, I contacted TWC records department and spoke to a representative, to follow-up on job request: 190621-008, regarding unemployment benefits. It was stated, "I didn't get the last request, but will reorder." I asked where the request was coming from, and the representative stated, "The Print Shop." I asked to speak to Gee, regarding the request that was mailed to me, which had nothing in it, and the representative stated, "She's gone for the day." I called to speak with G. Jones and questioned her regarding my file being blank and she stated, "I needed to speak with the ombudsman, then placed me on hold until she went to her desk. Ms. Johnson took a while to come back to the phone, so I hung up and called back.

August 5, 2019, I was contacted by email (refer to **Exhibit 284**), at 12:14 p.m., from Ms. Mills of TWC regarding the EEOC request. August 6, 2019, I was sent more mail from Texas Workforce Commission, Open Records Department, regarding the unemployment request, 190621-008. Now this request gave detailed information, which is listed under TWC unemployment. Aug 30, 2019, I asked for the name of the ombudsman, and was given a name, telephone number and TWC Civil Rights Department 512-463-2642. I spoke to a representative and was given the employment manager name K. Song and number. K. Song stated, "The charge may be in archive" and "If the EEOC can't give the information, then TWC would have to find the charge." She asked, "Are you suing." I told her, there is something ongoing.

I asked, Why do you have to know if I'm filing a lawsuit? She stated, "Because it may take hours to find and we would have to charge a fee." I told her, I paid for the service, and open records told me to call the ombudsman.

We hung up, but I called back to ask K. Song another question, regarding the federal system and she stated, "It's a paperless computer system." I spoke to a representative in the records department and was told, "We received paper in 2014 and filed it electronically. The retention policy is 4 years for unemployment and 3 years for CRD, Civil Rights Department files."

Resource and Information: Where there's a will, there's a way. My God always provides. To reiterate, contact Texas Workforce Commission, Open Records Department, by utilize the following link to request records https://apps.twc.state.tx.us/OpenRecords/submitform. If you don't live in Texas, you must contact your state regulation office, on guidance regarding obtaining public records request for unemployment, and civil rights employment discrimination.

On May 13, 2015, Centers for Medicare & Medicaid Services responded (refer to **Exhibit 285 & 286**) to my complaint, regarding my experience with CMS's call center contractor, General Dynamics Information Technology. I was asked to contact the Federal Acquisition Regulation (FAR). Information was given regarding the vision of FAR, and the contractors' responsibilities according to regulations. On July 30, 2015, I contacted (refer to **Exhibit 287**) Centers for Medicare & Medicaid Services by certified mail **(7015 0640 0006 5090 3426),** located at 7500 Security Blvd, Mail Stop B3-30-03 Baltimore, Maryland 21244-1850.

I wanted to know, what actions CMS would take to avoid such treatment, to future employees of call center contractors or any contractor. CMS did not respond. While researching to complete this book, I came across some information, which reminded me of the letter I submitted to HHS, Attention: SYLVIA MATTHEWS BURWELL located at 200 Independence Ave., SW Washington DC 20201, on April 10, 2015, by certified mail **(7011 0470 0003 5828 4862)**. I later learned someone tampered with my mail, because the postal service said my letter was never delivered.

Resource and Information: The information I came across said, "**Department of Health and Human Services (HHS)** The federal agency that oversees CMS, which administers programs for protecting the health of all Americans, including Medicare, the Marketplace, Medicaid, and the Children's Health Insurance Program (CHIP)." If you have an issue with CMS, contact HHS by utilizing the following link https://www.hhs.gov/about/contact-us/index.html. Hopefully, HHS will be better equip to assist.

Federal Bureau of Investigation (FBI)   **Journey for Justice**

After doing more research, I drafted a letter to the Federal Bureau of Investigation and attached supporting documents. I visited the FBI Houston location in person around 2:35 p.m., on October 26th. My letter (refer to **Exhibit 288 - 290**) was dated, October 22, 2015, concerning *public corruption*, with Vangent/General Dynamics Information Technology and U.S. Equal Employment Opportunity Commission. I submitted the exact documents, submitted to the EEOC, when I first filed my discrimination charge against Vangent/GDIT. I was not given information on how to follow-up with my case submission.

The staff who took my information would not give their names. Will I get justice through this government entity? OMG! Who can I run too, after such an experience of obstruction of justice, public corruption, collusion, and cover-up? Will I be saved? Who will vindicate me? Where is my reward for such persecution? How long must I endure and walk through this valley of the shadow of death? Hast thou forsaken me? My soul is at its depth of dryness. I'm cracking and peeling, yet still holding on. Who will quench my thirst for justice? When will I experience the righteousness for which my soul desires? I'm ready for the anointing, the flowing of olive oil, I long to be made whole, moisturize my soul.

Chapter 7: Faith and Works **What are you doing? – March 26**

The following is signs I created as I was protesting my injustice on social media.

March 2016, I created a website (www.ladyjusticetx.org), opened a business phone line, and uploaded a new video, which can be viewed at the following link https://www.youtube.com/watch?v=m-_Ny6w2zbE.

I ordered business cards, and I came up with the saying, Education by Information Giving Knowledge, for my business. One month prior to the *Spiritual* march around the City of Houston, all the following information was posted on social media.

You can also find information at the back of this book, regarding my protest on social media from 2015 to 2017. I expressed my truth, as well as provided information Facebook deleted, regarding my injustice truth. On March 10, 2016, I posted: There are some things that only you can accomplish through God. He will strategically guide you; no one can do it the way he has given it to you. There are many things I have asked people to help me with and I was either ignored or turned away. I'm grateful for that experience, should I have not had it, I wouldn't have known what I was totally capable of. I'm gifted and talented! All thanks to my father. And there are some things I have learned, if you want it done right, you have to do it yourself. I'm grateful for my gifts and the 'know how.' On March 11, 2016, I posted: The Lord has commanded us. (Proverbs 34:8,9 NLT)

On March 12, 2016, I posted: God is real, he's sitting high and looking low. They are not getting away but have gotten by for the mean time. On March 14, 2016, I posted: The people have cried out and God has answered. God will destroy the Pharaohs of this present land, just as he destroyed pharaoh of our ancestors.

(Isaiah 61:8 ESV)

On March 14, 2016, I posted: End government systematic oppression now.

On March 14, 2016, I posted: EEOC corrupt.

On March 14, 2016, I posted: Disabled demand hostile free working environments.

On March 15, 2016, I posted: Victory! "For the Lord your God is he who goes with you to fight for you against your enemies, to give you the victory." (Deuteronomy 20:4 ESV) On March 15, 2016, I posted: Right is Right! Join the Fight! Help the Disabled!

On March 15, 2016, I posted: My oppressors will not rest, may God bring terror to their homes and everything the oppressors put their hands to shall crumble; for they are children of Pharaoh and God will give them their just reward in Jesus' name, Amen. On March 15, 2016, I posted: BE CAREFUL HOW YOU TREAT AND JUDGE PEOPLE, When I was in a bad place in life, things kept happening to my children and I (Slumlords - taking my money and not repairing property, Broadway Square Apartments; Sexually harassed on the job - forced out at Sears Outlet Store (5901 Griggs Rd, Suite A, Houston) then harassed by supervisor over the phone, while attending HEB kids festival in 2006; violated by Houston Housing Authority staff while on public housing - entered apartment and stole kids items; Obstruction of Justice - After suing Houston Housing Authority in court - White attorney for Houston Housing Authority stated to judge, "If we pay her, we will have to pay others;" Hurricane Ike - My mother, kids and I were displaced; Slumlords - South Acres Ranch LTD - Staff told my mother, kids and I, "If you don't like the way you are treated, then move" became homeless; Nursing Home abuse/neglect - my mother was mistreated by staff at The Colonnades at Reflection Bay;

Medical Malpractice - my mother died as a result of doctors at Memorial Herman Hospital Medical Center - they would not listen to me, although I was the voice for my mother legally and by her choice, she was given medication she was allergic to, which caused massive blood clots; Police Misconduct - I was harassed by a police officer, summoned as a witness for the City of Houston against G. L Tolliver - daughter of S. J. Tolliver, she lied to the judge and after court I asked her for information, so she told the police officer I was stalking her; Medical Malpractice - doctors and specialist at Harris County Hospital District would not help me after suffering on the job of General Dynamics Information Technology; GDIT violated my civil rights and ignored policy and procedures concerning my disability; GDIT lied to Texas Workforce Commission when I filed for unemployment; EEOC violated my civil rights - denying due process, obstructed justice and I faced racism from Jeremy Crosby; GDIT lied to insurance carrier when I reported I was injured on the job; after contacting the President and Attorney General Lynch, I was treated with silence, no justice was served; I contacted the FBI- I have not been contacted regarding investigation of public corruption yet. U.S. Federal Court Judge - Violated my civil rights and obstructed justice as well. So you see, we just couldn't get a break. I have served the LORD since nine years old, so why has so much trouble come upon me.

All things above and not mentioned here was for God's glory. Some people spoke down to me, treated me like I was trash, thought I didn't know what they had been saying and doing. Yes it hurt, but I couldn't say a word. I couldn't tell anyone my assignment and the pain I was experiencing would not allow me to recall at the time, what the LORD showed me. I asked the LORD for strength and he provided. Nothing we have endured was overcome on our own.

Only when you have been broken to nothing can the LORD totally use you for his purposes.

I have no regrets. He has made me powerful in him. Everything I proclaim shall come to pass according to his will for his children in Jesus' name, Amen. Con March 15th, a friend told me, "I saw you at a podium in my dream." On March 16, 2016, I posted: Good Morning, So have I, now I wait patiently for my father in heaven. "Wait for the Lord; be strong, and let your heart take courage; wait for the Lord! (Psalm 27:14 ESV) "With God we shall do valiantly; it is he who will tread down our foes." (Psalm 108:13 ESV) On March 17, 2016, I posted: Amazing Song! God is Alive! I gave a sneak peak of my business card.

March 17th, I created and release the poem, Diamonds. It's Time To Shine Bright Black Citizens of American & African Descent! You have been under immense pressure…the heat at times has seemed unbearable. Someone who read and write Spanish was helping me transcribe my protest flyer to Spanish.

On March 21, 2016, I posted: IT'S TIME FOR CHANGE! Everything that we have done is not for our own benefit, but the benefit of millions. We have endured so much and it's time for the LORD to act. Please share, there is more to come, leading to April 10th. For all who can't make it to Houston, Texas, join us in solidarity at your City Hall. A website will be published April 23, feel free to print any sign from the Protest Gallery to utilize.

On March 22, 2016, I posted: The time is now! We have obeyed the instruction of the LORD. Every issue that we deal with as black people and people of injustice starts at the local level. The LORD will bring every culprit to ruin; they will know he rules and reign. They will know without a shadow of doubt, that they have offended the LORD with the oppression of his children. God is alive y'all!

On March 22, 2016, I posted: God is intentional, He will be magnified. I pray the LORD inhabits Houston, Texas and every city that has oppressed his children in Jesus name, Amen. Pharaoh wouldn't listen and was destroyed as a result. The LORD sent me on many occasions to various levels of government and they too would not listen, their hearts are hardened and rejected the words given to me by the LORD. The LORD will have the last dance. This was not my plan to endure this injustice, it was the plan of the LORD and he alone will see it through. If he brought me to it, he will bring me through it. I posted the photo: "When the righteous cry for help, the Lord hears….(Psalm 34:17-18 ESV)

On March 23, 2016, I posted: I LOVE THE LORD! Only by his spirit are many things made possible, not by the hands of man. Now thanks be unto God, which always causeth us to triumph in Christ, and maketh manifest the savour of his knowledge by us in every place. (2 Corinthians 2:14 KJV) I listed the song: God's Favor by Donald Lawrence and Tri City and posted: There is nothing greater than the favor of the LORD!

On March 23, 2016, I posted: I represent 3rd Ward, Houston, Texas and I'm proud of where I come from. To all my old neighbors, friends, classmates and family from 3rd Ward, 2nd Ward, 4th Ward, 5th Ward; Missouri City, Texas, SouthPark, Sunny Side and etcetera. Don't allow anyone to tell you what God can't do in your life, just because of where you came from. God is getting ready to make many people out of liars. He can use whomever he pleases. Don't allow people to limit God in your life. Minimize your circle and let God use you. On March 24, 2016, I posted: Just because you are going through hell don't mean you have to submit to it, you are not your circumstances. On March 27, 2016, I posted: To the people of injustice, who are truly ready for a change. It doesn't matter how long it's been. The LORD said to me, "Tell them to come." He also said, "If you are afraid, do not come." Follow the instructions under the Daily Agenda Tab, if you are ready for this move of God.

On March 27, 2016, I listed the song: Greater Is Coming by Jekalyn Carr and posted: "He's Preparing Me!" On March 27, 2016, I posted: Don't allow anyone, and I mean anyone, to tell you what God won't do for you. Remove people who don't support you and PUSH, until the LORD himself tells you to stop. He brought me to it and alone my father in heaven will bring me through it! He can bring you through as well. Know who you are in him and allow his SPIRIT to rest upon you, giving you all that you need to concur through him, the giver of all things, everything he has promised. On March 27, 2016, I listed the song: I'll Be The One by Bri (Briana Babineaux) and posted: Will you be the one? I said, "Yes" at age 9, I love the LORD and through this journey of life I have no regrets. I picked up my cross, carried it and follow Jesus. Yes, it's been a hard journey, I've been through hell. Even if I told you all the things I've been through you wouldn't believe me, it's because he has anointed, comforted and kept me for his good works. Because I suffered in him, I will reign in him. All Glory and Honor belongs to my father in heaven. Where would I be without you?

The Call   **Intercessors**

On March 28, 2016, I posted: Calling all Intercessors and Prayer Warriors!

On March 29, 2016, I posted: Don't Panic…

On March 29, 2016, I posted: A web page was created for prayer in unity before the protest. Part of my website says; *Do you want a breakthrough with injustice? Join us! Spread the word! On the website, I made an area for information:* **Praise, Prayer & Fasting and Protesting.** *I made an area for scripture to follow. It is titled,* **SCRIPTURES:** *Praising, Prayer, Fasting Courage, Victory and Protesting Preparation. I made an area and gave information on songs. It is titled,* **PRAISE & WORSHIP, RESTORATION & ENCOURAGEMENT** *and SONGS OF VICTORY. You can view the actual layout of the website at the following link* https://www.ladyjusticetx.org/justice-agenda. The information below was posted on a website page that I later disabled. It says, Protest Signs: Find a location near you and Join Us in Solidarity! The locations listed below are EEOC locations and have been tagged with a home or flag in the map above. The yellow homes represent the district office, the flags are local, area or a field office. The district office locations below will be in **bold print**. This government entity has grossly violated the laws of God. They have also refused to abide by their own written laws, rules, regulations, policy and procedures.

Many of you have been denied due process, by the EEOC after filing a complaint against your employer. Many of you have also been denied due process by other government agencies, including Federal and State Courts. **Please pay close attention to the following words. The LORD has instructed us on what the People of Injustice must do.** When you go to protest **start at your City or Town Hall**. The locations below are only EEOC locations; this is where you should end up after receiving the details, which will be **posted on April 10th. Go in numbers of 7 (seven) to your City or Town Hall. The addresses below do not include Suite #'s, they were intentionally left out. Do not enter buildings! Do not enter buildings!** The LORD will do his work from the outside. The first thing you are to do is **began praising and thanking God for who he is, Sing songs of praise to the LORD. You should be praising the LORD prior to April 10th.**

You can listen to songs under tab, **Daily Agenda** titled Praise & Worship at the bottom of page. If you are unsure what location is nearest you, click the button to the right and enter your zip code. Find EEOC Near Me: If for some reason this button provided does not work, the map above is interactive; so you can navigate it with arrows and the plus symbol to zoom in. Follow me on media sites for other important details. I will not list them at this time. Twitter@LadyJusticeEPR ; facebook /Ellenor P. Ratcliff. Make sure you follow the instructions in tab, **Daily Agenda** leading up to this **Move of God**!

Another friend gave me a message from God on March 29, 2016. My friend said, "This season is to great of a season to make mistakes." On March 31, 2016, I listed the song: Say Yes by Michelle Williams and posted: I told God, "Yes". If the LORD has instructed you, complete it to the end. He will handle everything else. On March 31, 2016, I posted: SURELY, THE LORD WILL ACT! "Take no part in the unfruitful works of darkness, but instead expose them." (Ephesians 5:11 ESV) PAY ATTENTION TO THE DATES. March 2016, I came up with the name Lady Justice Films. As I prepare for what's ahead, God instructed me on what to do, and I fasted and prayed before this march of victory for God to bring down the walls of injustice. I said everything God told me to say, on social media regarding justice.

Can You Praise God in Advance? **Crazy Faith – April 2016**

On April 1, 2016, I posted: Crazy Faith! Praise Him In Advance by Marvin Sapp. "That even though they're looking at the obstacle before them, they're not going to allow what they see, to hinder what they believe." Do you have Crazy Faith? I truly love God for who he is! On April 2, 2016, I posted: Good morning, The LORD is strong and mighty, he is mighty in BATTLE! THE LORD WILL GET IN THE FIRE WITH YOU! My most favorite living story, Jesus got into the fire with Shadrach, Meshach and Abednego, after they wouldn't obey King Nebuchadnezzar by worshipping an image. God has looked after his word all this time, nothing has changed. He looks after his word to see it fulfilled. A major change is coming to the United States of America, there will be a shift. Have your way LORD, this government has forsaken you. Come by your Spirit Father GOD and deliver like only you can in Jesus' name, Amen!

On April 2, 2016, I posted: For all who have been chosen according to his purposes. He called many of you for such a time as this. You must not rely on anyone but God. People will fail you every time, but God has promised to always be with you. This past Wednesday the Pastor taught on, "The Test of Love." The LORD asked Peter on more than three occasions, "Peter, do you love me?" and Peter caved under pressure when Jesus was going through his trial. I said that to say this, seek and allow God to move, he will place the people he want to help you, if he wants them to help. Don't seek out anyone on your own but allow the LORD to guide you. On April 2, 2016, I listed the song: A Change Is Gonna Come by Deitrick Haddon and posted: YES!

On April 3, 2016, I posted: Between 4:50 and 5:10 a.m., *The Holy Spirit said, "Anyone who has not received JUSTICE come, bring your family and friends, but only bring those whom are not afraid. Leave behind those who fear what man can do. Come before me in PRAISE."* On April 3, 2016, I listed the song: Days of Elijah (No God Like Jehovah) by Judy Jacobs and posted: I LOVE THIS SONG!!! HEY, THERE'S NOBODY LIKE JEHOVAH!!!

On April 4, 2016, I posted: Five Days Left! Obey God and he will give you Power and Authority. The same Power that raised Jesus from the dead, the same Power that heal the sick, that same Power that says, "Peace be still" in the midst of your storm, it resides within me. I don't know why he chose me, but I'm gonna run to the end. He has given me the Authority to speak what I want into existence. VICTORY IS OURS, WE HAVE ALREADY WON! God is Real! Don't allow the enemy to fool you because of your circumstances. Trust me. The LORD trumps your circumstances.

On April 4, 2016, I posted: "He uncovers the deeps out of darkness and brings deep darkness to light."(Job 12:22 ESV) Everything that you have done to me has also been done to my father in heaven. EXPOSED! EXPOSED! EXPOSED! THE LORD WILL ACT! The United States of America has partnered with GDIT and many other companies, together they have committed treason against American Citizens. DO THESE MISSION AND VISION statements below match all that I have provided in documentation to the public? The proof is in. The entire world will know that there is no integrity within the U.S. Our government is CORRUPTED at the highest levels. God has revealed you. You have oppressed his children, long enough and he will bring you to JUSTICE. Also FACEBOOK, my attorney and I are aware. The President and General Dynamics Information Technology has asked you to make it possible so that I can't tag their names or websites on my post. You too will answer, this is how the media has kept the evil of America out of the worlds view. But the destruction that will come will be a sure sign of the United States works against the people of God and all who participated will lose. God knows you and he has seen what you have done. YOU ARE ALL HEREBY EXPOSED and God will bring you to poverty because you have violated his laws. All this will happen by the Spirit of God through Jesus Christ, Amen.

On April 4, 2016, I posted: When God is moving in your life the devil will use all kinds of foolishness to distract you. Don't entertain that darn mess. Know what you're dealing with and cast down the enemy. He uses people that are willing. If you don't let God occupy, then the devil will. There is only room for one. On April 4, 2016, I posted: THE LORD says, "Your gifts will make room for you." STOP COMPETING. On April 5, 2016, I posted: When you call on the LORD, he will come see about you? There are so many that have cried out because of CORRUPTION. On April 5, 2016, I posted: Everything Has Been Exposed! Not one person can say they didn't know the truth. All the documents are true facts and have been provided on social media and many more areas. Whoever denied us in our suffering, will be denied in our victory. On April 5, 2016, I posted: Who's report will you believe? Man told us, "No". We believe the report of the LORD! God told us, "YES". There is not one that can change the plans of the LORD. For his plans are of old.

On April 6, 2016, I posted: THIS IS A SEASON OF REAPING! We are in a season, where God will honor the request of his obedient children, those who have withstood the test of time. God has been guiding many of you and God has told you to position yourself. POSITION YOURSELF!

There will be a season of famine in this land; in this season you must only sow where the LORD has instructed. There are people that can't go where you are going. Obey everything God has told you even if you don't like or understand it. He knows and can see things in people you can't see. Trust God's process and do not lean to your own understanding. Leaning to your own understanding sows doubt. This is not a season to doubt, are you will miss God. Don't let the enemy devour your harvest.

On April 6, 2016, I posted: Bring your own sign. Write the name of the Injustice you or your loved ones experienced. Examples on Daily Agenda Tab at www.LadyJusticeTx.org.

On April 6, 2016, I listed the song: You're Next In Line For A Miracle by Shirley Caesar and posted, Your Suffering Is Not In Vain. On April 6, 2016, I posted: He will come and see about his children. On April 6, 2016, I posted: It can only be done by the SPIRIT of GOD. On April 6, 2016, I listed the song: Holy Holy Holy Lord God Almighty by Agnus Dei and posted: HE REIGNS! On April 6, 2016, I listed the song: God's Favor by Donald Lawrence and Tri City and posted: No one or thing can change God's Favor in your life. On April 7, 2016, I posted: 3 Days Remaining; The LORD looks after his word to see it fulfilled, it will not return to him void. Come LORD Jesus, Come! For you have appointed a judgment against our oppressors.

On April 7, 2016, I posted: I'm Out Of My Comfort Zone; Feed yourself so you can grow spiritually. Marvin Sapp has this song on track five of HERE I AM. It speaks of coming out of your comfort zone, so God can bring you into your density in him. On April 7, 2016, I posted: 21st Century…

On April 7, 2016, I posted: Trust God! On April 7, 2016, I posted: At 6:50 p.m., *Thus says the LORD, "Before you come, if any of you lack any faith about what I can do, ask me to help you with your doubt." – God.* Sometimes our problems can be so egregious and seems as though it's too big for God to handle, but he is the best mathematician. He is the only one that can take all your suffering and add it up and turn it into your blessing. On April 8, 2016, I posted: Find a location near you and join us in solidarity. View Campaigns Tab at www.ljrstx.org. What injustice have you experienced? Bring it before the LORD, I don't care how long it's been, bring your petition before the LORD. If you fear what man can do, do not come. If you believe what the LORD will do, come boldly, proclaiming what he says about your life. Blessings.

On April 8, 2016, I listed the song: Send The Rain by William McDowell and posted: We need you LORD; We thank you for hearing the petition of your children. On April 8, 2016, I posted: Joy; Today I had the most beautiful experience I've had in a long time. I met a woman; we are like minded in regard to building up our communities. Of course, I started talking about how good God has been to me and how I was in 7 storms and how God brought me out. She then started telling me about her ambitions and how the LORD has blessed her. You know when you start talking about God and all of a sudden you get goosebumps, she had them, I had them and glorifying God brought his Spirit in the room. I became so overwhelmed with joy, I didn't know what to do with myself. Then the T-shirt company called and my proofs were in, it looked so amazing, I was overjoyed and felt the Spirit of God all over me. I'm so happy God is proud of us, we have been diligent in the LORD instructions. A change is coming! What have God told you? See it to completion. On April 9, 2016, I listed the song: Harvest Time by The Brown Boyz and posted: Good Morning! It's Harvest Time!

On April 9, 2016, I posted: The LORD said that vengeance is his, my father will avenge us. After you have done what has been instructed, stand firm. That's in the bible.

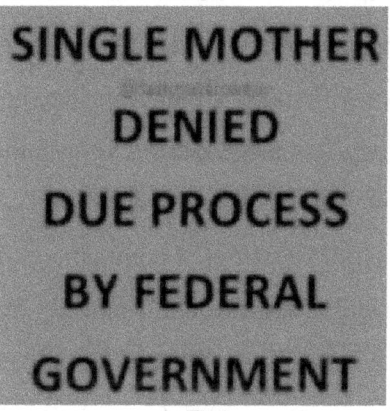

On April 9, 2016, I posted: God is up to something! Anyone who has experienced injustice come, but if you are afraid of what man can do, do not come. God is greater than man. Bring your sign listing the injustice you or a love one has experienced. On April 9, 2016, I posted: This is a spiritual uprising! It's Harvest Time! We want to represent God in excellence. Purple and Gold are colors of Royalty. The LORD said, "You are a royal priesthood". (1 Peter 2:9); But you are a chosen race, a royal priesthood, a holy nation, a people for his own possession, that you may proclaim the excellencies of him who called you out of darkness into his marvelous light. We are ready for this move of God. No weapons formed against us will prevail. The LORD will send the commander of his army to fight with us. God is for us and he's more than the world against us in Jesus' name, Amen!

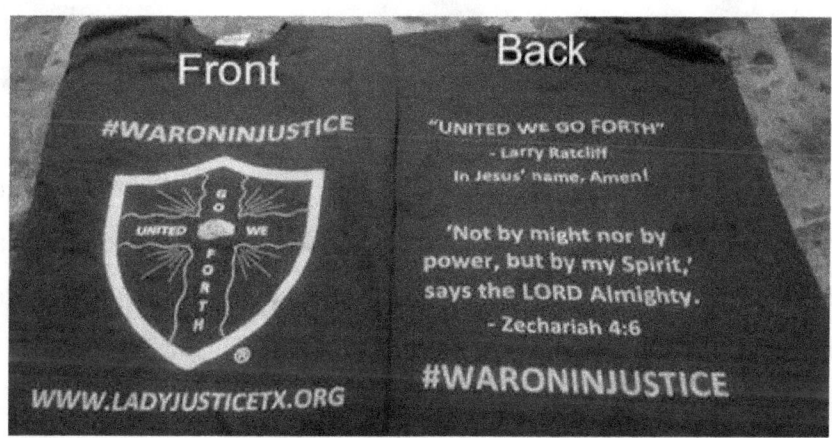

Do you know who you are?   **Walls of Injustice Come Down**

On April 10, 2016, I posted: April 10th-16th, 9:00 a.m.-12:00 noon; Join us & Walk in the light of justice; Jesus is the Light and he loves Justice. Find a location near you and join us in solidarity. View Campaigns Tab at www.ljrstx.org. What injustice have you experienced? Bring it before the LORD, I don't care how long it has been, bring your petition before the LORD. If you fear what man can do, do not come. If you believe what the LORD will do, come boldly, proclaiming what he says about your life. Blessings. I commented, Today was an awesome day, as soon as I place my foot on the pavement downtown, I felt this excruciating pain in my foot. I told the devil he was a liar. We walked around over 17 blocks and I walked with a limp. We praised God as we walked and sung songs, sweet to his ears. Come hell or hi water, we are getting this victory. My question to you is, How bad do you want what the LORD says is yours? Are you willing, by any means necessary? Will you allow the enemy to keep you in captivity?

On April 10, 2016, I posted: A Change Is Coming! Are you aware of what's getting ready to take place? You better position yourself, so you don't miss God. I met a man April 9, 2016, he told me about "government programs and how the majority pacifies the people, dumbing the people down for government. The group was protesting, and I wanted to know their story and it was about enriching our communities. The guy said, "Prosperity is talked about, but the people who claim to be us are not." I told him, "I hear people talking about prosperity, but they don't talk about Justice. There is no Prosperity without Justice". This brought me back to a conversation I had in 2014 with someone. Be careful what control you give the government over your business and etc., they can tell you what you can and can't say or do within your organization. Everything must come to a head for the LORD to fulfill his words. Don't be surprised, but God is getting ready. This is why he says in Hosea 4:6 ESV, "My people are destroyed for lack of knowledge; because you have rejected knowledge, I reject you from being a priest to me. And since you have forgotten the law of your God, I also will forget your children." Because man rejected God, they are overcome with destruction. In my early years I asked God, "How did we become slaves?, " The LORD answered, "Disobedience". Black people of long ago disobeyed God and that is why many of us don't know who we are. Disobedience of the leaders caused a major shift. You can't expect God to leave you in a position of power and let you remain there in disobedience. This is why the LORD says in (2 Chronicles 7:14 ESV)," If my people who are called by my name humble themselves, and pray and seek my face and turn from their wicked ways, then I will hear from heaven and will forgive their sin and heal their land." This is why the LORD will choose, "The least of these" to bring the people out of captivity.

April 10th was the 1st day of the protest. All was well when I woke up. We drove into town to prepare. As I put my foot to the pavement of Downtown Houston I felt this excruciating pain and I pulled my foot up quickly and took off my shoes to make sure I had not stepped on a nail. I put my shoe back on and put my foot down again but that pain was still there and it hurt so badly. I was determined to march around the City of Houston building and the U.S. Equal Employment Opportunity Commission. I told the devil, you are a liar and marched with a limp. On April 11, 2016, I posted: Protesting – Marching for God to bring justice to the United States of America. People of injustice rise up by any means necessary!

On April 11, 2016, I posted: God will look after his word to see it fulfilled, it's his word. Not mans. On April 11, 2016, I posted: A Change Is Coming! I will not post protest pictures here. Iron sharpens Iron. God sent some people who have affirmed what the LORD has said to me. The Holy Spirit was all over us. A shift is coming. On April 11, 2016, I posted: The People, we are the people; God will deliver; A change is coming; God has not tested us but have allowed situation for such a time as this. Today we met three people that have suffered injustice (employment discrimination, killing of parent- due to neglect of company and wrongful imprisonment). Surely my father in heaven has heard the cry of the people and he will deliver. A shift is coming to America.

On April 11, 2016, I posted: Father God we thank you for who you are, LORD you said you would fight for your people and we have taken the stand you commanded. Come LORD Jesus and render judgement upon our oppressors. Father we thank you for what has been promised in secret, that it will manifest in the human eye. They shall know that you are the Alpha & Omega, I am, The beginning and the end, El Shaddi and my banner. LORD we glorify your name, Jesus. There is none like you, (Image nor man). Show them your power so they may never forget who are. We ask you these things in the name of Jesus, Amen. On April 11, 2016, I posted: We have been naïve as a people; If you get close to God he will reveal everything he needs you to see.

On April 12th I posted: April 11th was the 2nd day of protesting. This sick feeling came upon me. I was begging the LORD to remove it and said, "We must finish." I began singing this song, "I Need Thee." We made a stop and I continued to sing as I walked into the building, I continued to sing as I came out and returned to the car, that feeling left me. We marched around the city still limping and signing praises to the LORD. We were marching pass EEOC and a black woman was standing outside smoking a cigarette and the person marching with me heard her say, "What the F**k does she think she's doing? A few moments later, another woman approached us from the federal building side where the firehouse is located. She walked up to us and asked us a question and a federal officer walk up to us saying we can't protest on federal property. We informed the male officer that the lady was asking us a question and the lady told the federal officer the same thing. We were on a public sidewalk, which was not federal property; we answered her question and proceeded on our way. In my depression, frustration and pain, Lady Justice and Lady Justice Resource Services were established.

On April 12, 2016, I posted: Today we met an atheist. Because he touched my flyer, I proclaim that he is now turned unto God in Jesus' name, Amen. On April 12, 2016, I posted: Today we met this group, protesting vaccine because of the proof of destruction to the people in our communities. The post I shared said, "Jamie Stephens *to* Vaccine Resistance Movement: VRM Updates & News From The Trenches; April 10 · Vaxxed is coming to Dallas!! Opening May 6th."

On April 12, 2016, I posted: Obedience to God yields blessings; I don't care how crazy the instructions of the LORD may seem, obey. It doesn't matter what others have to say, stand on the word of God. And anyone who goes against you in obedience to God, will answer to God. On April 12, 2016, I posted: Don't be naive......the LORD will act; Today, I was approached by several people and was asked have I been to city council and etc. I stated, if the President of the United States, a federal judge and the attorney general did nothing what is city council going to do. I went on to say, the mayor of this city knows about me, he knows who I am. I'm going to say something I haven't told anyone but one individual. No one knows this but God, the Mayor, that individual and I, unless the mayor has spoken to someone (I received a call and the person asked, "Is this Ellenor ...." I said, "Yes." I received that call before the Mayor was elected. I knew who he was when he called me, after all I voted for him, President Obama and many others who have these political positions. No one can tell me what God is getting ready to do to this nation. I know for myself, this is a wicked nation and the LORD is going to bring America to its knees. Pharaoh, you can't treat us any kind of way and don't expect our father to come and see about us. I pray the LORD acts; this country has slap God in the face. Every culprit shall be brought to justice and the LORD himself will cause them to suffer according to his words in Jesus name, Amen.

On April 12, 2016, I posted: For many of you who have relationships with these people and you uphold them in their wrong doing, the LORD will judge you as well. This judgement will not be when the LORD comes back, but you shall be judged in the here and now just as you participated.

On April 12, 2016, I posted: picture of myself holding 21st Century sign.

On April 12, 2016, I posted: picture of partner who joined me in protesting.

On April 12, 2016, I posted: I Love God… On April 13th I posted: April 12th was the 3rd day of protesting. I felt so sick and didn't want to get out of bed. *As I get myself together, at 6:38 a.m. I was in the mirror brushing my teeth and the LORD said to me, "Anyone who denies me before the people, I will deny them before my father."* And I wrote on social media: If you don't know him as your LORD and Savior accept him into your life. He died for you and it's time you live for him. Do you all know what time we are living in? God has to allow somethings for his word to be fulfilled. Get your house in order. As I moved about my foot was still hurting but we pressed our way and marched around the city protesting my injustice and singing praises to the LORD.

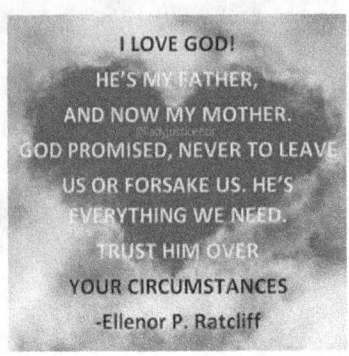

On April 13, 2016, I posted: This is our morning view. The sky was gray and it was going to rain. We still marched around the City of Houston, protesting our injustice and proclaiming our Victory through our LORD, Jesus Christ. On April 14th, I posted: April 13th was the 4th day of protesting, the same issue was present with my foot, but again we pressed our way. Later I learned there was a serious assault on one of my children at school. My child was choked by another student and bad thoughts immediately came to mind but I had to remember what I was marching for and couldn't make a bad choice. I brought myself under subjection and asked the LORD for forgiveness of my thoughts. On April 14, 2016, I listed the song: "I'll Be The One" by **Bri (Briana Babineaux)** and posted; Many are called, but few are chosen." The chosen will you run from God or will you be the one. He is truly searching for those he can trust to accomplish what he has set in motion from the beginning. There is no more time for talk but acting in obedience.

On April 14, 2016, I posted: Gideon Defeated the Midianites; The LORD told Gideon, "You have too many men....Now announce to the army, 'Anyone who trembles with fear may turn back and leave Mount Gilead....The LORD told Gideon, "There are still too many men. Take them down to the water, and I will thin them out for you there......" -Judges 7; This is not my work, but the work of the LORD. There is a post where I told everyone who would listen that the LORD said, "Come". Protesting our injustice – Marching for God to bring justice to the United States of America. People of injustice, rise up by any means necessary! I posted: April 10th-16th, 9:00 a.m.-12:00 noon; Join Us & Walk in the light of justice; Jesus is the Light and he loves Justice. It is time like never before to know the LORD. On April 14, 2016, I posted: Two days left; Bring your own sign. Write the name of the Injustice you or your loved ones experienced. Examples on Daily Agenda Tab at www.LadyJusticeTx.org. If you or you know someone that has been denied their God given rights, tell them to come. It doesn't matter how long the injustice has lingered over your life. God said, "COME".

On April 14, 2016, I posted: The Shift Is Coming! Y'all better get in position. Don't let anybody distract you from what the LORD has commanded you. I don't know why people think this is a game, but again, the LORD has sent another who knows him. There is about to be a major change. The LORD said, "If I be lifted up I will draw all men unto me." As my mother's favorite quote, "God is somebody!" On April 14, 2016, I posted: It can only be done by his Spirit. That's God word.

On April 14, 2016, I posted: God is strategic, follow him to completion.

On April 14, 2016, I posted: The Journey; We have had quite a difficult journey. I don't regret what I've been through. It has molded me into the Woman of God I am today. Yes, in the past I wanted to give up, it was just too much. I even asked God to take my children and I away from this earth. Then he reminded me of when I said, "Yes" and he showed me some really good things. I no longer asked the LORD to take me out of this world, but to give me strength to make it through. He has given me that strength. The LORD will set you up for his purposes. It may look so bad, but don't trust what is visible to the eye. Trust the LORD and his promises to you. Don't get upset when people won't help you, those persons don't have the capacity to walk where the LORD is taking you. This is why I have allowed the LORD to draw the people he wants to help me. If you have been pressed to the point of wanting to give up, lean on the LORD. I promise he will be everything you need. No amount of drugs, sex, alcohol, gambling or whatever it is you like to do, to take your mind off your problems will work, it's a temporary fix. Why get a temporary fix, when you can have a permanent solution. Trust God! April 14th was the 5th day of protesting, we were really hurting, the leg and foot condition did not change and I continued to walk with a limp. We met a Hispanic family that was passionate about my cause. We still marched around the city singing praises to God.

On April 15, 2016, I posted: One day left; Protesting before the LORD, asking him to bring justice to the United States of America by his spirit. We walk around the city singing praises to

God, for he will be glorified. "Oh magnify the LORD; for he is worthy to be Praised; Hosanna bless it be the Rock; Hallelujah..." He is coming to see about his children! On April 15, 2016, I posted: I like when people underestimate God. They are in for a rude awaking.

On April 15, 2016, I posted: The people still have a slavery mentality. People have been down so long, the realization of their state of being is unchanged. On April 15, 2016, I posted: Do you know what it means to "Prepare Ye the way of the LORD"? April 15th was the 6th day of protesting, my foot was still hurting we marched around the city once singing praises praises to God. On April 16, 2016, I posted: I listed the song Changed by Tramaine Hawkins and posted, He Changed Me; Once the LORD calls you unto himself and change your life, you are freed from HELL. He paid the cost on Calvary. Because he has done such a marvelous thing for me, I sit at his feet waiting for him to direct me. Whatever he tells me I will do, until he comes. There is a shift coming people. Get your house in order. The first will be last and the last will be first. This is the year of the LORD'S favor!

On April 16, 2016, I posted: This is a spiritual uprising, get up! He calls the deeps out of darkness and brings deep darkness to light. On April 16, 2016, I posted: You don't need all those people; The LORD said, "Verily I say unto you, Whatsoever ye shall bind on earth shall be bound in heaven: and whatsoever ye shall loose on earth shall be loosed in heaven. Again I say unto you, That if two of you shall agree on earth as touching anything that they shall ask, it shall be done for them of my Father which is in heaven." Through protesting my injustice and asking God to bring justice to the United States of America; I was asked, "Why didn't I contact this one or that one. True fact, I did contact a couple of people and there was no response. Then I told the LORD to draw who he wants and during this time of protesting, the LORD drew no one to help us. This is my view, the LORD said, "That if two of you shall agree on earth as touching anything that they shall ask, it shall be done for them of my Father which is in heaven." So, why do I need the popular activist, when my father in heaven has spoken to me and has already given me the Victory. He told me I had the Victory before the protesting even started which was April 10-16, 2016. *And please understand, I didn't protest for anyone else but my family. The invitation was given and rather you accepted or rejected that's on you.* I got my Victory. I will tell you exactly what the LORD told me, but I don't think it will be released here. If the LORD tells you to do a thing, you better do it with all your might. God is not begging people to get blessed, either you want it or you don't, the choice is yours. You don't need all those people to get the blessing God has for you.

On April 16, 2016, I posted: Where is your faith? Do you know the LORD will give you the Victories you read about in the bible? I believe everything he says I can have according to his will. The miracles I have asked for are huge, I don't ask God for little things, although I know he can do those as well, but I want him to do things that I can't do; things that will shake this nation. The LORD gave the Victory to Gideon, he also gave the Victory to Joshua, in the Battle of Jericho. All you have to do is be totally willing to obey God and he will give you the Victory over your enemy. I'm a witness. Because the LORD said it, it's already won. Because of the oppression of God's children in this land, there will be trouble for all the oppressors. He will remind all of them who he is, they will never again forget that God is Elohim, Yahweh-Jireh, El Shaddi, Jehovah Nissi and I AM. A Shift is coming!

On April 16. 2016, I listed the song: Sinking by Tye Tribbett and posted: We must have a personal relationship with God. Just like you have a relationship with the one you love. You must love God even the more. He is a jealous God and must be placed first in your life. On April 16, 2016, I listed the song: It's Working by William Murphy and posted: For your good. It's time to harvest. On April 16, 2016, I posted: Recognize the one who approaches; Today while walking around this city 7 times, the enemy approached me. She read my sign, then read the scripture that was on the front of my sign which said, "Whoever says to the wicked, "You are in the right," will be cursed by peoples, abhorred by nations, but those who rebuke the wicked will have delight, and a good blessing will come upon them." (Proverbs 24: 24-25 ESV). Then she said, "What?" And I offered her my flyer and told her to view the poem and video dedicated to The People of Injustice. She said, "We are all suffering injustice" she reminded me of those people who say, "All lives matter" due to protesting of Black Lives Matter. She wouldn't even take the flyer. Had she looked at the video she would have saw that it's about more than just black people. I recognized who I was dealing with and got back to my march around the city. The enemy will use anyone to move you off course.

On April 17th, I posted: April 16th was the 7th and final day of the march. On this morning I heard, "Get up! Get up, time for your breakthrough." As we marched around the city every day, I prayed and asked God to send the rain. We marched around the city 7 times, this time we did not sing, but played the shofar as we marched. Indeed, God heard me, and he sent the rain on the 7th day As I marched for the last time around the EEOC I remember feeling drops of water but as we finished, it began to pour down raining, God heard me and I just smiled. Read (Joshua 5:13-6:27) I can't remember which foot was hurting me; it was nothing but the devil. I marched with a limp for seven days; I couldn't let that pain stop me. I posted: April 10th-16th, 2016, we anointed our heads, prayed praised the LORD and marched for Victory.

On April 17, 2016, I listed the song: You are my strength by William Murphy and posted: You can make it! God will give you a song. We have all these beautiful songs unto the LORD. He has given his children words that will change lives. Find songs that minister to your life circumstance. You are a child of the King, so all things work for your good, that's the LORD's promise and "God is not a man, that he should lie; neither the son of man, that he should repent.." (Numbers 23:19 NIV). On April 17, 2016, I posted: We are in a Spiritual Battle. A shift is coming and it can't be prevented, no matter what the enemy attempts. This is the LORD'S promise to his people. There are many of you whom have suffered for the LORD, a season is coming and you will REIGN with the LORD on this side. You can't carry your CROSS and the LORD not BLESS you.

On April 17, 2016, I posted: On April 16, 2016, we called out to the army of the LORD, using the Shofar as we walked around the City of Houston on the 7th day. Look up the definition of what the shofar symbolizes. I tell you, a shift is coming. On April 17, 2016, I posted: The Door Has Been Opened; What do you want God to do for you? I want you to know in advance, God will require something of you. Follow what he tells you or has told you. Stop blocking your blessing and step out in faith.

On April 17, 2016, I posted: You Will Be Able To Laugh About Your Journey, One Day; Day 1 - We woke-up and all was well, until my feet touched the pavement of Downtown Houston. My foot had this excruciating pain as it was placed on the pavement; it hurt so bad, immediately I lifted my foot. When placed on the pavement again, the pain was there. I told the devil, "you are a liar," put my shoe on and marched around the city with a limp, singing praises to the LORD. Day 2 - This sick feeling came upon me. I was begging the LORD to remove it and said, "We must finish." I began singing this song, "I Need Thee." We made a stop and I continued to sing as I walked into the building, I continued to sing as I came out and returned to the car, that feeling left me. We marched around the city, still limping and singing praises to the LORD. Day 3 - We felt horrible and didn't want to get out of bed. My partner's leg was hurting and my foot was hurting, but we pressed our way and marched around the city. Protesting our injustice and singing praises to the LORD. Day 4 - Same physical feeling from day before, but we pressed our way. Later I learned there was a serious assault on one of my children at school. I nearly lost it, but had to bring myself under subjection.

Day 5 - We were really hurting, to the point we could barely move and the leg and foot condition did not change. We still marched around the city singing praises to God. Day 6 - Same physical condition exited. We marched around the city once singing praises to God. Day 7- With our foot and leg still hurting, we marched around the city 7 times. This time we did not sing, but played the Shofar as we marched. On April 17, 2016, I posted: You Will Be Able To Laugh About Your Journey, One Day and I said, Today we laughed! We laughed because my partner told me how I was marching with a purpose. He said, "You had your sign in one hand and every few seconds I heard the trumpet. When the LORD gives you the Power and Authority, you better walk in it. Below is a picture of our march around the city, outlined in red.

I commented, The LORD has given us the Victory. Every culprit will be brought to justice by the LORD and we will receive what is rightfully ours. "Beloved, do not avenge yourselves, but rather give place to wrath; for it is written, "Vengeance is Mine, I will repay," says the Lord." (Romans 12:19). On April 20, 2016, I posted: the Shofar is the musical instrument used for Spiritual Warfare.

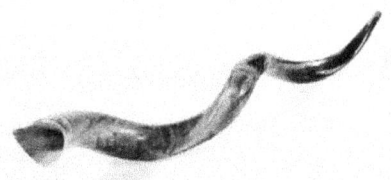

On April 21, 2016, I posted: Don't misunderstand and don't allow anyone to fool you. Once you're called, it's your choice to answer the call. You don't have to be a Preacher, Bishop, Reverend or Minister to be God's anointed and you don't have to have all the degrees behind your name. God needs those, whom have been down and out. Those who are unashamed of his gospel, no matter the place he sends them and regardless of affiliation.

Fasting and Praying   **Faith and Works - May 2016**

      At the end of April I posted, Seven Day Fast; May 1st-7th, fast and pray. Fast Preparation: For those with medical ailments, please make certain you speak with your medical provider on the proper way to fast before you began. Fasting is a sacrifice to the LORD. You must give up things you love for seven days to prove your commitment to the LORD. If you fall down, get up. Don't end the fast because you did something you committed not to do? Ask the LORD for strength and began again. What do you need from the LORD? He said, "If my people, who are called by my name, will humble themselves and pray and seek my face and turn from their wicked ways, then I will hear from heaven, and I will forgive their sin and will heal their land." (2 Chronicles 7:14) We will continue to bring the lost before the LORD. We will continue to ask the LORD to bring Justice to America.

      Continue to read and listen to praise & worship, things that exalt the LORD. You are welcome to read the Daily Agenda at www.ladyjusticetx.org. After this there is the 7th and 10th month remaining, updates will be provided the end of June and the end of September. May the LORD provide what you're in need of according to his will in Jesus' name, Amen. Blessings. On May 1, 2016, I posted: This is the first day of 7 day fast. What have you asked of the LORD? How serious are you about your request? Make a sacrifice to the LORD, take away the things you love the most for seven days. Pray and see if he won't answer. He's listening. Blessings.

      On, May 2, 2016, I posted: God has already concurred this world. Thank him for what he will do in your life, it's in your praise. People won't understand how you are making it through your problems, praise him through it all. On May 2, 2016, I posted: God gave me a beautiful dream about my end result. On May 4, 2016, I posted: A Ram In The Bush; There was a point in my life when I couldn't pray, nor could I cry. I was broken to nothing. I loved God and did my best to live by his word. One thing continued to get worse after the other, it was so dark. I didn't know what I did wrong. I received a call from Atlanta Georgia and my mentor prayed for me. She's an older women and I thank God for her obedient spirit. My ram in the bush. On May 4, 2016, I listed the song: "Grab and Hold" by Brian Courtney Wilson and posted, Have you ever felt thrown away, down-and-out, and no one to turn to, then grab and hold on to Jesus. He will do magnificent things after you have come out the fire.

Faith and Works **Are you willing to die?**

On June 13, 2016, I posted: I decree and declare. Every individual who played a part will be brought to ruin. You will not escape. I don't care how great you think you are, the LORD will give you your just reward in the here and now. There is not a place you can hide on earth. On June 13, 2016, I posted: I Will Pursue; My name is Ellenor P. Ratcliff and I have been oppressed by the United States of America. I have obeyed the law yet you have oppressed me and done things not pleasing in the sight of my father in heaven. My constitutional rights have been denied by The President of the United States, The Attorney General of the United States, The Federal Bureau of Investigation, Federal Court Judge Hughes, The Equal Employment Opportunity Commission in Houston, Texas and my past employer General Dynamics Information Technology. I will not cease to profess my injustice until you either kill me or surrender what belongs to me. If my father in heaven allows you to kill me then so be it, but you shall be terrified all the days of your life in Jesus name, Amen. What you have done to me has been done to my father in heaven. May he bring terror to your homes until you do right by me. You are evil men and women and you will release what's mine in the name of Jesus, Amen. April 2016 it rained because of our march around the City of Houston. This is no joke. All of you oppressors will soon account. As sure as the LORD called me unto Himself, so shall you suffer 100 fold, what you have brought upon the children of God.

Fasting and Praying **Faith and Works – July 2016**

The month of July 2016, I continued to work towards my destiny. On July 10, 2016, I posted: Day 1; Father God; Father we praise you and magnify your name. Father we exalt you, you are I AM, KING of Kings and LORD of Lords, you are the way, the truth and the light, you are El Shaddi, the soon coming KING. Father, please forgive us of our sins against you and please forgive us of the sin acts of our ancestors. LORD you know, we have been demonized and mistreated for centuries. LORD you said if we would humble ourselves, pray, seek your face and repent, then you would hear from heaven, forgive our sins and heal this land. We know you will work in your own timing, LORD. We want you to remember your promises to us, even before we were formed in the womb of our mothers. Remember LORD, you said we are the head and not the tail, we are lenders and not borrowers, we are above and not beneath. You said we are the salt of the earth. You created us to praise you LORD, and we magnify you, we boast upon your name, Yeshua. There is not one greater than you Father. LORD, let your plans be fulfilled in its entirety. Continue to expose all the leaders, whom have fooled your children, it's time for them to be removed, each and every one of them. LORD you commanded us to stand for righteousness and we stand boldly, as you fight in the heavens for justice on this wicked earth. Send your angels LORD to combat the attacks of spiritual forces. Father we thank you for binding every weapon against us. May your plans of old manifest and abolish this government of corruption in the mighty name of Yeshua, Amen.

On July 11, 2016, I posted: Day 2; Father God we come kneeling before you, thanking and praising your name. LORD, thank you for interceding for us at the right hand of the Father. Father, we thank you for shaking this nation. Father God we pray that you get the attention of every preacher you have called to service. Revive the Prophets you have called to lead and give them a spirit of boldness to stand completely on your word and not sugarcoat or back down from it. Father God, we pray right now that everything that does not align with your Word be removed. Every practice that is not of you, abolish it. LORD, you said your house is A HOUSE OF PRAYER, not for promoting worldly interests. We need you to lead Yeshua. LORD, discipline every pastor that has allowed the government (Politian's) to come and stand before your people in the house of God. LORD, you know what those people really came to do in your house and that's to make it a den of robbers and to sow discord. Your house has been perverted, everyone who you haven't called remove them from leading your sheep. LORD, weigh the motives of their hearts and move for your children in the mighty name of Jesus, we need COURAGEOUS and UNCOMPROMISING leadership. Raise up new leaders who will be UNCOMPROMISING. You called Christians to stand for righteousness and many have coward, due to worldly gain or fear, fix it Yeshua. We have grown tired and have vacated your house due to such acts. LORD, where are your MIGHTY MEN OF VALOR and WOMEN OF FAITH/VIRTUE? Father God, send your angles to cover all your servants, as we all do your bidding in the mighty name of Jesus, Amen.

On July 11, 2016, I posted: I'm sitting here at 6:24 p.m. This is what I heard. "God has called some of you to service. You know who you are, stop running and submit to him. You have already been equip to handle the task that will be placed before you." Stop running and submit. On July 12, 2016, I posted: Day 3 Prayer; Father we need you, and we thank you for your magnificent power. Father you said, we can come into you and be safe, our tower. LORD you said, you would expose the deeps of darkness and bring it to light. You said that you love justice. LORD, you promised to bring everyone who perverts justice to accountability. Father, America has committed treason against its citizens. What they planned in secret is manifesting. Father God, may your judgment come to America for its heinous Acts against your children. May all the participants who obstructed justice get their just reward soon. Father bind up the principalities and vindicate your children. LORD, comfort the families of the black men and women slain and bring every culprit to justice in the mighty name of Yeshua. LORD you said, pray for our enemies, we honestly don't know which ones are our enemies, until you reveal them. Father we pray that you make all the plans of our enemy known, we pray that once revealed the plans are abolished. LORD, we pray you abolished all the evil laws and practices of America. LORD, we pray for the innocent officers who were killed while serving the Dallas community during the rally. LORD, heal those officers who were wounded. Father God, you are able to do all things and we ask you to bring healing to their families. Father we pray all these things in the mighty name of Jesus, Amen.

On July 12, 2016, I posted: Please Pay Attention; We have spoken for months, telling everyone, "Change Is Coming," because that's what the LORD told us. Also you were told, "Get Close To God." We said that so you are not moved, due to what's to come. We told you, "Famine was coming to this land," it's not here yet. We also told you, "Spend your harvest wisely and ask God where to spend and how much to spend." I know I might curse because I'm pissed off and angry about what America has done to me and no one could or would help me, but please don't disregard what the LORD has given us to tell you. It will literally save your family for what's to come. Blessings.

On July 12, 2016, I posted: Delay Is Not Denial; Have you did all the right things and was still denied. I know man may tell you "No," but wait on God. On July 13, 2016, I posted: Day 4 Prayer; Father God, we come humbly to you, asking your forgiveness for our sins of omission and commission. Father, your children have suffered injustice in America and abroad. We have prayed for our political leaders to do right, yet when they get in office they turn away and ignore your people's plea for justice Incline your ear LORD and hear our petition. For you have knowledge of the senseless murders, misconduct, corruption, abuse of authority and extortion we face. We have been denied due process in America's judicial system. Father bring every culprit to justice, for they have broken your laws. LORD, act on behalf of your children. Deliver us from this great injustice with your mighty hand and by your spirit. The blood of the slain cries out to you. Avenge us father in Jesus' name, Amen.

On July 14, 2016, I posted: Day 5 Prayer; Father we need you. We come kneeling before you El Shaddi. Come LORD Jesus, we have been terrorized when all we have wanted was to have equality and live in peace. Lord you said, you love Justice, but America has forgotten your laws. They have perverted your word and have committed abomination against you. LORD you said, you would expose the deeps of darkness and bring it to light. LORD, you promised to bring everyone who perverts justice to accountability. LORD, you said you would go with us and fight our enemies for us. You said, when we cry to you, you will deliver us from this trouble we face in

America and abroad. Father God, may your judgment come to America for its heinous Acts against your children. May all the participants who obstructed justice get their just reward soon. LORD, you said we are a chosen race, a royal priesthood, a holy nation that will proclaim your glory. Father we are perplexed on every side and we need deliverance to worship and reverence you without worrying if our kids or loved ones is next to be killed. You said, not to be frightened, but to stand firm because you will destroy our opponents. Deliver us Father God. You promised if we would seek your kingdom that you would add unto us. LORD, politicians are making evil laws to uphold their wrong-doings. LORD, we pray you abolished all the evil laws and practices of America. This has been done so that truth does not shine forth. LORD, fix it Jesus. Send your angels, to bring terror into the homes of all those who make it possible for your children to be mistreated and slain. Father move this nation by your powerful spirit in the mighty name of Jesus, Amen.

On July 15, 2016, I posted: God is not to blame for the evil man does. He gave us a choice. He said love one and hate the other, we can't serve two masters. Please understand that God gave man dominion over the earth. God also gave us rules, in which we should abide. What we have to do is ask God to create circumstances that will destroy the plans of our enemies. We must continue to seek God through it all. When things go awry ask God, "What do you need me to do in accomplishing your plans?" Don't get upset, get in position. On July 15, 2016, I posted: Day 6; Prayer of Praise & Thanks; Father we come lifting our hands in surrender to you. You are worthy to be praised. Hallelujah! LORD we are so grateful for all the things you have done for us. We thank you for being our Father or Mother in our time of pain and need. Father thank you, we can't make it without you. Father, you are the true living God! Who can speak peace to our souls when deeply troubled? Who can answer our unspoken thoughts? Who makes a way out of no way? Who gives us his strength to stand against powerful enemies? Who encourages us to keep the fight and not be weary in well doing? Who tells the sun to gently fall and moon to rise to give us rest? Who heals our wounds? Thank you LORD for using us for your glory. Thank you for protecting us. Who has given us breath to witness all your beautiful works? LORD there is none equal to you. You walk and talk with us, we can't deny the truth, we know who you are. Thank you for allowing us to feel your soft spoken words to soothe. LORD of Glory, soon coming King, thank you for everything. Father may your plans of old be fulfilled to the end in Jesus' name, Amen.

On July 16, 2016, I posted: Day 7; Father God as we come to the conclusion of this fast, we thank you for all you have done for us, and what you plan to do for our future. We come humbly to you, asking your forgiveness for our sins of omission and commission. LORD we glorify you, we magnify your name, and there is none like you. We are grateful to have you fight for us as we stand firm on your words. LORD you commanded us to stand for righteousness and we stand boldly, as you fight in the heavens for justice on this wicked earth. Send your angels LORD to combat the attacks of spiritual forces. Father we thank you for binding every weapon against us. Father, your children have suffered injustice in America and abroad. Incline your ear LORD and hear our petition. Father God we pray that you get the attention of every preacher you have called to service. Father God we pray right now that everything that does not align with your word be removed, every practice that is not of you, abolish it. LORD, you said your house is "A HOUSE OF PRAYER," not for promoting worldly interest. LORD, discipline every pastor that has allowed the government to come and stand before your people in the house of God. We need COURAGEOUS and UNCOMPROMISING leadership. LORD, comfort the families of the black men and women slain and bring every culprit to justice. Father, America has committed treason against Black African Citizens. What they planned in secret is manifesting. LORD, politicians are making evil laws to uphold their wrong-doing. Continue to expose all the leaders whom have fooled your children, it's time for them to be removed, each and every one of them, for the senseless murders, misconduct, corruption, abuse of authority and extortion we face. Father God, may your judgment come to America for its heinous acts against your children. May all the participants who obstructed justice get their just reward, soon. LORD, we pray you abolished all the evil laws and practices of America. May your plans of old manifest in its entirety and abolish this government of corruption in the might name of Jesus, Amen. Blessings. Facebook family, may God grant the desires of your heart according to His will for your life. We are in a SPIRITUAL WAR. Stay prayed up and continue praying until the next fast which will resume in October. This evil we have encountered can only be moved by the spirit of God. Continue black on black support of your dollars in the earthly realms and let's change this nation.

Fasting and Prayer   **Faith and Works - October 2016**

On October 2, 2016, I made the following post, but Facebook deleted it: Victory: This week I had victory over a 4 year long wait, in a situation that violated my consumer rights. I Won! God will connect you with the right contacts. Even when something is not what you think it may be, go anyway. Someone holds the key to your breakthrough! Thank you Father! On October 4, 2016, I posted: This is the season. God has prepared many of you for such a time as this. It's time you go to war in the spirit. God has given you the power and authority. He has given you the gift to call things into existence. It's time you get off those gifts and get to work. Sacrifice 7 days for 3 Weeks; Let's fast, praise, pray and petition the LORD to come against the principalities. It will begin October 7th and end the 28th. Faith can move mountains. There has been a change in the atmosphere, we must continue to pray even beyond the 28th when this fast ends. God has made promises to you. Make a sacrifice and let's get close to him as one, Black African people.

On October 6, 2016, I made the following post, and Facebook deleted it: Good Morning! We have been commanded to stand for righteousness. On October 6, 2016, I posted: It Is Time! Join us to Petition the most high! Sacrifice 7 days for 3 weeks; these are Spiritual numbers that bare meaning. We must war in the Spirit for this great injustice and oppression forced upon us as Black African people. Then listen to the LORD as you fast, you must sacrifice to know the next move. He will speak to you, but you must sacrifice. Join us to petition the LORD from October 7th - 28th. We must seek him in unity. Stay posted for more information later today. By the Spirit of Yeshua, the Black African people will have victory. On October 7, 2016, I posted: *Sacrifice; Pray these individual daily prayers in addition to meditating to the scriptures on website under justice agenda tab, www.ladyjusticetx.org.* Repeat the prayer for 3 weeks.

October 7th, 14th and 21st; Day 1 Praise, Forgiveness and Deliverance Prayer; Repeat prayer from July, Day 1. On October 8, 2016, I posted: October 8th, 15th and 22nd; Day 2 Pastors and Impostors Prayer; Repeat prayer from July, Day 2. On October 9, 2016, I posted: October 9th, 16th and 23rd; Day 3 Exposure, Judgement, Comfort Prayer; Repeat prayer from July, Day 3. On October 10, 2016, I posted: October 10th, 17th and 24th; Day 4 Injustice Prayer; Repeat prayer from July, Day 4. On October 11, 2016, I posted: October 11th, 18th and 25th; Day 5 Prayer Deliverance; Repeat prayer from July, Day 5. On October 12, 2016, I posted: October 12th, 19th and 26th; Day 6 Prayer of Praise & Thanks; Repeat prayer from July, Day 6. On October 13, 2016, I posted: October 13th, 20th and 27th; Day 7; Repeat prayer from July, Day 7. On the 28th a different prayer will be posted. Black African people we can and will get justice. Sacrifice for our change as a unit.

On October 28, 2016, I posted: Day 23; *Change is coming! Justice is coming!* Thank you for sacrificing in Unity for God to bring Justice to America and abroad. The prayer petitions will be on the website by next week. If you are in a Battle for Justice visit the website anytime to refer to scripture and prayers at www.ladyjusticetx.org, select Justice Agenda tab. Blessings and victory in your journey. Father we thank you for who you are. El Shaddi, our Banner, KING of Kings and LORD of Lords. You are all powerful. There is none like you. Thank you for loving us. Thank you for forgiving our sins of omission and commission, as well as the sins of our ancestors. Thank you for making a covenant with your people. Thank you for your awesome greatness. Thank you for inclining your ear to hear our petition. Thank you LORD for going before us to fight this injustice on our behalf. Thank you for your plans of old, to give us a future and a hope. Thank you father for guiding us in the way you would have us go. We thank you for strengthening your soldiers for battle and for raising up new leaders who won't comprise your word or your people. Thank you for sending the Commander of your army to stand with us against powers and principalities. Thank you for who you are, you are awesome Father. We praise, honor and give you all the glory in the name of Yeshua, The Messiah, Amen.

Resource and Information: When God has given you an assignment, complete it to the best of your ability. Ask for guidance as you work in obedience. If you need help, ask God to send you help. As you can see from my experiences, things will not be easy when you are working towards a great calling; you will have great opposition, but you must remain in God. Don't lean to your own understanding. You cannot tell everyone what God has commanded you. God will send messenger along the way to encourage you. Some will provide you great detail at the appointed time, some will tell you about visions and even dreams. God has allowed those people to see and speak to uplift you. Truly I have been uplifted, and I thank God for his obedient servants.

Chapter 8: Baytown Police Misconduct /Auto Accident   Unforeseen Circumstance #3

December 10, 2016, I was involved in a car accident on the freeway in Baytown, Texas. During the accident, my head and right side of my body was resting on the door and the window. I saw white approaching in my peripheral vision; the man hit us with the left front side of his truck, then the back of his dully truck came up in the air and took of the right passenger mirror.

We pulled over to the left shoulder of the freeway, and he jumped out the truck with his phone to his head, walked over to us and said, "You hit me." I asked for his insurance and driver's license, which the driver did provide, but he was not on the insurance. We called the police, and at that time, was asked to safely exit the freeway. Things went from bad to worst.

We pulled off the freeway and waited for the police. The Hispanic man who hit us parked far away from us. I felt a little dizzy, my head and knee was hurting. The driver hit his head on the window. The other passenger was elderly and sitting straight up in his seat. Baytown ambulance came and made sure everyone was okay. The paramedic asked, if I wanted to go to the hospital and I said yes. When everyone questioned the elderly man, he stated he was okay. He didn't realize we had been involved in an accident. Officer O. Martinez came to the location where we pulled over, and asked us questions regarding our insurance, if anyone was hurt and how the accident took place.

We informed the officer we had rental insurance through our Capital One Bank card, and two of us were injured. My driver explained how the other driver hit us. The Hispanic officer proceeded to question the Hispanic driver. The officer and the driver were mostly laughing, and the driver drove off. When the officer came back to our vehicle, he stated, "I concluded that you caused the accident and will give you a citation." The driver of our vehicle stated, "How are you going to give me a ticket, and he is not even on the car insurance? He caused the accident?" After disputing the ticket with the officer, the officer said, "I'm giving you a warning." Now, the officer allowed the other driver to leave and he actually caused the accident. The officer did not give him a ticket but wanted to give the black veteran driver a ticket. I knew the officer was bias and that something was wrong. Even the paramedic stated, "He really banged up your vehicle." When the ambulance learned we were from SW Houston, they wouldn't drive me to the hospital in my area, only to a hospital in Baytown, Tx. I went to the hospital later.

December 16, 2016, contact was made with the Records Department of Baytown Police Department on December 14th, to follow-up on crash report #2016 – 69135, and the report had not yet been submitted by the police officer. Contact was made again on December 16th and December 28th, the report was still not ready. January 5, 2017, while visiting the Ophthalmologist, I had a general conversation with the assistant, and we somehow brought up the subject of auto accidents. He explained his experience and I told him about my experience. Then I said, Do you know an attorney? The guy mentioned, "Law Offices of Tuan Khuu & Associates," now called Global Law Group.

Resource and Information: To reiterate, if you experience police misconduct file a complaint. You can file a complaint with the Chief of Police, and send a copy to Internal Affairs of your local police department. To ensure you are not ignored, remember to submit the complaint to the Department of Justice. Utilize the following link for information on filing a complaint https://www.justice.gov/crt/addressing-police-misconduct-laws-enforced-department-justice. Be very careful of who you get your attorney referral from. Do your research first.

While fighting this great battle for justice, I was asked for help. An elderly man was being exploited, and I assisted the family. Truly I was sympathetic regarding this seasoned man circumstances. Upon agreement, I advocated by contacting APS, the Attorney General's office and other agencies. I must tell you, I had never seen such manipulation and abuse. God always makes a way. The police department where he lived was contacted regarding items stolen from the elderly man, but the officers refused to file the police report. We were extremely successful with recovering money stolen from the elderly man, with the help of other government entities.

Resource and Information: Make time to help others, you will be blessed. Work the gift God has given you. You are more than equipped. If you notice an elderly person is being neglected, abused or exploited, report to the proper authorities. In Texas, you can report behavior against the elderly by utilizing the following link https://www.texasattorneygeneral.gov/consumer-protection/seniors-and-elderly/how-spot-and-report-elder-abuse-and-neglect. Select the appropriate link for the situation you have witnessed. If you don't live in Texas, you must contact your states attorney general, for guidance on reporting elderly abuse, neglect or exploitation.

Baytown Police, Allstate & Who did I hire to represent me?   Unforeseen Circumstance #4

January 6, 2017, I consulted with Law Offices of Tuan & Associates now called Global Law Group, for the accident of 2016, and sent over all my paperwork (police report, pictures and Allstate notice). I was hopeful, but things later took a turn for the worst. Upon completing the contract for representation, I was given the name of my attorney. I informed the paralegal about the bias officer behavior, and how he purposely omitted information (injured parties and insurance information) from the report. In all this time I contacted and waited on the law office to respond. I assumed things were being properly handled. The police crash report was still not corrected; the law firm was under obligation to handle this issue, but instead I was forced to file an internal investigation, with the Baytown Police Department Internal Affairs Office.

When the investigation was filed I spoke to B. Thompson on July 18, 2017, I explained the officers' actions at the scene of the accident, and told the investigator, Officer O. Martinez was biased. Officer Thomas stated he would contact me upon completion of the investigation. The attorney's office was informed of the internal investigation. I followed up with Internal Affairs on August 2, 2017, and August 4, 2017. I explain to B. Thomas again, that Officer Martinez was biased. The investigator asked, "Why do you feel the officer was biased." I said, first the driver was Hispanic, he didn't have insurance in his name, the officer laughed and talked with him and let the driver go. The officer came over to us and insisted on giving the aboriginal dark skin driver a ticket. The officer omitted our insurance and passengers from the report. The investigator stated, "Officer Martinez does recall you and the other passenger being in the vehicle, a supplement report will be completed and I spoke to Officer O. Martinez and his supervisor, to ensure the omitted information would be added. Everything should be on file in the electronic system." I said to myself, *Now that I have raised hell the officer all of a sudden recall us being in the vehicle.* August 30, 2017, I contacted Txdot.gov to get a copy of the supplement crash report.

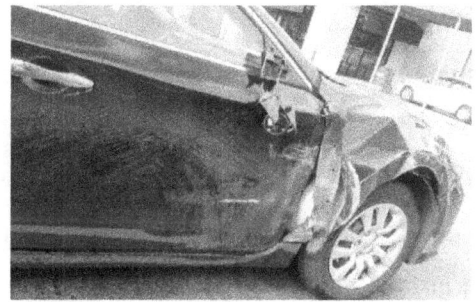

September 13, 2017, I sent my attorney the new crash report, along with the proof of insurance through Capital One and Amica. Between the time I hired the law firm and getting the last crash report, I asked to speak with Attorney Tuan Khuu on a consistent basis, and the staff gave me the run around. I was asked to lie on the stand, so the case would go in my favor but I refused. I informed the law firm that I would be leaving Houston for a job. October 2017, I was deployed to Dallas for briefing, training and federal clearance. I went back home to Houston and then I was sent to Florida. Well, little did I know the law office was doing some unethical things. My insurance company contacted me and informed me that someone filed a claim, at that time I was deployed. I learned the law office sent a letter of no representation to my insurance company, released information to the insurance company, then the law office sent another letter to the insurance company stating they do represent me.

When I found out what had been done, I contacted the law firm to question them about the checks they received and about the letters they sent to the insurance company. The law firm lied to me and gave me the run around. On July 6, 2018, I mailed a request, for Tuan Khuu, Dallas/ Houston office to release my file. The request was sent certified mail on July 10, 2018. On July 7, 2018, I heard, "You don't have a choice, it's mandatory. You either fall in line or fall behind." November 16, 2018, I mailed a certified release to Tuan Khuu & Associates, now called Global Law Group. This was to request my file again, because the trust was lost after all the lying.

Since I was having such an issue with Allstate after an improper denial, for the auto accident of December 2016, I decided to research and contacted the Texas Department of Insurance. After asking certain questions, I informed the department of insurance of what was taking place, and I was informed of a possible improper denial on part of Allstate. I called over 15 lawyers to get help with the issue of the Baytown Police Department, but no one would help me. My claim was in jeopardy, because of a lie and what was I going to do. I started the process of filing a lawsuit myself, but mentally, I was not capable to finish, I was already stressed to the limit and was dealing with the effects of an assault.

While going through this whole ordeal, I contacted Allstate on November 29, 2018, to gather information and I learned some interesting things, and informed the adjuster I was no longer represented by Khuu & Associates. Allstate was only interested in knowing if I was represented by another attorney, and I believe I was lied to regarding some information, but all is well. I asked a question about the name of the insured and the adjuster said, she didn't have to provide that information. The adjuster informed me that she received my case in August. Several calls were made to Allstate to verify the policy number. In one of our conversations, I was informed, "Police officers always leave names off crash reports, then it has to be corrected." When she made that statement it struck me as odd.

While in the fight for justice once again, I find myself reaching out for help. On December 18, 2018, I contacted the NAACP (refer to **Exhibit 291**) located in Baltimore, MD & ACLU (refer to **Exhibit 292**) located in New York NY, regarding the misconduct (officer purposely omitted information from the crash report and failed to ticket the driver who caused the accident) of the Baytown Police Officer. To reinerate, the individual name was not on the insurance policy, although the vehicle was insured under his mother's name, he was on his phone and jumped out his vehicle after the accident and said, you hit me. No one came to my aid. Well, as I was going through this ordeal of having an attorney I couldn't trust and dismissing the law firm, I prayed to God. I asked him to lead me to the right attorney and indeed this law firm was a Godsend.

Allstate didn't count on me obtaining another attorney, nor did Allstate take me seriously. Due to the unforeseen incidents and accidents of my life the last 5 years, the horrible law firm I hired to help me prior, and my decline to lie on the stand, has reduced my 2.5,000,000.00 case to a settlement of 20 something thousand (before all fees, cost and etc. are subtracted) with Allstate. It's depressing but looks as if I will come out with less than 6 thousand for all the pain and suffering, as well as the medical cost I incurred out-of-pocket, having surgery and seeing the specialist for my knee.

In all my years of driving and dealing with police prior to 2016 accident, I never, had an officer of the law, to omit pertinent details on a crash report. It made me wonder, *How many times have this behavior gone unchecked and How often does this happen? How many claims have been denied because of this issue?* Initially, my claim was denied for coverage because, Allstate said, "Your name was not on the crash report," go figure. Is this a new way for claims to be denied? Is there collusion taking place in auto accidents? Why are officers leaving names and insurance information off crash reports? What is happening? Are the American people facing a new level in obstruction of justice or has this always been?

Resource and Information: Be consistent, don't allow anyone to violate your rights and continue. *A violator will only continue*, speak up and report to the proper authorities or to agencies who help those of your particular situation. Keep a record of all your conversations, regarding auto accidents, the insurance company and everyone involved in your case. Be your own advocate as best as you can, then seek help with the information you have gathered. If an insurance company gives you an improper denial, always contact the Texas Department of Insurance 1-800-252-3439, and get help with consumer protection. You can view several insurance categories in which you can get assistance regarding improper denials. Utilize the following link to contact TDI https://www.tdi.texas.gov/consumer/index.html. Select the appropriate link for filing a complaint. If you live in another state you can contact the Federal Insurance Office (FIO) by utilizing the following link https://home.treasury.gov/policy-issues/financial-markets-financial-institutions-and-fiscal-service/federal-insurance-office. FIO can give you guidance if you have not been successful with contacting your State Department of Insurance, regarding how to file a complaint.

Den of Robbers   **Revelation**

June 2, 2016, God gave me a revelation, and I was irked. To warn others I made a Facebook post. What do you do when you realize the truth? Who willingly allows robbers to enter into their homes? Jesus was furious and he began destroying their things. Robbers have come into the church and have deceived the people. Many have seen this happen and I have seen it with my own eyes for years. Except this year, 2016 the LORD spoke and showed me the truth. What has happened to the LORD'S house? I'm done with the church! Because I know the truth, it irks me to sit in a place of worship, where God's word is partially given. I just can't do it anymore.

So many, are compromising with the world because of affiliation, numbers, and money. The youth sees right through, and I understand why the youth stay away from the church. It's not what it once was. I pray that eyes are opened, and people are saved before God's coming. I love going to church and worshiping with others, but it's not the same anymore. Our leaders are not obeying God, once again. Bad things come from disobedience. Due to my injustice experience (Vangent/ GDIT and EEOC) and me following God's instruction, I was searching for a new place to worship, after God told me to leave a place. God had been showing me so much.

The scripture of Jesus overthrowing tables and throwing people out of the temple court came to me. It says in (Mark 11:15-17) "Jesus entered the temple courts and began driving out those who were buying and selling there. He overturned the tables of the money changers and the benches of those selling doves and would not allow anyone to carry merchandise through the temple courts. And as he taught them, he said, "Is it not written: 'My house will be called a house of prayer for all nations' But you have made it 'a den of robbers." I couldn't understand why God was showing me this scripture. God then, related it to the pastors, allowing the politicians, to come into Gods house, before the people, to get a vote. The church building (Gods place of worship today) represents the temple court. The sellers who went into the temple court were the politicians of today. The people buying represent the church body (children of God). The money changers are the pastors and leaders in the church building. The goods that were sold back then, represent the political vote of today.

I must say, any church leaders who have participated with this robbery, has defiled God's house and the blood of the people are on your hands. Repent, because you know it was not written for you to allow such wickedness to enter into the temple courts of God. I had no idea how angry God was with the leaders. For years, I have set under pastors, allowing politicians to enter God's house, to get a vote. I was so ignorant to this fact before God revealed the whole set up to me.

Resource and Information: Leaders have brought nations to ruin. There is only one way to write this wrong, and it is to repent for the great disobedience that has sacrificed the lives of many. We must ask God to make a new covenant with us, the obedient children of God. God must have obedience, it's the only way.

Well, as I was seeking a new group to worship with outside my home, I visited this particular church body on separate occasions. It seemed as though the pastor was on point and following God. The praise and worship experience was amazing, I was in such a good place after God made me leave another place of worship. One day, something happened. The praise & worship and prayer was amazing as usual, but something happen that changed my whole spirit, and I couldn't understand it at first.

The pastor introduced a political candidate before the people, and a spirit of sudden anger arouse within me, this was not me, and it was so powerful. I stood up from my seat, and told everyone with me, We have to leave! From that day forward, I never returned to that church for a Sunday service. This is when God told me, "Leaders are bring nations to ruin." God gave a command and responsibility. When the spiritual leaders chooses to disobey God, regarding leading the people, God will punish each and every one of them, but not before some of the people parish. *Disobeying God in your personal life, is not as fatal as disobeying God concerning his people.* Your disobedience is costing lives and blood is upon your hands.

Why is it, that you hear preaching about prosperity, but don't hear preaching about justice? I've heard preaching in the past about Jesus and his miracles, hoes, pimps, prostitutes, adulterers, sexual immortality, and so many other things, but nothing on *Justice*. I'm forty-two years old. I don't think I have amnesia. Everything that should be taught isn't, and that is why we must read the word of God for ourselves. There are over 90 scriptures teaching on justice in the bible. Over

90!

Resource and Information: Are you so obedient to your church leaders that you are disobedient to God? If you have done such a thing, you must repent, because that very behavior will lead you to death in more than one way.

Make The Pain Stop   **My Heart Bleeds**

There are some who come to pour salt on your open wound, to further pain your already broken existence. On February 22, 2017, I made a post and included a picture of all (Z Boise, Z Wentz, Jeremy Crosbie, Martin Ebel, CMS, Broadspire, M Martin, President Obama, Loretta Lynch and Judge Lynn N. Hughes) the people I contacted for help, that turned a blind eye, and deaf ear to my suffering. The post said: They were all willing participants, They were all willing participants in corruption and government collusion.

Because I have been placed in this position to come against the powerful corrupt, I know many won't tell my story because they glorify some of these individuals.

C Alex Forrest decided to comment, and he said, "All this is political nonsense;" in response I told him, No, C Alex Forrest! This is what I, as a law abiding citizen have experienced like so many others. You must be one of their followers. I'm against injustice no matter if the oppressors are Black, African American, White or European. It's nonsense because you lack understand. You want to know the whole truth visit www.ladyjusticetx.org and take a walk in my shoes. Above you will see the words of salt poured upon my already bleeding heart. This was a hard and difficult time for me, and at this point I was desperate and willing to do anything legal to get justice.

This man had the audacity to call my journey for justice "political nonsense." He had no idea the pain and suffering my family and I had experienced from September 2013 to February 22, 2017, yet he made that statement out of pure ignorance. Even when the naysayers come, continue to stand on the words of God. It might hurt but continue to do the work for which you have been called. God told us to resist the devil, and he will flee. That individual never again commented on any of my post.

Make The Pain Stop   **Keep Fighting**

Sometimes I really get tired, but I know others are depending on me. I've read some of their pleas to this country, and truly only God will deliver. I know my children are depending on me and most of all, God is depending on me to hold until our change comes. God said, "Change is coming," it seems like so long to wait. It's like a child waiting for that favorite ice cream treat. The first step was asking and believing. The second step is waiting. The third step is preparation (this step has many steps within itself: taking the ice cream out the freezer, placing it on the counter, getting a scoop, parent ask if you want a bowl or a cone, the first scoop is taken then the second), you're just sitting and watching, then you receive your treat. The anticipation seems like hours, when it has only been minutes. And you savor the moment by eating small bits at a time and your parent watches your delight. God is our father, whatever you are going through, fight and don't give up. He is preparing a table for you. Hold on to his spoken promises. God will fulfill it, he can't lie. I pray you have the faith to wait on God in Jesus name, Amen.

| UN Humanitarian Council | Complaint of Human Rights Violation |

I submitted an inquiry to get help from the UN Humanitarian Council, and there were several phone communications between the person who presented himself in the emails. In fact, what comes to memory is when the individual stated he would be in Houston on business, and we could meet. On June 5, 2017, at 6:55 p.m., I received an email (refer to **Exhibit 293**) from the UN Humanitarian Council regarding my organization and a request for information. The email says, "Dear Ellenor, I trust you and your family are doing great? Send your bank account details, copies of your identification and a letter indicating who you are and who directed you (Mr Staffan de Mistura) by fax to the UN Humanitarian Council, #3 Whitehall Ct, Westminister, London SW1A 2EL UK. Tel: +44 20 338 ***** Fax: +44 20 768 *****; Notify me once you fax the details to them. Remain blessed! Mr Staffan."

On June 6, 2017, at 2:03 p.m., I faxed a letter to the UN Humanitarian Council regarding my organization, birth out of my experience. The letter says, … "Dear United Nation Humanitarian Council, I would first like to thank you in advance, I'm truly grateful. During my experience of Human Rights violations in the United States, Lady Justice was founded. Lady Justice was intended for speaking out. It was truly unbelievable what I was experiencing. As I began to research, my heart was broken, there were hundreds of citizens dealing with similar if not the same violations, that is when Lady Justice Resource Services was founded. These violations are extremely prevalent in the African community; I knew something had to be one to help those whom are facing human rights violations as well. My injustice experience took place from 2013 to 2016; I have yet to receive justice for the acts against me, but I will continue to fight on. This experience has encouraged me to fight for others. Your assistance will aid Lady Justice to move at a faster pace, to help thousands of citizens receive human rights services, that will enable justice. Mr. Staffan De Mistura directed me to the UN Humanitarian Council. May the blessings of the Lord be with you, for enabling great works around the world. Sincerely…

On June 7, 2017, at 11:11 p.m., I received another email (refer to **Exhibit 294**) from the UN Humanitarian Council. The email says, "Dear Ellenor, As a matter of urgency our office in London is ready to transfer the total sum of Seven Hundred Thousand United States Dollars to you first and once you receive it they will transfer another until the Two Million Dollars is completely transferred. This is because according to them the total amount cannot be transferred at one time following the instruction and advice from the US Treasury Department. But before the transfer takes place, you need to get a Donation Approval from the Buckingham Palace approving the outward remittance to your account following the monetary regulations of UK. Unfortunately I am still in hospital and therefore won't be able to go to London to represent you and I am sure you too won't be able to go, so if you could allow them to assign a lawyer who would go and get the approval that would be better, but according to them, the Donation Approval and Stamp-Duty would cost One Thousand Seven Hundred Dollars while the Lawyer's fee is Three Hundred and Seventy Dollars. The Total is therefore Two Thousand Seventy Dollars. You should send this amount to them through Western Union Money Transfer or Moneygram and fax the receipt to them. The receiver's name is John Howard. If they receive the fee today the transfer of your donation will commence today. If you have a relative in London and would want them to handle this on your behalf, that would be perfect. In Christ, Sir Staffan.

On June 8, 2017, at 7:50 a.m., I typed a letter responding to the email I received from the UN Humanitarian Council but I never sent the email (refer to **Exhibit 295**). The email reads, Dear Staffan, Didn't know you were still in hospital. I pray all is well. Unfortunately, I don't have family in London that can assist me with representation and I don't have the funds to hire an attorney to represent me either. I truly thank you for your assistance in helping with my efforts. If it's meant God will make a way.

On June 8, 2017, at 7:52 a.m., I sent an email (refer to **Exhibit 296**) to the UN Humanitarian Council's "infoDesk" portal regarding my suspicion of a scheme in the name of the UN Humanitarian Council. The letter says, Good Morning, My name is Ellenor and I have an organization called Lady Justice, in which was founded due to the human rights violations I faced. In my organization I fight for the rights of my people who's human rights have been violated and educate on human rights.

Please give this email to the proper authorities. I strongly believe an imposter is portraying to be Staffan de Mistura. This person has offered me financial assistance to further my work and is asking that I provide information to receive help from United Nations Humanitarian Council. I became a little suspicious after he asked me to send money for attorney fees to receive money from London (But before the transfer takes place, you need to get a Donation Approval from the Buckingham Palace approving the outward remittance to your account following the monetary regulations of UK.). Please contact me, I have greater details in regard to the correspondence between the individual and I. Sincerely, Ellenor P. Ratcliff; United States Resident of Houston Texas …

Resource and Information: When God has given you an assignment, complete it to the best of your ability. Ask for guidance as you work in obedience. If you need help ask God to send you help. As you can see from my experiences, things will not be easy if you are working towards a great calling; you will have great opposition, but you must remain in God. Don't lean to your own understanding. You cannot tell everyone what God has commanded you. God will send messengers along the way to encourage you. Some will provide you great detail at the appointed time, some will tell you about visions and dreams. God has allowed those people to see you and to keep you encouraged. Truly I have been uplifted and I thank God for his obedient servants.

Chapter 9: School Assault by Students/ Bully Teacher   Unforeseen Circumstance #5

How do we protect our children when not in our presence? Parents send children to school to get an education, at least it was my intention, when I sent my daughter to school in Cypress Fair District. I truly thought my child would have a more positive experience, when she attended 2016-2019 school year. Truth revealed, the school system was no better than the prior, in regard to bullying and reporting. My child was in choir, with two girls she befriended, and both girls were guest in my home on separate occasions. Well, after the girls came to our home things changed. Their behavior changed towards my child and I told her, "If they are truly your friends talk with them to see what's going on." My child did in fact talk with the shorter "friend" first and my child told me, the girl acted like she wanted to fight her. Now, I took this girl and my child to an eventful place for fun and this was how she repays my daughter. I told my daughter don't deal with her, and make sure to report it to the AP, so if any problems arise, the school is aware.

Well, this girl moved back out of town with her family. My daughter talked to me about the taller friend. My child allowed this girl to borrow clothes and other things. I told my child to talk with her friend to see what was going on. April 26, 2018, the day my daughter went to talk to her "friend" before class started, the girl lied and said my daughter came to the class to jump her with some other girls. Now my child has been bullied a great majority of her school tenor (elementary to high school) and bullying was not her thing. Now, the girl was almost 6 feet and about 200 - 230 pounds.

The morning my daughter went to talk with her "friend," the girl went and got her older sister, who was in another class. This girl was short and about 250 pounds. After learning everything, I found out this girl lied and told her sister my daughter came to jump her. The girl and her sister came to my child's cosmetology class and jumped my daughter. My child was kicked in the face, head and neck, while the teacher set back and watched. My child started having migraines. Then the girls were going around lying saying they didn't jump my child, and there were over 10 witnesses. I strongly believe the small-minded girls were jealous of my child's living environment and the little things my baby had, which I don't understand. My child had been through so much mentally, and I know she talked to her friends about her experiences. For them to turn on her was just too much.

To make matters worse, my child's cosmetology teacher does not like black people, my child was not graded fairly and the teacher bullied my child over and over. She taunted my child about the fight and other small things. She happens to tell my child we are all in slavery. When I talked to Torres, she compared working on her job, as binging in slavery. I told her, that is not the same thing. Many parents had been to the school about this teacher, and students even tried to get her removed by writing letters.

This teacher bullied my child to the point of making my baby drop out of cosmetology and my child loved cosmetology, but she couldn't take it anymore. It also caused my child to have a mental breakdown. The school called me, pretending they were worried about my child, after knowing all the things going on with this monster teacher from hell. When my child dropped out of cosmetology, the teacher called the police. My child visited the classroom to get her cosmetology items, that were paid for by us. This teacher had the audacity to approach my child, and tried to make my child accept her apology, for all the pain and suffering she caused my baby. But I should have known better than letting my child to return for the 2018-2019, school year. I felt it in my spirit, but I was so stressed behind the things I was going through myself.

Resource and Information: If your child is dealing with bullying by the teacher, please keep a record of each occurrence. Do you know if your child is displaying signs of bullying by teacher? Visit the following link https://www.thoughtco.com/signs-your-child-s-teacher-is-a-bully-4178674. Read the signs of bullying by teacher. Notify the principal of your child's school, the school board and contact the Department of Education's Office of Civil Rights https://www2.ed.gov/about/offices/list/ocr/docs/howto.html. Utilize the following link to locate information by state regarding laws, policies and regulations regarding bullying. https://www.stopbullying.gov/laws/index.html. If you live in another state, contact your school's headquarters to find out how to file a complaint, and you can also use the following link https://www.stopbullying.gov/laws/index.html.

It saddens me to think about how close to death many of us have been, while under the care of some doctors whom hide their medical mistakes and are then working on our families. Integrity is scares. I'm reminded of when my mother was sick and how I told the doctor my mother's stomach was hurting her and the doctors ignored her stomach pain and were only focused on getting her blood pressure down, not realizing there was an internal problem which was causing her body to have various symptoms. At the end of everything my mother's bowel was leaking into her body, and the doctors at the hospital would not listen. After the surgeon's examination, he stated, "There is about 5 feet of dead bowel in your mother's body," which they would remove and give her a colostomy bag.

I knew there was something more serious before it came to this difficult point because I saw a hole prior. I asked the doctor to do what he could to save her because my mother was prior full of life at the time of her illness. It was like she got this burst of energy from somewhere. In the end our mother's heart was not strong enough and the odds were totally against her. The morning my mother died, I was not at the hospital. I was lying on the sofa at home. I heard, "Ellenor" in my mother's voice and I set up. She was letting me know that she was gone.

The spiritual realm is real, and I've known it for years. But that was my first experience with a love one who physically died and was telling me goodbye. Prior to her passing I do remember my mother telling me, "God told me, he's giving me beauty for my ashes." At that time I didn't know what that meant nor did I consider my mother leaving us, because I was so busy caring for her and my children, but there were so many signs and dreams now that I look back. At the time I didn't comprehend but it all makes perfect since now. The beauty of it all is, God will provide a ram in the bush for your needs. My mother helped many people and, in the end, God provided.

My child was having a procedure done June 5, 2018, and instead of the doctor giving the proper medication for sedation, my child was woke. In the office the doctor made it seem minute. When I got my baby home, my child asked me, "Why did they do this to me?" Can you imagine how frightened I was? The doctor cut my babies mouth during the procedure, and my child felt the pain and tried to push the doctor off, in an effort to stop the procedure. When my child told me this I was horrified and couldn't believe it. If doctors don't report their medical error, I believe lives are at stake, and there's no integrity. If you survive a medical error, you should report it. Please do not be silent, it could save someone else.

Resource and Information: To file a complaint against a hospital utilize the following link https://www.tha.org/Services/Consumer-Information/Hospital-Information/What-To-Do-If-You-Have-A-Complaint. Select the appropriate link for the facility you are complaining regarding. To file a complaint against a physician, who chose to neglect your medical need contact Texas Medical Board by utilizing the following link http://www.tmb.state.tx.us/page/place-a-complaint. If you live in another state, use the link below to contact the Federation Of State Medical Boards, and locate your states Medical Board to file a complaint. https://www.fsmb.org/contact-a-state-medical-board/ To file a complaint against a dentist in Texas, contact State Board of Dental Examiners by utilizing the following link http://tsbde.texas.gov/. If you live in another state and have a complaint, utilize the following link https://www.ada.org/en/education-careers/licensure/licensure-dental-students/state-dental-boards. Follow the option to file a complaint under your respective state.

Chapter 10: Breach of Contract   Unforeseen Circumstance #7

While physically viewing the dwelling everything looked in place, then I looked a little closer. Northpoint Asset Management was managing the property. Never lease a home and or apartment that does not have utilities connected. A tenant can encounter vast problems with landlords. Many of us assume, if we pay our rent or lease, and take care of the property as if it's our own, everything else would be fine. Tenants must consider the fact, "I may have to force the landlord to maintain their property should issues arise." It's only wishful thinking, when assuming a landlord will automatically do what is right. I viewed this house online through a home finder service. The listing said, "Ready for MOVE-IN This home includes a gas stove, granite kitchen counters, neutral paint throughout, title and wood flooring…NO smoking and NO Section 8 vouchers accepted."

From the pictures online everything looked to be in place. When we visited the dwelling, no utilities were connected. The unit was not clean and needed minor repairs (light fixtures were broken; the yard was not cut and the fence needed fixing). A moving company was hired to move us and everything was setback. The realtor didn't check the property before advertising on the home finder website. It caused a major delay. After I connected utilities, and we were getting settled, I began to notice many things were not repaired. We didn't have a dishwasher for a while because the owner "Wanted to make sure the unit was occupied first." It was one thing after another. While living at 7911, one day God gave me a dream about court, and there were snakes (evil people of the enemy) in the courtroom. This dream caused me to pray against every demonic force and that God annihilate every plan of the enemy. It made me think about the attorney, and landlord regarding the house where I slipped and fell.

The electrical outlets were not working and the light bulbs kept blowing out, come to find out there was a serious electrical issue, which took about four to six months to repair. Always complete the inventory form of what is damaged on a landlord's property. Send a separate note of everything you listed on the inventory form that you want repaired. A landlord once told me, "The inventory list is not a request for repairs." Now you would think, the landlord would repair what's not properly working before another tenant occupies. There are so many slumlords, it's unbelievable. February 8, 2018, I wrote a letter (refer to **Exhibit 297 - 300**) requesting repairs. After the landlord and the agent would not accept my certified letters by mail, I did some research and found the California owners address (refer to **Exhibit 301**). This address is the same as the address on the letters I sent, why would she not receive (accept) my mail, regarding her property.

A request was made for the landlord/agent to get us the proper keys for the mailbox and it was never done. Well, as time passed it came to 3 months with no access to the mailbox assigned to the house.

February 14, 2018, I visited the postal location assigned to the area and completed a "Customer Key Order Request." The postal station contacted me to pick up the keys. On February 28, 2018, we finally had access to the mailbox (refer to **Exhibit 302**). The owner told me not to pay the company who managed the property prior. She stated, "The company is not paying me the rent money." Now, I'm a tenant and this realtor and landlord have me in the middle of their affairs. One day I was praying, I walked around and anointed every door and window in my house, to ward off bad spirits. As I neared the end, I open the front door and commanded every spirit not of God, to be removed in the name of Jesus, then I walked to the back door and opened the door to say the same thing. As I opened the door, I felt God blow on me and immediately I started crying and praising God. I guess God was covering me. God knew what I was getting ready to experience, and how it would affect me.

A new realtor from Crown Eagle Realty came and introduced himself in March. When he came to visit the property, I informed him I was not happy because of all the repairs needed, and we had been paying the rent. While looking over the unit, he tripped going up the stairs and his phone flew out his hand, he almost fails on the stairs, but put his hand down to break the fall. The stairs were a huge problem, and I complained about it many times prior to his visit. When he was finished and I told him how I felt about what the landlord was doing, Aleksander Koronowski gave me a 3-day notice to move out or pay rent (refer to **Exhibit 303**).

How was he going to give me a notice, and he just introduced himself as the new agent? Aleksander Koronowski retaliated against me for saying what needed to be repaired on the property. While he was looking at the property outside, he saw the trash cans in front of the gate. We were never informed the trash cans were supposed to be moved behind the gate. I believe he called the association to give me a fine, and he emailed me the paper with the owners' name and address marked out. Crown Eagle Realty was, I guess, a better choice for the owner, but he didn't know the law or maybe he just didn't give a care. Who knew I would have such problems when leasing this property? Well, one night I had a dream and God did warn me that something would take place. I prayed for covering and asked God to keep me. I dreamed I was falling through the floor of my bedroom. That dream really had me shook up, because I was already dealing with a leg injury from the auto accident, and I didn't need to go through any more physical pain. Well as time passed different events began to unfold.

Assault by Aleksander Koronowski of Crown Eagle Realty

On two occasions, we arranged meeting places for the rent to be paid. Aleksander Koronowski felt comfortable enough and allowed us to bring the payments to his home address (refer to **Exhibit 304**). I was not given one receipt from March to July, I asked for receipts. Under consumer law (if I'm paying for a product, service or making a purchase), I'm supposed to receive a receipt. I informed the realtor of the consumer law. After traveling to his neighborhood to make the payment, I couldn't remember his address. I called him on the phone and asked what his street number was, he became upset and told us, "You can't come to my house, this is private property, not a business." Now we drove all the way to him.

This man gets pissed off, because I tell him about consumer law, and asked for receipts. We left the area and I had to put the payment in the mail. In August, we mailed a check and was unaware, the payment didn't go through. I was unaware of another transaction, which came through the account and caused the rent payment not to be processed. Instead of him contacting me to inform me there was a problem with the payment, he just popped up. I was totally caught off guard and wasn't dressed properly. And I had not seen this man face in months. I really didn't remember what he looked like to be honest. I don't open my door to anyone. When I was in the garage working, I thought I heard knocks. I fixed my clothes and walked to look out the window and I didn't see anyone.

I said to myself, who was knocking at the door. I open the door and I stepped out to find out what was going on, I see this man walking the driveway and this woman was recording. I hurried up and stepped back into the house, I didn't know what was taking place. The man was banging on the door like a lunatic and called me a f***ing b***h repeatedly, it was scaring my children and honestly I was worried. I told him, I'm not a f***ing b***h, and he just kept saying it. When I thought he calm down, I open the door and a paper fell, he came back to the door and through the paper at me and called me a f***ing b***h and I closed the door. I open the door again and walked out to take pictures because my children said they were getting in a car. I took a picture of the car. He jumped out, and ran up to me, I felt threatened and he called me a f***ing b***h again.

I told him I was calling my attorney and he said f**k your attorney you f***ing b***h.

Harris County Constable Precinct 5   **Press Charges/ Fraud/ Investigation**

I went in the house and called the police because I didn't know what this man was capable of or if he was on drugs. When I was on the phone line with the Sheriff Department I was told, "Don't open the door, and don't answer if he comes back. Call us but don't say we are coming." When the deputy arrived, she asked me what happened, I explained and gave the description of the vehicle, as well as his address. The officer asked me what was on the paper and I picked it up and it was another 3-Day Notice "To Pay Rent Or Move Out" (refer to **Exhibit 305**) from Crown Eagle Realty dated for 8/14/18. Now, this is the same man who said, I couldn't bring him the payment before.

The deputy went back to her patrol car and called someone else, then she came back to me. The officer asked me if I wanted to file charges, but I was worried about my children and if I press charges he could come back and harm us. I told the deputy, I need to call my partner and I want to move because he was managing the property. The officer came back with a report number of terroristic threat (refer to **Exhibit 306**). September 8, 2018, God gave me a song and I went out looking for another place to live. September 11, 2018, I signed a lease for a new place to live.

September 12, 2018, A. Koronowski called, and asked, "Can we work something out." My head would hurt every time I thought about what he did to me on that day; I couldn't talk about it because it made me feel bad. It was totally stressing me out. I didn't know how bad I was affected until my friends called and told me what was happening to them regarding an eviction. They never received a final notice. The notice wasn't on the door of their apartment and it wasn't placed inside the unit. The couple was home. Thinking about my situation and what my friends were experiencing broke me down. While I was driving one day, tears filled my eyes and I cried uncontrollably. I wanted to go and talk with a therapist because I was so disturbed, but I had to save all the money to move. I couldn't take care my mental need at that time.

Truly, I know I was traumatized; tears fill my eyes as I write to tell you this part of my story on August 9, 2019, at 11:09 p.m. We mailed the rent payment and the return check fee. Although we were unaware the first check didn't go through properly, due to an unexpected draft, it was still our responsibility. Due to the above assault, I did visit Precinct 5 in September 2018, once I moved off the property. The location was closed at the time of my visit. Finally on two separate occasions 10/19/18, and 10/22/18, I requested report of the assault. There was also phone communication between Precinct 5 and I, in 2018, and on August 21st, November 8, 2019, November 9th and other days. When I visited the precinct, a deputy was called to the lobby. I told the deputy my request. He said to me, "It would seem like retaliation if you press charges now, and the District Attorney may not press charges now." I told the officer, I wanted to make sure my family and I were in a safe place.

Harris County District Attorney   **Refusal**

After getting nowhere with Precinct 5, I wrote Harris County District Attorney and sent the letter (refer to **Exhibit 307)** certified mail (refer to **Exhibit 308)**. After waiting for a response and dealing with so many life events, I finally called the District Attorney office to follow-up on my letter, and was told, "We don't accept charges from the public. Only an enforcement office can bring charges." I told the receptionist; the police department was saying I needed to speak with the District Attorney office and I informed her that I was just getting the run around from the precinct. She stated, "You need to contact that precinct." I called the precinct office and left a message regarding me getting the run around, and said I want to speak to someone in the internal investigations' department, since I was getting the run around from the precinct. An investigator did call me back in November regarding my request to press charges from 2018.

Resource and Information: To reiterate, there are certain things a landlord must do according to the law. If you are a tenant dealing with a landlord who is not on a federal program, and you have inhabitable issues or the landlord won't repair conditions which affect the health and safety of your family, contact the Health Department or City Housing Code Inspector. You can contact City of Houston, Fair Housing Office by utilizing the following link https://www.houstontx.gov/housing/tenant_law_intro.html. Select, "Who Do I Call About…," the link should direct you to a phone number. If you live in another city, contact your City Housing Code Inspector to get guidance on reporting landlord issues, which cause health and safety concerns.

Crown Eagle Realty   **Cashed My Check - Retaliatory Eviction**

Crown Eagle Realty cashed the check on the 20th of August (refer to **Exhibit 309**), and he filed a wrongful eviction (refer to **Exhibit 310 & 311**) on the same day. It was nothing but retaliation after all the hell my family and I experienced with repairs, falling on the faulty stairs, and assault by Aleksander Koronowski. Why did we have to go through this? Haven't we suffered enough? We received the citation by posting on the door from the constable. We went to court and the judge ordered the company owner to remove his name (Aleksander's name was not on the original contract that was signed) from the court papers. Aleksander was to correct it and bring the citation back to the court. We did not clearly understand, that the judge was resuming the case at the time, the owner was bringing back the updated citation to the court for filing. It was quite confusing, we sat and watched how others were given the opportunity to come on a day which fit their schedule and my partner had to work the following day. We missed the court date due to the miss understanding, and we did not receive any written documentation to come back to court. God came through as he always does. I didn't see a way out and mentally, I was outdone. God had given me a dream about a red building.

While going through this wrongful eviction, I was looking for another place to live. Once we visited the court to find out what was happening, we received a paper from the clerk that showed a judgement was made on the initial day, we were in court. How could a judgement be made already, and how could it be ruled for the owner? Crown Eagle Realty hadn't even removed his name from the original citation as the judge ordered, and he had not return the correction to the court. God sent word by a messenger. The messenger said, "You won't have to go through this again." We asked for an appeal, and we wrote a letter to the judge, especially since a judgment was made on the day we were there in court and no notification was mailed. This error legally gave us the option to sue the court, and the owner of Crown Eagle Realty.

After writing the judge and pleading my case we received a notification that the wrongful eviction was corrected. After we were finished and had the place cleaned out. Later, the neighbor told me her little boy said, "I feel bad for her, I saw everything that man did." Aleksander Koronowski of Crown Eagle Realty assaulted me. My neighbor's child witnessed the assault, and I didn't even know someone was outside. While checking for packages and mail, I saw the owner immediately moved someone else into the unit. There was not just cause for the landlord to keep my deposit. Due to the treatment I received, I filed a lawsuit against the landlord. At the last minute she decides to hire an attorney to represent her, and I was served with interrogatories.

I searched for an attorney to no avail. Since I am representing myself, I visited the law library, and did some research in an effort to answer the interrogatories. Later I searched for an attorney and finally was successful but was informed the attorney didn't handle tort cases. While dealing with pressing issues and doing all the foot work for my workman comp case, I received a call one day. It was the same attorney, and I was a little shocked. Maybe God was opening a door for me. We met with the attorney November 8, 2019. During our meeting the attorney noticed something very strange, in fact, the attorney never seen anything like it. This attorney has been in practice for 30 plus years and brought the issue to our attention.

The wrongful eviction that the court said was "corrected" was a lie. We were sent blank documents on September 20, 2018, which said corrected, but nothing was checked. I visited the court as the attorney instructed me, and learned there was some serious, and corruptible behavior taking place. I showed the clerk the blank documents which were mailed to me. The document should have showed a judgment but didn't. I asked the clerk, what was the paper supposed to say, and what judgment was actually made? The clerk went back into the office and printed the correct document. The clerk went on to tell me it was human error.

The judge denied our appeal, and we never received notice of the judgment. When the manager called us asking, "Can we work something out?" that was the only way we knew a judgment was made. As stated before, we were confused about the judge allowing the manager to remove his name from the wrongful eviction, then to bring the corrected eviction citation back to court and refile. We received no documentation by hand to return to court, the judge gave a default judgment, and ignored the fact that I was assaulted by the manager, and we never received anything by mail lawfully. I asked the clerk who regulates this court, and I was given the number to Judicial Conduct Commission, Austin, Texas 1-877-228-5750. This made me very upset to the point of crying, I'm so sick of these crooked people. They need to be annihilated. All the hell I went through with the slumlord, and her manager and this is what my family gets.

Resource and Information: It is totally against the law for a landlord or management company to retaliate against a tenant, for things a landlord or management company should provide by law. A lease agreement does not override the law. If you are at the point of danger dealing with a landlord or agent, call the police and report the behavior. Make the best decision that will protect your family from danger. Texas law prohibits landlord retaliation. If you are retaliated against, get an attorney. "Under **Texas law**, it is illegal for a **landlord** to **retaliate** against you for complaining in good faith about necessary repairs for a period of six months from the date you made such a complaint. § 92.331-§92.335." Visit the following link https://www.texasattorneygeneral.gov/consumer-protection/home-real-estate-and-travel/renters-rights. Learn more about your rights of protection from retaliation. If you live in another state, visit your Attorney Generals government website. Verify if there are any protections for tenants from retaliation by landlords. Also, research your states property code for landlord tenant issues.

Chapter 11: Oppressed and Traumatized   Where Can I Get Healed?

Due to the oppression and trauma as well as personal life events, I was so broken. I didn't care at times, I didn't feel and my heart was just a heart pumping to make this body and mind live. Often, I prayed for healing and restoration because I felt nothing. I stop taking care of bills, I stop cooking and communicating. I didn't care anymore but somehow, my mind was on my Father's business, so that's where I put my focus. One day, I was invited to an assembly of saints, and I was a little hesitant. After sacrificing to travel 34 miles to church on some Wednesdays, Sundays and at special events, my family and I left that ministry. The church wouldn't help my family when in urgent need. This was the time we faced the illegal eviction; their response made my decision very easy.

While attending services here and there, I saw the power of God exhibited. I witness prayers of deliverance, breakthrough and saw/ heard spiritual gifts coming forth at a time when I was mentally terrorized by the events of my life. I was so traumatized and broken. My deliverance was at **Prevailing Life Kingdom Center,** in Houston, Texas. The spiritual leaders prayed for me and God spoke through them both. Things were spoken that I had forgotten about. I can't tell it all but God has used these leaders to minister to me in ways they can't even imagine. I haven't spoken of my purpose. I have literally seen God move. Because of the leaders obedience to God, deliverance is in the house. I'm delivered from oppression and I needed it! Now I can go forth and do the work for which I had been called. If you have been oppressed and you need deliverance, enter into this house of God, where obedient leaders abide.

Are you tired of the games and want to encounter true worship with Gods spirit? Go and allow God to minister to you at **Prevailing Life Kingdom Center**. Do you want your children to be equipped spiritually, and you don't know how to do it? Find a ministry where God abides and get your children equipped in God. We have entered into a time when man will seek God like never before. Truthfully, God is alive. All this playing church will end and all the fake prophets will be exposed. If you can't deliver the healing of God and you say you stand in his name, you will give an account. God came that we might have life and have it more abundantly, so if you don't speak to the oppression of Gods people, yet you say you represent God, you are an agent of the enemy. Did you not know that God loves justice? Surely, if you have been called to preach the word, you need to repent and preach all the words, even the word on justice. There is no prosperity without justice. God can't lie!

A gentleman asked for my assistance with the complaint process against the same attorney who represented us both. I assisted a navy veteran with completing his complaint. His grievance was initially completed July 5, 2018 and was sent (refer to **Exhibit 312**) via certified mail **(7017 1450 0001 0829 2403)** to State Bar of Texas, 1414 Colorado Street, Austin, Texas 78701 on July 9, 2018. During his battle with the same law firm, the veteran was requesting his records and never received them from Tuan Khuu & Associates, now called Global Law Group. July 12th, State Bar of Texas received (refer to **Exhibit 313**) the letter of complaint. On July 27th, the veteran received (refer to **Exhibit 314 & 315**) the complaint back from State Bar of Texas with a letter dated July 26, 2018, with the correct procedure on filing a grievance.

After contacting the State Bar of Texas in July, all of a sudden the veteran received a letter (refer to **Exhibit 316**) dated August 2, 2018, from Tuan and Associates, which was a release as their client.

On February 14, 2019, I assisted the veteran with gathering and organizing supporting documentation and submitted it to Office of the Chief Disciplinary Counsel by fax (refer to **Exhibit 317 - 320**). On March 11, 2019, the veteran received a letter from State Bar of Texas, the Office of Chief Disciplinary Counsel – T.J. Baldwin, Administrative Attorney and the investigator introduced himself as J. McPoland. The letter says, "The Office of Chief Disciplinary Counsel of the State Bar of Texas has reviewed the above referenced grievance and determined that the information provided alleges professional misconduct or a disability, or both. The lawyer will be provided a copy of your complaint, directed to file a response, and provide you a copy of the response within thirty (30) days of receiving notice of the complaint. After receipt of the lawyer's written response, the Office of Chief Disciplinary Counsel shall investigate the complaint to determine whether there is just cause to believe that the lawyer has committed professional misconduct or suffers from a disability. During this time, it is important that you keep us informed of any changes to your address, telephone number, or employment, and that you cooperate fully with our investigation. You will be notified in writing of further proceedings in this matter. Please know that the Office of the Chief Disciplinary Counsel maintains confidentiality in the grievance process as directed by the Texas Rules of Disciplinary Procedure."

On March 14, 2019, the veteran received a letter from State Bar of Texas, the Office of Chief Disciplinary Counsel – E. Hsu, Assistant Disciplinary Counsel regarding Tuan Khuu. The letter says, "The Office of the Chief Disciplinary Counsel of the State Bar of Texas has examined the grievance concerning the above-referenced individual and determined that this person is not licensed as an attorney in the state of Texas. Under the Texas Rules of Disciplinary Procedure, we do not have jurisdiction to take action against an individual not licensed to practice law in the state of Texas. Accordingly, this matter has been dismissed as an inquiry. Please know that the Office of the Chief Disciplinary Counsel maintains confidentiality in the grievance process as directed by the Texas Rules of Disciplinary Procedure. By copy of this letter, the grievance form and any documents you have provided are being forwarded to the Texas Supreme Court's Unauthorized Practice of Law Committee, which investigates allegations against individuals who practice without a license. Please address all future correspondence concerning this matter to: Zara Stanfield, Legal Assistant, Unauthorized Practice of Law Committee, 1414 Colorado, Ste 200, Austin, Texas 78701. If you have any questions about the dismissal of your grievance, I can be reached at (877) 953-****."

On May 15, 2019, Attorney Purinton sent the veteran gentleman copies of documents filed in court. On July 29, 2019, The veteran received a letter from State Bar of Texas, the Chief Disciplinary Counsel – J. S. Brannon, Assistant Disciplinary Counsel. The letter says, "You are hereby notified that the referenced Complaint has been placed on a summary disposition panel docket. The summary disposition panel is an independent panel of grievance committee members comprised of both volunteer lawyers and public members. The panel will review all information, documents and evidence submitted during the investigation and determine whether the complaint should be dismissed or should proceed. The rules of disciplinary procedure provide that, at the summary disposition proceeding, the chief disciplinary counsel will present the complaint without the presence of the complainant or the respondent. You will be notified of the results by letter."

On July 29, 2019, the veteran received a letter from State Bar of Texas, the Chief Disciplinary Counsel – J. S. Brannon, Assistant Disciplinary Counsel. The letter says, "Upon completion of its investigation of your grievance, the Chief Disciplinary Counsel has determined that there is no just cause to believe that the above named lawyer has committed professional misconduct. In accordance with the Texas Rules of Disciplinary Procedure, following this determination by the Chief Disciplinary Counsel your complaint was presented to a summary disposition panel of the District 4 Grievance Committee. The panel which is comprised of volunteer lawyers and public members has the option to dismiss the complaint or vote to proceed should they believe the case should go forward. This is solely their decision to make on any complaint presented to them. The panel has voted to dismiss the complaint after reviewing all the evidence submitted and obtained during the investigation. Please know that the Office of the Chief

Disciplinary Counsel maintains confidentiality in the grievance process as directed by the Texas Rules of Disciplinary Procedure. Although there is no appeal of the panel's decision to dismiss your grievance the State Bar of Texas maintains the Client-Attorney Assistance Program (CAAP), which you may have contacted prior to filing your grievance. Please be advised that even after a grievance has been dismissed, CAAP can still attempt to assist you through alternative dispute resolution procedures unless the attorney at issue is deceased, disbarred, suspended or not your lawyer. CAAP is not a continuation of the attorney disciplinary process, and participation by both you and your attorney is voluntary. Should you wish to pursue that option, CAAP may be reached at 1-800-932-1900."

Resource and Information: You must protect yourself. First contact your local U.S. Department of Veterans Affairs, Office of General Counsel at the following link https://www.va.gov/OGC/LegalServices.asp. Select the link to the right, which says Legal Help for Veterans. Veterans can also get help from Texas Lawyers for Texas Veterans, select the following link https://www.texasbar.com/Content/NavigationMenu/AboutUs/StateBarPresident/TexasLawyersforTexasVeterans/default.htm. Before you file with the Chief Disciplinary Counsel of State Bar of Texas, look into the resources above. If you live in another state, contact your local Veterans Affairs or resources to find out if there is free to low cost attorney assistance available to you. Fight for your rights!

State Bar of Texas - Who are you really?　　　　　　　　　　　　　　　　　　**I see you!**

　　　　The first thing I want to tell every individual is, get an attorney to help you even in filing a grievance against another attorney. If you are not knowledgeable it's high likely you will be taken advantage of. December 2018, I contacted State Bar of Texas by phone, I wanted to file a complaint against the law firm, but I learned you can only file a grievance against individual attorneys within the law firm. This firm has done some totally unethical things, and I was well within my right to file a complaint, and even sue all attorneys involved in the legal misconduct. I have dealt with attorneys before, but never, in all my years, had I ever experienced such misconduct as listed in this book.

　　　　December 2, 2018, at 10:27 p.m., I submitted an online grievance form (refer to **Exhibit 321 & 322**) against Attorney C. Purinton with 21 supporting documents. December 3, 2018, at 2:52 p.m., I submitted an online grievance form (refer to **Exhibit 323**) against Attorney Tuan Khuu with 21 supporting documents. December 13, 2018, at 1:14 p.m., I faxed (refer to **Exhibit 324**) supporting document to the Chief Disciplinary Counsel against Tuan Khuu. December 13, 2018, at 1:23 p.m., I faxed (refer to **Exhibit 325**) supporting document to the Chief Disciplinary Counsel against C. Purinton. December 14, 2018, I faxed additional supporting documents to the Chief Disciplinary Counsel against Tuan Khuu (refer to **Exhibit 326**) & C. Purinton (refer to **Exhibit 327**). On January 2, 2019, a letter (refer to **Exhibit 328 & 329**) was received from State Bar of Texas, Chief Disciplinary Counsel, and the investigator over my grievance introduced himself and addressed C. Purinton.

　　　　January 2, 2019, a letter (refer to **Exhibit 330 & 331**) was received from State Bar of Texas, Chief Disciplinary Counsel regarding Tuan Khuu and was informed the attorney was not licensed to practice in Texas. On January 29, 2019, C. Purinton addressed and mailed (refer to **Exhibit 332 - 335**) a letter responding to my grievance, and provided email communications, in which Purinton agreed to file petition. The email communications provide evidence of legal malpractice on part of Tuan & Associates, now called Global Law Group, as well as misconduct on the part of the attorney who first filed my case in court. This was like totally mind boggling to me, and I can't believe such behavior exist in law offices. Exhibit A is when I contacted C.D. Purinton on June 5, 2018, regarding approval for a loan to help me out with bills, since I was involved in an auto accident on December 10, 2016 and couldn't do physical demanding work at the time of my request. Attorney Purinton responded on June 5, 2018 at 9:18 am. Exhibit B is email communication between

Attorney Purinton & Law Office Tuan & Associates dated February 15, 2018.

June 7, 2018, there was communication between Attorney Purinton and THOMPSON COE COUSINS & IRONS, L.L.P., which Attorney Purinton forwarded the conversation to Jan in Oklahoma. On June 27, 2018, there was communication between Jan and Attorney Purinton. On October 15, 2018, Attorney Purinton forwarded a motion that was filed in court, to Jan in Oklahoma with Tuan & Associates, and on that same day there was communication between Purinton and THOMPSON COE COUSINS & IRONS, L.L.P., in this email. There was a question of who is in charge at Tuan & Associates Law Office. October 16, 2018, there was communication between Purinton, THOMPSON COE COUSINS & IRONS, L.L.P. and Tuan & Associates Law Office, which Attorney Purinton forwarded a notice that I filed in court.

On November 13, 2018, there was communication between Jan and Attorney Purinton. On January 31, 2019, a letter was received (refer to **Exhibit 336 & 337)** from State Bar of Texas, Chief Disciplinary Counsel informing me of Attorney Purinton response to my grievance, and I was asked to notify the State Bar Association if I don't receive the documents from Attorney C. Purinton. On February 20, 2019, a letter was received (refer to **Exhibit 338 & 339)** from State Bar of Texas, Chief Disciplinary Counsel informing me of C. Purinton supplemental response, and I received the exact documentation C. Purinton sent to State Bar. On February 26, 2019, I wrote my rebuttal and filed February 28, 2019, by fax in response to Candy Purinton. On April 3, 2019, a letter was received (refer to **Exhibit 340)** from State Bar of Texas, Chief Disciplinary Counsel informing me of an investigatory hearing. May 15, 2019, Attorney C. Purinton sent me a copy of the release I filed in court. May 29, 2019, a letter was received (refer to **Exhibit 341)** from State Bar of Texas, Chief Disciplinary Counsel regarding attorney of record change.

On June 5, 2019, I arrived for the investigatory hearing against Attorney C. Purinton. As we arrive for the hearing, we sign in and set in the lobby area. I picked up a Texas Bar Journal to read it, and as I flip through the pages it mentioned Legal Malpractice Defense and Grievance defense. One thing we must realize is that not every attorney is diligent in their performance; some are right out horrible professionals. Some are skilled, and they have the gift, and some are there taking up space. The investigator pulled me in to speak with me, and I learned there were over 800 grievances filed against attorneys in Texas a year. This I couldn't believe, but I know it was true. My experience has taught me a bit much and it's amazing what people think they can get away with, as if you would never find out.

I filed a grievance in hope that justice would prevail, after all, I was filing with the State Bar of Texas, but oh, was I in for a surprise. When I entered the room there were two European mean, and two men who look to be of color, who were the panel making the decision on dismissing my grievance or charging the attorney. If you file against an attorney, make sure you have an attorney representing you in the hearing. My experience, and others experience is that this is but another corrupt organization, especially if you don't have counsel. You are ill-equipped and don't know the law, I promise you, the panel will take advantage especially if your skin is dark. I encourage you to file a complaint if you have problems and keep records as I have kept records. In the hearing I learned some really shocking facts.

The attorney admitted there was no attorney to handle her client's cases, after she left Tuan Khuu practice. She admitted to not contacting her clients or introducing her clients to another attorney, who would be handling the cases. Attorney Purinton admitted having several grievances filed against her by other clients. She admitted to not following the law regarding her client's communication. She admitted to managers and paralegals running the law office. She admitted to violating several Texas laws. The attorney admitted to finding the law firm on Craig's List.

On June 12, 2019, a letter was received (refer to **Exhibit 342 & 343**) from State Bar of Texas, Chief Disciplinary Counsel regarding dismissal of my grievance, filed against C. Purinton on December 13, 2018. As I sat at my desk looking over the details for State Bar of Texas, to choose what I would add to the last draft of this book, I heard the words, "Yea, though I walk through the valley of the shadow of death, I will fear no evil."

Resource and Information: If you have knowledge that the Chief Disciplinary Counsel ("CDC") knowingly violated your rights, and not rightful charged an attorney for professional misconduct, file a complaint with the authority who oversees the entity. If you have issues with the State Bar of Texas, contact The Commission for Lawyer Discipline, regarding the behavior of participants deciding on your case. View the link below to gather the information needed to file a complaint https://www.texasbar.com/AM/Template.cfm?Section=DisciplinaryProcessOverview& Template=/ CM/HTMLDisplay.cfm&ContentID=29473. Contact the American Bar Association at the link below, if you are still not satisfied with the results in your case https://www.americanbar.org/ groups/professional_responsibility/resources/report_archive/mckay_report/ "The ABA Board Of Governors charged the Commission to examine all aspects of lawyer discipline." If you live outside of Texas, contact your State Bar for assistance with attorney misconduct and contact American Bar Association should you need additional assistance with the regulation of the local State Bar. Fight for your rights!

Chapter 12: You Are Important to God!   **Shareholders of Injustice**

There was an event taking place from February 18th – March 1, 2019. This was great because I had been waiting for such a program, people wanted to learn how to do business. This company was from England and I learned so many amazing things, I mean it sparked my interest, and I was able to incorporate new ideas into my social justice organization. The company elaborated greatly on bartering, which is something that I've talked about before with my mentor and practiced. Well, it was a ten-day class and on the last couple of days, we were preparing to display in Memorial Mall for business. There was a huge group of entrepreneurs. I regret not going around to all the tables to view the displays. Prior to this event, we were asked to submit our information to be interviewed by PBS. I don't know why I submitted my information because the media didn't want anyone to know how I was using my experience in Houston, Texas to help others. It's funny how PBS spent many hours talking to particular people, and they didn't once come my way nor was I selected prior to be interviewed. If not mistaken the company who held the event did interviews. This was for everyone who wasn't interviewed by PBS. <u>The shareholders of your injustice will not televise your revolution</u>.

Resource and Information: Those who benefit from your oppression will not televise your injustice experience.

God Answers!

As I was going through the process of writing my book, on July 7, 2019, I asked God, what is a good title for my book? I love God so much! You all have no idea how awesome and amazing God really is. God normally wakes me early in the morning, and I sometimes, pray, praise or I just listen. On the morning of July 8, 2019, God woke me at 3:08 a.m., I was listening, and I heard, "You Are A Champion" (I knew this was the title for my book).

What are you doing here?   **Thriving and Surviving**

One day, I was driving to an event. The traffic was bumper to bumper everywhere I turned; I decided to take some short cuts. Why did I do that? There was even more traffic, but in the end I was on the side of I-10, and I saw this tree as I was driving bumper to bumper again. I hurried and snapped a picture and my creative began to flow. Many of you are like this tree. The foundation of this wall was built for one purpose. This tree was out of place by the plans of the builder. How on God's green earth did this tree get here? Who or What put the seed there and when was it planted?

This tree wasn't supposed to grow from this structure, however many of you are like this tree, living, and thriving. Despite the organized foundation that was built against you, to affect every area of your life, you are still breathing, and God has shined his light on you. Look at yourself, you are flourishing, and branching out into the world. Look how God has revealed and annihilated the plans of your enemies. Give God the praise and glory, had it not been for God's guidance, you wouldn't be successful. All praises and glory belong to the Most High God. Thank you, Father! For watering, pruning, and trimming my will for your destiny to be fulfilled. But most of all, thank you for the sun, that has enabled our growth in every season. "This little light of mine, I'm going to let it shine."

Death and Resurrection　　　　　　　　　　　**You Will Never Be Seen The Same Again!**

When you have died to your old self, God must bury you within himself, which is a repositioning that will birth a new you. And this birth is different from being born again. It is a spiritual awaking once you have moved to a higher level, after suffering persecution. God will prepare you as you follow every command. God is preparing you for himself. In September, God told me to go and do something important. Remember the different times in this book, when I told you what friends and others have come to tell me, God said. You can't feed a baby solid food, for there are levels of growth that must be achieved.

Resource and Information: You must be attentive to the things surrounding you. I've heard people say, "that's life" when certain things happen, but I don't believe that saying is true. If someone violates you, report them. Do not allow anyone to continue with such behavior. You have an obligation to yourself, your children, and your grandchildren, as well as every individual in your demographic. You have been commanded to stand for righteousness. Obey the order. The God I serve is strong and might, he's mighty in battle. God has given you everything you need, stop dumbing down the power within you, and learn how to use it. You all do know they expected me to give up, right. As a girl, I remember reciting this scripture to myself almost every day. "The LORD is my shepherd; I shall not want. He maketh me to lie down in green pastures: he leadeth me beside the still waters. He restoreth my soul: he leadeth me in the paths of righteousness for his name's sake. Yea, though I walk through the valley of the shadow of death, I will fear no evil: for thou art with me; thy rod and thy staff they comfort me. Thou preparest a table before me in the presence of mine enemies: thou anointest my head with oil; my cup runneth over. Surely goodness and mercy shall follow me all the days of my life: and I will dwell in the house of the LORD forever." (Psalms 23: 1-6) Teach your children that scripture, birth to 18 years of age.

Friends Through Adversity **Thank You!**

    To all my friends I have meet through adversity: Thank you for your support, power and strength to persevere! Well, there is a couple of good things that have come about since using Facebook, and it's the meeting and connecting with individuals who struggled and suffered like myself. It's different when you have others who can identify with you, I have been encouraged, and we support one another. I'm so grateful for the support given to me, and knowing that I'm not alone, in the physical. It's my understanding not all people can identify with us, but can symptomize, with the hurt and pain of such betrayal by the government. Father you said, "If I be lifted up, I will draw all men unto me." (John 12:32 KJV) I pray that I have pleased you, I have done my part in this journey. All praises to the King, Lord God, to you be the glory.

Social Media Injustice Protest   **Facebook**

For authentication purposes I did not allow editing of this section. My injustice protesting began September 2015 on Facebook. Provided is selected post from, September 2015 – January 2017, later post will be provided in part 2 of this book. As a forewarning, you may read some of the language on my post expressing my hurt, hatred, pain, anger, joy and my faith. There are post that I shared on Facebook, as well as my own post, which I found out Facebook deleted from my page (You will see the word **Facebook Deleted** in bold).

On September 21, 2015, I posted: Good morning Facebook, Justice shall prevail! Isaiah 45:21 "Declare and present your case; let them take counsel together! Who told this long ago? Who declared it of old? Was it not I, the Lord? And there is no other god besides me, a righteous God and a Savior; there is none besides me." Make every official aware of your situation. When God brings justice, they too shall be held accountable.

On November 9, 2015, I posted: Who Are You? "Who Are You?" was the name of an old facebook page of mine. Many may have wondered why that was my facebook name or what it meant. "Who Are You?" was a reminder to remind me who I was. What are you doing to remind yourself of, who you are or who's are you? Do you know why our ancestors were beaten, when they were caught reading? Do you know why Black History has been removed from text books or why it's distorted? Do you know why the media portray us as animals? Do you know why the Judicial System is set against us? Do you know why our black men and women are killed in rampant numbers? Do you know who's you are? If you know who's you are, you know who you are.

On November 19, 2015, I posted: Part 1 of 3; Public Corruption in Elected Offices and Courts Share, if you know someone who has a "disability" or a "record of perceived disability," and was denied due process by Equal Employment Opportunity Commission. Then Comment on this post of corruption. My prior employer General Dynamics Information Technology violated my ADA and ADAAA Rights. I was harassed after asking company to enforce company policy. The employer discriminated against record of perceived disability and I constructively discharged.

On November 19, 2015, I posted: African-American Citizens; If you know someone with a disability or anyone who files with the EEOC be careful. EEOC is not in place to protect your rights. EEOC created an intake questionnaire to disqualify blacks. Today I visited the EEOC. There is a new Director in place. Martin S. Ebel was either fired or given the option to resign. He was the director over my case. This man along with Jeremy Crosbie is a Racist. Jeremy Crosbie has not been fired, better yet, why aren't these men in prison. If it were a black man who violated the law, that black man would be in prison. Jeremy Crosbie made a certain statement to me, after that I knew he was a racist. I have called upon the federal government to deal with their employees, who I have proof of rights violations. Before you consult with the EEOC, contact an attorney, hopefully that attorney is not in their pocket. Also, consider filing with Texas Workforce Commission. I'm not sure of their practices, but I know EEOC is not Just, they are Corrupt. Fight like hell for your rights. It won't be given easily but must be pursued.

On November 23, 2015, I posted: Treason against American Citizens by government officials. As a past childcare owner, I was instructed to develop policy and procedures to care for children in my home. The State of Texas has many requirements for childcare centers and homes. When you choose to care for children, you must abide by the law. If I were to receive a violation of the law, it was posted to help parents make an informed choice. So, why is the United States of America allowing General Dynamics Information Technology and the EEOC to get away with this blatant discrimination. This company has a policy and blatantly discriminated against me and others. Is it because GDIT was given a government contact? Aren't there requirements that contractors must abide and enforce? EEOC and GDIT made a conscious choice to violate civil rights and disability rights. EEOC and GDIT, YOU ARE NOT ABOVE THE LAW. God told man to obey the laws of the land. We The People of the United States, must abide by the law. So, what is the government going to do about this mess, that GDIT and EEOC has created. Are you going to act or do you want God to act? If God acts, there will be destruction. Officials have committed great treason against the citizens of America. God is angry and you have been warned. No longer will God allow time to pass, before you are held accountable.

On November 25, 2015, I posted: Keep doubters out your life. When God says a thing is so, it is what he says it is. There is no hate in my heart. I just happen to know who's I am and what God has promised me. There is no Justice when you keep your mouth closed, I have never heard such a thing. Now if you are afraid, ask God to strengthen your faith. Don't rain on my parade. Let me school some people who obviously don't know any better. Martin Luther King, Rosa Parks, Harriett Tubman, Fredrick Douglas and etc. fought for our rights. They prayed then got to work, faith without works is dead. I've obeyed, prayed and protested here on Facebook. There is something larger coming. Do what you must by any means necessary.

FACEBOOK DELETED - On December 15, 2015, I posted: For all Citizens who have encountered Government Corruption, please read. If you see in a province the oppression of the poor and the violation of justice and righteousness, do not be amazed at the matter, for the high official is watched by a higher, and there are yet higher ones over them. -Ecclesiastes 5:8 ESV Thus says the Lord: "Keep justice, and do righteousness, for soon my salvation will come, and my deliverance be revealed. -Isaiah 56:1 ESV When the righteous cry for help, the Lord hears and delivers them out of all their troubles. The Lord is near to the brokenhearted and saves the crushed in spirit. -Psalm 34:17-18 ESV Come to me, all who labor and are heavy laden, and I will give you rest. -Matthew 11:28 ESV The people of the land have practiced extortion and committed robbery. They have oppressed the poor and needy, and have extorted from the sojourner without justice. -Ezekiel 22:29 ESV It is time for the Lord to act, for your law has been broken. - Psalm 119:126 ESV "Cursed be anyone who perverts the justice due to the sojourner, the fatherless, and the widow.' And all the people shall say, 'Amen.' -Deuteronomy 27:19 ESV God will move, the United States of America is Corrupt and his anger will be brought upon all whom have oppressed the people of God. The people have cried out and the Lord has inclined his ear. EEOC corruption is in every state of the USA. Now, that the people have cried out to the Lord he is ready to act. Father God have your way, bring every culprit to Justice in Jesus' name, Amen.

On December 28, 2015, I posted: FATHER YOUR CHILDREN ARE CRYING OUT TO YOU, INCLINE YOUR EAR TO US LORD. WE PETITION THEE. FATHER, GOD BRING YOUR MIGHTY HAND, SEND YOUR ANGLES TO BRING TERROR TO OUR OPPRESSORS. YOUR CHILDREN ARE BEING KILLED IN ASTRONOMICAL NUMBERS.

On January 27, 2016, I posted: The Lord said, "Many of you are battling with what I have instructed you to do. You have already been instructed, stop fighting with me and obey my voice. Get people's opinions out of it and do as I said, you know my voice." Facebook, I don't know who that was for, but please obey God. It's for your benefit. I don't know what God has attempted to free you from, or whom he has attempted to free you from. Obey God. Please obey. I was awaken out my sleep. I personally pray you hearken to the Lord and that you are set free, in Jesus' name Amen.

On March 10, 2016, I posted: I posted a photo of MLK statue with the words, "I HAVE A DREAM TOO!"

On March 13, 2016, I posted: It's okay when people count you out. God is going to use it for your good. Let him do it through his son, Jesus Christ. All the gossip, lies and slander will be taken care of by God. My daddy said, " I got this." He's real Y'all! I use to get mad and bring it in the open on facebook when I found out what people had been doing and saying in secret against me. God will make your enemies your foot stool and it's not for you to mistreat them, but for God to be glorified. Because you are his, everything works together for your good. I'm grateful to be a child of the King.

On March 15, 2016, I posted: God is going to do it again! He's real Y'all. Many proclaim to love God and Jesus Christ. But can he count on you to carry out his commands. Any assignment God has given you, do it to the fullest and with all your might." "let it be known to all of you and to all the people of Israel that by the name of Jesus Christ of Nazareth, whom you crucified, whom God raised from the dead—by him this man is standing before you well. And there is salvation in no one else, for there is no other name under heaven given among men by which we must be saved." Acts 4:10,12 ESV

On March 15, 2016, I posted: America has forgotten about God, America has elected officials who scratch their wicked desires. Surely the LORD will act. People, God is not asleep nor is he dead. He sits high and looks low.

On March 16, 2016, I posted: "Put on then, as God's chosen ones, holy and beloved, compassionate hearts, kindness, humility, meekness, and patience." -Colossians 3:12 ESV

On March 17, 2016, I posted: FOR HIS NAME SAKE! The Lord Is My Shepherd, A Psalm of David. "The Lord is my shepherd; I shall not want. He makes me lie down in green pastures. He leads me beside still waters. He restores my soul. He leads me in paths of righteousness for his name's sake." Psalm 23:1-3 ESV

On March 27, 2016, I posted: Standing Alone; Ladies and Gentlemen of God, The LORD has taught me, it's okay to stand alone. He would rather have a few that will totally trust him, than a thousand that believe in him, but doubt his magnificent power. He will do marvelous things through the few of them. Because he stood alone, nailed to that Ole Rugged Cross, I will never be alone. By his Spirit, the LORD goes before us in battle and gives us victory!

On March 29, 2016, I posted: ENCORE LORD! ENCORE LORD! The LORD has been tired and ready to act. People of Injustice, Are you tired and truly ready for the LORD to act? When the Israelites and our ancestors were really tired, they cried out to the LORD. They were mistreated by the governing authorities and God sent a mighty change. Have you cried out for the LORD to heal our people? He has heard me and he will deliver! On March 31, 2016, I posted: As humans, many of us speak of what we have done for others, much of the time boasting. Did you give to boast about yourself or Did you give because you truly love God?

On April 2, 2016, I posted: The LORD will bring justice swiftly without ending for those, who have sought him. And showed a photo which said, "Let justice roll down like a river..." Amos 5:24

On April 2, 2016, I listed the song: A Change Is Gonna Come by Deitrick Haddon. On April 3, 2016, I listed the song: You're Next In Line For A Miracle by Shirley Caesar and posted OUR MIRACLE IS COMING!!!! "A SUPERNATURAL GIFT ONLY GOD CAN GIVE, YOU HAVE KEPT THE FAITH, TODAY IS YOUR DAY FOR YOUR MIRACLE I DON'T CARE WHAT THE DEVIL HAS TOLD YOU, YOUR NEXT IN LINE!!!!!!!!!!" HALLELUJAH!!!!!!!!!!!!! On April 4, 2016, I posted: We claim we love God, but are we willing to suffer for God?

On April 4, 2016, I posted: A MAJOR SHIFT IS COMING! "COME CLOSE" – JESUS: HOW MANY OF YOU HAVE HEARD THE LORD SAY, "COME CLOSE?" IF THE LORD HAS TOLD YOU "COME CLOSE" HE WANTS TO REVEAL TO YOU. DO NOT RUN, BUT GET CLOSE. IT WILL BE FOR THE BENEFIT OF YOU AND YOUR FAMILY. WHEN YOU BECOME CLOSE TO GOD, HE WILL SHOW YOU THINGS THAT ONLY HE KNOWS. OBEY GOD!

On April 4, 2016, I posted: SHOW THIS NATION WHO YOU ARE LORD! FATHER, YOU COMMANDED US AS CHRISTIANS AND SO MANY HAVE COWARD IN THE FACE OF INJUSTICE. MILLIONS HAVE BEEN OPPRESSED....

On April 5, 2016, I posted: CHANGE IS COMING!!!!!! BEHOLD HE COMES, THERES NOBODY LIKE JEHOVAH!!! BECAUSE HE IS STRONG AND MIGHTY, HE IS MIGHTY IN BATTLE. HE WILL BRING AN OVERWHELMING VICTORY TO HIS CHILDREN! HE REIGNS FOREVER!

On April 20, 2016, I posted: Do not be fooled by this government and never forget. Jesus instructed for us to give to Ceasar what belongs to Ceasar (taxes) and give to God what belongs to God (tithe and offering service). "Render to Caesar the things that are Caesar's, and to God the things that are God's." - Mark 12:17 ESV "And he commanded the people who lived in Jerusalem to give the portion due to the priests and the Levites, that they might give themselves to the Law of the Lord. As soon as the command was spread abroad, the people of Israel gave in abundance the firstfruits of grain, wine, oil, honey, and of all the produce of the field. And they brought in abundantly the tithe of everything." - Chronicles 31:4-5; I said that to say this, the LORD said pay your taxes and bring your tithe, which is a tenth of your earnings. People didn't have money before so, requested was first fruit, which were animals & crops. Today first fruit is a tenth of your income. I learned to tithe when I was a young girl, my mother taught us and for it we have been blessed. Stop getting twisted up in what the Pastor is doing with the money, you bring tithe to the LORD. Your Pastor must and will give an account to the most high. Don't miss your blessing worrying about what others are doing, do your part. You Have Been Commanded, So Listen To The LORD. We have been instructed by the LORD to also follow the law of the land and to follow his law. When the world has ignored God's laws, he will act. America must pay for making a mockery of God. He's alive!

On April 26, 2016, I posted: LEADERS CAN BRING DEVASTATION TO A NATION: We have been instructed to pray for our leaders. All the words of the LORD have great meaning. Leaders can bring death to a nation. Be careful whom you follow in this world, they could be leading you down the wrong path. What good leader would bring devastation upon his people? It is the leader who does not have the guidance of the LORD, but of pride. The LORD is getting ready to shake this nation. For too long, good people have set on the sidelines and watched evil men bring pain to the people. Do you not know? The LORD is real and he has come to see about his children. He will repay each one of them their just reward. Father bring justice by any means necessary to your people. Do what you must, this is an evil nation and you have seen their deeds. LORD, you have commanded us to obey the laws of the land and this land we live about has defied every law known to man. We have been oppressed and killed. LORD, do you not hear the blood of the slain, which cries out to you. Father God, avenge your children as promised. Man has defied the Laws of God, God will act by the power of his Spirit in Jesus Name, Amen.

On May 25, 2016, I posted: 30 years ago, the LORD called me unto himself. When you belong to the LORD, he got your back. I have had so many dreams, too many to tell. You are born with a purpose. It doesn't matter how many times you fall down, God will pick you up. And he will give you a glimpse of your future too keep you strong, courageous and motivated. There is no one like God.

On July 3, 2016, I posted: GOD of WRATH; I know many of you don't want to believe it, but God will destroy all he hates. Once the people get tired and call upon him, he will change things. Yes, he gives grace and mercy, but he also gives wrath to his enemies and disobedient children. So many are afraid to stand up for what's righteous and you will have to account for it. You can't stand by the wayside thinking you're safe because you kept your mouth closed. God has commanded all Christians to stand for righteousness. When God kept pushing me to expose the crimes committed against me by America, he was also exposing some people. I have seen pastors, lawyers, artist and many elected officials who claim to be Christians cower. I'm truly shameful for supporting such people, because they are black and I thought more of them. We are fooled by people and I'm truly discussed and disappointed. God will send warriors, it's not for the faint at heart.

On July 4, 2016, I posted: I'm awake and I can't turn back, even if it means death. God said, we perish because we lack knowledge of him. Please get close to God, I know it's just something to do to many, but he's real y'all. He has showed me things I never would have learned on my own. Trust God enough to follow him even when it seems crazy.

On July 6, 2016, I posted: The bible says there is "a time for war, and a time for peace." - Ecclesiastes 3:8 and said IT'S TIME TO STOP TALKING AND BEGGING FOR THEM TO STOP KILLING US. IT IS TIME FOR WAR. #AltonSterling

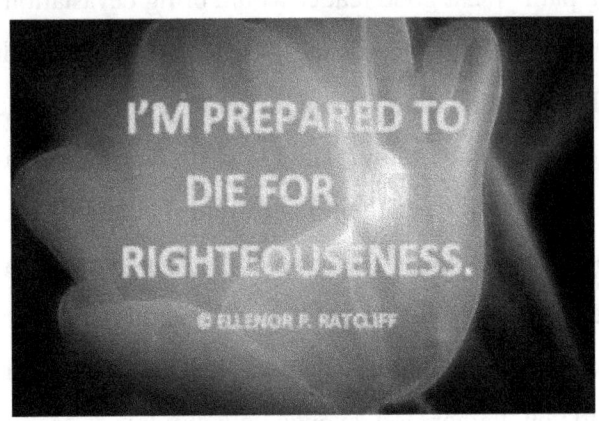

On July 6, 2016, I posted: FATHER GOD, FATHER WE ARE TIRED, WE HAVE OBEYED THE LAWS AND THIS GOVERNMENT CONTINUES TO KILL US AND OPPRESS US. I HAVE BELIEVED IN YOU AND DONE THE THINGS YOU REQUIRED OF ME. I'M ASKING YOU TO DO SOMETHING, BRING TERROR TO OUR OPPRESSORS BLACK AND WHITE. DON'T ALLOW NOT ONE OF THEM TO ESCAPE WHAT THEY HAVE DONE. MAKE AN EXAMPLE OUT OF THEM LORD. GIVE A WORD TO THOSE YOU WILL USE FOR BATTLE, WHO WILL FIGHT FOR RIGHTEOUSNESS. IT'S TIME GOD, SEND YOUR ANGELS TO TEAR DOWN THIS EVIL NATION IN JESUS NAME, AMEN. #AltonSterling

On July 7, 2016, I posted: IT'S REALLY TIME FOR WAR, SERIOUSLY. Many Of You Know I Have Fought For Justice. And You Are Aware That The Government Still Denied My Constitutional Rights. Go To My twitter: @LadyJusticeEPR, Instagram, Google and Facebook. Read my post and documents I posted regarding this American Government and it's Corruption. Strait Prejudice. God told me expose then all and I have. You can see my documents better on Instagram. But read everything on Blogger. Google my name and look at the images. I HAVE FRIENDS WHO'S FAMILY WAS ALSO KILLED BY POLICE. THIS AINT RIGHT AND

YALL BETTER GET SOME COURAGE BECAUSE IT DONT MATTER ABOUT YOUR CLASS OR DEGREE'S. WE BLACK AND WE HATED.

FACEBOOK DELETED - On July 7, 2016, I posted, the video of Philando Castile killing by police officer and said: IT'S TIME FOR WAR. #PhilandoCastile; WE ARE NOT SAFE. TAKE A STAND NOW. WE ARE BLACK WE ARE HATED.

FACEBOOK DELETED - On July 7, 2016, I posted: SOCIAL JUSTICE AWARENESS; 3 YEARS MAN TOLD ME "NO," GOD TOLD ME, "GRANTED." SO GUESS WHAT, I'M GOING IN HARD. THIS IS OUR EXPERIENCE TODAY. THREE YEARS I ASKED FOR JUSTICE. PRESIDENT OBAMA, GENERAL DYNAMICS INFORMATION TECHNOLOGY, ATTORNEY GENERAL LYNCH, U.S. EQUAL EMPLOYMENT OPPORTUNITY, AND U.S. FEDERAL COURT WHAT ARE YOU GOING TO DO NOW. Y'ALL SUPPORT THIS CORRUPTION AND HAVE SUPPORTED IT FOR YEARS. THE TIME IS NOW. GIVE ME WHAT'S MINE. YOU OWE ME!!! WE OBEYED YOUR LAWS AND YOU VIOLATED US. YOU WILL HAVE NO PEACE and I posted a picture of the conversation I had with a government troll.

Ellenor P. Ratcliff IT'S TIME FOR WAR! REDISTRIBUTE THE PAIN. We have stood for truth, we helped citizens, we voted, we did everything right and still they kill us.
Like Reply 14 15 hrs

Evan Charles Time for war? Against who? ALL COPS? All White people? Why? Because less than 1% of all police commit police brutality against Blacks? Because of the perception that most white people are racist? Please. First you preach peace, then you call for War? Absurd.
Like Reply 4 hrs

 Ellenor P. Ratcliff Ive never preached peace. There is no peace without justice. There is a war coming. Others have told me so many months ago. Our Pastors preach prosperity, but don't preach justice. All this is the direct result of them letting the wolves -POLITIONS into God's house to fool God's sheep. For three years, hell maybe longer I have been oppressed. God has revealed the devils to me, the white men and the black people who's done his bidding. They will all pay.

> I've prayed for God to bring terror to the home of every oppressor black and white. We walked this city for 7 days around Houston City Hall and Equal Employment Opportunity Commission. The United States as a whole is Corrupt. The White House, U.S. Attorney General Lorretta Lynch, U.S. Equal Employment Opportunity Commission, U.S. Federal Courts, Center for Medicaid and Medicare and The Federal Bureau of Investigation, police Departments. OUR ENTIRE GOVERNMENT IS CORRUPT. Look at my Facebook, intagram and twitter. Go all the way back and read. AMERICA SHITTED ON ME AND MANY LIKE ME. WHEN YOU LOOK AT THE MURDER OF #ALTONSTERLING IT'S BECAUSE ALL YALL DO IS UPHOLD VIOLENCE, ITS ALL YOU UNDERSTAND. When we have been law-abiding, voted, helped others and paid taxes and you still kill us, GOD SAID ITS TIME FOR WAR. IM HIS CHILD AND YALL THINK YALL CAN KEEP KILLING, HURTING AND VIOLATING OUR GOD GIVEN RIGHTS, YOU ARE MISTAKEN. IF WE ARE GOING TO DIE, WE ARE GOING TO DIE FIGHTING. IT'S TIME. NICE IS OUT, WAR IS IN. God Gave Us Wisdom And Knowledge, WE ARE HUMAN GOT DAMMIT! ITS TIME FOR WAR.

FACEBOOK DELETED - On July 7, 2016, I posted: FOURTH OF JULY; MY POEM KEPT RINGING IN MY EARS. I KEPT HEARING IT AND HEARING IT AND HEARING IT; JUSTICE, WHERE ART THEE? www.ladyjusticetx.org

On July 7, 2016, I posted: THEY PRETEND TO BE PATRIOTIC, BUT THEY'RE ACTIONS ARE OF PURE EVIL. IT'S TIME FOR THE LORD TO ACT. WE ARE NOT SAFE, EVEN IF WE DO WHAT'S RIGHT.

> IT'S HYPOCRISY
> IT'S NOT PATRIOTIC,
> NO JUSTIFICATION.
> IT'S TIME!!!

On July 7, 2016, I posted: FACEBOOK DO NOT VIOLATE MY RIGHTS TO FREE SPEECH. REMOVE THE LIMITATION YOU PLACED ON MY PAGE. I KNOW A WHILE BACK YOU MADE IT WHERE I COULDN'T TAG GENERAL DYNAMICS INFORMATION TECHNOLOGY, THE PRESIDENT AND ZANDRA BOSIE IN MY POST. YOU ARE VIOLATING MY RIGHTS. STOP NOW. WITH FACEBOOK PICTURE: WHY ARE YOU

STAGNATING MY ABILITY TO PASTE COMMENTS

> **facebook**
>
> Why are you stagnating
> My ability to paste Comments.
> Is it under the President's Order?
> STOP NOW!!!
> YOU ARE VIOLATING MY RIGHTS TO FREE SPEECH.
> THANK YOU KINDLY!
> @ladyjusticeepr

On July 8, 2016, I posted: Good Morning America; God said, "A CHANGE IS COMING." I CRIED OUT BECAUSE I WAS TIRED OF FIGHTING THIS GOVERNMENT. ONCE HE EXPOSED ALL THE PEOPLE I CONTACTED FOR HELP, I WAS SAD AND IN DISBELIEF. HOW DARE THE MEN AND WOMEN TAKE AN OAT, AND DON'T HOLD TO GOD'S WORD, Y'ALL PLACED Y'ALL HAD ON GOD'S WORD THE BIBLE. DON'T Y'ALL KNOW GOD WON'T BE PUT TO SHAME. All this is the fault of our GOVERNMENT or the people behind it. I know they think their winning, but God will get the glory. It will get worse before it gets better, much worst. Christians can't sit down and not challenge these corrupt leaders, this is their faults, all of them. It will take chaos. I have been talking about this kind of stuff for years. PASTORS Y'ALL BETTER START PREACHING ABOUT JUSTICE. FOR THOSE OF YOU WHO WON'T THIS IS YOUR FAULT AS WELL AND GOD WILL JUDGE YOU. ANY SERVANT OF THE LORD WHO WON'T STAND FOR RIGHTEOUSNESS WILL BE JUDGED, BUT YOU WILL SUFFER ON THIS SIDE.

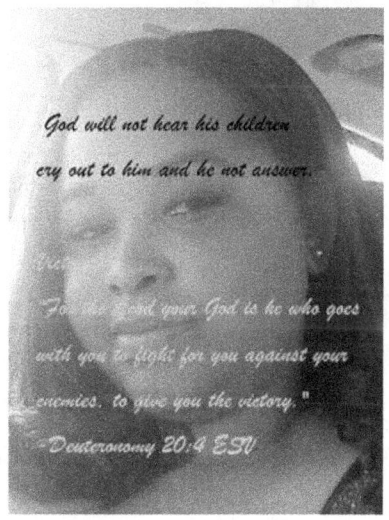

FACEBOOK DELETED - On July 8, 2016, I posted: Y'ALL AFFILIATIONS GONE GET Y'ALL IN TROUBLE WITH GOD.

FACEBOOK DELETED - On July 8, 2016, I shared a post from a Facebook friend of a friend and he said: "PLEASE PRAY FOR MY FRIENDS FAMILY." There was a video and everyone was asked to google, "Jerry Williams ashville nc" Jerry Williams a 35 year old father of 5 black male was killed in the mountains of North Carolina by police officers Saturday. Meet us this Friday at Moore square park in downtown Raleigh from 6:30pm to 8pm for a vigal and community conversation about the problem and solutions. #Justiceorelse #COMPus #Policymattersnc #raleighloc #JerryWilliams #Akieldenkins #Altonsterling Allan X Fuller Amon Muhammad Kelvin Bahr Jervay Assatta X Indeya Niecee Cornute Shakem Amen Akhet" I also shared the post of another person, related to Jerry Williams and it said, "While my family was peacefully protesting the death of my murdered family member. Asheville Police Department had snipers on the roof ready to kill more of us! Wake up people they put targets on our backs!! Report this! WLOS ABC 13"

On July 8, 2016, I posted: HOW WILL YOU BETTER OUR PEOPLE? COMING SOON! I have CHANNELED my ANGER to HELPING our people by LAUNCHING an organization come 2017, called LADY JUSTICE RESOURCE SERVICES. We have also used a SEPARATE ORGANIZATION name LADY JUSTICE, to SPEAK TRUTH TO POWER.

On July 8, 2016, I posted: TODAY I WAS ALLOWED TO COPY AND PASTE AGAIN. THANK Y'ALL FOR GIVING ME MY RIGHTS BACK.

> **facebook**
> Why are you stagnating
> My ability to paste Comments.
> Is it under the President's Order?
> STOP NOW!!!
> YOU ARE VIOLATING MY RIGHTS TO FREE SPEECH.
> THANK YOU KINDLY!
> @ladyjusticepr

************July 8 · ***********

FACEBOOK DELETED - FASTING; GOD SAID CHANGE WAS COMING. We have fasted for April and May; Normally I post this at the beginning of the mouth but something happened. We are suppose to fast this month. This is the seventh month, the next and final fast is the tenth month. If you wish to join you can find the fasting information at www.ladyjusticetx.org on the Daily Agenda tab. We have already protested before the LORD in April, so excuse that portion of the Daily Agenda. God has really been speaking to us. It's really live when he wants something done. It's a shame people doubt him, thank God that we know too much about him. God does move on his own timing. All this is a result to our dedication to obeying what God said. This fast is for 7 days straight, do not skip days. We will fast July 10 to July 16. You must make a sacrifice and give up the things you love the most for 7 days. If you have a medical issue, please consult your doctor. Give up things you love, like facebook, junk food, watching tv, gambling or etc. Tell God what you plan to give up and stick to what you say. Ask God for what you have need of, ask him to make a way for you. I'm telling you God will move for you. Don't expect him to move how you want him to move. Tell the LORD to have his way and you allow him to have his way. Somethings only change by prayer and fasting. We have been praying for God to bring justice to this country for his children. They not treating us right and I will not pray for peace, this is not a time for peace but a time for the LORD to shake this country up and bring it to it's knees. America has slapped God in the face, we are tired of hurting and crying for the injustice we face on a daily basis. "Not by MIGHT nor by POWER, but by my SPIRIT, says the LORD ALMIGHTY." - Zechariah 4:6 #WARONINJUSTICE #GODISKING #WEAREHISCHILDREN #UNITEDWEGOFORTH

On July 8, 2016, I posted: SPREAD THE WORD, WE NEED TO KNOW THE TRUTH! Jerry Williams a 35 year old father of 5, was shot 7 times on July 2, 2016, by Asheville Police Department off Deaverview Rd at Deaverview Apartments in Asheville, NC. The first shot blew his arm off his body. He did not have a weapon. First Responders did not help him as he lay in the street per witnesses. The shooting was caught on police body camera. Stories are conflicting and the family needs answers. A Justice Rally was organized, once Mayor Manheimer found out snipers were ordered and were on the building near Buncombe County Sheriff's Office. Manheimer has yet to release video footage. #justice4jerry #JerryWilliams

FACEBOOK DELETED - On July 9, 2016, I shared a facebook post: "Due to Police shooting of #JerryWilliams #justice4jerry Hundreds gather for Black Lives Matter rally in Raleigh Though the Dallas shootings had dominated the news for much of the day, several hundred people gathered in downtown Raleigh on Friday evening to remember 500 other lives lost in officer-involved shootings this year. newsobserver.com"

FACEBOOK DELETED - On July 9, 2016, I posted: Everyone switch to black banks. Black On Black Support!

FACEBOOK DELETED - On July 9, 2016, I posted: 7 DAY FASTING; GOD TOLD MY HUSBAND AND I CHANGE WAS COMING. On July 16th, I will tell you the song the LORD spoke to us on April 16th, which was the last day of our 7 day march around the City of Houston and U.S. Equal Employment Opportunity. View our 7 day march of Praise, Prayer and Protest on the map below. We have fasted for April and May. This is the seventh month, the next and final fast is the tenth month. If you wish to join us, you can find the fasting information at www.ladyjusticetx.org on the Daily Agenda tab. We have already protested before the LORD in April, so excuse that portion of the Daily Agenda. God has really been speaking to us. It's really live when he wants something done. It's a shame people doubt him, thank God that we know too much about him. God does move on his own timing. All this is a result to our dedication to obeying what God said. This fast is for 7 days straight, do not skip days. We will fast July 10 to July 16. You must make a sacrifice and give up the things you love the most for 7 days. If you have a medical issue, please consult your doctor. Give up things you love, like facebook, junk food, watching tv, gambling, sex or etc. Tell God what you plan to give up and stick to what you say. Ask God for what you have need of, ask him to make a way for you. I'm telling you God will move for you. Don't expect him to move how you want him to move. Tell the LORD to have his way and you allow him to have his way. Somethings only change by prayer and fasting. We have been praying for God to bring justice to this country for his children. They not treating us right and I will not pray for peace, this is not a time for peace but a time for the LORD to shake this country up and bring it to it's knees. America has slapped God in the face, we are tired of hurting and crying for the injustice we face on a daily basis. Blessings and may God supernaturally protect your families in the mighty name of Jesus, Amen. "Not by MIGHT nor by POWER, but by my SPIRIT, says the LORD ALMIGHTY." -Zechariah 4:6 #WARONINJUSTICE #GODISKING #WEAREHISCHILDREN #UNITEDWEGOFORTH

On July 10, 2016, I shared a picture of the Fact sheet and posted: BLACK FAMILY HARRASSED BY APD, AFTER SLAUGHTER OF #JerryWilliams. LORD, you know what has been done against #JerryWilliams. We present facts before you and all America. Bring every culprits to justice in the media, police department, the mayor's office and the fire department. LORD you said you love justice and we stand boldly professing your word. Father hear the pleas of this family. LORD bring terror to every person who is doing Satan's bidding. Supernaturally protect every family member. Expose the truth and give the Williams family justice. Avenge your children as you have promised, #JerryWilliams blood is crying out to you LORD. Remember your word to us LORD, in the mighty name of Jesus, Amen. #JerryWilliams #UNITEDWEGOFORTH

I shared another post that said, "Asheville Black Lives Matter Community; Fact sheet passed out yesterday at the march/rally through downtown. It was put together by the family with support from Asheville Black Lives Matter. Please share with as many people as possible so we can get Jerry's story out there. Note: Tuesday, July 12th is Jerry's birthday."

On July 10, 2016, I posted: EXPOSE; The devil must move once exposed. God said ,when we resist, he will flee. Resist the hell he brings in your life by keeping your trust in the LORD. Praise God through it all. The enemy must surrender what belongs to you in the name of Jesus. Stand firm on the promises of God, regardless of how things look.

FACEBOOK DELETED - On July 12, 2016, I posted: ELITE; They don't care about the hood. They don't care about what you are suffering. They promote other elites even when they are wrong but pretend they don't. The elite knows what their "political friends are doing but because they get dropped some dollars, they sell out our communities. Don't let these people fool you. If they gave a darn, our communities would be thriving. DON'T LET THEM FOOL YOU TWICE. COMING SOON, MY DECLARATION TO ENDING OPPRESSION IN AMERICA.

On July 14, 2016, I posted: TO EVERY ACTIVIST..WATCH FOR THE GOVERNMENT TROLLS. Everyone on my page is shielded, I did that long ago, so no one can view my friends list unless I allow them to be a friend. Someone posed as a friend on facebook to get access to my page. Well, I was suspicious so, I allowed it for about 10 minutes. Why is facebook leaking information to the government? The government has to ask permission to get my information. TO THE PUBLIC, facebook has to notify you if your account has been logged in from another source. If it has more than likely it's the government looking at your information. KNOWLEDGE IS POWER Emailed me about some government grants and what was I up to, remember I told you they posed as a friend. They thought I would actually tell them what the LORD was up to.

Whomever you are, wait and see what the LORD has in store for you. Signed off, Child of the KING.

FACEBOOK DELETED - On July 16, 2016, I posted: STAY AWOKE; This is the conversation I told you all about on FACEBOOK. The first picture is facebook or the government posing as one of you who are on my friends list. NOW PAY CLOSE ATTENTION. I have my friends list blocked so only friends can see it. Someone asked to be a friend two weeks ago and I allowed them, I felt funny about the person. So I watched. This week someone posed as one of you and I spoke to them only to learn of course it was the government. WHEN WE ARE BLACK, FIGHTING FOR AND DEMANDING CHANGE THIS IS WHAT OUR GOVERNMENT DOSE. The person I allowed two weeks ago removed themselves, it was the government. The second picture is facebook supposedly shutting down the page. Our government is corrupt and they have been trying to get popular people and others to sale or the government has facebook block us from using certain functions within facebook. Y'ALL BETTER WAKE UP! THEY WANT TO KEEP US DOWN, BUT IT'S TIME TO RISE! TAKE YOUR PLACE! I showed two pictures how Facebook was pretending to be a fake friend asking me questions in messenger.

On July 17, 2016, I posted: I can't tell you how many times, I've heard the words POLICY AND PROCEDURES. I have worked since I was 13 years old. The SCHOOLS have POLICY AND PROCEDURES. The CHURCH has POLICY AND PROCEDURES. CHILD CARES CENTERS have POLICY AND PROCEDURES. BUSINESSES have POLICY AND PROCEDURES. GOVERNMENT has POLICY AND PROCEDURES. WHY DO OUR LOCAL CITIES AND GOVERNMENT, NOT MAKE CERTAIN ALL VIOLATORS REGARDLESS OF RACE AND CLASS, ARE EQUALLY GIVEN DUE PROCESS IN THE MURDERS AND OTHER VIOLATIONS AGAINST CITIZENS? THEY HAVE CREATED EVIL LAWS, TO UP HOLD THEIR WRONG, AGAINST GOD AND CITIZENS. THERE'S SOMETHING TRULY WRONG IN THIS COUNTRY! ONLY GOD WILL FIX IT, ONLY HE CAN. HE WILL.

FACEBOOK DELETED - On July 18, 2016, I posted: I once loved this country, but their hate for us has become more realized; as they kill our brothers and sisters and are at the least, given a slap on the wrist. And to see those of my African background participating in these crimes against its own, is far beyond me. Our people are truly strong and we know how to survive, but at this level of corruption, who can thrive. God will send his army, they are awaiting in our midth, to do the bidding of the father and end this madness. It must be torn down to build again and the rolls will change. All who perverted justice will meet poverty, they will stare it in the face and wish it wasn't so, but its the path they created and must go. The first will be last and the last will thirst. This is the way, it has to be rebuilt again, but this time upon those who will boldly do God's will and when he speaks will be still. Not doing the deeds of evil that throws cash his way, but remaining steadfast never to sway. We need powerful and strong leadership. AMERICA UNDERMINDS BLACKS.

FACEBOOK DELETED - On July 19, 2016, I posted: Revelation; God will reveal what our enemies have done, stay close and follow his guidance. Remember the devil doesn't have new tricks, he has new faces. I have showed you the faces of my oppressors. Don't be shocked, be ready and get into position. God is going to turn this nation upside down. "He uncovers the deeps out of darkness and brings deep darkness to light." - Job 12:22 ESV

FACEBOOK DELETED - On July 19, 2016, I shared a post and said: I know it's the truth! Darn, people thought I was lying! Breakfast Club added a new video: Dr. Omar Johnson On How Obama Has Failed Black America. On the 18th of July, Dr. Umar Ifatunde says "black americans have failed to hold Barack Obama accountable for ignoring black issues. Watch the full interview here: http://bit.ly/29GJCC6"

FACEBOOK DELETED - On July 19, 2016, I posted: Only He Can Deliver; When God has to give you justice, he will bring things against your oppressors, every last one of them. It will hurt them, when injustice was done unto me, it was also done unto my father in heaven. All of my oppressors must pay for what they have done. You can't bring harm to me and not expect my father to protect his child. You shall pay 100 fold the hurt and pain you have brought to my life. I obeyed your rules and you denied me. As sure as the LORD called me unto himself at the age of 9 years old, you will get your just reward for the hand you have dealt. May my father in heaven bring terror to your homes until you do right by me.

FACEBOOK DELETED - On July 19, 2016, I posted: Y'all Better WAKE UP! LISTEN TO HIS WORDS CAREFULLY! You need to pray to God and seek him really. Like you have never sought him before, the devil is showing himself, your job is to seek the LORD and stay armed. Don't let folks fool you. Listen carefully, you will see why I choose not to walk for peace in the City of Houston on July 10th, after the shootings of 4 black men, one took place right here in Houston Texas. These people have lied to us long enough and wishes to destroy us. I shared a post of the Navy Seal interview with Fox News and he warns all America and the post said, "Navy SEAL Drops Bombshell On FOX: Says Government Is CREATING Conditions To Impose MARTIAL LAW Navy SEAL Drops Bombshell On FOX: Says Government Is CREATING Conditions To Impose MARTIAL LAW Ex-US Navy SEAL Ben Smith joins Fox News and drops a…secretsofthefed.com"

FACEBOOK DELETED - On July 20, 2016, I posted: It's not against God's laws to protect your family. When the LORD called for war, he selected men that had their hands on their swords and drunk from the river with one hand. Those whom were scared, and those whom put down their swords to drink were not fit for battle. Get to know the LORD your God, he has called us to stand in this day of evil against our opponents. The LORD will dash your enemies to pieces, get in position and await the voice of the LORD. He will speak to you, we live in a time were God will call men to serve and the LORD God Almighty, will slay our enemies. God only needs a few good men, to slay thousands and it will be done by his Spirit. Oh my God, if y'all really knew his power. They will tremble with fear as the LORD'S army is released for battle. There is not an army greater than the LORDS, COME LORD JESUS! Show the nations so they may never forget your magnificent power, bring this nation to its knees, for they have mocked you and make evil laws against your people. COME LORD JESUS, SO WE CAN WORSHIP YOU WITHOUT WORRING IF OUR MEN ARE NEXT TO DIE BY THIS GOVERNMENT, COME LORD JESUS, COME.

On July 20, 2016, I shared a post from World Truth TV and there was a picture with the facebook logo and the words, Central Intelligence Agency – United States of America and I said: Y'all Better Recognize; Yeah, we already know. That's why I don't talk on the phone or on Facebook message box. I know they have been doing this. I was referring to the following text, "CIA Admits Full Monitoring of Facebook and Social Networks | World Truth.TV Most people use social media like Facebook and Twitter to share photos of friends…worldtruth.tv|By Eddie Levin"

FACEBOOK DELETED - On July 22 2016, I posted: WE DEMAND JUSTICE! *Jerry Williams was shot and killed* Don't Give Up! I pray you are empowered to continue your fight for justice.#UNITEDWEGOFORTH #Justice4Jerry To everyone, we want to know your experience with injustice, email your experience to bornblackroyalty@gmail.com. To receive a copy of this poem: Justice, Where Art Thee? Visit www.ladyjusticetx.org and make a donation of $4.00 through PayPal. The funds will be utilized to cover paper, envelope and postage. Justice is a right, it's not an option!

On July 24, 2016, I posted a poem and said: This country of America, I despise.

DREAMS
"You Can Be Anything You Choose To Be"

The words of a mother to her daughter, who demonstrated great potential. What can hardworking, dedication and loyalty get you?

On July 27, 2016, I posted: WHAT HAVE YOU DONE? The Church has sinned against God. The leaders refused to obey God, but allow the government to enter the church of God, parading before God's people. The leaders refuse to obey God and have forsaken his teaching on truth. You have sinned against God. Do you not know what the LORD will do now? Have you forgotten his commands and his promises for such perversion? There is not one who can save you from his judgment.

FACEBOOK DELETED - On July 28, 2016, I posted: CIA and FBI we demand justice. This act has caused terrorist to succeed in their acts. You said, Public Corruption threatens U.S. Borders. These terrorist are in U. S. Office. Arrest them at once and hold them accountable. Our borders are in jeopardy.

FACEBOOK DELETED - On August 5, 2016, I shared a post and photo then I said: Ladies and Gentleman, Accountability is Everything. The shared post said, "Facebook just set a dangerous precedent with the police. Facebook deactivated Korryn Gaines' FB on police request. Then police killed her. Now the company has some serious explaining to do. d.shpg.org"

On August 5, 2016, I posted a photo of Attorney General Loretta Lynch at "Facebook Live Town Hall On Community Policing" the other wording in the picture says: "Attorney General Loretta E. Lynch traveled to Los Angeles as part of her national Community Policing Tour aimed to highlight law enforcement's efforts to use social media and technology to increase transparency, curb violent crime, and build stronger bonds with the communities they serve. While in Los Angeles, the Attorney General held a live town hall at Facebook at their new Playa Vista Campus, taking questions from an audience of students and officers about policing strategies and innovative solutions to build mutual respect and coordination between law enforcement and members of the community. The town hall was also streamed on Facebook Live on the Department of Justice Facebook page." And I said in my post, I told you all, I read everything. This is why police and government are trolling our pages and deleting our post. It's even going down on Instagram.

On August 5, 2016, I shared a posted of Korryn Gains with her son in a picture. The post was dated August 5 and said: " #RIP #KORRYNGAINES .... Soooo you mean to tell me that you need swat team to serve a warrant for a #trafficticket on a 130lb female in the house with her son that you claim she held hostage and shoot her in the head and shot her son wounding him(he's gonna survive) and she had a lawsuit pending against Baltimore PD. This sounds like a few other cases... THIS IS STR8 BULLSHIT #RIP #korryngaines She documented everything on her Facebook and somehow her page was deleted..."

FACEBOOK DELETED - On August 10, 2016, I shared a post and photo. The photo was regarding the "Black Facebook News" which featured a "New Black Facebook Website" and of course it was created by one of our own and the post said: "Black Social Network Community Breaking News! - Black Facebook Website - Register Now! http://www.blackfbook.com/news/news.php…"

On August 11, 2016, I posted: ARE YOU READY, REALLY? When the rubber meets the road! Are you prepared to obey the LORD, even until death? Are you? You have to be willing to do what the LORD says, even until death. Who are you really?

On August 19, 2016, I posted: He Has Your Back "Yea, though I walk through the valley of shadow of death, I will fear no evil: for thou art with me..." We walk through a valley as the ingenious people and you should not fear what the enemy does, God is with us and he's preparing the way. I promise, he's preparing a way.

FACEBOOK DELETED - On August 21, 2016, I posted: *Black Woman Scorn; All I wanted was peace, they refuse to let me be. Scorn by a country, relentlessly. You lie, you steal, you cheat, you kill. Never will we forget what you have done. Raped and violated our men, women and children. Castrated many of our men because of your guilt, that the same would happen to your wives and daughters. You have not gotten away, you have deepened your pit, upon it you will be slit. Never forgetting all the evil you've done, a woman scorn, she is the key. You have opened the wrong door. Terror will be your rest, it will terrorize you until death. All the evil all the lies, all the killings we despise. You will not rest, it will haunt you until your last breath. You betrayed us, we trusted you. The things that await is nothing compared to what you have done. A black woman scorn. We Won!*

On August 29, 2016, I posted: America; It has been extremely difficult fighting for justice. Our government is full of deceitful ways. This thing that has been done to so many and myself is hypocrisy. All I ever wanted was to live my life, complete without government denying my rights.

Enforcing the laws not only for whites. America has told me by action, "You are a black woman and you don't matter. Sometimes, I truly wish this was not my experience. After all, I lived according to the law. But I learned America never intended to protect my black skin. You have lied, killed and stolen what doesn't belong to you. He will make you surrender all you have stolen, it doesn't belong to you. The evil plans you delivered will be brought unto your own. They will wonder, "What have we possibly done?" They will come to the knowledge of the evil acts you have delivered them into. The hypocrisy and slaughter of a people. It will haunt them unto death. Never again will they ignore the pain we felt. It will come upon them like flood waters but it will never cease. Eternally they will be tormented, it will never end. They only have you to thank, their beginning is your end.

FACEBOOK DELETED - On September 11, 2016, I posted: I Appreciate You! I want to take this opportunity to thank the individuals whom have supported me consistently through my current fight of injustice. Truly it's only a very few of you. You have supported me when others though I was lying, even after presenting the facts here on Facebook and other social sites. Your support will never be forgotten. It's often difficult and scary for one to support you after coming against powerful people. You will always be remembered and may God overflow you with blessings! Thank you and I appreciate you. Blessings to the few!

On September 11, 2016, I posted: Facebook is controlled by Government now and they are specifically targeting African Americans. Y'all think it's a joke but pay attention. All kind of things have been happening and believe me, it will get worst.

FACEBOOK DELETED - On September 21, 2016, I posted: Amerikkka the Babylon.

FACEBOOK DELETED - On September 21, 2016, I posted: How to defeat America; This place called Amerikka is bring death unto itself. They don't have enough sense to do right. There is only one way to fix this. God will do it. Before you strike you must know where to hit your enemy. God always gave direction in wars against the savage people and victory was won. Don't go on what you know but listen to God. You can have victory but you must ask how. We have been in a war but are you ready to win God's way.

On September 21, 2016, I posted: Get In Position; Without the most high, there is no victory. You not just fighting against humans. Wake up, these are dark forces, until you know how to pray and counter act the enemy all the talk is pointless. First, repent for saying there is no God beg the most high for forgiveness. Second, ask him to save the people from the enemy and to give an overwhelming victory. Third, bring a sacrifice unto the Lord. Forth, fast for what we collectively need as a people. Commit no sin while fasting. Fifth, wait for his answer. Only move on what the

Lord has told you. Then watch him move by his spirit. Stop doubting and position yourself.

On September 28, 2016, I posted: FACEBOOK; Why are you deleting truth from my page? I still have a copy. I want to say, Thank you. Now I know for sure what to build on.

FACEBOOK DELETED - On September 29, 2016, I posted: FACEBOOK; I'm aware that you deleted my prayers for the fast in July on the 5th and 6th day. I have copies of them and I know why you deleted those prayer. What you have done was not done unto us, but to our father in heaven. May he terrorize you for terrorizing his people. You probe our facebook pages because we are the original people and you don't want the truth revealed. You will suffer for what you have done. Every act you commit against the Black Africans will come into your life 100 fold. LORD you have seen the unjust actions of Facebook and this government. Pay them 100 fold their action in the name of Yahushua, Amen. - Ellenor P. Ratcliff

On September 29, 2016, I posted: FACEBOOK users, COPY ALL YOUR WORK! **FACEBOOK DELETED -** On September 29, 2016, I posted: Injustice Prayer; Father God we come humbly before you. We praise you and magnify your name. We adore you LORD, you are KING of Kings and LORD of Lords, you are El Shaddi and I Am. Father please forgive our sins against you and please forgive the sins of our ancestors. Come by your spirit and rescue your people. Father God we need you to tear down the walls of injustice in this world. Father you said you would curse those who oppress your people. Come LORD Yahushua and show yourself faithful. Thank you for inclining your ear to hear our petition. We love you and thank you for who you are, All Mighty. Father as you lead us into victory, I decree and declare that every individual will be set free from the bonds of injustice in the mighty name of Yahushua, Amen. Please listen to this song below as we come into the fasting month of October. We are excited about what God has promised his people. This will be a 31 day fast. Please stay posted for information regarding the fast. Blessings, William McDowell feat. Trinity Anderson "Spirit Break Out."

FACEBOOK DELETED - On October 4, 2016, I posted: It's all Systematic and many fail to realize the truth. Only through God, once you really connect with him in praise, he will Shift the Atmosphere. All God needs is a few good men and women to act on their faith. He will turn it around for the good of his chosen people.

FACEBOOK DELETED - On October 4, 2016, I posted: Yes! The time is now!

On October 4, 2016, I posted: FACEBOOK; If you remove any more of my post of prayer or anything opposed to these evil times, I pray that you lose the activity of your limbs. We bind the demonic authorities who are participating with these acts. May my father bring his Spirit against you, that you may never again forget who he is. May God give you your just reward in the name of Yeshua, Amen.

FACEBOOK DELETED - On October 5, 2016, I posted: Speak It! What do you want God to do for his chosen people? Speak it into Existence!

FACEBOOK DELETED - On October 6, 2016, I posted: Prayer is power. It must be used now against our enemies for God to show himself mighty as always. My prayers were deleted by Facebook, but I will post them here one time for the 7 days. In these prayers I oppose everything that doesn't line up with the word of God in the name of Yeshua, Amen. For everything, there is a season. We will petition for the LORD to come against our oppressors and bring justice to America by any means necessary.

FACEBOOK DELETED - On October 16, 2016, I posted: Our Faith and Works; Our oppressors don't understand, there is a greater power behind the drive of the Black African movement of today. Just as Pharaoh hands were forced to his destruction so shall our oppressors of today. He will do it by his Spirit as promised.

FACEBOOK DELETED - On October 17, 2016, I posted: There is not a place you can hide, he will pursue you to the ends of the earth. I decree and declare, by the spirit of God shall he come against every oppressor. May he terrify them and give them their just reward 100 fold. Father move by your spirit and chase down our oppressors in the mighty name of Yeshua The Messiah, Amen.

FACEBOOK DELETED - On October 18, 2016, I posted: FACEBOOK;

*******REMINDER******* If you remove any more of my post of prayer or anything opposed to these evil times, I pray that you lose the activity of your limbs. We bind the demonic authorities who are participating with these acts. May my father bring his Spirit against you, that you may never again forget who he is. May God give you your just reward in the name of Yeshua, Amen.

FACEBOOK DELETED - On October 19, 2016, I posted: God is Strategic; When the LORD tells you to move on a certain thing, you better move. I don't care how crazy it may sound, obey then get out his way until further instruction. Move when he says move and stop procrastinating!

FACEBOOK DELETED - On October 21, 2016, I posted: JUST OBEY, EVEN WHEN YOU DON'T FEEL LIKE FIGHTING. In one year God has exposed so many people. He has truly uncovered the deeps of darkness in my Case of Injustice. I can honestly say, I'm ashamed that some of these people are the same skin color as myself. 2013 to 2016, It ain't over until God says it's over! You will get knocked down but stand your ground. You are VICTORIOUS!

FACEBOOK DELETED - On October 22, 2016, I posted: Change Is Coming! Why Couldn't You Do Right? All General Dynamics Information Technology had to do was obey federal laws. I enjoyed helping people and my employer made it a living hell. I gladly woke at 3:30 a.m., stood outside alone at 4:30 a.m. in the morning to ride the bus, which arrived at 4:49 a.m. Black people are not lazy nor are we ignorant to your discrimination and evil tactics. GDIT you will pay for what you've done.

FACEBOOK DELETED - On October 22, 2016, I posted: Why have Black African People not received Reparations? President Obama just awarded Reparations to Non-Blacks this year 2016. mtholyoke.edu History of Reparations Payments.

FACEBOOK DELETED - On October 22, 2016, I posted: As a people we have been led astray for wicked gain. God even told his servants don't welcome bribery. That is why you see the black community drowning while the church is financially growing. He will fix this mess, allowed.

FACEBOOK DELETED - On October 24, 2016, I posted: Day 18; Father God we come kneeling before you, thanking you for making a way out of no way, thank you for your awesome greatness, thank you for guiding your children even when the enemy attempts to trick us. Thank you for leading us in righteousness for your name sake. LORD you know all things. We come asking forgiveness of our sins as well as the sins of our ancestors. LORD you have seen the plans of our enemies and you have made them known, please continue to expose the deeps of darkness. Come LORD Yeshua and strike down our enemies with a mighty blow. Repay them 100 fold what they have delivered unto your chosen people. Father give us victory over injustice in America, just like you gave Jericho into the hands of Joshua. Father you stood in the fire with Shadrach, Meshach and Abednego when Nebuchadnezzar ordered their death by fire. Come Father and show yourself faithful just as you did of old. Show America and the world that you are El Shaddi, come to our rescue and punish our enemies. They are evil, vile creatures that have mocked your name. Come

Father and avenge your people. Have your way, magnificent one in the mighty name of Yeshua The Messiah, Amen.

FACEBOOK DELETED - On October 26, 2016, I posted: Day 20; JUSTICE IS COMING! SACRIFICE October 7-28 : 7 days for 3 weeks: JOIN US at www.ladyjusticetx.org, select Justice Agenda tab. Father we love you, we come praising and magnifying your name. You are KING of Kings and LORD of Lords, you are I Am, the soon coming KING. There is none like you. You are the LORD our God, you are strong and mighty, mighty in battle. We take refuge in you El Shaddi. We come humbly kneeling before you. Thanking you for who you are, our Banner. Father please forgive our ancestors sins and please forgive our sins of omission and commission against you. LORD we come to you, sacrificing for you to make a new covenant with your chosen people of today. LORD, you said you love Justice and hate robbery and wrong doing. You promised by your faithfulness that you would make an everlasting covenant with us. Father forget not your words of old. We thank you for inclining your ear to hear our petition. Come by your Spirit and Fight for us giving us an overwhelming Victory against America and the powers and principalities operating. You have seen their evil deeds of murder, rape, corruption, extortion, bribery, collusion and they refuse to do right by your people. Come LORD, send the Commander of your army and grant our petition of bringing Justice to this wicked land; hold every one of them accountable, they have ruled by greed and the love of money. Father teardown America's evil systems and every place that defy your commands. Replace the leaders including pastors, who refuse to abide in your word before you and your people. Raise up soldiers whom are not afraid to carry out your commands, appoint leaders who will not compromise your word or compromise your people. Strike down our enemies with a mighty blow, never to be in any form of authority as long as they shall live. Come Father by your Spirit in the mighty name of Yeshua The Messiah, shake the nations that have come against you and us, your chosen people, Amen.

FACEBOOK DELETED - On October 27, 2016, I posted: Day 22; JUSTICE IS COMING! SACRIFICE October 7-28 : JOIN US at www.ladyjusticetx.org, select Justice Agenda tab. Father we come thanking you for your magnificent power. As we conclude LORD we come humbly praising and magnifying your name. You are El Shaddi, KING of Kings and LORD of Lords. There is none that can measure to your awesome greatness. Father thank you for forgiveness of our sins of omission and commission. Thank you for forgiving the sins of our ancestors. We thank you for inclining your ear to hear our petition. Father you have witnessed the great oppression to your people by America and abroad places. Their evil deeds of murder, rape, corruption, extortion, bribery, collusion and they refuse to do right by your people. Father you said you would go before us and fight for us. You said we can come into you and be safe. Father you said all things work together for the good of those who love you. You said if we would seek first your kingdom you would add unto us. You said the wealth of the wicked is laid up for the righteous. You said eyes haven't seen and ears haven't heard the blessings stored up for your people. Father we have sacrificed unto you for you to make a new covenant with your chosen people of today. LORD, you said you love Justice and hate robbery and wrong doing. You promised by your faithfulness that you would make an everlasting covenant with us. Father forget not your words of old. Come by your Spirit and Fight for us giving us an overwhelming Victory against America and the powers and principalities operating. Come LORD, send the Commander of your army and grant our petition of bringing Justice to this wicked land; hold every one of them accountable, they have ruled by greed and the love of money. Father teardown America's evil systems and every place that defy your commands. Replace the leaders including pastors, who refuse to abide in your word before you and your people. Raise up soldiers whom are not afraid to carry out your commands, appoint leaders who will not compromise your word or compromise your people. Strike down our enemies with a mighty blow, never to be in any form of authority as long as they shall live. Come Father by your Spirit in the mighty name of Yeshua The Messiah, shake the nations that have come against you.

FACEBOOK DELETED - On October 28, 2016, I posted: I can never return to whom I use to be. America has made me over. Blind and naive no longer.

On November 3, 2016, I shared my post and said: Do y'all remember this? Today I'm going to show you every post Facebook deleted. They have a price to pay for putting a hand to the things of the children of Israel. FACEBOOK: **********REMINDER************* If you remove any more of my post of prayer or anything opposed to these evil times, I pray that you lose the activity of your limbs. We bind the demonic authorities who are participating with these acts. May my father bring his Spirit against you, that you may never again forget who he is. May God give you your just punishment in the name of Yeshua, Amen.

On November 4, 2016, I posted: Facebook was warned, this is what they deleted from my page.

Facebook Deleted My Post

October 8 at 2:13am ·

God is Strategic

Sacrifice and Obey God, he will lead you in this season.

On November 4, 2016, I posted: God won't be mocked Facebook, you have a price to pay.

> *Facebook Deleted My Post*
> October 8 at 2:39am ·
> LORD Yeshua, send the commander of your army of heavenly forces.

November 4, 2016 · I was only the messenger. Look what the enemy did Black African people, they don't want you to know you are a Royal Priesthood.

> *Facebook Deleted My Post*
> October 9 at 6:52am ·
> He's Listening
> Are you sacrificing? Black African people, you are a royal priesthood.
> "I am with you and will rescue you, declares the LORD."
> - Jeremiah 30:11

On November 8, 2016, I posted: Facebook deleted while Fasting and Praying October 7th - 28th, while asking God to bring Justice, which the Pastors won't preach about.

> *Facebook Deleted My Post*
> October 10 at 5:02am ·
> Black Clergy, God has a word for you.
> Ten times out of ten,
> God has already spoken to you.

On November 13, 2016, I posted: Devotion to our culture and economic development is part of nation building. #BuyTheBlock.

FACEBOOK DELETED - On November 14, 2016, I shared a post from Buy Black Economics and I said: Give me Black Quality business and I will support you. Point Blank. The picture I shared said, "Eat at black restaurants more. Hire black attorneys. Encourage and support black men and women to run for public office. Tutor black students. Wear cosmetics made by black women. Patronize more small black businesses. Tip the black waitresses/waiters at these black restaurants. Get your manis/pedis at black owned salons. When you travel to a new city find the black owned businesses and patronize them. We are really all we have."

FACEBOOK DELETED - On November 14, 2016, I shared a post from 11Alive.com News Station. The post said: "Facebook is taking steps to eliminate fake news and hoaxes that some critics have suggested might have influenced the 2016 presidential election, CEO Mark Zuckerberg says." The bottom of the picture says, "Zuckerberg vows to weed out Facebook 'fake news' My response to this post was, This means, all black people reporting crimes by government will be shut down. Facebook police is already deleting our post thinking we are not knowledgeable. WE SEE YOU!

FACEBOOK DELETED - On November 15, 2016, I posted: NOTIFICATION; If you have sided with my oppressors, you have also become my oppressor, therefore you are my enemy.

FACEBOOK DELETED - On November 15, 2016, I posted: Wake Up! Black people of African descent, who are you? When will you wake from your slumber? When will you reclaim your throne? When will you come to yourself? Return to the house of your father so he can throw a feast in celebration of your awakening. WAKE UP!

FACEBOOK DELETED - On November 17, 2016, I posted: THE FBI; OUR NATION IS AT THE HANDS OF TERRORIST IN OFFICE. They did nothing to help me after I reported mass corruption of the EEOC, General Dynamics Information Technology. They are also participants. I found out the GENERAL DYNAMICS INFORMATION TECHNOLOGY IS A MAJOR CONTRACTOR FOR THE UNITED STATES GOVERNMENT. GDIT was responsible for the roll out of The Affordable Care Act (Obama Care). It has all been exposed and many now know who is tied to whom.

FACEBOOK DELETED - On November 17, 2016, I posted: Employers; If you want a company that will ensure obstruction of justice to your employees, HIRE Broadspire by CRAWFORD & COMPANY. They are the lowest of the low and they will do everything to make sure your employee claims are denied.

FACEBOOK DELETED - On November 17, 2016, I posted: Why do I keep catching people in lies? On November 18, 2016, I posted: Where is your faith?

FACEBOOK DELETED - On November 19, 2016, I posted: Good Morning, When God gave specific instructions to us regarding the March around the city in Praise, Prayer and Protest not one person who experienced injustice joined us. Maybe they thought it was about me, maybe they didn't like me exposing truth, maybe I hurt their feelings, maybe they were afraid, maybe they lost their faith in God. God is specific, regardless of what you may have thought. Many people missed God on those days. I have seen people in the church miss God because they were respecters of people, instead of being respecters of God. He will uproot the church because it has turned to being lovers of self and self-pleasing. Anything done for the people is not about the individuals doing it to get the worlds praise, it should be about God gaining the glory. The faith of the people is not where is should be and that's a bad thing.

On November 19, 2016, I posted: Den of Robbers!

On November 19, 2016, I posted: Ask your Pastor, "Dose God love Justice?" Prosperity without Justice is a Lie. On November 20, 2016, I posted: Get close to God.

FACEBOOK DELETED - On November 21, 2016, I posted: What good is a degree, if you are not helping your people?

FACEBOOK DELETED - On November 20, 2016, I posted: Chosen People; Don't let anyone fool you and tell you, you are treated that way because you are not educated. The fact remains that you are very knowledgeable and because you are black they treat us in such a way. Education and Knowledge are two different things. You can have the most educated person and they don't have knowledge. There are things that I know that far exceed the educated mind, but they would call me crazy until they see it for themselves. Sad.

FACEBOOK DELETED - On November 22, 2016, I posted: For His Glory!!! I'm telling y'all. The connections I have made are making moves. Nothing we go through is for granted. If I didn't go through, how then could I tell others they can make it through.

FACEBOOK DELETED - On November 27, 2016, I posted: Exposure; I'm telling y'all, we are seeing them more and more. God said it would come.

FACEBOOK DELETED - On November 27, 2016, I posted: Good Morning, God will expose all, he must before he acts. Not one can hide from his majesty. He will render them to ruin. All they have gained wickedly will be lost within a blink of an I. I decree and declare a mighty change is coming. They will receive 100 fold their giving, and they will know that he is El Shaddi. Father have your way and avenge your people in the name of Yeshua The Messiah, Amen.

On November 28, 2016, I posted: I think it's been about a week now. Facebook asked me to complete a questionnaire. I was asked, "Do facebook care about its users?" Of course you know I said, "No facebook does not care about it's users." All the terrorist groups of America delete and hide truth so the world can remain blind. But we can't be silenced. Someone will tell our story, even when you cut our bodies to pieces and churn our flesh into oil. That's what you did to our ancestors, yet they still speak out against you. Nothing you have done will remain hidden. It must come from the deeps of darkness.

On November 29, 2016, I posted: FACEBOOK TERRORIST; Stop screwing with my controls, once again the Federal government has blocked me from submitting my web address. I WILL EXPOSE YOU EVERYTIME! I have posted 4 times and it's not showing up, but this post showed up.

FACEBOOK DELETED - On December 11, 2016, I posted: King of Glory!

FACEBOOK DELETED - On December 11, 2016, I posted: "Choose Ye This Day" Will they be frightened when the truth is learned?

FACEBOOK DELETED - On December 12, 2016, I posted:

FACEBOOK DELETED - On December 12, 2016, I posted: People of African Descent: Get out of Debt! Save your money! Don't make unnecessary purchases. Look for products and services that promotes your growth, not your material want. Get out of Debt! Save your money!

FACEBOOK DELETED - On December 12, 2016, I posted: Hang In There! When you have a calling on your life the enemy will fight you every step of the way, but God.

On December 16, 2016, I posted: I HAVE A DISABILITY! EEOC IS CORRUPT AND ALL OF THESE PEOPLE AND ORGANIZATIONS HAVE PARTICIPATED IN TERRORISM AGAINST THE PEOPLE OF AFRICAN DESCENT. THE EEOC IS CORRUPT! ASK GENERAL DYNAMICS INFORMATION TECHNOLOGY I'M DISABLED, EEOC STAFF ARE TERRORIST. Father: Come, delivering a mighty blow against America. They have oppressed your people. Nothing but evil is on their hearts, their tongues and they devise evil schemes to make more money daily. Father take their wealth and deliver it unto the oppressed. Pay back the U. S. Equal Employment Opportunity Commission, General Dynamics Information Technology, U.S. District Court, The Department of Justice, The White House and all of its participants, ravage them financially to zero. Bring upon them all they have brought upon your people. Send the commander of your army to come against this wicked nation and all the culprits in Houston, Texas. All the leaders that have hid the truth of this RACIST city. Come and fight for your people. We petition thee, fulfill your promises made unto your people in the mighty name of Yahushua, Amen.

FACEBOOK DELETED - On December 20, 2016, I posted: ARE YOU READY TO WALK IN MY SHOES: Public Corruption in Elected Offices and Courts: Share, if you know someone who has a "disability" or a "record of perceived disability," and was denied due process by Equal Employment Opportunity Commission and Federal Court. Then Comment on this post of corruption. My prior employer General Dynamics Information Technology violated my ADA and ADAAA Rights. I was harassed after asking company to enforce company policy. The employer discriminated against record of perceived disability and I constructively discharged.

On December 21, 2016, I posted: Don't you just love FACEBOOK! I'm blocked from posting on U. S. Equal Employment Opportunity Commission Facebook page.

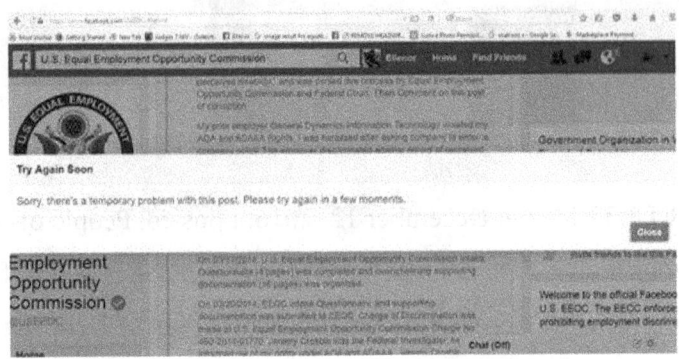

FACEBOOK DELETED - On December 25, 2016, I posted: Father fulfill your plans of old, in the name of Yahweh, Amen.

On December 29, 2016, I posted: Who Are You? If you're not broken, God can't use you.

FACEBOOK DELETED - On December 27, 2016, I posted: the picture of the town hall meeting DOJ had on Facebook live and said, FACEBOOK: WHY ARE YOU POLICING THE PEOPLE TELLING THE TRUTH? WHY ARE YOU DELETING OUR POST? WHY ARE YOU MAKING IT SO WE CAN'T POST TO GOVERNMENT FACEBOOK PAGES? FACEBOOK YOU DON'T CARE ABOUT YOUR USERS!

FACEBOOK DELETED - On December 27, 2016, I posted: TRAITORS; Any black leader who undermines the black community is a traitor. You are either for us or against us, there is no in-between.

FACEBOOK DELETED - On December 28, 2016, I posted: Broken; When you are broken in God...You will say what he tells you. You will be his anointed vessel. You will be covered supernaturally. You will be despised by his enemy. You will be known by those who know him. You will have the power to curse and bless. You will obey regardless of what man thinks. You will be used to bring the debts of darkness to light. You will be whom he destined from the beginning of time. You will be granted the spiritual ability to call to the nations. Do not be afraid of what God has called you to, it is a blessing, embrace it and live for God.

FACEBOOK DELETED - On December 29, 2016, I posted: wording from GDIT Facebook page, "General Dynamics Information Technology; December 28, 2016 at 1:40pm; Interested in a career supporting the #Intel Community? Search for a new opportunity with #GDIT www.gdit.com/careers/ic-jobs/" and I said, As an employee with a record of perceived disability you violated and harassed me. Although I trusted that you had integrity it was not so. You violated me and refused to enforce company policy and procedures. I decree and declare as sure as God called me unto himself at the age of 9, this company shall lose every government contract given by Centers for Medicare and Medicaid; and your stocks shall plummet until you do right by me in the name of Yahushua The Messiah, Amen.

FACEBOOK DELETED - On December 29, 2016, I shared a post which said: "DNA Doesn't Lie." In the picture was an Aboriginal black woman with five children beside her and their color of skin varied. The words of the picture said, "THE EVE GENE: (Above) Black Brazilian mother with her 5 children, three of which are albino & the father is also black. Scientifically, the black woman is the only organism that possesses the mitochondrial DNA that has all variations possible for every different kind of human being on this Earth (the African, the albino, the European, the middle eastern, etc.) When the DNA of a black woman mutates all other types of human beings comes about. This is called the "Eve Gene" and is ONLY found in black women."

FACEBOOK DELETED - On December 29, 2016, I posted: Everyone Looking Up: What have these black leaders done? They refuse to call out the leaders which whom they associate. They refused to warn the community of the false sense of hope. They have failed the people and have been bribed by the enemy. Then my brothers and sisters, What good are they, if not to lift the community? They shall be relinquished of their position and God shall appointment leaders whom can't be persuaded by the enemy.

FACEBOOK DELETED - On December 29, 2016, I posted: These men are prostituted by the enemy. They have given their souls and communities for wasteful gain.

FACEBOOK DELETED - On December 29, 2016, I posted: God come and set balance in this wicked place. Destroy, uproot and send your commander throughout this land. Deliver our enemies into our hands as you did long ago. Remove every leader that has defied your children, bring such men and women to destruction. Nothing but evil has been planned against us, come delivering a mighty blow to our oppressors.

FACEBOOK DELETED - On December 30, 2016, I posted: Complacency is Dangerous.

FACEBOOK DELETED - On December 30, 2016, I shared a post and it's a picture with a presented wasteland in Africa with three humans walking in the waste. The picture had 9,248,140 views and the words on the post said: "Corporate America! Al Jazeera English added a new video: Suing Shell. November 28, 2016 · A Nigerian tribal king has taken oil giant Shell to court in London. Here's why.

FACEBOOK DELETED - On December 30, 2016, I posted: You Must Always Be

Ready! God has sought for those who will keep their hands on their swords, while eating. For in the time of battle you must always be ready.

FACEBOOK DELETED - On December 30, 2016, I posted: Are you serving for God or the Pastor? The people don't know who they are and are not aware of who's they are. When you are a child of the King, your job is not to be in the leader's face. Your job is to serve. Matter of fact, I stay far away from the leaders as possible. Find a position you love and serve. It's also not your job to mention everything you do for the Kingdom, get out your flesh. God is sick and tired of everyone wanting to be seen. You want to be seen, serve and let God see you doing so. Your praise don't come from the leaders, it comes from God. Know who you are and move away from the fleshly situations created. It's time to stop playing church.

FACEBOOK DELETED - On December 30, 2016, I posted: God has exposed many people this year. I didn't know the involvement of many of these government organizations and corporations before God showed me. I don't care what anyone says, GOD IS REAL. Many of the lies the people have told are even being exposed. That was indeed my prayer for everything done unto the children of God to surface. Next punishment will be delivered. You can't touch the children of God and think there is no consequence.

FACEBOOK DELETED - On January 1, 2017, I posted: Reflection; For two days I have reflected on my post. And again, FACEBOOK HAS DELETED TRUTH that I have shared with the world. You may ask the following question: How do you know FACEBOOK DELETED your post? My Answer is : I copy all my work.

FACEBOOK DELETED - On January 21, 2017, I posted: Facebook Deleted this picture (picture of CMS.gov and Broadspire, protesting how they ignored my complaints and plea for justice) from my photo's, so sick of those bastards. Centers for Medicare and Medicaid gave General Dynamics Information Technology a call center contract. I contacted CMS on 5/13/15 & 7/30/15. Under the contract all participants must develop and abide by the policy and procedures submitted to CMS. How do I know this you asked? As a participant of Texas Department of Human Services, and a small business owner, I was required to developed policy and procedures which I had to submitted with my application to the state, so with that being said, I'm knowledgeable of the law. This is the end of the Facebook post. When God calls you to stand, you stand, regardless of what the enemy brings.

Documents - Leaving a paper trail.

Exhibit 1

September 5, 2013

ELLENOR PERKINS
8700 BROADWAY ST #
HOUSTON, Texas 77061

Dear ELLENOR:

Vangent, Inc., a General Dynamics company (Vangent) is pleased to offer you employment as a temporary, non-exempt Assoc Specialist, Cust Svc at an hourly rate of $11.88. Your anticipated start date will be 09/23/2013 reporting to Maureen Argus and your worksite location will be TX-Houston-5959 Corporate Dr. This is a temporary assignment for our peak period call volume. Your approximate end date will be reviewed with you during training and throughout the course of the assignment. End dates may vary through the course of the assignment due to an increase or decrease in anticipated call volume projections. Schedules are typically reviewed at the end of peak season and could change based on business needs.

This position is covered by the Service Contract Act (SCA) and classified as a General Clerk I within the Department of Labor's Directory of Occupations. Your wages will be paid in accordance with the applicable wage determination. As an SCA employee, in addition to the base wage outlined above, the company will also provide you a health and welfare fringe benefit of $3.71 per hour for hours paid up to 40 hours per week. As defined by the Department of Labor this fringe benefit obligation is provided to you in bona fide fringe benefits. Details regarding the calculation of your health and welfare benefit will be provided to you during orientation. You will have 14 days from your start date to review these materials and make your benefit selections.

It is the company's policy to conduct background investigations on all new hires. Your continued employment with Vangent is contingent upon verification of your educational and employment background as well as criminal history and possibly your credit history and driving record, depending on the position. Your employment with Vangent is also contingent on successful completion of all training requirements including evaluations, assessments, and/or certifications. You will also be required to successfully pass a drug test prior to moving from temporary status to a regular status position within the company, or upon hire if contractually required. Regular status is not guaranteed and based on business needs.

Your continued employment may be contingent upon your obtaining and retaining a specified security clearance within a reasonable time period, as determined at the sole discretion of the company. Due to the nature of certain work performed at Vangent, a security clearance may be required for this position and this offer is contingent upon your obtaining and/or the successful verification, transfer and retention of that clearance.

Under federal law, the Company is required to verify employment eligibility of all new hires and complete the Employment Eligibility Verification (Form I-9). You will receive an email to your home email address from DoNotReply@perfectcompliance.com. This has been established to provide our new employees with an efficient and secure way to complete Section 1 of Form I-9 online in advance of their first day. Please follow the instructions provided in the email to access the website, and complete Section One.

Vangent is committed to providing equal employment opportunity to all employees and applicants for employment without regard to race, color, religion, national origin, sex, age, disability, pregnancy, sexual orientation, gender identity, veteran status, or membership in any other protected group. As an affirmative action employer with federal contracts, we are required to report demographic information about our employees and job applicants to various agencies of the United States government.

Exhibit 2

By accepting this offer, you acknowledge and agree that no promise, representation, or inducement, except as set forth above, has been made with respect to your accepting employment with Vangent. The terms of this offer letter cannot be varied except in writing expressly noting the amendment and approved by the undersigned. It is important for you to know that employment with Vangent is "at will" and that Vangent does not guarantee your employment for any specific period of time. This means that there is no written or unwritten agreement of employment between you and Vangent. Both you and the company have the choice of ending your employment at any time, for any reason, with or without notice. No oral representation shall supersede this offer letter. Vangent reserves the right to modify or terminate any of its benefits and compensation plans, including but not limited to any of the plans described in this letter.

To indicate your understanding and acceptance of this offer of employment at will, please electronically sign where indicated below, retain a copy for your records. If any aspect of this letter raises questions, please contact Z   Wentz at (602) 718-   . This offer is contingent upon verification of your application data and is valid through 09/05/2013, unless extended by mutual agreement.

On behalf of the entire management team, I would like to welcome you to Vangent.

Sincerely,

Z   Wentz, Hiring Manager
Vangent, Inc., a General Dynamics company

My signature below signifies that I agree to the terms and conditions as set forth in this letter.

Exhibit 3

Fw: Ellenor Perkins Urgent- New Hire Orientation   Yahoo/Sent

Ellenor Perkins <e   @yahoo.com>   Sep 7, 2013 at 1:03 PM
To: e   @hotmail.com, J   .Gladney@wrksolutions.com
Cc: j   .quinones@wrksolutions.com

Sent from Yahoo! Mail on Android

∨ Hide original message

Exhibit 4

Please complete Friday afternoon. Thank you.

Workforce Solutions — Verification of Hours

Name: **Ellenor Perkins**   Social Security Number: _____

Employer/School Name: **General Dynamics**

Employer/School Address: **5959** (Street) **Corporate Dr** (City, State) **Houston, TX** **77036** (ZIP Code)

Supervisor/Professor/Other Contact Person Name: **Z___ B___ /HR Generalist**

Supervisor/Professor/Other Contact Telephone Number: **713 231___**

Check one:
- [x] Employed
- [ ] Community Service
- [ ] Work /Experience
- [ ] Attending School
- [ ] Workfare
- [ ] Other (list) _____

Week beginning Sunday **9 8 2013** (date)   Week ending Saturday **9 14 2013** (date)

Total Hours this week: **40**

Enter number of hours paid for holidays, vacation or sick leave: **0**

Satisfactory Progress: The individual is attending school and making satisfactory progress. [ ] Yes [ ] No [x] Not attending school

I certify that the information provided above is true and correct. I understand that Workforce Solutions may ask to verify this information.

_____
Signature of Supervisor/Professor/Other contact person   **REQUIRED**

Fax to **713-644-___** (Fax number)   On **Friday** (Day of Week)

Providing false information on this form or over the telephone for the purpose of inappropriately obtaining benefits may result in civil, criminal, or administrative penalties.

Received by: _____   Date: _____

WS Verification of Hours Form (REV 3/11/11)

Exhibit 5

Summary of Today's Visit

Perkins, Ellenor

10/03/2013 visit with M   M   , DO

Treatment
- Start Flonase : 50 MCG/ACT 2 sprays in each nostril Nasally once a day (for: Nasal congestion)
- Start Ibuprofen : 600 MG 1 tablet as needed Orally Three times a day with food (for: URI-Acute upper respiratory infections of unspecified site)
- Start Bromfed DM : 30-2-10 MG/5ML 10 ml as needed Orally every 6 hrs (for: URI-Acute upper respiratory infections of unspecified site)
- Start ProAir HFA : 108 (90 Base) MCG/ACT 2 puffs as needed Inhalation every 4 hrs (for: Asthma, unspecified, with (acute) exacerbation)
- Start Advair Diskus : 250-50 MCG/DOSE 1 puff Inhalation every 12 hrs (for: Asthma, unspecified, with (acute) exacerbation)
- Start Singulair : 10 mg 1 tablet in the evening Orally once a day (for: Asthma, unspecified, with (acute) exacerbation)
- Taking Albuterol : 2 MG 1 tablet Orally Three times a day (for: Others)
- Taking Loratadine : 10 MG 1 tablet Orally once a day (for: Others)

Patient Instructions:
Increase in fluid intake and rest. Reassurance (for: URI-Acute upper respiratory infections of unspecified site)
Reassurance. (for: Nasal congestion)
Pt states she is not depressed and does not want medicine. (for: Screening for depression)

Tests ordered/performed today
Labs:
- CBC With Differential/Platelet on 10/03/2013 (for: URI-Acute upper respiratory infections of unspecified site)

Your Next Appointment(s)
- 10/21/2013 at 08:00 AM

You are Diagnosed with
- 465.9   URI-Acute upper respiratory infections of unspecified site
- 786.2   Cough
- 786.07 Wheezing
- V85.35 Body Mass Index 35.0-35.9, adult
- 784.0   Headache
- V79.0   Screening for depression
- 493.92 Asthma, unspecified, with (acute) exacerbation
- 478.19 Nasal congestion

Fairway Medical Clinic   4910 Telephone Road   Houston, TX 770873504   713-641-3900

Note generated by

Exhibit 6

FAIRWAY MEDICAL CLINIC
4910 Telephone Rd Houston, TX 77087
Tel. (713) 641-3900 Fax (713) 641-3901

Mr. /Mrs. /Ms. Ellenor Perkins

Has been under my care for Medical Treatment on 10-3-13

And is able to return to Work/School on 10-4-13

Restrictions: ______________________

____

Fairway Medical Clinic
4910 Telephone Rd.
Houston, TX 77087
713-641-3900

Dr. ______________________ Date 10-3-13

Exhibit 7

Ellenor

To: Z   Bosie 10/4/13 6:03 pm

Ellenor Perkins
PO Box
Houston, Texas

Human Resources
5959 Corporate Dr
Houston, Texas 77036

Dear Z   Bosie,

On yesterday I missed work due to my Asthma. I made a visit to the doctor's office and was told my breathing is restricted. On my second week of training I began coughing and it became sever. I had no idea the cold was affecting me in this manner amoung other things and never have I viewed my asthma as a disability until now. I'm really uncomfortable. In training, I asked if the temperature could be elevated, on several occasions. Candice instructed us to bring a coat. I'm fine with bringing a coat, that is not relieving the issue at hand.

I'm contacting you to ask for a reasonable accomidation. Is there an area that people such as myself who suffer from Asthma can sit. I'm under vents on a consistant bases and it is really uncomfortable and makes it hard to breath.

Exhibit 8

URGENT- E   Yahoo/Sent

E
To: D   perez@wrksolutions.com   Oct 11, 2013 at 9:16 AM

Good Morning,

Ms. Perez, My name is Elleror Perkins and my Social is _____. The office in my area is the hobby office, they are closed. Several times I have emailed J_____ Herbert and J_____ Gladney. Gladney did respond last week and told me to contact the Astrodome office.

However, I emailed J_____ my check stub prior to J_____ telling me to contact your office. I visited the hobby office before they closed. I was told by J_____ that my childcare would revert to a fee and that fee would be based on a percentage. I need my childcare ASAP. I was just dropped and nothing else was done.

I work for GDIT and it's a hassle. They don't sign any verifications and I can't access the GDIT site outside of work. I was instructed my someone at your office to submit verification of work hours although company won't verify and submit my check stubs.

I need a caseworker who will respond. If u can email me the name and email address for a worker I would appreciate it. I have to leave home for 7:00 am on Metro in order to make it for work. 9:30. It's not possible at this time for me to visit the Workforce Office. I'm off work at 6:00 pm.

Thank you for your assistance

Exhibit 9

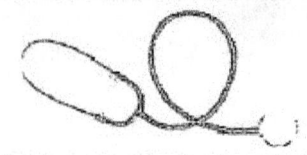

Summary of Today's Visit

Perkins, Ellenor

10/17/2013 visit with M_____ M_____, DO

Treatment
- Continue ProAir HFA : 108 (90 Base) MCG/ACT 2 puffs as needed Inhalation every 4 hrs (for: Asthma, unspecified, with (acute) exacerbation)
- Continue Advair Diskus : 250-50 MCG/DOSE 1 puff Inhalation every 12 hrs (for: Asthma, unspecified, with (acute) exacerbation)
- Continue Singulair : 10 mg 1 tablet in the evening Orally once a day (for: Asthma, unspecified, with (acute) exacerbation)
- Continue Bromfed DM : 30-2-10 MG/5ML 10 ml as needed Orally every 6 hrs (for: URI-Acute upper respiratory infections of unspecified site)
- Taking Flonase : 50 MCG/ACT 2 sprays in each nostril Nasally once a day (for: Others)
- Taking Albuterol : 2 MG 1 tablet Orally Three times a day (for: Others)
- Taking Ibuprofen : 600 MG 1 tablet as needed Orally Three times a day with food (for: Others)

Patient Instructions:
Couseled on Diet, Exercise, and Weight Loss (for: Body Mass Index 34.0-34.9, adult)

Your Next Appointment(s)
- 10/24/2013 at 08:00 AM

Fairway Medical Clinic   4910 Telephone Road   Houston, TX 770873504   713-641-3900

Note generated by

Exhibit 10

FAIRWAY MEDICAL CLINIC
4910 Telephone Rd Houston, TX 77087
Tel. (713) 641-3900 Fax (713) 641-3901

Mr./Mrs./Ms. __Ellenor Perkins__

Has been under my care for Medical Treatment on __10-17-13__

And is able to return to Work/School on __10-17-13__

Restrictions: _____

Dr. __M__   Date __10-17-13__

Exhibit 11

10/29/2013 From: Ellenor Perkins To: Z Bosie
Subject: HR Policy Emailed 3:24 PM

Hello,

On yesterday, a co-worker came back to their desk after smoking. This person was loaded with perfume; this person was not seated on either side of me. I was sitting at my desk and I begin having an asthma attack (my breathing became restricted). I did not make a scene, but I medicated myself. There is a growing problem with co-workers wearing fragrances that you can smell twenty feet away. I understand people want to smell nice; however, it should not be at the expense of others health. The fragrances are worn very heavy. Many people are not taking into consideration that there are some who suffer from Asthma and allergies. I'm not the only one who has spoken about this issue. Can you please address these issues?

I also have a follow up appointment for my asthma on November 1, 2013, due to mold exposure in my apartment at the beginning of this month and due to difficulty I'm facing on the call center floor.

Thank you,

Ellenor Perkins

Exhibit 12

11/8/2013 From: Ellenor Perkins To: A Clem CC: W Reimer
Subject: Medical Condition, Can you move me for now? Emailed 12:25 PM

Good Morning,

I would like to know, if there is possibly any virtual positions available (working from home)? I was diagnosed with asthma sometime ago. I enjoy working here at GDIT, however, the perfume, smoke and etc., that I smell are becoming unbearable.

My breathing becomes restricted and I began to have a difficult time (this is one of the reasons I have missed days from work). I don't want to resign, that's my reason for asking, if there is a position I can work from home. Please inform me if there is a way I can transfer to another position, where I'm not exposed to smoke/perfume. I'm aware that I must contact my supervisor and the Human Resources Recruiting Representative, regarding my interest in a new position in accordance with GDIT's Instaff Transfers and Promotions Policy #406.

Sincerely,

Ellenor Perkins

Exhibit 13

11/8/2013   From: Ellenor Perkins   To: A   Clem
Subject: Medical Condition   Emailed 12:28 PM

Z   did not respond to the email. I understand if there is nothing GDIT can do. I do need a response one way or the other.

Thanks.

Ellenor Perkins

Forwarded email I sent to Z   on 10/29/13 @ 3:24 PM

Exhibit 14

11/8/2013   From: A   Clem   CC: W   Reimer   To: Ellenor Perkins
Subject: Medical Condition, Can you move me for now?   Emailed 12:45 PM

A   Responded to 11/8/13, 12:25 email

Ellenor,

I do not think that virtual will be possibility, but let me get with Bill and see if there is anything that can be done here. I saw your other emails as well. I know it ties directly in to this. So we will see what we can do to accommodate.

Thanks.

A   Clem
Contact Center Supervisor
General Dynamics Information Technology
Health and Civilian Solutions
Houston, Texas 770
Desk# 832-

Exhibit 15

11/8/13 From: Ellenor Perkins To: A   Clem
Subject: I'm not feeling well. Emailed 3:31 PM

Someone has sprayed on more perfume. I begin feeling good the first part of the day. I'm not feeling well and I don't want it to get worst. Can I leave?

Exhibit 16

11/8/13 From: A   Clem   To: Ellenor Perkins
Subject: RE: I'm not feeling well. Emailed 3:32 PM

Yes and we will just need to adjust your time card accordingly on Wednesday. And I will get with B   first thing Monday for you. I'm sorry it's been so rough up here for you definitely do not want you to feel so out of sorts at work and I really want to see what can be done for you.

A   Clem
CCS
GDIT
Health/Civilan Drive

Exhibit 17

Fowarded to Ellenor Perkins

11/12/13 From: W   Reimer   To: Bair, L
Subject: FW: Medical Condition, Can you move me for now?   Emailed 6:03 PM

L   , is virtual workplace a possibility? Just asking. Thx

Exhibit 18

11/13/13　　　From: Bair, L　　(CNV)　　To: William R　　(B)

Subject: FW: Medical Condition, Can you move me for now?　　　Emailed 7:38 AM

No, Sorry.
Sr. Manager, Customer Service.

11/13/13　　　From: William R　　(B)　　To: A　　Clem　　Emailed 10:01 AM
Subject: FW: Medical Condition, Can you move me for now?

FYI

Exhibit 19

11/18/13　　　From: Clem A　　　To: Ellenor Perkins

Subject : FW: Medical Condition, Can you move me for now?　　　Emailed 9:51 AM

Just want to let you know we tried to see what could be done as far as virtual. If things continue on please let us know and we will see if there is another area you might be able to be moved to?

Thank you
A　　Clem

Exhibit 20

Harris Health System
P.O. Box 66769, Houston, Texas 77266-6769

To Whom It May Concern:

Ellenor Perkins was seen in our clinic on 11/19/2013. She has been having recurrent asthma exacerbations that have been difficult to control. Environmental allergens are one of the major contributors for these exacerbations. It will be very important for her to have an environment and living situation free of mold and other environmental exacerbants. Any assistance with this for Ms. Perkins would be greatly appreciated.

Thank You,

J Khan, MD

Exhibit 21

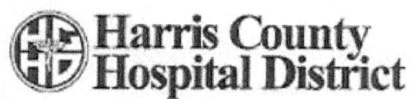 

We will create a healthier community and be recognized as one of America's best community-owned healthcare systems.
P.O. Box 66769, Houston, TX 77266-6769   www.hchdonline.com

MLK
FAMILY PRACTICE MLK
3550 Swingle Rd
Houston TX 77047
713-547-1020

Certification to Return to Work/School

12/19/2013

Ellenor Yvette Perkins was seen in the clinic today by Ms. C   Okusanya Nurse
Practitioner and is able to return to work/school on tomorrow.

A Parker
Licensed Vocational Nurse

Exhibit 22

Exhibit 23

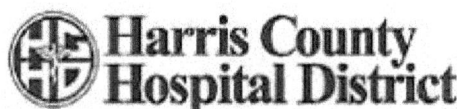

We will create a healthier community and be recognized as one of America's best community-owned healthcare systems.

P.O. Box 66769, Houston, TX 77266-6769   www.hcbdonline.com

MLK
FAMILY PRACTICE MLK
3550 Swingle Rd
Houston TX 77047
713-547-1020

Certification to Return to Work/School

12/31/2013

Ellenor has been under my care on 12/31/13 and is able to return to work on 1/7/14.

℞   L Ramage, PA-C

Exhibit 25

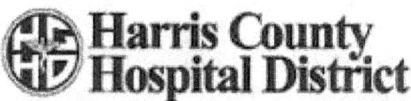 

We will create a healthier community and be recognized as one of America's best community-owned healthcare systems.
P.O. Box 66769, Houston, TX 77266-6769   www.hchdonline.com

MLK
FAMILY PRACTICE MLK
3550 Swingle Rd
Houston TX 77047
713-547-1020

Certification to Return to Work

2/10/2014

Ellenor   has been under my care on 2/7/14 and is able to return to work
on 2/10/14.

R   /Ramage, PA-C

Exhibit 26

We will create a healthier community and be recognized as one of America's best community-owned healthcare systems.
P.O. Box 66769, Houston, TX 77266-6769   www.hchdonline.com

Certification

Today's Date: 2/13/2014

Ellenor   (DOB   ) was evaluated in the Pulmonary Clinic at Smith Clinic today, 2/13/2014 and is currently being evaluated for the possibility of Asthma. Several tests have been ordered and are pending at this time.

N   Hanania, MD
Pulmonary/Asthma Clinic
Smith Clinic

Exhibit 27

gdit resign

Ellenor Perkins
Po Box
Houston, Texas 77221

@yahoo.com

yahoo.inbox
Feb 20 2014 at 4:29 PM

General Dynamics
5959 Corporate Dr.
Houston, Texas 77036

February 17, 2014

Dear Z   Boise, Human Resources Department:

Effective today, I will resign. I have done my very best under the circumstances. I have spoken with you on numerous occasions in regards to CSR's spraying perfume on the call center floor. I have not seen one email addressing this issue, it is not being enforced. When we met as a group in the large conference room, this was addressed in September, once. The dress code has been enforced on a number of occasions. My condition has worsened instead of getting better.

An email was sent to Royal, Reimer and Clem they are all aware. I have spoken to   Clem, my superior on numerous occasions as well. I asked for accommodations and was told it was nothing GDIT could do. Z   . I stated on numerous occasions, "I understand your company can't stop CSR's from wearing perfume." However, they should have not been allowed to spray it on the call center floor. There are other CSR's who have witnessed this action as well. They should not have to suffer with this issue either. The last notice from doctor that I delivered to you shows, I haven't been diagnosed with Asthma as of yet, so there is clearly something wrong.

This is why I must resign. I have done everything within my power to cope with the issue (wearing a mask throughout the call center, which raised alarm and staying in my seat much as possible. I was smelling the perfume although I wore a mask) and my health is declining because of the exposure. This is why I couldn't give you a report of the duration of time it would take for me to return to my desk after being exposed and medicating myself. I know I was penalized because of this, but it was completely out of my hand. I was given verbal warnings and that was not fare, since GDIT never sent out a notice for employees not to spray perfume on the call center floor. I stopped taking my breaks downstairs so I wouldn't be exposed to spoke as well GDIT would not accommodate me and this is the end result. I truly wished it could have been a different outcome. Again, there was no resolve.

Disappointedly,

Ellenor Perkins

Exhibit 28

Ellenor Perkins
Po Box
Houston, Texas 77221

CM# 7013 0600 0002 4184 4828

General Dynamics
5959 Corporate Dr.
Houston, Texas 77036
Attn: Z   Bosie
CC: E   Okon

March 3, 2014

Dear   Bosie, Human Resources Department:

On February 17, 2014, I sent an email to you and three other staff. The email contains brief information. The email I sent stated, "I will send a formal letter as well, explaining the reason and whom I conversed with. Effective today, I will resign. I have done my very best under the circumstances. I have spoken with you on numerous occasions, in regards to CSR's spraying perfume on the call center floor. I have not seen one email addressing this issue, it is not being enforced. My condition has worsened instead of getting better."

The first time that we had the conversation regarding CSR's spraying perfume you stated, "We can't stop CSR's from wearing perfume." I informed you that in the HR briefing, which was conducted in September, addressed the issue along with GDIT HR Policy-305. Since the briefing, the dress code and secure floor policy (no leggings or tight fitting clothing can be worn, no cell phone, paper, jacket on back of set and etc) was enforced on a number of occasions.

The day I resigned, A   Clem my previous supervisor walked me to the new supervisor. I wore my mask as usual. As we walked through an area in the call center the perfume was very strong. It was as if the perfume was freshly applied. An email was sent to the new supervisor, R   William and A   Clem they are all aware; I had spoken with A   Clem, my superior on numerous occasions as well.

I asked for accommodations and was told it was nothing GDIT could do, other than to switch shifts. That does not negate the fact that, I would still be exposed to CRS's spraying perfume on the call center floor. Z   , I stated on numerous occasions, "I understand your company can't stop

1 | Page

Exhibit 29

CSR's from wearing perfume." However, they should have not been allowed to spray it on the call center floor. There are other CSR's who have witnessed this action as well. They should not have to suffer with this issue either. The last notice from doctor that I delivered to you shows, I haven't been diagnosed with Asthma as of yet, so there is clearly something wrong.

This is why I was forced to resign. I did everything within my power to cope with the issue (wearing a mask throughout the call center, which raised alarm and staying in my seat much as possible, I was smelling the perfume although I wore a mask) and my health was declining because of the exposure. This health issue is very much new to me and this is why the doctor, wouldn't give me a statement of the duration of time it would take for me to return to my desk after being exposed and medicating myself. I know I was penalized because of this, but it was completely out of my hand. I was given verbal warnings and that was not fare, since GDIT never sent out a notice for employees not to spray perfume on the call center floor. I stopped taking my breaks downstairs so I wouldn't be exposed to smoke as well. GDIT would not accommodate me and this is the end result. I truly wished it could have been a different outcome. Again, there was no resolve.

Disappointedly,

Ellenor Perkins

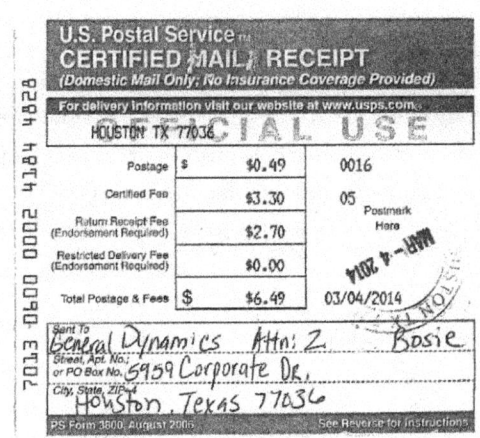

Exhibit 30

How To File A Charge　　3A　Page 1 of 2

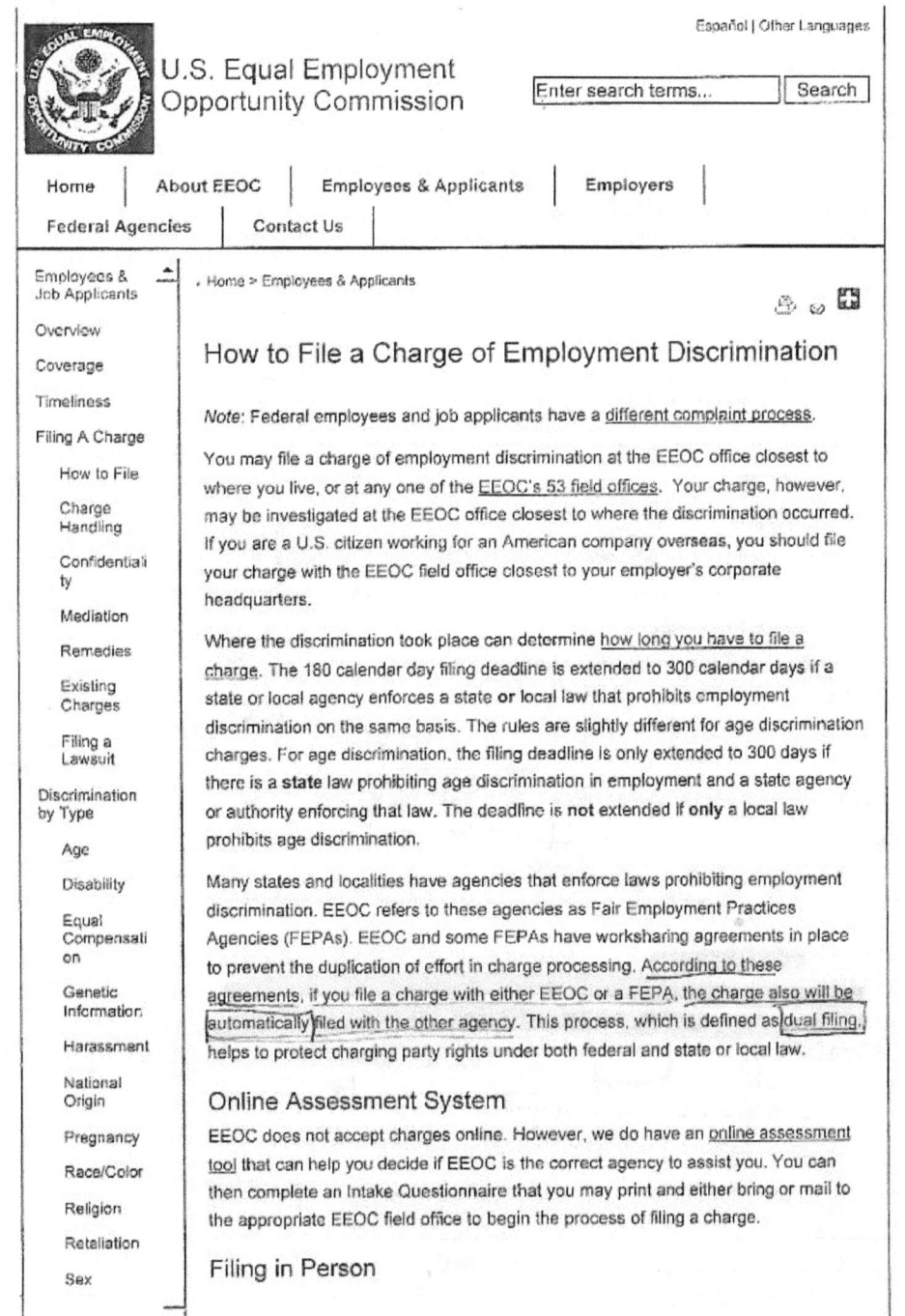

http://www.eeoc.gov/employees/howtofile.cfm　　3/10/2014

Exhibit 32

EQUAL EMPLOYMENT OPPORTUNITY COMMISSION
INTAKE QUESTIONNAIRE

Please immediately complete the entire form and return it to the U.S. Equal Employment Opportunity Commission ("EEOC"). **REMEMBER**, a charge of employment discrimination must be filed within the time limits imposed by law, generally within 180 days or in some places 300 days of the alleged discrimination. Upon receipt, this form will be reviewed to determine EEOC coverage. Answer all questions as completely as possible, and attach additional pages if needed to complete your response(s). If you do not know the answer to a question, answer by stating "not known." If a question is not applicable, write "n/a." Please Print.

1. Personal Information

Last Name: Perkins   First Name: Ellenor   MI:

Street or Mailing Address: PO Box   Apt Or Unit #: N/A

City: Houston   County: Harris   State: Texas   ZIP: 77221

Phone Numbers: Home: (832)   Work: (N/A)

Cell: (832)   Email Address: @gmail.com

Date of Birth: Sex: Male ☐ Female ☒   Do You Have a Disability? ☒ Yes ☐ No

Please answer each of the next three questions.   i. Are you Hispanic or Latino? ☐ Yes ☒ No

ii. What is your Race? Please choose all that apply.   ☒ American Indian or Alaska Native   ☐ Asian   ☐ White
☒ Black or African American   ☐ Native Hawaiian or Other Pacific Islander

iii. What is your National Origin (country of origin or ancestry)? USA

Please Provide The Name Of A Person We Can Contact If We Are Unable To Reach You:

Name: Relationship: Pa

Address: City: Houston   State: Tx   Zip Code: 77096

Home Phone: (832)   Other Phone: (N/A)

2. I believe that I was discriminated against by the following organization(s): (Check those that apply)

☒ Employer   ☐ Union   ☐ Employment Agency   ☐ Other (Please Specify)

Organization Contact Information (If the organization is an employer, provide the address where you actually worked. If you work from home, check here ☐ and provide the address of the office to which you reported.) **If more than one employer is involved, attach additional sheets.**

Organization Name: General Dynamics Information Technology/ Vangent/ Pearson Government

Address: 3211 Jermantown Road   County:

City: Fairfax   State: VA   Zip: 22030   Phone: (703) 995-

Type of Business: Information Technology   Job Location if different from Org. Address: 5959 Corporate Dr. Hou, Tx 77036

Human Resources Director or Owner Name: P   Novakovic   Phone: 1-800-242-

Number of Employees in the Organization at All Locations: Please Check (√) One

☐ Fewer Than 15   ☐ 15 - 100   ☐ 101 - 200   ☐ 201 - 500   ☒ More than 500

3. Your Employment Data (Complete as many items as you can)   Are you a Federal Employee? ☐ Yes ☒ No

Date Hired: 09/09/2013   Job Title At Hire: Associate Specialist, Customer Service

Pay Rate When Hired: $11.88   Last or Current Pay Rate: $13.88

Job Title at Time of Alleged Discrimination: Associate Specialist, Customer Ser Date Quit/Discharged: 02/17/2014

Name and Title of Immediate Supervisor: A   Clem, Supervisor then Dana Royal.

Exhibit 33

If Job Applicant, Date You Applied for Job 09/05/2013 Job Title Applied For Customer Service

4. **What is the reason (basis) for your claim of employment discrimination?**
FOR EXAMPLE, if you feel that you were treated worse than someone else because of race, you should check the box next to Race. If you feel you were treated worse for several reasons, such as your sex, religion and national origin, you should check all that apply. If you complained about discrimination, participated in someone else's complaint, or filed a charge of discrimination, and a negative action was threatened or taken, you should check the box next to Retaliation.

☐ Race ☐ Sex ☐ Age ☒ Disability ☐ National Origin ☐ Religion ☐ Retaliation ☐ Pregnancy ☐ Color (typically a difference in skin shade within the same race) ☐ Genetic Information; choose which type(s) of genetic information is involved:

☐ i. genetic testing ☐ ii. family medical history ☐ iii. genetic services (genetic services means counseling, education or testing)

If you checked color, religion or national origin, please specify: _____

If you checked genetic information, how did the employer obtain the genetic information? _____

Other reason (basis) for discrimination (Explain). GDIT would not enforce policy. View attachment 1 and Exhibit A, B and C.

5. **What happened to you that you believe was discriminatory?** Include the date(s) of harm, the action(s), and the name(s) and title(s) of the person(s) who you believe discriminated against you. Please attach additional pages if needed.
(Example: 10/02/06 - Discharged by Mr. John Soto, Production Supervisor)

A) Date: 10/04/2013   Action: Email, Asked for Reasonable Accommodation, Z didn't respond.

Name and Title of Person(s) Responsible: Z   Bosie, HR Generalist

B) Date: 10/10/2013   Action: Email, Notice regarding breathing issues.
VIEW ATTACHMENT 2.

Name and Title of Person(s) Responsible: A   Clem, Supervisor

6. **Why do you believe these actions were discriminatory?** Please attach additional pages if needed.
Under GDIT HSCD, Dress Code Standards it states, "Overly strong or offensive odors or scents such as perfumes and cologne, unclean attire, or body odor will not be allowed in the workplace. The above statement has not been enforced by GDIT. On many occasions, I asked for assistance in regards to CSR's spraying perfume on the call center floor, I then asked if there was a virtual position. VIEW ATTACHMENT 3.

7. **What reason(s) were given to you for the acts you consider discriminatory? By whom? His or Her Job Title?**
"We can't stop CSR's from wearing perfume." Z   Bosie, Hr Generalist There was also another Hr person in her office as well, she was a female of color.
Supervisor apologized for CSR's spraying perfume, but never spoke with team regarding the issue. A   Clem Supervisor

8. Describe who was in the same or similar situation as you and how they were treated. For example, who else applied for the same job you did, who else had the same attendance record, or who else had the same performance? Provide the race, sex, age, national origin, religion, or disability of these individuals, if known, and if it relates to your claim of discrimination. For example, if your complaint alleges race discrimination, provide the race of each person; if it alleges sex discrimination, provide the sex of each person; and so on. Use additional sheets if needed.

Of the persons in the same or similar situation as you, who was treated *better* than you?

A. Full Name	Race, sex, age, national origin, religion or disability	Job Title

Description of Treatment

B. Full Name	Race, sex, age, national origin, religion or disability	Job Title

Description of Treatment

Exhibit 34

Of the persons in the same or similar situation as you, who was treated *worse* than you?

A. Full Name	Race, sex, age, national origin, religion or disability	Job Title

Description of Treatment

B. Full Name	Race, sex, age, national origin, religion or disability	Job Title

Description of Treatment

Of the persons in the same or similar situation as you, who was treated the *same* as you?

A. Full Name	Race, sex, age, national origin, religion or disability	Job Title
M Browne	African American	Associate Specialist, Customer Serv

Description of Treatment   CSR's sprayed scents in the area where we seat as a team.

B. Full Name	Race, sex, age, national origin, religion or disability	Job Title
Mrs. E on S Johnson Team	African American	Associate Specialist, Customer Serv

Description of Treatment   witness the overly strong scents CSR's would spray and stated it was too strong.

Answer questions 9-12 **only** if you are claiming discrimination based on disability. If not, skip to question 13. Please tell us if you have more than one disability. Please add additional pages if needed.

9. Please check all that apply:
   - [X] Yes, I have a disability
   - [ ] I do not have a disability now but I did have one
   - [ ] No disability but the organization treats me as if I am disabled

10. What is the disability that you believe is the reason for the adverse action taken against you? Does this disability prevent or limit you from doing anything? (e.g., lifting, sleeping, breathing, walking, caring for yourself, working, etc.).

IGE, Allergic Asthma according to testing dated, 02/12/2013. When exposed to allergens (perfume) it prevents me from breathing, working and other duties.

11. Do you use medications, medical equipment or anything else to lessen or eliminate the symptoms of your disability?

    Yes [X]   No [ ]

If "Yes," what medication, medical equipment or other assistance do you use?

I currently medicate with

12. Did you ask your employer for any changes or assistance to do your job because of your disability?

    Yes [X]   No [ ]

If "YES", when did you ask? 10/04/2013   How did you ask (verbally or in writing)? Writing and Email

Who did you ask? (Provide full name and job title of person)

Z   Bosic, HR Generalist

Describe the changes or assistance that you asked for:

Asked for reasonable accommodation due to restricted breathing.

How did your employer respond to your request?
She did not respond to the email. Other times I was told verbally, "We can't stop CSR's from wearing perfume." VIEW ATTACHMENT 4, COMMUNICATION BETWEEN MYSELF AND GDIT. View doctor statements dated for 11/19/2013 and 02/13/2014.

Exhibit 35

13. Are there any witnesses to the alleged discriminatory incidents? If yes, please identify them below and tell us what they will say. (Please attach additional pages if needed to complete your response)

A. Full Name	Job Title	Address & Phone Number
S Deal	Associate Specialist, Cus	currently employed at GDIT

What do you believe this person will tell us?

never received an email asking CSR's not to wear or spray overly strong or offensive odors or scents such as perfumes and cologne.

B. Full Name	Job Title	Address & Phone Number
A Clem	Supervisor	currently employed at GDIT

What do you believe this person will tell us?

never received direction from HR to inform CSR's not to wear or spray overly strong or offensive odors or scents such as perfumes and cologne. There was never an email or verbal communication sent to CSR's or Supervisor's. VIIEW ATTACHMENT 5

14. Have you filed a charge previously in this matter with EEOC or another agency? Yes ☐ No ☒

15. If you have filed a complaint with another agency, provide name of agency and date of filing:

16. Have you sought help about this situation from a union, an attorney, or any other source? Yes ☐ No ☒
Provide name of organization, name of person you spoke with and date of contact. Results, if any?

Please check one of the boxes below to tell us what you would like us to do with the information you are providing on this questionnaire. If you would like to file a charge of job discrimination, you must do so either within 180 days from the day you knew about the discrimination, or within 300 days from the day you knew about the discrimination if the employer is located in a place where a state or local government agency enforces laws similar to the EEOC's laws. If you do not file a charge of discrimination within the time limits, you will lose your rights. If you would like more information before filing a charge or you have concerns about EEOC's notifying the employer, union, or employment agency about your charge, you may wish to check Box 1. If you want to file a charge, you should check Box 2.

Box 1 ☐ I want to talk to an EEOC employee before deciding whether to file a charge. I understand that by checking this box, I have not filed a charge with the EEOC. I also understand that I could lose my rights if I do not file a charge in time.

Box 2 ☒ I want to file a charge of discrimination, and I authorize the EEOC to look into the discrimination I described above. I understand that the EEOC must give the employer, union, or employment agency that I accuse of discrimination information about the charge, including my name. I also understand that the EEOC can only accept charges of job discrimination based on race, color, religion, sex, national origin, disability, age, genetic information, or retaliation for opposing discrimination.

_____ March 17, 2014
Signature   Today's Date

PRIVACY ACT STATEMENT: This form is covered by the Privacy Act of 1974; Public Law 93-579. Authority for requesting personal data and the uses thereof are:
1. **FORM NUMBER/TITLE/DATE.** EEOC Intake Questionnaire (9/20/08).
2. **AUTHORITY.** 42 U.S.C. § 2000e-5(b), 29 U.S.C. § 211, 29 U.S.C. § 626, 42 U.S.C. 12117(a), 42 USC §2000ff-6.
3. **PRINCIPAL PURPOSE.** The purpose of this questionnaire is to solicit information about claims of employment discrimination, determine whether the EEOC has jurisdiction over those claims, and provide charge filing counseling, as appropriate. Consistent with 29 CFR 1601.12(b) and 29 CFR 1626.8(c), this questionnaire may serve as a charge if it meets the elements of a charge.
4. **ROUTINE USES.** EEOC may disclose information from this form to other state, local and federal agencies as appropriate or necessary to carry out the Commission's functions, or if EEOC becomes aware of a civil or criminal law violation. EEOC may also disclose information to respondents in litigation, to congressional offices in response to inquiries from parties to the charge, to disciplinary committees investigating complaints against attorneys representing the parties to the charge, or to federal agencies inquiring about hiring or security clearance matters
5. **WHETHER DISCLOSURE IS MANDATORY OR VOLUNTARY AND EFFECT ON INDIVIDUAL FOR NOT PROVIDING INFORMATION.** Providing of this information is voluntary but the failure to do so may hamper the Commission's investigation of a charge. It is not mandatory that this form be used to provide the requested information.

Exhibit 36

Additional Information

Attachment 1

Continued Answer to Question 4

This information is from handouts CSR's received from GDIT/Vangent in September of 2013. Please review attachment, Exhibit A and B.

"Revised 2-1-12, VANGENT expects all employees to maintain personal hygiene that does not impede their ability to perform assigned duties, or negatively have an effect on others in the workplace. Overly strong or offensive odors or scents such as perfumes and cologne, unclean attire, or body odor will not be allowed in the workplace."

"Revised 6-12-2013 (Version 2), "GDIT HCSD expects all employees to maintain personal hygiene that does not impede their ability to perform assigned duties, or negatively have an effect on others in the workplace. Overly strong or offensive odors or scents such as perfumes and cologne, unclean attire, or body odor will not be allowed in the workplace."

Exhibit 37

Additional Information

Attachment 2

Continued Answer to Question 5

    10/29/13 - Emailed, 3:24 p.m., Subject: HR Policy, Body: CSR's spraying perfume. Z   Bosie, HR Generalist

    10/30/13 – Emailed, Forwarded 11/8 10:56 a.m. Z   HR Policy, no response. Z   Bosie, HR Generalist

    11/08/13 – Emailed, 12:25 p.m., Subject: Medical Condition, Can you move me for now? Body: My enjoyment at the job, CSR's spraying perfume; unbearable condition asked if I can transfer to virtual if available.   A   Clem, Supervisor   CC: W   Reimer

    11/08/13 – Emailed, 12:28 p.m. Subject: Medical Condition, Body: Z   didn't respond, I demanded a response from A   . Email sent to Z   on 10/29 was also forwarded in email to A   Clem, Supervisor

    12/20 Emailed, 1:21 p.m. Responded to verbal Warning   A   Clem, Supervisor

Exhibit 38

Additional Information

Attachment 3

Continued Answer to Question 6

Human Resources Department didn't respond to my emails, basically ignoring me. My supervisor attempted to help me, but without instructions from human resources, our team was not addressed regarding the issue, nor was any other team addressed, this is why I believe I was discriminated against. There was never an email or verbal communication, asking CSR's not to wear or spray overly offensive scents (perfume and etc) on the call center floor.

10/4/13 – Emailed, 6:03 p.m. Notice regarding restricted breathing, asked for reasonable accommodation. Z Bosie, HR Generalist

10/10/13 – Emailed, Notice regarding breathing issues. A Clem, Supervisor

10/29/13 - Emailed, 3:24 p.m., Subject: HR Policy, Body: CSR's spraying perfume. Z Bosie, HR Generalist

10/30/13 – Emailed, Forwarded 11/8 10:56 a.m. Z HR Policy. Z Bosie, HR Generalist

11/08/13 – Verbal, Medical Condition. A Clem, Supervisor

11/08/13 – Emailed, 12:25 p.m., Subject: Medical Condition, Can you move me for now? Body: My enjoyment at the job, CSR's spraying perfume; unbearable condition asked if I can transfer to virtual if available. A Clem, Supervisor CC: W Reimer

11/08/13 – Emailed, 12:28 p.m. Subject: Medical Condition, Body: Z didn't respond, I demanded a response from A . Email sent to Z on 10/29 was also forwarded in email to A Clem, Supervisor

Exhibit 39

Continued Answer to Question 12

10/4/13 – Emailed, 6:03 p.m. Notice regarding restricted breathing, asked for reasonable accommodation.   Z   Bosie, HR Generalist

   10/10/13 – Emailed, Notice regarding breathing issues.   A   Clem, Supervisor

   10/29/13 - Emailed, 3:24 p.m., Subject: HR Policy, Body: CSR's spraying perfume.   Z   Bosie, HR Generalist

   10/30/13 – Emailed, Forwarded 11/8 10:56 a.m. Z   HR Policy. Z   Bosie, HR Generalist

   11/08/13 – Verbal, Medical Condition. A   Clem, Supervisor

   11/08/13 – Emailed, 12:25 p.m., Subject: Medical Condition, Can you move me for now? Body: My enjoyment at the job, CSR's spraying perfume; unbearable condition asked if I can transfer to virtual if available.   A   Clem, Supervisor   CC: W   Reimer

   11/08/13 – Emailed, 12:28 p.m. Subject: Medical Condition, Body: Z   didn't respond, I demanded a response from Austin. Email sent to Z   on 10/29 was also forwarded in email to A   Clem, Supervisor

   11/08/13 – Email Response, 12:45 p.m. Subject: Medical Condition, Can you move me for now? Body: A   responded, unsure of virtual possibility. Will check with   W   Reimer, Manager). Acknowledged other emails. Will see how GDIT can accommodate.
   CC: W   Reimer

   11/08/13 – Emailed, 3:31 p.m., Subject: "I'm not feeling well. Body: Someone sprayed on more perfume. Can I leave?   A   Clem, Supervisor

   11/08/13 – Email Response, 3:32 p.m., Subject: I'm not feeling well. Body: Yes, we'll adjust time. Will speak with Manager and apologized for the rough time I was having at work.
   A   Clem, Supervisor

   11/12-11/13 – Email Response, No virtual possibility. Communication between A   Clem,   W   Reimer   and L   Bair.   A   Clem, Supervisor

Exhibit 40

Attachment 4

Question 12 continued.

11/18- Emailed, 9:51a.m., Subject: Fw: Medical Condition, Can you move me now? Body: Attempted to assist me as far as a virtual possibility. If things continue on please let us know and we will see if there is another area you might be able to be moved to? A   Clem, Supervisor

11/18 – Verbal, I may have to resign. A   Clem, Supervisor

*11/19 – Emailed, 9:40a.m., before shift began feeling ill downstairs, departed 9:40 a.m. Urgent visit to Doctor Juneja 10:40 a.m. apt
A   Clem, Supervisor

**11/21 – Emailed/ Verbal, 1:18p.m., Medical Condition, Dr. Statement dated 11/19/2013
        A   Clem, Supervisor**

*12/19 Respiratory System, in distress – Dr. Okusanya , Extrinsic asthma with exacerbation/ Allergic rhinitis.

12/20 Emailed, 1:21 p.m. Responded to verbal Warning   A   Clem, Supervisor

12/27 Emailed, 12:37p.m. Feeling ill. S   Johnson, back up Supervisor

12/30 Emailed, 3:38 p.m., Attendance - forgot to log into phone.   A   Clem, Supervisor

*12/31 Respiratory System, in distress – Dr. Ramage , Extrinsic asthma with exacerbation. Excuse for work from 12/31/2013 to 1/7/2014

*1/6/14 9:00 a.m. Respiratory follow up. Si   White, Reactive airway disease.

1/7 12:25 p.m. Regarding Issues on call center floor (CSR's spraying perfume) Z   Bosie, HR Generalist

02/13/14 – Verbal Medical Condition, Dr. Statement dated 02/13/14   Z   Bosie, HR Generalist

Exhibit 41

Attachment 5

Continued Answer to Question 13

Pa	Associate Specialist, Customer Service
Oc	Associate Specialist, Customer Service
Mi	Associate Specialist, Customer Service
Se:	Associate Specialist, Customer Service
Ka	Associate Specialist, Customer Service
La	Associate Specialist, Customer Service
Jul	Associate Specialist, Customer Service
Joe	Associate Specialist, Customer Service
De	Associate Specialist, Customer Service
Mr	Associate Specialist, Customer Service
Au	Supervisor
Shi	Supervisor
Wi	Manager
Rya	Manager
Zar	HR Generalist

Other witnesses, anyone employed before December 2013.

All witness can attest that CSR received a single document, which stated NO CELL PHONES ALLOWED. This was because CSR's would have phones on their person and that was against the rules. In fact, many employees were fired for such actions. There was an HR briefing in September 2013. In this briefing CSR's received two packets, the first packet contained information regarding: Helpful Contact Information, Employee Acknowledgement Form, GSA 14-Day Benefits Statement of Understanding and Dress Code Standards. The second packet contained: Human Resources Guideline #H301- Attendance Guidelines, this packet has five pages. CSR's received no verbal, electronic or written communication for wearing Overly strong or Offensive odors or scents such as perfumes and cologne, prior to February 17, 2014. CSR's can attest to the fact that former CSR's were fired for violating dress code standards (wearing clothing too short or too tight) and having cell phones in restricted area (call center floor). Secure floor policy and dress code were enforced on consistent bases through email and verbalization from supervisor. CSR's completed mandatory training, time sheet, testing and etc. based on information sent through email and Ethernet. CSR's often received emails on a daily, weekly or annual basis.

Again, there was no email sent addressing CSR's not to spray or wear overly offensive or strong scents.

Exhibit 42

EEOC Form 5 (11/09)

CHARGE OF DISCRIMINATION	Charge Presented To:	Agency(ies) Charge No(s):
This form is affected by the Privacy Act of 1974. See enclosed Privacy Act Statement and other information before completing this form.	[ ] FEPA [X] EEOC	460-2014-01770

Texas Workforce Commission Civil Rights Division and EEOC
State or local Agency, if any

Name (indicate Mr., Ms., Mrs.): Ellenor Perkins
Home Phone (Incl. Area Code):
Date of Birth:

Street Address: P. O. Box
City, State and ZIP Code: Houston, TX 77221

Named Is the Employer, Labor Organization, Employment Agency, Apprenticeship Committee, or State or Local Government Agency That I Believe Discriminated Against Me or Others. (If more than two, list under PARTICULARS below.)

Name: GENERAL DYNAMICS INFORMATION TECHNOLOGY
No. Employees, Members: 500+
Phone No. (Include Area Code): (832)
Street Address: 5959 Corporate Dr., Houston, TX 77036

DISCRIMINATION BASED ON (Check appropriate box(es).):
[ ] RACE [ ] COLOR [ ] SEX [ ] RELIGION [ ] NATIONAL ORIGIN
[ ] RETALIATION [ ] AGE [X] DISABILITY [ ] GENETIC INFORMATION
[ ] OTHER (Specify)

DATE(S) DISCRIMINATION TOOK PLACE
Earliest: 10-04-2013
Latest: 02-17-2014
[ ] CONTINUING ACTION

THE PARTICULARS ARE (If additional paper is needed, attach extra sheet(s)):

I began my employment on September 9, 2013, as an Associate Specialist, Customer Service. On February 17, 2014, I was forced to resign from my position after my employer failed to provide me with a reasonable accommodation.

Specifically, on October 4, 2013, I advised Zandra Bosie (HR Generalist) by email with a Doctor's letter, that I was requesting an accommodation due to my disability. I simply asked them to address their company policy on excessive use of cologne or perfume because it caused complications with my disability. My request was essentially ignored until I was advised by Zandra that they could not stop employees from wearing perfume or cologne. After informing Zandra, CSR's applied it on the call center floor.

I believe the respondent failed to provide me with a reasonable accommodation due to my disability and forced me to resign, in violation of Title I and V of the Americans with Disabilities Act of 1990, as amended.

I want this charge filed with both the EEOC and the State or local Agency, if any. I will advise the agencies if I change my address or phone number and I will cooperate fully with them in the processing of my charge in accordance with their procedures.

I declare under penalty of perjury that the above is true and correct.

Date: Mar 20, 2014
Charging Party Signature

NOTARY — When necessary for State and Local Agency Requirements

I swear or affirm that I have read the above charge and that it is true to the best of my knowledge, information and belief.
SIGNATURE OF COMPLAINANT

SUBSCRIBED AND SWORN TO BEFORE ME THIS DATE (month, day, year)
March 20, 2014

ARTURO MEDINA III
MY COMMISSION EXPIRES
June 28, 2017

Exhibit 43

CP Enclosure with EEOC Form 5 (11/09)

PRIVACY ACT STATEMENT: Under the Privacy Act of 1974, Pub. Law 93-579, authority to request personal data and its uses are:

1. **FORM NUMBER/TITLE/DATE.** EEOC Form 5, Charge of Discrimination (11/09).

2. **AUTHORITY.** 42 U.S.C. 2000e-5(b), 29 U.S.C. 211, 29 U.S.C. 626, 42 U.S.C. 12117, 42 U.S.C. 2000ff-6.

3. **PRINCIPAL PURPOSES.** The purposes of a charge, taken on this form or otherwise reduced to writing (whether later recorded on this form or not) are, as applicable under the EEOC anti-discrimination statutes (EEOC statutes), to preserve private suit rights under the EEOC statutes, to invoke the EEOC's jurisdiction and, where dual-filing or referral arrangements exist, to begin state or local proceedings.

4. **ROUTINE USES.** This form is used to provide facts that may establish the existence of matters covered by the EEOC statutes (and as applicable, other federal, state or local laws). Information given will be used by staff to guide its mediation and investigation efforts and, as applicable, to determine, conciliate and litigate claims of unlawful discrimination. This form may be presented to or disclosed to other federal, state or local agencies as appropriate or necessary in carrying out EEOC's functions. A copy of this charge will ordinarily be sent to the respondent organization against which the charge is made.

5. **WHETHER DISCLOSURE IS MANDATORY; EFFECT OF NOT GIVING INFORMATION.** Charges must be reduced to writing and should identify the charging and responding parties and the actions or policies complained of. Without a written charge, EEOC will ordinarily not act on the complaint. Charges under Title VII, the ADA or GINA must be sworn to or affirmed (either by using this form or by presenting a notarized statement or unsworn declaration under penalty of perjury); charges under the ADEA should ordinarily be signed. Charges may be clarified or amplified later by amendment. It is not mandatory that this form be used to make a charge.

NOTICE OF RIGHT TO REQUEST SUBSTANTIAL WEIGHT REVIEW

Charges filed at a state or local Fair Employment Practices Agency (FEPA) that dual-files charges with EEOC will ordinarily be handled first by the FEPA. Some charges filed at EEOC may also be first handled by a FEPA under worksharing agreements. You will be told which agency will handle your charge. When the FEPA is the first to handle the charge, it will notify you of its final resolution of the matter. Then, if you wish EEOC to give Substantial Weight Review to the FEPA's final findings, you must ask us in writing to do so <u>within 15 days</u> of your receipt of its findings. Otherwise, we will ordinarily adopt the FEPA's finding and close our file on the charge.

NOTICE OF NON-RETALIATION REQUIREMENTS

Please **notify** EEOC or the state or local agency where you filed your charge **if retaliation is taken against you or others** who oppose discrimination or cooperate in any investigation or lawsuit concerning this charge. Under Section 704(a) of Title VII, Section 4(d) of the ADEA, Section 503(a) of the ADA and Section 207(f) of GINA, it is unlawful for an *employer* to discriminate against present or former employees or job applicants, for an *employment agency* to discriminate against anyone, or for a *union* to discriminate against its members or membership applicants, because they have opposed any practice made unlawful by the statutes, or because they have made a charge, testified, assisted, or participated in any manner in an investigation, proceeding, or hearing under the laws. The Equal Pay Act has similar provisions and Section 503(b) of the ADA prohibits coercion, intimidation, threats or interference with anyone for exercising or enjoying, or aiding or encouraging others in their exercise or enjoyment of, rights under the Act.

Exhibit 44

Ellenor Perkins
PO Box
Houston, Texas 77221-1168

EEOC
Total Plaza
1201 Louisiana, 6th Floor
Houston, Texas 77002

Charge No: 460.2014.01770

NOTICE

March 27, 2014

On the week of March 17 and on yesterday, March 26, I was informed GDIT will be permanently closing the Houston location. This is vital information; many of the witnesses currently work at the Houston location.

Also, I have someone that is willing to come forth for the claim I have filed against GDIT. This witness is willing to testify to the practice of GDIT, while employed by GDIT. She was also discriminated against. My former co-worker is name T   Singletary, her phone number is 254.

Sincerely,

Ellenor Perkins

Exhibit 45

U.S. EQUAL EMPLOYMENT OPPORTUNITY COMMISSION
Houston District Office

1201 Louisiana Street, 6th Floor
Houston, TX 77002
Intake Information Group: (800) 669-4000
Houston Direct Dial: (713) 651-4900

March 27, 2014

Ellenor Perkins
Post Office Box
Houston, Texas 77221

Charge No.: 460-2014-01770
Respondent: GENERAL DYNAMICS INFORMATION TECHNOLOGY

Dear Ms. Perkins:

I am the Investigator assigned to investigate your charge to determine if there is sufficient evidence to support your allegations. You need to do nothing further at this time.

If you have additional information concerning your charge, you may contact me at the above address or at my **direct number** below. Please refer to the above charge number and the name of the firm you filed against when calling or writing.

EEOC regulations require that you notify us of any change in address and keep us informed of any prolonged absence from your current address. Your cooperation in this matter is essential.

Sincerely,

Jeremy Crosbie (713) 651-4919
EEOC Federal Investigator

Enc:
Charging Party Reminder Letter

U.S. EQUAL EMPLOYMENT OPPORTUNITY COMMISSION
Houston District Office

JEREMY CROSBIE

713 651 4919

460-2014-01770

Exhibit 46

U.S. EQUAL EMPLOYMENT OPPORTUNITY COMMISSION
Houston District Office

1201 Louisiana Street, 6th Floor
Houston, TX 77002
Intake Information Group: (800) 669-4000
Houston Direct Dial: (713) 651-4900

CHARGING PARTY REMINDER

You have filed a charge.

What happens to your charge next:

1. It is important that you keep the charge number assigned to your charge handy as you should refer to it when communicating with our Office. In most instances, the Investigator that counseled you will be the assigned Investigator for your charge. Therefore, you should also keep her/his name and telephone number handy.

2. The employer named in the charge will be given a copy of your charge within ten (10) days from the date that you signed the charge.

3. The majority of charges filed with our Office are sent to our Alternative Dispute Resolution Unit for mediation prior to an investigation into your allegations of employment discrimination. Mediation is a voluntary program to expeditiously resolve your charge. However, you and the employer must agree to mediation. Once both parties agree, a Mediator will contact you to schedule a meeting with you and the employer.

4. Once it is determined that mediation is not appropriate or an agreement to mediate between both parties is not reached, your charge will be forwarded to an Enforcement Unit for investigation. (The processing time between Mediation and Enforcement is approximately 60-90 days.) The assigned Investigator will begin the investigation process by contacting the employer for a response to the allegations that appear on your charge of employment discrimination. The assigned Investigator may also contact you, the employer or any witnesses to obtain facts or additional information about the allegations of your charge. It is important that you or your witnesses immediately respond to the assigned Investigator's attempt to communicate regarding your charge of employment discrimination.

5. After the Investigator has obtained sufficient information to make a recommendation regarding the allegations you have raised in your charge, you will receive a call or a letter outlining the outcome of the investigation. If it is determined that a violation has occurred, the District Director will send you a Letter of Determination addressing the specific violations and an invitation to resolve the issues through conciliation. If the evidence does not support a violation of the law, you will receive a Dismissal and Notice of Right to Sue. It is your responsibility to file a lawsuit within 90 days from receipt of the Dismissal and Notice of Right to Sue.

6. The amount of time to complete an investigation depends on the complexity of the charge. Our Office attempts to complete our investigations within 180 days; however, if we have not made a determination on the merits of your charge within 180 days, you may request a Notice of Right to Sue in order to file a lawsuit in a Federal District Court.

OPTIONS FOR COURT ACTION:

Title VII of the Civil Rights Act of 1964, as amended, and the Americans with Disabilities Act (ADA) of 1990 requires EEOC to issue a Dismissal and Notice of Right to sue before you can bring suit in Federal District Court. The petition must be filed within 90 days of receipt of the Dismissal and Notice of Rights. Failure to file a lawsuit within 90 days after the Dismissal and Notice of Rights may result in the right to file being lost. The 90 days cannot be extended or restored by EEOC. If you request a Notice of Rights to Sue after your charge has been on file for 180 days, EEOC will take no further action on your case. You are responsible for retaining your own attorney to represent you or file on your own.

The Age Discrimination in Employment Act of 1967 (ADEA) allows, that after 60 days have passed after you file with the EEOC, you may file in Federal District Court if you wish to do so. You should notify this office if you file. Should the EEOC dismiss your case or otherwise terminate proceedings on your case, you will receive your Dismissal and Notice of Rights, and have 90 days from the date of receipt to file in Federal Court. Failure to file within 90 days may result in loss of your right to file and it cannot be extended or restored.

The Equal Pay Act of 1963 (EPA) does not require that you complain to any Federal agency before bringing an EPA lawsuit in court. The EPA requires that you file a lawsuit within two years from the date of the alleged underpayment (or three years for a willful violation). If you file a complaint with the EEOC under the EPA, your complaint will be investigated and you will be notified of the results and any action that EEOC will take.

If any additional information is required, you may contact the assigned Investigator at the number given to you during the Intake interview or contact the Intake Unit at (713) 651-4900.

Exhibit 47

HARRIS HEALTH
SYSTEM

Harris Health System
P.O. Box 66769, Houston, Texas 77266-6769

4/24/2014

TO WHOM IT MAY CONCERN

Re: Ms. Ellenor

Ms. Perkins has been evaluated at Smith Clinic of the Harris Health System for possible asthma and allergic rhinitis, She reports significant upper airway symptoms made worse by certain exposures such as perfumes and strong odor. Allergy evaluation shows sensitivity to Ragweed, dust mites, cat hair dander and cockroach. She was advised to avoid exposures to these triggers both at work and home. She is to be evaluated by the ENT service and Allergy Immunology services to determine any further management of her allergic rhinitis. This letter was given to her upon request.

Hanania, MD, MS
Pulmonary and Critical Care Medicine
Baylor College of Medicine
713566

Exhibit 48

Please call me

Texas Health and Human Services Commission
Medical Release/Physician's Statement
Form H1836-A
April 2003

SECTION I — TO BE COMPLETED BY STAFF

Name of Patient: Ellenor Perkins	Date of Birth:	Social Security No.
Name (caregiver):	Case No.	Patient's Usual Job
Advisor's Name	BJN	
Office Address/Mail Code/FAX No.		

SECTION II — TO BE COMPLETED BY PHYSICIAN

The patient named above has applied for benefits with our agency. Federal and state regulations require that persons receiving benefits work or participate in activities to prepare them for work unless they are physically or mentally incapable of working. This patient claims that disability. Please complete the appropriate parts. After you complete the form, you may give it to the client or mail it to HHSC at the address in Section I.

PART A – PERSONAL DISABILITY:
To what extent is the individual able to work or participate in activities to prepare for work? Please check **one** of the following boxes:

1) The individual is able to work, or participate in activities to prepare for work, **without restrictions**:
   a) ☐ Full time (40 hours/week)
   b) ☐ Part time at ___ hours/week

2) ☒ The individual is able to work, or participate in activities to prepare for work, **with restrictions**: (Please complete Part B and C)
   a) ☐ Full time (40 hours/week)
   b) ☒ Part time at 20 hours/week

3) The individual is unable to work, or participate in activities to prepare for work, at all (Please complete Part C)
   a) ☐ The disability is permanent.
   b) ☐ The disability is not permanent and is expected to last more than 6 months.
   c) ☐ The disability is not permanent and is expected to last 6 months or less.

PART B – ACTIVITY RESTRICTIONS
What can this individual do now? Check the appropriate boxes that are applicable during a workday:

Maximum hours per workday:	2	4	6	8	Other
Sitting	☐	☐	☐	☐	
Standing	☐	☐	☐	☐	
Walking	☐	☐	☐	☐	
Climbing stairs/ladders	☐	☐	☐	☐	N/A
Kneeling/Squatting	☐	☐	☐	☐	
Bending/Stooping	☐	☐	☐	☐	
Pushing/Pulling	☐	☐	☐	☐	
Keyboarding	☐	☐	☐	☐	
Lifting/Carrying	☐	☐	☐	☐	
Other (please describe)					Pt has asthma triggered by strong smells and is advised to work in indoor environment avoid dust/chemicals/strong cleaning agents

The individual may not lift/carry objects more than ___ lbs. for more than ___ hours per day.

Individuals with employment limitations may still be assigned to complete community work in an office environment with little physical strain or demand (answering phones, filing while seated, etc.) Others may be assigned to complete employment related activities in a classroom setting. In your opinion, can this individual participate in activities of this nature?
☐ Yes ☐ No

Any other remarks, recommendations or restrictions? **No mobility restrictions**

PART C – DIAGNOSIS — Environmental allergies

Primary disabling diagnosis: Allergic Rhinitis triggering asthma	Secondary disabling diagnosis: Asthma

Comments:

Name of Physician (please type or print): Juneja MD	Physicians License No.	Signature-Physician	Date: 7/28/14
Office Address (Street or P.O. Box, City, State, ZIP): 6630 DeMoss St, Houston, TX 77074		Telephone Number (Include Area Code)	

Exhibit 49

E\
to Cindy

Mon, Jun 22, 2015, 2:35 PM

Hello Cindy

Can you also send me the inquiry that I submitted to DisabilityRights Texas for help?

Sincerely,

Ellenor Perkins

Houston, Texas
P: 832-618-
E:

Exhibit 50

E\
to Cindy

Jun 22, 2015, 3:00 PM

Have you viewed the spelling of first name? She spelled it two different ways, we verbally spoke about this over the phone months ago.
Have you received any calls in relation to the employer? How much is the skip trace since the first one was done earlier in the year?

Thanks

Exhibit 51

EEOC Form 161 (11/09)	**U.S. EQUAL EMPLOYMENT OPPORTUNITY COMMISSION**

DISMISSAL AND NOTICE OF RIGHTS

To: Ellenor Perkins - Ratcliff
Houston, TX

From: Houston District Office
Total Plaza
1201 Louisiana, Suite 600
Houston, TX 77002

[ ] On behalf of person(s) aggrieved whose identity is CONFIDENTIAL (29 CFR §1601.7(a))

EEOC Charge No.	EEOC Representative	Telephone No.
460-2014-01770	Jeremy Crosbie, Investigator	(713) 651-4919

THE EEOC IS CLOSING ITS FILE ON THIS CHARGE FOR THE FOLLOWING REASON:

[ ] The facts alleged in the charge fail to state a claim under any of the statutes enforced by the EEOC.

[ ] Your allegations did not involve a disability as defined by the Americans With Disabilities Act.

[ ] The Respondent employs less than the required number of employees or is not otherwise covered by the statutes.

[ ] Your charge was not timely filed with EEOC; in other words, you waited too long after the date(s) of the alleged discrimination to file your charge

[X] The EEOC issues the following determination: Based upon its investigation, the EEOC is unable to conclude that the information obtained establishes violations of the statutes. This does not certify that the respondent is in compliance with the statutes. No finding is made as to any other issues that might be construed as having been raised by this charge.

[ ] The EEOC has adopted the findings of the state or local fair employment practices agency that investigated this charge.

[ ] Other (briefly state)

- NOTICE OF SUIT RIGHTS -
(See the additional information attached to this form.)

Title VII, the Americans with Disabilities Act, the Genetic Information Nondiscrimination Act, or the Age Discrimination in Employment Act: This will be the only notice of dismissal and of your right to sue that we will send you. You may file a lawsuit against the respondent(s) under federal law based on this charge in federal or state court. Your lawsuit **must be filed WITHIN 90 DAYS** of your receipt of this notice; or your right to sue based on this charge will be lost. (The time limit for filing suit based on a claim under state law may be different.)

Equal Pay Act (EPA): EPA suits must be filed in federal or state court within 2 years (3 years for willful violations) of the alleged EPA underpayment. This means that backpay due for any violations that occurred **more than 2 years (3 years)** before you file suit may not be collectible.

On behalf of the Commission

Martin S. Ebel,
Acting District Director

MAR 2 6 2015
(Date Mailed)

Enclosures(s)

cc:
L. P. Marlin
Assistant General Counsel
GENERAL DYNAMICS INFORMAITON TECH.
3211 Jermantown Road
Fairfax, VA 22030

Lowell Keig, Division Director
TWC – Civil Rights Division
101 East 15th Street, Room 144-T
Austin, TX 78778-0001

Exhibit 52

Enclosure with EEOC
Form 161 (11/09)

INFORMATION RELATED TO FILING SUIT
UNDER THE LAWS ENFORCED BY THE EEOC

*(This information relates to filing suit in Federal or State court under Federal law.
If you also plan to sue claiming violations of State law, please be aware that time limits and other
provisions of State law may be shorter or more limited than those described below.)*

PRIVATE SUIT RIGHTS -- **Title VII of the Civil Rights Act, the Americans with Disabilities Act (ADA), the Genetic Information Nondiscrimination Act (GINA), or the Age Discrimination in Employment Act (ADEA):**

In order to pursue this matter further, you must file a lawsuit against the respondent(s) named in the charge **within 90 days** of the date you *receive* this Notice. Therefore, you should keep a record of this date. Once this 90-day period is over, your right to sue based on the charge referred to in this Notice will be lost. If you intend to consult an attorney, you should do so promptly. Give your attorney a copy of this Notice, and its envelope, and tell him or her the date you received it. Furthermore, in order to avoid any question that you did not act in a timely manner, it is prudent that your suit be filed **within 90 days of the date this Notice was *mailed* to you** (as indicated where the Notice is signed) or the date of the postmark, if later.

Your lawsuit may be filed in U.S. District Court or a State court of competent jurisdiction. (Usually, the appropriate State court is the general civil trial court.) Whether you file in Federal or State court is a matter for you to decide after talking to your attorney. Filing this Notice is not enough. You must file a "complaint" that contains a short statement of the facts of your case which shows that you are entitled to relief. Your suit may include any matter alleged in the charge or, to the extent permitted by court decisions, matters like or related to the matters alleged in the charge. Generally, suits are brought in the State where the alleged unlawful practice occurred, but in some cases can be brought where relevant employment records are kept, where the employment would have been, or where the respondent has its main office. If you have simple questions, you usually can get answers from the office of the clerk of the court where you are bringing suit, but do not expect that office to write your complaint or make legal strategy decisions for you.

PRIVATE SUIT RIGHTS -- **Equal Pay Act (EPA):**

EPA suits must be filed in court within 2 years (3 years for willful violations) of the alleged EPA underpayment: back pay due for violations that occurred more than **2 years (3 years)** before you file suit may not be collectible. For example, if you were underpaid under the EPA for work performed from 7/1/08 to 12/1/08, you should file suit **before 7/1/10** – *not* 12/1/10 -- in order to recover unpaid wages due for July 2008. This time limit for filing an EPA suit is separate from the 90-day filing period under Title VII, the ADA, GINA or the ADEA referred to above. Therefore, if you also plan to sue under Title VII, the ADA, GINA or the ADEA, in addition to suing on the EPA claim, suit must be filed within 90 days of this Notice **and** within the 2- or 3-year EPA back pay recovery period.

ATTORNEY REPRESENTATION -- **Title VII, the ADA or GINA:**

If you cannot afford or have been unable to obtain a lawyer to represent you, the U.S. District Court having jurisdiction in your case may, in limited circumstances, assist you in obtaining a lawyer. Requests for such assistance must be made to the U.S. District Court in the form and manner it requires (you should be prepared to explain in detail your efforts to retain an attorney). Requests should be made well before the end of the 90-day period mentioned above, because such requests do **not** relieve you of the requirement to bring suit within 90 days.

ATTORNEY REFERRAL AND EEOC ASSISTANCE -- **All Statutes:**

You may contact the EEOC representative shown on your Notice if you need help in finding a lawyer or if you have any questions about your legal rights, including advice on which U.S. District Court can hear your case. If you need to inspect or obtain a copy of information in EEOC's file on the charge, please request it promptly in writing and provide your charge number (as shown on your Notice). While EEOC destroys charge files after a certain time, all charge files are kept for at least 6 months after our last action on the case. Therefore, if you file suit and want to review the charge file, please make your review request **within 6 months** of this Notice. (Before filing suit, any request should be made within the next 90 days.)

IF YOU FILE SUIT, PLEASE SEND A COPY OF YOUR COURT COMPLAINT TO THIS OFFICE.

Exhibit 53

EQUAL EMPLOYMENT OPPORTUNITY COMMISSION
HOUSTON DISTRICT OFFICE
TOTAL PLAZA
1201 LOUISIANA STREET - 6TH FLOOR
HOUSTON, TX 77002

OFFICIAL BUSINESS
Penalty for Private Use, $300

N HOUSTON
TX 773
26 MAR '15
PM 1 L

02 1P
0000605339   MAR 26 2015
MAILED FROM ZIP CODE 77002

77096999955

Exhibit 54

Justice

@yahoo.com

Apr 9, 2015 at 8:15 AM

State Regulations
We believe these findings are wrong and wish to appeal the decision made by Jeremy Crosbie. We would also like to express our request for a different EEOC Federal Investigator.

Mr. Jeremy Crosbie, stated in a conversation over the phone, "GDIT was not obligated to enforce the perfume issue and that they gave reasonable accommodation." We do not agree with his statement. GDIT provides services to CMS as a government contractor. GDIT was responsible for enrolling citizens into the Affordable Care Act program. Every company or organization that operates within government affairs are regulated to develop policies and procedures and enforce such policies and procedures. In order to be a contractor, each company or organization must then submit such policies and procedures over to the state with an application for review to gain permission to operate as a contractor of the government. Any entry who is granted permission under the regulations of the state, as well as their own policies and procedures.

GDIT made the effort only to enforce certain policies and procedures, such as the ones that were in the best interest of the company. The policies and procedures that were enforced was dress code (no leggings and revealing clothing) and secure floor policy (no cell phones) Employees had to read and sign off on these policies and procedures on a consistant basis, electronically. Employees signed off on the mentioned policies and procedures at least fifty (50) times. GDIT also walked around each group on the call center floor with a word to detect who had a cell phone on the call center floor. If a phone was detected that employee was then fired. Employees who didn't have their badge to enter was instructed to return home and retrieve it. GDIT began to monitor at the entrance for employees who were not dressed properly and sent such employees home to change. Employees who were habitual offenders of these policies were fired, except for the cell phone rule, they were terminated immediately. This was in an effort to protect PII, Personal Identifiable Information.

GDIT penalize me for being off the phone for the period of time that exceeded their standards. Once exposed to the fragrances it restricted my breathing causing me to have an asthma attack. I would medicate myself and return to the call center floor. It made me feel very weak and it took a little time to recover after exposed. This situation also caused the composition of my voice to change, because my lungs were restricted. The customers could not understand me on the phone. You may ask, "Why did she stay on the job so long? I stayed because, I needed to support my family.
On many occasions I worked overtime and stayed late. I worked at a time when the weather was horrible and only a small number of workers came in. I worked when GDIT allowed workers to go home because the phones where not as busy. The statement I made pertained to different times of day.

The issues began after employees were moved from the training rooms to the call center floor. I began to wear a mask after the company wouldn't address the car and supervisors apllieing perfume and cologne on the call center floor. I felt alienated because our csr kept asking me what was wrong, was I sick? The mask didn't help much because it didn't allow ventilation therefore I felt like I was suffocating. Once I made it to my desk I removed the mask so I could breath properly.
GDIT offered to move me to a different group and did so. That did not help because GDIT refused to address the issue of car applying their fragrance on the job of an open floor. There is a difference from someone applying perfume or cologne at home verses applying it on the call center floor.

This company was operating under a government contract and there are rules and regulation this company agreed to when accessing the contract. Under state regulation, a company does not have a chioce on which policies they want to enforce. GDIT must enforce all policies and procedures according to Texas Department of Human Services.

I only asked what was already written in GDIT policies and procedures under Dress Code Standards, to be enforced. What I asked, at no time caused GDIT undue hardship. GDIT made a choice, and that choice was to not enforce their own policy, therefore causing injury. I was forced to resign, as a result of not being able to tolerate the fragrances sprayed on the call center floor and due to my health declining. I was not accomodated. You can't move someone all over and not address policy. I know I didn't matter then, but I matter now and so well the rights of others matter to GDIT. You discriminated against many individuals and I have spoken with them the entire time I worked there. It's a crime to discriminate and you will be brought to justice. Justice shall prevail. I decree and declare that Justice will not be perverted.

FYI
This was my transit to work once hired by GDIT. My training started at 7:00 a.m. I woke at 3:30 in the morning. I stood outside alone at 4:30 in the morning. My first bus arrived for 4:49 a.m. I arrived to the second stop, then transferred to the last bus stop to arrive for work at the scheduled time of 7:00 a.m.

Exhibit 55

Ellenor Perkins-Ratcliff

Houston, Texas

U.S. EQUAL EMPLOYMENT OPPORTUNITY COMMISSION
1201 Louisiana Street, 6th Floor
Houston, Texas 77002

April 10, 2015

NOTICE OF RIGHT TO REQUEST SUBSTANTIAL WEIGHT REVIEW

We believe these findings are wrong and wish to appeal the decision made by Jeremy Crosbie, regarding charge no. 460-2014-01770. We would also like to express our request for a different EEOC Federal Investigator. Mr. Jeremy Crosbie, stated in a conversation over the phone, "GDIT was not obligated to enforce the perfume issue and that they gave reasonable accommodations." We do not agree with his statement. U.S. Department of Health and Human Services has strict regulations which contractors agreed to and are to enforce.

GDIT provides services to CMS as a government contractor. GDIT was responsible for enrolling citizens into the Affordable Care Act. Every entity that operates under the jurisdiction of any government agency, are required to develop policies and procedures to protect clients as well as employees. The entity must enforce such policies and procedures, and abide by the rules and regulations of HHS. In order to be a contractor, each company or organization must submit such policies and procedures, with an application to the state for review, to gain permission to operate as a government contractor. Any entity that is granted permission, must operate under the regulations of the state, as well as enforce their own policies and procedures.

GDIT made the effort only to enforce certain policies and procedures, such as the ones that were in the best interest of the company. The policies and procedures that were enforced were dress code (no leggings and reviling clothing) and secure floor policy (no cell phones). Employees had to read and sign off on these policies and procedures on a consistent basis,

Exhibit 56

electronically. Employees signed off on the mentioned policies and procedures, at least fifty (50) times. GDIT authority also walked around each group on the call center floor, with a wand to detect who had a cell phone on the call center floor. If a phone was detected, that employee was immediately fired.

Employees, who didn't have their badge to enter, were instructed to return home and retrieve it. GDIT began to monitor at the entrance, for employees who were not dressed properly and sent such employees home to change. Employees who were habitual offenders of these policies were fired, except for the cell phone rule, they were terminated immediately. This was in an effort to protect CMS and the Personal Identifiable Information of citizens.

GDIT penalize me, for being off the phone for the period of time that exceeded their standards. Once exposed to the fragrances it restricted my breathing, causing me to have an asthma attack. I would medicate myself and return to the call center floor, still feeling sick. It made me feel very weak and it took time to recover after exposed. This situation also caused the composition of my voice to change, due to my lung restriction. The customers could not understand me on the phone. This exposure took place from 10/4/2013 to 02/17/2014; I dealt with this issue as long as possible before resigning.

You may ask, "Why did she stay on the job so long?" I stayed on the job, because I needed to support my family. On many occasions I worked overtime and stayed late. I worked at a time when the weather was horrible and only a small number of workers came in. I worked when GDIT allowed workers to go home, because the phones were not as busy. I worked various times of the day. The issues began after employees were moved from the training rooms to the call center floor. **I began to wear a mask after the company wouldn't address the customer service reps or supervisor's regarding applying perfume and cologne on the call center floor.** I felt alienated because of the treatment from GDIT. Customer service reps., kept asking me, "What was wrong, was I sick?" The mask didn't help much, because it didn't allow ventilation therefore, I felt like I was suffocating. Once I made it to my desk, I removed the mask so I could breathe properly.

Exhibit 57

GDIT offered to move me to a different group and did so. That did not help because GDIT refused to address the issue of csr's applying their fragrance on the job of an open floor. There is a difference from someone applying perfume or cologne at home verses applying it on the call center floor. Z   stated, **"We can't stop csr's from wearing perfume."** I never asked for Human Resources to tell staff not to wear perfume, **I asked Z   to enforce their policy and procedures and ask staff not to spray it on the call center floor.**

My condition was new as of 2013 and I was under evaluation by my pcp and specialist, never the less I expressed my concerns to Human Resource Department and was ignored. I only asked what was already written in GDIT policies and procedures under Dress Code Standards, to be enforced. **What I asked, at no time caused GDIT undue hardship.** GDIT made a choice, and that choice was to only enforce certain areas of their own policy for the benefit of the company, ignoring their written standards as a whole which caused injury. **That was very negligent of GDIT.** I was forced to resign, as a result of not being taken seriously regarding my illness and unable to tolerate the fragrances sprayed on the call center floor. **I was not accommodated. You can't move someone all over and not address policy.**

GDIT was operating under a government contract and there are rules and regulation this company agreed to when accepting the contract. Under state regulation, a company does not have a choice on which policies they want to enforce. GDIT must enforce all policies and procedures according to U.S. Department of Health and Human Service. **To GDIT**, I know you felt I didn't matter then, but I matter now and so will the rights of others. You discriminated against many individuals with different medical needs. I rode the bus and conversed with some of the employees you discriminated against. It's a crime to discriminate and you will be brought to justice. **Justice shall prevail. I decree and declare that Justice will not be perverted in Jesus name, Amen.**

For informational purposes only, this was my routine to make it to work on time once hired by GDIT. My training started at 7:00 a.m. I woke at 3:30 in the morning. I stood outside alone at 4:30 in the morning. My first bus arrived for 4:49 a.m. I arrived to the second stop, then transferred to the last bus stop to arrive for work at the scheduled time of 7:00 a.m.

Exhibit 58

Sincerely,

Ellenor Perkins-Ratcliff

cc: U.S. Department of Health and Human Services, Centers for Medicare & Medicaid Services and Media.

State of Texas

County Of Harris

The foregoing instrument was acknowledged before me this day of April 10th 2015 by Ellenor Perkins-Ratcliff, who has Produced Texas Driver's License as identification.

_____
Notary

_____
Name typed, printed or stamped)

Notary Public
_____
Title

_____
License number

Exhibit 59

Exhibit 60

Exhibit 61

Exhibit 62

U.S. EQUAL EMPLOYMENT OPPORTUNITY COMMISSION
Houston District Office

1201 Louisiana Street, 6th Floor
Houston, TX 77002
Intake Information Group: (800) 669-4000
Intake Information Group TTY: (800) 669-6820
Houston Status Line: (866) 408-8075
Houston Direct Dial: (713) 651-4900
TTY (713) 651-4901
FAX (713) 651-4902

3E

April 29, 2015

Ms. Ellenor Perkins-Ratcliff

Houston, TX 77

Dear Ms. Perkins-Ratcliff:

This is in response to your letter dated April 10, 2015, concerning your request that the Commission reconsider its final findings on her charge of employment discrimination filed with the U.S. Equal Employment Opportunity Commission (EEOC) against General Dynamics Information Technology - GDIT (EEOC Charge No. 460-2014-01770).

The EEOC has no obligation to reconsider the final findings we have issued on a charge. EEOC Directors, therefore, may decline to review a request to reconsider an EEOC final finding unless the Charging Party presents substantial new and relevant evidence, or a persuasive argument that the EEOC's prior decision was contrary to law or the facts.

I have thoroughly reviewed the handling of your charge in light of your expressed concerns and the information that you provided. Based on my review of the investigative file, you alleged that you were denied a disability accommodation and forced to resign from your position as Customer Service Representative. The evidence reflects that in accordance with the company's policies and procedures, you requested a disability accommodation to work from home. The company engaged in the interactive process and a decision was made that it was not feasible for you to conduct the company's business from your home due to the confidential and sensitive information of beneficiaries and consumers. On November 21, 2014, you again requested a disability accommodation to relocate from your work station to a closed cubicle. You were given the option to move to a work station at the end of a row where you would be as isolated as possible from others working or moving throughout the contact center. It was also suggested that you wear a mask at the company's expense while at work, especially when you needed to walk through the contact center. You indicated that you would provide your on mask. In early 2014, while visiting the Human Resources to discuss the attendance policy, you broadly generalized your concern that the scents in the workplace were still strong and that you would be consulting with your doctor. On January 29, 2014, you alerted the Human Resources about an alleged incident where a coworker was spraying perfume in the call center near your locker. You informed the Human Resources that you would obtain supporting documentation for your absences which impacted the attendance policy and other performance metrics such as schedule adherence. There is no evidence that you followed up with your physician's documentation. A few weeks later you requested a schedule change, changed your mind and then tried to rescind it. Because the schedule change had already been granted, your request to change it was denied.

Exhibit 63

You then informed your new and former supervisors that it would be your last day and that you were resigning. Your resignation was tendered on February 17, 2014. Based on my review, I have determined that no appropriate evidence was overlooked or misinterpreted in evaluating your charge. The evidence indicates that the company engaged in the interactive process and provided you with an accommodation. You failed to provide medical supporting documentation to further evaluate your accommodation request. Therefore, the evidence does not establish a violation of the Americans With Disability Act. Your request for reconsideration is hereby denied.

It is important to note that a request for reconsideration does not extend or eliminate the statutory 90-day period for pursuing this matter in court. If a private lawsuit is not filed within 90 days of receipt of the **March 26, 2015,** final dismissal notice, the right to sue for the charge will be lost and cannot be restored by the EEOC.

I hope this information is helpful to you.

Sincerely,

Martin Ebel
Acting District Director

Exhibit 64

EQUAL EMPLOYMENT OPPORTUNITY COMMISSION
HOUSTON DISTRICT OFFICE
TOTAL PLAZA
1201 LOUISIANA STREET - 6TH FLOOR
HOUSTON, TX 77002

OFFICIAL BUSINESS
Penalty for Private Use, $300

N HOUSTON
TX 773
30 APR '15
PM 9 L

$ 000.48

Ms. Ellenor Perkins-Ratcliff

7709625090

Exhibit 65

NOTICE OF REPRESENTATION OR WITHDRAWAL OF REPRESENTATION
GENERAL CLAIM AND REPRESENTATIVE IDENTIFICATION INFORMATION

Send form to DWC and a copy to insurance carrier
Texas Department of Insurance
Division of Workers' Compensation
7551 Metro Center Drive, Suite 100
Austin, Texas 78744

CLAIM # _____
Carrier Claim # _____

Section I. Injured Employee Information

1a. Last Name	1b. First Name	1c. Middle Name	1d. Name Suffix
Perkins-Ratcliff	Ellenor		

2. Date of Birth (mm/dd/yyyy)	3. Social Security Number	4a. Phone Area Code	4b. Phone Number	4c. Phone Extension	5. Date of Injury (mm/dd/yyyy)
		832			10/4/2013

6a. Street Address	6b. City	6c. State	6d. Zip Code
	Houston	TX	

Section II. Beneficiary Information (if represented person is a beneficiary)

7a. Last Name	7b. First Name	7c. Middle Name	7d. Name Suffix

8. Date of Birth (mm/dd/yyyy)	9. Social Security No. (last 4)	10a. Phone Area Code	10b. Phone Number	10c. Phone Extension	11. Relation of Injured Employee
	XXX-XX-				

12a. Street Address	12b. City	12c. State	12d. Zip Code

Section III. Representative Information

13a. Last Name	13b. First Name	13c. Middle Name	13d. Name Suffix
CURRY	M.	L	

14a. Street Address	14b. City	14c. State	14d. Zip Code
	HOUSTON	TX	77024

15. Email Address

16. Firm Name: LAW OFFICE OF ... CURRY

17. Representative's State Bar #	18. Date of License (mm/dd/yyyy)	19a. Phone Area Code	19b. Phone Number	19c. Phone Extension	20. Fax Number
		713	2		71

NOTICE OF REPRESENTATION

NOTE: Both the claimant and the representative must sign and date the Notice of Representation below before the relationship becomes effective. Send this form to DWC at the address shown above and a copy to the insurance carrier.

I certify that I am representing the interests of the above named claimant's workers' compensation claim for the above date of injury under the following circumstances: (PLEASE CHECK THE APPROPRIATE BOX)

☒ My representation began on: May 14, 2015. I am not aware of any other person or attorney representing this injured employee at this time.

☐ My representation began on: _____. I am aware that _____ was previously representing this claimant. I hereby certify I have verified that the previous representative has withdrawn representation for the above referenced claimant.

By signing below, I affirm that I qualify as a representative either as an attorney, or, if other than an attorney, I affirm that I qualify as a non-attorney representative under the Texas Workers' Compensation Act and the Workers' Compensation Rules, and that as a non-attorney representative, no fee or remuneration shall be received by me either directly or indirectly from a claimant.

By signing below the claimant acknowledges the person indicated above will represent the claimant for the above date of injury.

Claimant's Signature	Date Signed	Representative's Signature	Date Signed
	5/14/2015		

NOTICE OF WITHDRAWAL OF REPRESENTATION

NOTE: Either the representative or the claimant may terminate this representation relationship at any time, however, Rule 152.1(e) states," A Client who discharges an attorney does not, by this action, defeat the attorney's right to claim a fee." The party terminating the relationship must sign below and provide a copy to the other party, the insurance carrier, and the DWC field office handling the claim.

By my signature below, I am terminating this representation relationship effective the date indicated below. I will provide a copy of this Representation withdrawal notice to the other party, the insurance carrier, and the DWC filed office handling the claim.

Claimant's Signature	Date Signed	Withdrawing Representative's Signature	Date Signed

DWC FORM-150 (Rev. 10/05) Page 1   DIVISION OF WORKERS' COMPENSATION

Exhibit 66

E Wed, May 20, 2015, 5:02 PM
to M

5/20/2015

Hi N

Thank you for contacting me regarding my medical records. I will be available to pick them up on tomorrow.

During the meeting with Attorney Curry I forgot to ask the fee for representing me. We talked about many things concerning my case, but we didn't discuss his fee for representation. Please ask him that question and respond via email.

Thanks a million.

Mrs. Ellenor Perkins Ratcliff

Exhibit 67

E May 26, 2015, 5:25 PM
to M

Hi,

Stay safe during this horrendous flooding. I hope you all are doing well.

On last week I left a voice message regarding GDIT contacting me. When Attorney Curry asked for me to get information from Texas Department of Insurance, it was stated that I needed to contact the company for Policy number regarding Workman Comp. I had to file a claim to get information from the insurance company itself. So, GDIT was responding to my email when I was probing for information.

Basically, I wanted to know if Attorney Curry wants me to converse with GDIT regarding the claim. Z Wemtz at 602-718- contacted me again today 5/26/2015. Z Wemtz wanted to ask questions to complete the claim on his end so that he could give me the information regarding the Policy number and etc., at least that is what he stated to me. I informed Z that I would contact him once I speak with my attorney.

Exhibit 68

Attorney Fees

E Tue, Jun 2, 2015, 2:24 PM
to M

Hello N

I know we spoke over the phone regarding an email I sent you regarding attorney fees. Can you please provide that information to me in an email once you come from vacation?

Thanks.

Ellenor Perkins Ratcliff

Exhibit 69

Ms. Ellenor Perkins - Follow up to your inquiry Legal

Wentz, Z <@gdit.com>   Jun 2, 2015, 4:56 PM
to me

Ms. Perkins –

This is in follow-up to your web inquiry regarding your desire to file a Worker Compensation claim. Upon receiving your inquiry, I had initially contacted you by phone on 5/21/15 and left a voice message at the telephone number you listed in your web inquiry. Upon not receiving a return call, I contacted you via phone again on 5/22/15. When speaking to you on 5/22/15, you asked to return my call later that day because you were driving. I did not receive a return phone call, so I contacted you again on Monday, 5/24/15. During this discussion, you indicated you did not wish to provide me details about your claim of workplace injury at that time, but that you would contact your legal representative and then contact me back with additional details. To date, I have still received no contact or further information from you. If I do not receive additional information from you, I will assume that you no longer wish to pursue a workers' compensation claim.

Regards,

Z   Wentz
Manager Human Resources – Health Sector
Health & Civilian Solutions Division
General Dynamics Information Technology

Phoenix, AZ 85021
(o) 602-718-
(f) 602-718-
(m) 480-435

www.gdit.com

Exhibit 70

E
to M , Z ▾
Ellenor Perkins-Ratcliff

<I.com>

Jun 3, 2015, 4:49 PM

General Dynamics Information Technolog

Phoenix, AZ 85021

June 3, 2015

Mr. Z Wentz

This is in follow-up to your email regarding my web inquiry. My inquiry was forwarded to you. Prior to you contacting me, I made contact with Texas Department of Insurance. As I informed you on the phone, "I filed a claim." "Yes I did state, "I needed to speak with my legal representative." As a result of the inclement weather in Houston, Texas my attorney was not available. On June 3, 2015, I was able to make contact with the staff and I was informed to direct any questions from General Dynamics to my attorney. My legal representative information is listed below.

M   ATTORNEY AT LAW

Houston, Texas 77024
T: (713) 222-
F: (713) 222-

Sincerely,

220

Exhibit 71

Wentz, Z <@gdit.com>   Jun 4, 2015, 3:54 PM

to me

Ms. Perkins,

Thank you for your reply. You are welcomed to pursue any claims you deem appropriate with the State, but if you wish to file a workers' compensation claim through GDIT, we will need to be provided additional information in order to assist you. You may reach me at your convenience, if you wish.

Exhibit 72

E <@gmail.com>   Jun 4, 2015, 4:08 PM

to M

Ellenor Perkins-Ratcliff

M

Houston, Texas 77024

Dear Attorney Curry,

The following email was received from Z H Wentz on today. I spoke to Norma earlier this week and she informed me to direct Mr. Wentz to you.

Sincerely,

Ellenor Ratcliff

Exhibit 73

E
to z
Ellenor Perkins-Ratcliff

Jun 5, 2015, 5:28 PM

General Dynamics Information Technolog

Phoenix, AZ 85021

June 5, 2015

Mr. Wentz,

Broadspire has informed me that for this employer I can't file a workers' compensation claim without first speaking to GDIT. The representative was blocked from entering any information and received a message stating, "Contact GDIT." Your human resource department is aware of everything that took place from 10/13 to 02/14. If a claim needed to be filed by GDIT, why didn't human resources file it then? Honestly, I don't see GDIT doing anything to help me, after the repeated negligent behavior of staff ignoring policies and procedures causing tremendous suffering. What is the best time to contact you?

So, I'm now contacting you regarding the information you stated I needed for GDIT to assist me. "You are welcomed to pursue any claims you deem appropriate with the State, but if you wish to file a workers' compensation claim through GDIT, we will need to be provided additional information in order to assist you. You may reach me at your convenience, if you wish."

Ellenor P. Ratcliff
832-

Exhibit 74

Wentz, Z <@gdit.com>
to me

Jun 8, 2015, 10:50 AM

Ellenor – I will attempt to contact you today between the time frame of 3:00-3:30pm Central time so we may partner on the claim submission information. If I am unable to reach you, I will leave a voice message, but please feel free to suggest an alternate time if this does not work for you. I will be as flexible as possible to ensure we connect soon.

Thank you,

Exhibit 75

E
to M

Jun 9, 2015, 8:51 AM

Good Morning Attorney Curry,

On yesterday I did have a conversation with Mr. Wentz. He informed me that a claim number will be generated by the end of today. Mr. Wentz and I agreed that he could send this information by email. I will forward it over to you once I receive it.

Sincerely,

Ellenor Perkins-Ratcliff

Exhibit 76

E
to Z

Wed, Jun 10, 2015, 11:07 AM

Good Morning,

This is a follow up on our conversation for 6/8/2015. I'm contacting you regarding the claim number and claim you filed on my behalf on 6/8/2015. Per our verbal conversation you stated the claim number would be generated on 6/9/2015.

As we agreed you may send all information via email.

Thank you,

Ellenor Perkins-Ratcliff
832-

Exhibit 77

E
to M

Jun 10, 2015, 6:56 PM

Good Evening Attorney Curry,

I have provided for you below, the email from Mr. Wentz with the Worker's Compensation claim number. Please call me if you have any questions.

Exhibit 78

Broadspire Claim 1   001

E   Wed, Jun 24, 2015, 7:36 AM
to M

Good Morning N

Please retain for your records. Please update "CLIENT INFORMATION SHEET", I didn't accurately add all doctors.

You may contact me at anytime should you have any questions.

Sincerely,

Ellenor Perkins Ratcliff

Houston, Texas
832-

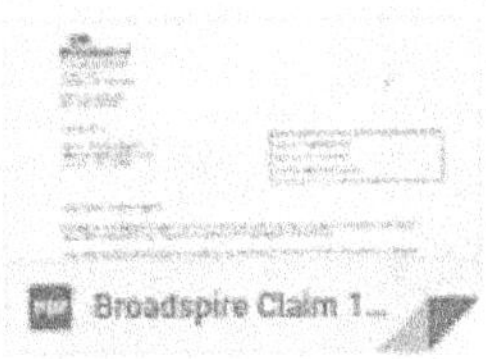

Broadspire Claim 1...

Exhibit 81

Número de reclamo: 188029923-001

¿Para quién trabajaba? General Dynamics Information Technology
Resigned 2/17/2014, due to repeated Exposure.
¿Cuál es su trabajo? Assisted with enrollment into Affordable Care Act. Title: Assoc. Specialist, Cust Svc
¿Cuando se lesionó? mes 10 día 4 año 2013 AM/PM break / break
¿Donde ocurrió? Call Center floor near desk and at lockers.
¿Que estaba haciendo? On break at locker, Team member applied perfume.
At desk/work station, different team member sat on opposite side. 4ppl down was loaded with perfume.
Passing down the isle to workstation, Supervisor was loaded with perfume so, I avoided walking near her desk.
¿Que sucedió? (Responda en la forma más completa.)
Employees applied perfume & cologne on the Call center floor on a daily basis.
I informed my supervisor, A Clem and he apologized. Contacted HR and was told "We can't stop CSR's from wearing perfume." per Z Bosie.

Indique por favor las heridas sostenidas en consecuencia de su herida de trabajo:
Injury was to my lungs. Once exposed experienced chest tightning and shortness of breath, I was coughing and wheezing, I felt so ill and weak. On many occasions I was forced to leave the job because I couldn't handle the Exposer.

¿Nombre y dirección del médico que le está tratando?
Kopas, MD 6624 Fannin Suite 1730
Houston Texas 77030

¿Ha regresado a trabajar? Yes
¿Si ha regresado indique la fecha? 10/7/2013

Firma:
Fecha: 6/24/2015

Exhibit 84

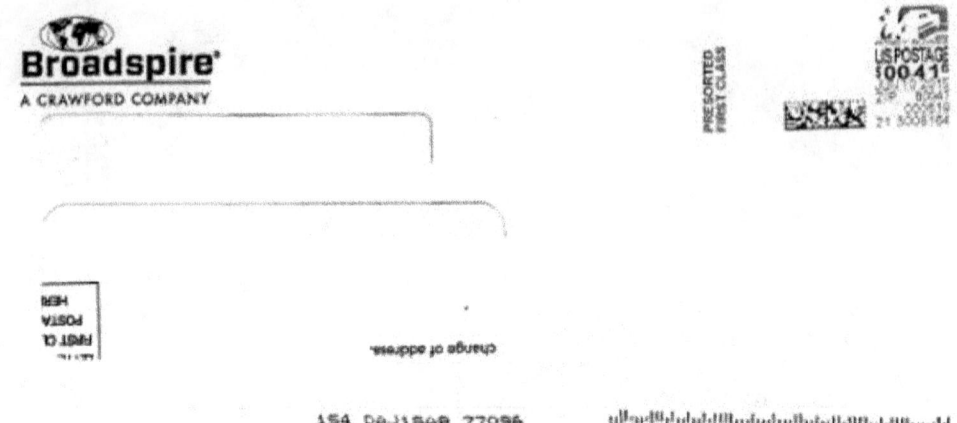

Exhibit 86

Exhibit 87

228

Exhibit 88

A CRAWFORD COMPANY
PO Box 14351
Lexington, KY 40512-4351

NOTICE OF DENIAL OF COMPENSABILITY/LIABILITY AND REFUSAL TO PAY BENEFITS

July 9, 2015

Ellenor Perkins Ratcliff

Houston, TX 77

RE: DATE OF INJURY: 10/4/2013
NATURE OF INJURY:
PART OF BODY: LUNG - Lungs
EMPLOYEE SSN: XXX-XX-
CLAIM #:
CARRIER NAME/TPA NAME: New Hampshire Insurance Co / Broadspire
CARRIER CLAIM #: 188029923-001
EMPLOYER NAME: General Dynamics
EMPLOYER ADDRESS: Gdit Vangent, Inc.
EMPLOYER CITY, STATE, ZIP: Houston, TX 77

On 6/9/2015 we received notice that you reported an on the job injury. We are denying your claim for workers' compensation benefits. Workers' compensation benefits, including medical benefits, are not being paid because:

The Carrier disputes the claimant's alleged injury did not arise out of or in the course and scope of employment for the Employer. No medical to substantiate that an injury occurred within course and scope employment with Employer. Claimant did not report any injury within 30 days to the Employer when she assumed it was a work related injury.

If you do not agree with the denial and refusal to pay benefits, please contact me:

Adjuster's Name: D
Toll Free Telephone #: (2   1 / 8
Fax #/E-mail Address: (8   / D

If we are unable to resolve the issue to your satisfaction, you may contact the Texas Department of Insurance, Division of Workers' Compensation for further assistance. You have the right to request a Benefit Review Conference. You can contact the Division office handling your claim at 1-800-252-7031.

If you would like to receive notices such as this by facsimile or e-mail, please contact me and provide your facsimile number or e-mail address.

Please note that making a false or fraudulent workers' compensation claim is a crime that may result in fines and/or imprisonment.

Cc:

Exhibit 89

Ellenor Perkins Ratcliff

Houston, TX

77096250902

Exhibit 90

Case Status

E :om>   Thu, Jul 16, 2015, 6:54 PM
to M

Good Evening,

Attorney Curry, I spoke with Norma on June 29, 2015. She informed me that I should receive a call by Friday, July 3 and if not by then surly Monday, July 6. July 17 will make it precisely two weeks, this is according to business days since I heard from N   a

I understand you are busy and I would very much appreciate a call on the status of my case. I have and will continue to patiently wait on your call. We are approaching the two years for me to file in court.

Prior to filing my case with you I informed you of the EEOC claim. I need to speak with you in regards to them. I have current information relating to that claim.

Appreciatively,

Ellenor Perkins-Ratcliff

Exhibit 91

E   com>   Fri, Jul 17, 2015, 1:03 PM
to d

Good Afternoon,

I contacted you via phone on July 6 at 10:01a.m., in regards to the claim I email on Jun 26, 2015. I contacted you to verify if the claim was received, since you had not responded. You stated it was received and will be denied, then you told me bye and hung up the phone. As of today my attorney nor I have received a letter of denial. I would like to know why the letter of denial has not been mailed.

Sincerely,

Exhibit 92

Status on Letter of Denial   Inbox x

E   com>   Fri, Jul 17, 2015, 1:06 PM
to d   , M

Good Afternoon,

I contacted you via phone on July 6 at 10:01a.m., in regards to the claim I email on Jun 26, 2015. I contacted you to verify if the claim was received, since you had not responded. You stated it was received and will be denied, then you told me bye and hung up the phone. As of today my attorney nor I have received a letter of denial. I would like to know why the letter of denial has not been mailed.

Sincerely,

Ellenor Perkins Ratcliff

Exhibit 93

Broadspire Notice

E   :om>   Wed, Jul 22, 2015, 2:03 PM
to M

Good Afternoon,

Attorney Curry I have attached the notice dated for July 9, 2015. The envelope is stamped for July 15, 2015.

Appreciatively,

Ellenor Perkins Ratcliff

Exhibit 94

E   :om>   Jul 22, 2015, 2:30 PM
to M

Attorney Curry,

Also, I forgot to mention my recent search to locate the Supervisor whom was over me at the time of working for GDIT. I located him   , his name is A Clem and he works for I   . I   numbers are 888.808.   and 866.715.:   Mr. Clem witnessed the difficult time I was having with GDIT. Mr Clem informed me to speak with HR regarding CSR's spraying perfume at the lockers and desk

Thank you,

EPR

Exhibit 95

D   @choosebroadspire.com   Jul 23, 2015, 1:24 PM
to me, M

I will send another copy, sorry what is your address

D   S. Fields
Senior Claims Examiner-Dallas Service Center
Claim
Broadspire- Dallas Branch

Lexington, KY 40512-4351
phone: 214-640-
fax: 678-937-

Exhibit 96

D   @choosebroadspire.com   Jul 23, 2015, 1:25 PM
to me

Make sure, I have the correct address   please confirm   thanks

D   S. Fields
Senior Claims Examiner-Dallas Service Center
Claim
Broadspire- Dallas Branch

Lexington, KY 40512-4351
phone: 214-640-
fax: 678-937-

Exhibit 97

E _____ com> Jul 23, 2015, 3:18 PM
to D ___ Fields

Hello,

The envelope dated for July 15, 2015, has been received.

Thank you

Exhibit 98

Witness

E _____ om> Wed, Jul 29, 2015, 7:18 AM
to M

Good morning,

I'm aware my claim was initially denied.

I have another witness that can discredit the statement of Z____, on behalf of the HR department.

Z____ lied about helping and this person has proof. Co-worker who worked with me at Gdit is willing to testify.

Sincerely,

Ellenor Perkins Ratcliff

Exhibit 99

Send form to DWC and a copy to insurance carrier
Texas Department of Insurance
Division of Workers' Compensation

CLAIM # Unknown
Carrier Claim # 188029923-00

NOTICE OF REPRESENTATION OR WITHDRAWAL OF REPRESENTATION
GENERAL CLAIM AND REPRESENTATIVE IDENTIFICATION INFORMATION

Section I. Injured Employee Information

- 1a. Last Name: Perkins-Ratcliff
- 1b. First Name: Ellenor
- 1c. Middle Name: Yvette
- 2. Code: 832
- 5. Date of Injury: 10/14/2013
- 6b. City: Houston
- Zip: 77086

Section III. Representative Information

- 13b. First Name: Marlo
- 13c. Middle Name: L
- 14b. City: Houston
- 14c. State: TX
- 14d. Zip Code: 77024
- 16. Firm Name: Law Office of ML Curry
- 19a. Phone Area Code: 713

NOTICE OF REPRESENTATION

☒ My representation began on: May 14, 2015. I am not aware of any other person or attorney representing this injured employee at this time.

Date Signed: 5/14/2015
Representative's Signature — Date Signed: 5·14·15

NOTICE OF WITHDRAWAL OF REPRESENTATION

Date Signed: 8·21·15

DWC FORM-150 (Rev. 10/05) Page 1   DIVISION OF WORKERS' COMPENSATION

Exhibit 100

Law Office of Curry
Houston, TX 77024

NORTH HOUSTON TX 773
28 AUG 2015 PM 2 L

Ms. Ellenor Perkins-Radcliff
Houston, Texas

77096250902

Exhibit 101

6B

ATTORNEYS AND COUNSELORS AT LAW

STUART
August 26, 2015

VIA FIRST CLASS MAIL

Ellenor Perkins Ratcliff

Houston, TX 77

Re: **Potential Case**

Dear Mrs. Ratcliff,

After a careful review of the facts you have provided this Firm, we have decided that we cannot assist you with your potential claim.

I certainly understand and respect the wrong you feel has been done to you. The decision not to take on your case was a difficult one to make. A variety of factors, many of which have nothing to do with the nature or quality of your potential case, entered into the decision. Nothing we have discussed or have set forth in this letter is an expression of our view of the likelihood of success or the desirability of filing suit. Thus, if you wish to pursue this matter, you should promptly seek the advice of other counsel.

Please note that this Firm has not taken any formal action on your behalf, nor will we be taking any action. Your claim may be subject to one or more statutes of limitation, meaning a lawsuit on your claims must be filed within a certain period of time, or your claim will be forever barred. Because of this, it is important that if you are interested in pursuing this matter through another law firm, that you do so immediately if you wish to preserve your right to sue.

Mr   has asked me to personally thank you for considering our Firm for representation. We hope we have been of some assistance to you and again thank you for allowing our Firm the opportunity to consider your case. Please feel free to contact us in the future. Since we are not undertaking representation, we are closing our file regarding this matter.

Sincerely,

(
For the Firm

(

Exhibit 102

Exhibit 103

Exhibit 104

EEOC documentation and Resignation letter

E   com>   Fri, Sep 4, 2015, 2:31 PM
to secretary

Hello,

Attached is a copy of the following.

EEOC Intake Questionnaire. 4 pages.
Additional Information, Attachment 3 to question 6 on Intake Questionnaire. 1 page
Resignation Letter. 2 pages
EEOC Right to Sue. 2 pages Form161
Charge of Discrimination. 2 pages Form 5

GDIT Case Informa...

Exhibit 105

6C

THE   LAW FIRM, PLLC

ATTORNEY AT LAW

*Board Certified-Labor and Employment Law
Texas Board of Legal Specialization

HOUSTON, TX 77098

September 8, 2015

Ms. Ellenor Perkins Ratcliff   <u>Via E-mail</u>

Houston, Texas 77...

RE: Potential Claims

Dear Ms. Ratcliff:

I have reviewed the information and documents you provided to me. This letter shall serve to confirm that after careful consideration, I have determined that I will be unable to take your case. This decision is not an indication or evaluation of the merits of your potential case and you are encouraged to seek alternate counsel should you wish to pursue this matter further. Therefore, this letter shall serve to confirm that The   Law Firm, PLLC does not currently represent you in this matter or any other.

In addition, please be advised that there are statutes of limitation as well as certain administrative deadlines applicable to any claims you may seek to assert. We have not attempted to determine when your claim(s) arose or what time constraints apply to your specific case. Should you desire to further pursue your potential claim(s), please note the deadline found on your right to sue letter from the Equal Employment Opportunity Commission (E.E.O.C). More specifically, you have 90 days from the date you received your right to sue letter from the EEOC in which to bring a lawsuit in a court of competent jurisdiction on these claims. Should you fail to take timely action, you will be barred from pursuing such claims for damages. Thus, it is important that you act promptly to insure that your rights are protected. You may also choose to contact your initial referring attorneys or the Houston Lawyer Referral Service at 1-800-289-HLRS for assistance in locating other attorneys that may be able to assist you in this matter.

Wishing you success in your future endeavors, I remain.

Very truly yours,

Exhibit 106

E   :om>   Wed, Oct 7, 2015 at 11:04 AM
To: M   l@aol.com>

Good morning,

I'm aware my claim was initially denied.

I have another witness that can discredit the statement of Z   , on behalf of the HR department.

Z   lied about helping and this person has proof. Co-worker who worked with me at Gdit is willing to testify.

Sincerely,

Ellenor Perkins Ratcliff

Exhibit 107

Ellenor   :om>   Wed, Oct 7, 2015 at 11:58 AM
To: M   @aol.com>

Good Morning,

Thank you for responding to the email. However, I am pursuing the company on my own in federal court. The EEOC will also be dismantled.

God is on my side and he's more than the EEOC and Gdit against me.

I wish you all blessings and I'm grateful for receiving your assistance.

Sincerely,

Ellenor Perkins Ratcliff

Exhibit 108

E   :om>   Tue, Jan 19, 2016, 4:04 PM
to M

This is the action others and myself are taking. We are standing to the end, just as God has instructed.

Exhibit 109

RE: Findlaw FirmSite Message From .com : Contact

to me

@amglaw.com

Feb 27, 2018, 4:05 PM

Dear Ms. Ratcliff:

I am in receipt of your e-mail. Unfortunately due to our office's present caseload and trial commitments, we are unable to consider representing you in any claims you may have as outlined in your email. If you desire to pursue further action, I strongly recommend you seek legal counsel immediately to advise you with respect to the statute(s) of limitations (time restrictions in which you may file legal claims) and to provide representation without delay. One source of referral to counsel willing to review matters such as yours is your local County Bar Association.

Neither this office nor any referring lawyer are your lawyers. We only agreed to review this case and have no obligation to file a lawsuit or claim to protect your rights. No written attorney/client retainer has been entered into. Our statements are a matter of opinion only and we can make no guarantees. You are free to obtain and solicit other legal advice and we encourage you to do so. Wishing you the best of luck in your pursuit of justice, I am

Very truly yours,

Los Angeles, CA 90048

Exhibit 110

U.S. EQUAL EMPLOYMENT OPPORTUNITY COMMISSION
Houston District Office

1201 Louisiana Street, 6th Floor
Houston, TX 77002
Intake Information Group: (800) 669-4000
Intake Information Group TTY: (800) 669-6820
Houston Status Line: (866) 408-8075
Houston Direct Dial: (713) 651-4900
TTY (713) 651-4901
FAX (713) 651-4902

July 7, 2105

Ms. Ellenor Perkins-Ratcliff

Houston, TX 77

Dear Ms. Perkins-Ratcliff:

This is in response to your April 10, 2015, inquiry to President Obama concerning the charge of employment discrimination you filed with the Equal Employment Opportunity Commission (EEOC), against General Dynamics Information Technology – GDIT (EEOC Charge No. 460-2014-01770). The President has asked this office to respond directly to you.

You forwarded a copy of a "claim" to the President and asked for action. As you know, we responded to your April 10, 2015, "NOTICE OF RIGHT TO REQUEST SUBSTANTIAL WEIGHT REVIEW" by letter dated April 29, 2015. A copy of that letter is attached. We treated that correspondence as a request for reconsideration and ultimately denied that request, because we did not believe there was enough evidence to conclude that a violation of the statutes we enforce had occurred.

You were not accorded a substantial weight review, because that process only occurs where a Fair Employment Practices Agency (FEPA)(such as, for example, the Texas Workforce Commission) has made a determination on a charge that was dual filed with both a FEPA and the EEOC. Your charge was not filed with a FEPA, but rather was filed directly with the EEOC, so a substantial weight review is not possible.

It is important to note that your request did not extend or eliminate the statutory 90-day period for pursuing this matter in court. If you do not (or did not) file a private lawsuit in this matter within 90 days of your receipt of the **March 26, 2015,** final dismissal notice, your right to sue for this charge will be (or was) lost and cannot be restored by the EEOC.

We hope this information is helpful to you.

Sincerely,

Martin S. Ebel,
Acting District Director

enclosure

cc: The White House

Exhibit 111

EQUAL EMPLOYMENT OPPORTUNITY COMMISSION
HOUSTON DISTRICT OFFICE
TOTAL PLAZA
1201 LOUISIANA STREET - 6TH FLOOR
HOUSTON, TX 77002

OFFICIAL BUSINESS
Penalty for Private Use, $300

Exhibit 112

Ellenor Perkins Ratcliff

Houston, Texas 77

President Barack Obama
The White House
1600 Pennsylvania Avenue, NW
Washington, DC 20500

August 6, 2015

Dear President Obama:

Thank you for instructing the EEOC to respond to my complaint. The EEOC has failed to give me justice, despite the documentation that was submitted when I filed the charge. Honestly, the EEOC is bias and corrupt. I'm asking for a federal investigation to be launched against the EEOC. My case was not handled accordingly. We are requesting for my charge to be handled by the governing authority of EEOC. March 20, 2014, the charge was recorded by EEOC. Enclosed are copies of the application packet (1A) – EEOC Intake Questionnaire, additional information packet (1B) – submitted with EEOC Intake Questionnaire, supporting documentation packet (2) – submitted to GDIT, 10/3 and 10/17 are copies of patient summary for doctor visit, I misplaced two excuses for those days but they were submitted to GDIT; Correspondences packet (3) – web printout on EEOC dated 3/10/14 and conversations between EEOC and I.

In the month of March 2015, I had a verbal conversation with Jeremy Crosbie. I was told, "GDIT is not obligated to enforce their policy." There is a witness who heard the entire conversation.

Per Mr. Cosbie, GDIT stated I provided no supporting documents. Packet (1A) and (13) has highlighted details to support charge. There is inaccurate information in the letter that was dated for April 29, 2015, from the EEOC. My first concern is, in the letter EEOC claims, GDIT suggested I wear a mask at the expense of the company, which was a lie. My second concern is, I first contacted Zandra Bosie regarding CSR's spraying perfume after I spoke with my supervisor and informed him Zandra was not responding to the email sent on October 29, 2013. I contacted Zandra by email October 29, 2013, not January 29, 2014. EEOC stated GDIT has disputed everything in my claim.

1

Exhibit 113

This leads me to believe EEOC didn't investigate properly. How could they have missed the packet with the emails and the letters that I submitted from my doctor? President Obama, that email is listed in packet (1B) page 6. My third concern is, supporting documentation was obtained and given to my supervisor, Austin Clem. Zandra Bosie also informed me that she received the doctor excuses and statements. Packet (2) contains the supporting documents that were given to GDIT, except for pages dated 4/14/2014 and 7/28/2014. In packet (1B) EECC was given two of the supporting documents. I don't believe EEOC requested to speak with any of the employees who worked for GDIT. EEOC never stated it requested contact information of staff listed in my charge.

The findings of the EEOC are contrary to the law and the facts are inaccurate.

1. In the beginning of this process with EEOC, I asked, "Do I need to file with the other agency, FEPA?" I was told, "No, the information would be shared."
2. The packet labeled (3A) has information regarding filing a charge. It states, "... if you file a charge with either EEOC or a FEPA, the charge also will be automatically filed with the other agency. This process, which is defined as dual filing, helps to protect charging party rights under both federal and state or local law.
3. Packets (3B) and (3C), has a form on the last page, it's the CP Enclosure. On this form it gives information on, NOTICE OF RIGHT TO REQUEST SUBSTANTIAL WEIGHT REVIEW.
4. Packet (3D), Written request for SUBSTANTIAL WEIGHT REVIEW, although EEOC didn't follow the law.
5. Packet (3E), dated April 29, 2015 states, "The EEOC has no obligation to reconsider the final findings we have issued on a charge. EEOC Directors, therefore, may decline to review a request to reconsider an EEOC final finding unless the Charging Party presents substantial new and relevant evidence, or a persuasive argument that the EEOC's prior decision was contrary to law or the facts."
6. Packet (3F), Is the letter I received after you asked EEOC to handle this issue directly. In this letter I was told, "You were not accorded a substantial weight review, because that process only occurs where a Fair Employment Practices Agency (FEPA) (such as , for

Exhibit 114

example, the Texas Workforce Commission) has made a determination on a charge that was dual filed with both FEPA and the EEOC. Your charge was not filed with a FEPA, but rather was filed directly with the EEOC, so a substantial weight review is not possible."

The verbal response from Mr. Crosbie and packets (3A), (3B), (3C), (3E) and (3F) are all contradictory.

I'm requesting for a federal investigation of the EEOC. My expectations are for the charge to be reopened, reviewed by the governing authority of EEOC and statues set forth by EEOC be removed based on corruption and inaccurate information. EEOC has acted contrary to the law and has chosen to ignore documents which contained information to support my charge. I no longer believe justice will come from the EEOC acting on it's on.

President Obama, I'm only asking for justice to be served.

Sincerely,

Ellenor Perkins Ratcliff

7015 0640 0006 5089 8715

U.S. Postal Service™
CERTIFIED MAIL® RECEIPT
Domestic Mail Only

For delivery information, visit our website at www.usps.com

WASHINGTON, DC 20500
OFFICIAL USE

Certified Mail Fee $ $3.45

Extra Services & Fees (check box, add fee as appropriate)
- Return Receipt (hardcopy) $ $0.00
- Return Receipt (electronic) $ $0.00
- Certified Mail Restricted Delivery $ $0.00
- Adult Signature Required $ $0.00
- Adult Signature Restricted Delivery $ $0.00

Postage $ $2.74

Total Postage and Fees $ $6.19

0039
09

Postmark Here

08/06/2015

Sent To President Barack Obama, The White House

Street and Apt. No., or PO Box No. 1600 Pennsylvania Ave, NW

City, State, ZIP+4® Washington, DC 20500

PS Form 3800, April 2015 See Reverse for Instructions

3

Exhibit 115

Ellenor Perkins Ratcliff
Houston, Texas 77

Certified Mail#7015 0920 0002 0409 1466

1E

Attorney General Lynch
U.S. Department of Justice
950 Pennsylvania Avenue, NW
Washington, DC 20530-0001

September 1, 2015

Dear U.S. Attorney General Loretta E. Lynch:

Congradulations on your nomination! There is a situation that I would like to address with you. I've faught for justice from the beginning. My past employer, General Dynamics Information Technology, neglected to protect my rights as a human, an employee and as an individual with a disability. The EEOC has violated my Civil Rights. A charge was filed with the EEOC, but the EEOC has fail to deliver justice, even after President Obama instructed EEOC to handle the issue. This is my last resort. The EEOC failed to contact witness and only used the statement of GDIT alone. Honestly, the EEOC is bias and corrupt. I'm asking for a federal investigation to be launched against the EEOC. My case was not handled accordingly. We are requesting for my charge to be handled by the governing authority of EEOC. March 20, 2014, the charge was recorded by EEOC. Enclosed are copies of the application packet (1A) – EEOC Intake Questionnaire, additional information packet (1B) – submitted with EEOC Intake Questionnaire, supporting documentation packet (2) – submitted to GDIT, 10/3 and 10/17 are copies of patient summary for doctor visit, I misplaced two excuses for those days, but they were all submitted to GDIT; Correspondences packet (3) – web printout on EEOC dated 3/10/14 and conversations between EEOC and I.

In the month of March 2015, I had a verbal conversation with Jeremy Crosbie. I was told, "GDIT is not obligated to enforce their policy." There is a witness who heard the entire conversation. Per Mr. Cosbie, GDIT stated I provided no supporting documents. Packet (1A) and (1B) has highlighted details to support charge. There is inaccurate information in the letter that was dated for April 29, 2015, from the EEOC. My first concern is, in the letter EEOC claims, GDIT suggested I wear a mask at the expense of the company, which was a lie. My second

Exhibit 118

Ellenor Perkins Ratcliff Certified Mail#7015 0920 0002 0409 1473

Houston, Texas 77(

General Dynamics Information Technology
Attn: Lesley P. Marlin
3211 Jermantown Road
Fairfax, VA 22030

September 11, 2015

Settlement Letter

Dear Lesley P. Marlin:

General Dynamics Information Technology neglected to protect my rights as a human, an employee and as an individual with a disability. GDIT violated my Civil Rights. We have asked for a federal investigation to be launched. GDIT will be held accountable for its inactions, one way or another. The actions we are prepared to take will make national news. This will not rest until the Lord delivers GDIT into my hands. GDIT has 10 business days, from the date of this letter to respond. We can settle out of federal court. Otherwise, we are prepared with witnesses, employees and documentation that will prove GDIT's negligence.

As a previous employee of GDIT, I was employed from September 9, 2013 to February 17, 2014. I suffered due to the inactions of GDIT. It began the month of October, after CSR's were moved to the call center floor. GDIT refused to comply with federal rules and regulations. GDIT's, human resource department has given false statements regarding my difficulty on the job. We have never experienced such negligence. We are going to fight for the correction of such behavior, in an effort to prevent others from suffering the same fate. GDIT showed blatant disregard for my rights, I could have died.

Not one time after the briefing, did GDIT instruct CSR's regarding your section on personal hygiene, nor were supervisors asked to enforce such standards; yet you enforced secure floor policy and dress code (acceptable attire) on a weekly, if not daily basis. GDIT managers walked the floor with a wand, to detect electronic devices and fired employees who violated secure floor policy. GDIT even fired employees who violated dress code on a consistent basis (acceptable attire).

Exhibit 119

We are demanding   dollars as an out of court settlement. The settlement will only be accepted in the form of a cashier's check. The settlement can be mailed to: Ellenor Perkins Ratcliff,   Houston, Texas 77   . If we proceed to court, that amount will double and possibly triple. We will file for gross negligence due to the reckless inaction of GDIT. We will ask the judge for punitive and compensatory damages. Every conversation and every form of documentation has been recorded; it has been delivered to individuals who will take this case upon themselves should any situation arise, preventing me from doing so.

GDIT's management ignored my plea; all I asked for was the enforcement of policy. GDIT blatantly disregarded my rights. GDIT will be brought to justice. On April 10, 2015, the Lord said to me, "Anyone who plans to harm my family, friends or associates for standing up for my rights will be cursed. The plans you make to harm us, will be carried out into the lives of your own. You will be cursed and that of your children." Justice shall prevail in Jesus name, Amen!

Sincerely,

Ellenor Perkins Ratcliff and Counsel

Enclosed: Correspondences between CMS and I.

CC: President Barack Obama, Attorney General Loretta E. Lynch and Counsel

248

Exhibit 120

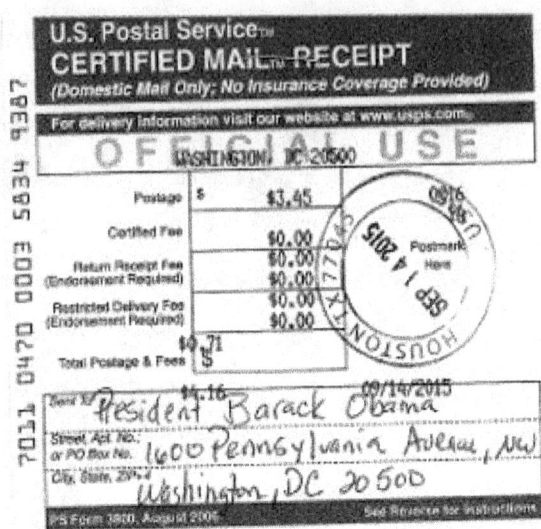

Ellenor Perkins Ratcliff

Houston, Texas

President Barack Obama
The White House
1600 Pennsylvania Avenue, NW
Washington, DC 20500

September 14, 2015

Dear President Obama:

Thank you once again for your assistance in the matter of U. S. Equal Employment Opportunity Commission and General Dynamics Information Technology. The last packet we sent to you was dated August 6, 2015; the packet contained detailed information regarding my claim of injustice and corruption among EEOC and GDIT. The enclosed documents are correspondences between General Dynamics Information Technology, CMS and I. We have contacted Attorney General Loretta Lynch in an effort to launch a federal investigation. We will await the findings of the attorney general's investigation of EEOC and GDIT, as we move forward in pursuit of GDIT in federal court, should the matter be taken to that extent.

Sincerely,

Ellenor Perkins Ratcliff

Exhibit 121

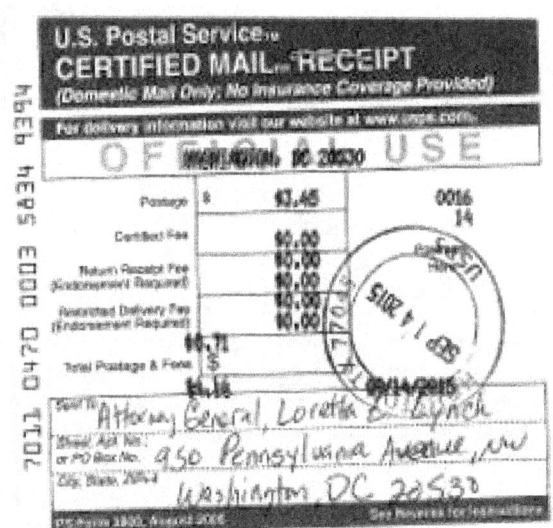

Ellenor Perkins Ratcliff

Houston, Texas

Attorney General Lynch
U.S. Department of Justice
950 Pennsylvania Avenue, NW
Washington, DC 20530-0001

September 14, 2015

Dear U.S. Attorney General Loretta E. Lynch:

Please excuse the grammar errors that were in the packet sent on September 1, 2015. The enclosed documents are correspondences between General Dynamics Information Technology, CMS and I. We are going to await the findings of your investigation of EEOC and GDIT, as we move forward in pursuit of GDIT in federal court, should the matter be taken to that extent.

Sincerely,

Ellenor Perkins Ratcliff

Exhibit 122

GENERAL DYNAMICS
Information Technology

L   Pate Marlin
Assistant General Counsel
Direct Dial: (703) 995-
@gdit.com

September 25, 2015

VIA FEDERAL EXPRESS
Ellenor Perkins Ratcliff

Houston, Texas

Re: Your Demand Letter

Dear Ms. Ratcliff:

I am writing on behalf of General Dynamics Information Technology, Inc. ("GDIT") in response to your September 11, 2015 letter demanding $100,   as "an out of court settlement."

GDIT has previously responded to your claims when they were pending before the Equal Employment Opportunity Commission ("EEOC"). The EEOC thoroughly investigated your claims, and based on its investigation, it found no probable cause to support your claims.

Quite simply, GDIT regards this matter as closed.

Sincerely,

L   Marlin

Exhibit 123

How to Submit an Employment Discrimination Complaint

Get MS Word Viewer or MS Excel Viewer.

On this page:

- Overview
- Complaint Requirements
- How to Submit a Complaint

Overview

If you believe you may have been discriminated against in employment and meet the complaint requirements listed on this page, you may submit a discrimination complaint through the TWC Civil Rights Division.

The Civil Rights Division conducts neutral investigations and gathers information to determine if discrimination has occurred under the Texas Labor Code. We work in cooperation with the federal Equal Employment Opportunity Commission (EEOC) to resolve employment discrimination allegations.

When you submit an employment discrimination complaint with the Civil Rights Division, it is automatically submitted with EEOC through our Worksharing Agreement. You cannot submit with both the Civil Rights Division and the EEOC.

These are a few of the most common employment discrimination allegations:

- I was not hired because of my disability.
- I was demoted because of my national origin.
- I was terminated because of my race.
- I was harassed by co-workers because of my age.
- I was denied benefits because of my pregnancy.

Return to Top

Complaint Requirements

How to Submit a Complaint

You can submit an employment discrimination complaint to us by e-mail, by postal mail or in person (not by phone). You must submit your complaint within 180 days from the date of the discrimination.

Exhibit 124

HR received record of perceived disability from 10/4/13 to 2/13/14. GOIT made the employment decision to violate company policy and harass through excessive couching and given a difficult time forcing me out. GOIT was asked to accomodate by the enforcement of policy on perfume/cologne which "negatively effect others in the workplace." My Asthmatic condition was aggravated on a daily basis.

Employment decision to violate company policy is discrimination against record of perceived disability and constructive discharge.

Violations of ADA & ~~ADAAA~~ ADAAA has taken place and this amendment must be handled accordingly.

"Every individual who puts a hand or mouth to this and does nothing for the justice of my family and I will be cursed. The Lord will bring Terror upon your house and you will lose all you treasure." — Jesus

Exhibit 125

AMENDED-EPR   1A

U.S. EQUAL EMPLOYMENT OPPORTUNITY COMMISSION

Thank you for using the EEOC Assessment System. The information you gave us indicates that your situation may be covered by the laws we enforce. If you want to file a charge, you can start the process by filling out the Intake Questionnaire, signing it, and either bringing it or mailing it to the EEOC office listed below right away. If you live within 50 miles of the EEOC office listed below, we recommend that you bring the completed questionnaire with you to this office to discuss your situation.

EEOC Houston District Office
Total Plaza
1201 Louisiana, 6th Floor
Houston, TX 77002

If you would like to bring the questionnaire to us in person instead of mailing it to us, please click http://www.eeoc.gov/field/index.cfm to find out the office hours of the EEOC office closest to you. If you would like to fax the questionnaire to us, please click http://www.eeoc.gov/field/index.cfm to find out the fax number of the office nearest to you.

You should be aware that filing a charge can take up to two hours. If you find that you are having difficulty completing the questionnaire on your own, you may call the number below for assistance.

Please be sure to:

- Answer all questions as completely as possible.
- Include the location where you work(ed) or applied.
- Complete all pages and sign the last page.
- Attach additional pages if you need more space to complete your responses.

You can find out more information about the laws we enforce and our charge-filing procedures on our website at www.eeoc.gov.

If you want to file a charge about job discrimination, there are time limits to file the charge. In many States that limit is 300 days from the date you knew about the harm or negative job action, but in other States it is 180 days. To protect your rights, it is important that you fill out the questionnaire, sign it, and bring it or send it to us right away.

Filling out and bringing us or sending us this questionnaire does not mean that you have filed a charge. This questionnaire will help us look at your situation and figure out if you are covered by the laws we enforce. If you live within 50 miles of the office listed above, we recommend that you bring the completed questionnaire to us to discuss your situation. If you mail the completed questionnaire to us, someone from the EEOC should contact you by mail or by phone within 30 days. If you don't hear from us in 30 days, please call us at 1-800-669-4000.

Sincerely,

U.S. Equal Employment Opportunity Commission

Phone: 1-800-669-4000   TTY: 1-800-669-6820   Internet: www.eeoc.gov   Email: info@eeoc.gov

I, Ellenor Perkins Ratcliff_____ have sent a copy of this document to all parties in Case: 4:15-cv-03038.

Exhibit 126

AMENDED EEER,

The EEOC failed to process my complaint properly.
The EEOC didn't advise me of Record Of Perceived Disability. – Ellenor P. Ratcliff

EQUAL EMPLOYMENT OPPORTUNITY COMMISSION
INTAKE QUESTIONNAIRE

Please immediately complete the entire form and return it to the U.S. Equal Employment Opportunity Commission ("EEOC"). **REMEMBER**, a charge of employment discrimination must be filed within the time limits imposed by law, generally within 180 days or in some places 300 days of the alleged discrimination. Upon receipt, this form will be reviewed to determine EEOC coverage. Answer all questions as completely as possible, and attach additional pages if needed to complete your response(s). If you do not know the answer to a question, answer by stating "not known." If a question is not applicable, write "n/a." Please Print.

1. **Personal Information**

Last Name: Perkins Ratcliff   First Name: Ellenor   MI: Y
Street or Mailing Address: _____   Apt Or Unit #: ____
City: Houston   County: Harris   State: Texas   ZIP: ____
Phone Numbers: Home: (___) _____   Work: (N/A)
Cell: (___) _____   Email Address: _____
Date of Birth: _____   Sex: Male ☐ Female ☒   Do You Have a Disability? ☒ Yes ☐ No

Please answer each of the next three questions.   i. Are you Hispanic or Latino? ☐ Yes ☒ No
ii. What is your Race? Please choose all that apply.   ☒ American Indian or Alaska Native   ☐ Asian   ☐ White
☒ Black or African American   ☐ Native Hawaiian or Other Pacific Islander
iii. What is your National Origin (country of origin or ancestry)? African Native American (Blackfoot)

Please Provide The Name Of A Person We Can Contact If We Are Unable To Reach You:
Name: _____   Relationship: _____
Address: Same   City: Houston   State: Tx   Zip Code: _____
Home Phone: (___) _____   Other Phone: (N/A)

2. **I believe that I was discriminated against by the following organization(s):** (Check those that apply)
☒ Employer   ☐ Union   ☐ Employment Agency   ☐ Other (Please Specify) _____

Organization Contact Information (If the organization is an employer, provide the address where you actually worked. If you work from home, check here ☐ and provide the address of the office to which you reported.) **If more than one employer is involved, attach additional sheets.**

Organization Name: General Dynamics Information Technology
Address: 3211 Jermantown Road   County: Fairfax
City: Fairfax   State: VA   Zip: 22030   Phone: (703) _____
Type of Business: Information Technology   Job Location if different from Org. Address: 5959 Corporate Dr. Hous., Tx 77036
Human Resources Director or Owner Name: Zack Wentz   Phone: _____
Number of Employees in the Organization at All Locations: Please Check (√) One
☐ Fewer Than 15   ☐ 15 - 100   ☐ 101 - 200   ☐ 201 - 500   ☒ More than 500

3. **Your Employment Data** (Complete as many items as you can)   Are you a Federal Employee? ☐ Yes ☐ No
Date Hired: 09/09/2013   Job Title At Hire: Associate Specialist, Customer Service
Pay Rate When Hired: $11.88   Last or Current Pay Rate: $13.88
Job Title at Time of Alleged Discrimination: Associate Specialist, Cus Service   Date Quit/Discharged: 02/17/2014
Name and Title of Immediate Supervisor: Austin Clem then transferred to Dana Royal

Every individual who puts a hand or mouth to this complaint and does nothing for the justice of this family will be cursed. My father in heaven will bring TERROR upon your house and you will lose all you treasure in Jesus' name, Amen.

Exhibit 127

AMENDED-EPR, The EEOC failed to process my complaint properly.
The EEOC didn't advise me of Record Of Perceived Disability. – Ellenor P. Ratcliff

If Job Applicant, Date You Applied for Job 09/05/2013   Job Title Applied For Customer Service

4. What is the reason (basis) for your claim of employment discrimination?
FOR EXAMPLE, if you feel that you were treated worse than someone else because of race, you should check the box next to Race. If you feel you were treated worse for several reasons, such as your sex, religion and national origin, you should check all that apply. If you complained about discrimination, participated in someone else's complaint, or filed a charge of discrimination, and a negative action was threatened or taken, you should check the box next to Retaliation.

☐ Race ☐ Sex ☐ Age ☒ Disability ☐ National Origin ☐ Religion ☐ Retaliation ☐ Pregnancy ☐ Color (typically a difference in skin shade within the same race) ☐ Genetic Information; choose which type(s) of genetic information is involved:

☐ i. genetic testing ☐ ii. family medical history ☐ iii. genetic services (genetic services means counseling, education or testing)

If you checked color, religion or national origin, please specify: _____
If you checked genetic information, how did the employer obtain the genetic information? _____

Other reason (basis) for discrimination (Explain). Harassed constantly for Record Of Perceived Disability, ADA/ADAAA Violations.

5. What happened to you that you believe was discriminatory? Include the date(s) of harm, the action(s), and the name(s) and title(s) of the person(s) who you believe discriminated against you. Please attach additional pages if needed.
(Example: 10/02/06 - Discharged by Mr. John Soto, Production Supervisor)

A) Date: 02/17/2014   Action: Constructive Discharge

Name and Title of Person(s) Responsible: Zandra Bosie- HR Business Partner, William Reimer- Manager, Austin Clem- Supervisor
B) Date: 10/3/2013 to 02/13/2014 Action: Harassment for Record Of Perceived Disability, which caused Constructive Discharge.

Name and Title of Person(s) Responsible: Austin Clem- Supervisor and GDIT HR department

6. Why do you believe these actions were discriminatory? Please attach additional pages if needed.
HR received Record Of Perceived Disability from 10/4/13 to 2/13/14. GDIT made the employment decision to violate company policy and harass, through excessive coaching and giving a difficult time forcing me out. GDIT was asked to accommodate by the enforcement of policy, regarding perfume/cologne which, "negatively effect others in the workplace." My Asthmatic condition was aggravated on a daily basis. Violations of ADA and ADAAA has taken place and this amended complaint must be handled properly.

7. What reason(s) were given to you for the acts you consider discriminatory? By whom? His or Her Job Title?
Continued from question 6. Employment decision to violate company policy is Discrimination against Record Of Perceived Disability and Constructive Discharge.

N/A to question 7.

8. Describe who was in the same or similar situation as you and how they were treated. For example, who else applied for the same job you did, who else had the same attendance record, or who else had the same performance? Provide the race, sex, age, national origin, religion, or disability of these individuals, if known, and if it relates to your claim of discrimination. For example, if your complaint alleges race discrimination, provide the race of each person; if it alleges sex discrimination, provide the sex of each person; and so on. Use additional sheets if needed.

Of the persons in the same or similar situation as you, who was treated *better* than you?

A. Full Name	Race, sex, age, national origin, religion or disability	Job Title
N/A		
Description of Treatment		

B. Full Name	Race, sex, age, national origin, religion or disability	Job Title
N/A		
Description of Treatment		

Every individual who puts a hand or mouth to this complaint and does nothing for the justice of this family will be cursed. My father in heaven will bring TERROR upon your house and you will lose all you treasure in Jesus' name, Amen.

Exhibit 128

AMENDED-EPR, The EEOC failed to process my complaint properly.
The EEOC didn't advise me of Record Of Perceived Disability. – Ellenor P. Ratcliff

Of the persons in the same or similar situation as you, who was treated *worse* than you?

A. Full Name	Race, sex, age, national origin, religion or disability	Job Title
N/A		
Description of Treatment		

B. Full Name	Race, sex, age, national origin, religion or disability	Job Title
N/A		
Description of Treatment		

Of the persons in the same or similar situation as you, who was treated the *same* as you?

A. Full Name	Race, sex, age, national origin, religion or disability	Job Title
N/A		
Description of Treatment		

B. Full Name	Race, sex, age, national origin, religion or disability	Job Title
N/A		
Description of Treatment		

Answer questions 9-12 <u>only</u> if you are claiming discrimination based on disability. If not, skip to question 13. Please tell us if you have more than one disability. Please add additional pages if needed.

9. Please check all that apply:
   - [X] Yes, I have a disability
   - [ ] I do not have a disability now but I did have one
   - [ ] No disability but the organization treats me as if I am disabled

10. What is the disability that you believe is the reason for the adverse action taken against you? Does this disability prevent or limit you from doing anything? (e.g., lifting, sleeping, breathing, walking, caring for yourself, working, etc.).

   Asthmatic Condition

11. Do you use medications, medical equipment or anything else to lessen or eliminate the symptoms of your disability?
   Yes [X]   No [ ]
   If "Yes," what medication, medical equipment or other assistance do you use?

   Privileged information between my doctor and I.

12. Did you ask your employer for any changes or assistance to do your job because of your disability?
   Yes [X]   No [ ]
   If "YES", when did you ask? Please Contact Employer   How did you ask (verbally or in writing)? Verbally/ Email
   Who did you ask? (Provide full name and job title of person)
   Zandra Bosie- HR Business Partner, Will Reimer- Manager and Aust em- Supervisor were asked.
   Describe the changes or assistance that you asked for:

   Please contact employer.

   How did your employer respond to your request?

   Please contact employer.

[Margin text, left side:] Every individual who puts a hand or mouth to this complaint and does nothing for the justice of this family will be cursed. My father in heaven will bring TERROR upon your house and you will lose all you treasure in Jesus' name, Amen.

[Margin text, right side:] Every individual who puts a hand or mouth to this complaint and does nothing for the justice of this family will be cursed. My father in heaven will bring TERROR upon your house and you will lose all you treasure in Jesus' name, Amen.

Exhibit 129

AMENDED-EPR, The EEOC failed to process my complaint properly.
The EEOC didn't advise me of Record Of Perceived Disability. – Ellenor P. Ratcliff

13. Are there any witnesses to the alleged discriminatory incidents? If yes, please identify them below and tell us what they will say. (Please attach additional pages if needed to complete your response)

A. Full Name	Job Title	Address & Phone Number
N/A		

What do you believe this person will tell us?

B. Full Name	Job Title	Address & Phone Number
N/A		

What do you believe this person will tell us?

14. Have you filed a charge previously in this matter with EEOC or another agency? Yes ☐ No ☒

15. If you have filed a complaint with another agency, provide name of agency and date of filing:
Amended complaint, filing under disability- Harassment and Constructive Discharge due to being forced out. EEOC 03/20 /14

16. Have you sought help about this situation from a union, an attorney, or any other source? Yes ☒ No ☐
Provide name of organization, name of person you spoke with and date of contact. Results, if any?

Who I have spoken with is Attorney-Client privileged.

Please check one of the boxes below to tell us what you would like us to do with the information you are providing on this questionnaire. If you would like to file a charge of job discrimination, you must do so either within 180 days from the day you knew about the discrimination, or within 300 days from the day you knew about the discrimination if the employer is located in a place where a state or local government agency enforces laws similar to the EEOC's laws. If you do not file a charge of discrimination within the time limits, you will lose your rights. If you would like more information before filing a charge or you have concerns about EEOC's notifying the employer, union, or employment agency about your charge, you may wish to check Box 1. If you want to file a charge, you should check Box 2.

Box 1 ☐ I want to talk to an EEOC employee before deciding whether to file a charge. I understand that by checking this box, I have not filed a charge with the EEOC. I also understand that I could lose my rights if I do not file a charge in time.

Box 2 ☒ I want to file a charge of discrimination, and I authorize the EEOC to look into the discrimination I described above. I understand that the EEOC must give the employer, union, or employment agency that I accuse of discrimination information about the charge, including my name. I also understand that the EEOC can only accept charges of job discrimination based on race, color, religion, sex, national origin, disability, age, genetic information, or retaliation for opposing discrimination.

_____   November 17, 2015
Signature   Today's Date

PRIVACY ACT STATEMENT: This form is covered by the Privacy Act of 1974: Public Law 93-579. Authority for requesting personal data and the uses thereof are:
1. FORM NUMBER/TITLE/DATE. EEOC Intake Questionnaire (9/20/08)
2. AUTHORITY. 42 U.S.C. § 2000e-5(b), 29 U.S.C. § 211, 29 U.S.C. § 626. 42 U.S.C. 12117(a), 42 USC §2000ff-6.
3. PRINCIPAL PURPOSE. The purpose of this questionnaire is to solicit information about claims of employment discrimination, determine whether the EEOC has jurisdiction over those claims, and provide charge filing counseling, as appropriate. Consistent with 29 CFR 1601.12(b) and 29 CFR 1626.8(c), this questionnaire may serve as a charge if it meets the elements of a charge.
4. ROUTINE USES. EEOC may disclose information from this form to other state, local and federal agencies as appropriate or necessary to carry out the Commission's functions, or if EEOC becomes aware of a civil or criminal law violation. EEOC may also disclose information to respondents in litigation, to congressional offices in response to inquiries from parties to the charge, to disciplinary committees investigating complaints against attorneys representing the parties to the charge, or to federal agencies inquiring about hiring or security clearance matters
5. WHETHER DISCLOSURE IS MANDATORY OR VOLUNTARY AND EFFECT ON INDIVIDUAL FOR NOT PROVIDING INFORMATION. Providing of this information is voluntary but the failure to do so may hamper the Commission's investigation of a charge. It is not mandatory that this form be used to provide the requested information.

Exhibit 130

EEOC Form 5 (11/09)

CHARGE OF DISCRIMINATION	Charge Presented To:	Agency(ies) Charge No(s):
This form is affected by the Privacy Act of 1974. See enclosed Privacy Act Statement and other information before completing this form.	☐ FEPA ☒ EEOC	460-2016-00589

Texas Workforce Commission Civil Rights Division and EEOC
State or local Agency, if any

Name (indicate Mr., Ms., Mrs.): Mr. Elienor Perkins - Ratcliff
Home Phone (Incl. Area Code):
Date of Birth:

Street Address — **City, State and ZIP Code**: Houston, TX 77

Named is the Employer, Labor Organization, Employment Agency, Apprenticeship Committee, or State or Local Government Agency That I Believe Discriminated Against Me or Others. (If more than two, list under PARTICULARS below.)

Name: GENERAL DYNAMICS INFORMATION TECHNOLOGY
No. Employees, Members: 500 or More
Phone No. (Include Area Code):
Street Address: 3211 Jermantown Rd, Fairfax, VA 22030

DISCRIMINATION BASED ON (Check appropriate box(es).):
☐ RACE ☐ COLOR ☐ SEX ☐ RELIGION ☐ NATIONAL ORIGIN
☐ RETALIATION ☐ AGE ☒ DISABILITY ☐ GENETIC INFORMATION
☐ OTHER (Specify)

DATE(S) DISCRIMINATION TOOK PLACE
Earliest: 10-04-2013   Latest: 02-17-2014
☒ CONTINUING ACTION

THE PARTICULARS ARE (If additional paper is needed, attach extra sheet(s)):

Human Resources received a Record of Perceived Disability from October 4, 2013 to February 13, 2014. General Dynamics Information Technology (GDIT) made the employment decision to violate company policy and harass, through excessive coaching and giving a difficult time, forcing me out. GDIT was asked to accommodate by the enforcement of policy, regarding perfume/cologne which, "negatively effect others in the workplace." My Asthmatic condition was aggravated on a daily basis. Violations of ADA and ADAA has taken place and this amended complaint must be handled properly.

Employment decision to violate company policy is discrimination against Record of Perceived Disability and Constructive Discharge.

I want this charge filed with both the EEOC and the State or local Agency, if any. I will advise the agencies if I change my address or phone number and I will cooperate fully with them in the processing of my charge in accordance with their procedures.

I declare under penalty of perjury that the above is true and correct.

Date: Nov 19, 2015

NOTARY – When necessary for State and Local Agency Requirements

I swear or affirm that I have read the above charge and that it is true to the best of my knowledge, information and belief.
SIGNATURE OF COMPLAINANT

SUBSCRIBED AND SWORN TO BEFORE ME THIS DATE (month, day, year)

Exhibit 131

November 20, 2015 at 9:35am

President Barack Obama and Attorney General L Lynch

Good Morning,

Prior communication with you and AG Lynch has been conducted in private and there has been no resolve.

We are asking for every charge Jeremy Crosbie of EEOC, allegedly investigated to be reviewed by an outside Auditing Agency. This agency must have no business or financial connections with the U.S. Government.

Also, I'm asking for you to reinstate my charge. Jeremy Crosbie is a racist and I was not given due process. General Dynamics Information Technology Violated ADA and ADAAA Violations.

There is proof and we will not rest until General Dynamics Information Technology, Jeremy Crosbie and Martin S. Ebel are brought to Justice.

Jeremy Crosbie and Martin S. Ebel have participated in public corruption and political rights violations.
We demand JUSTICE!

To all listed in hashtag, please join me in this fight for justice. Some of you have received my support through voting and etc; now I stand in the need of your support. Thank you, for your support in advance.

#EndPublicCorruptioninAmerica #EndPoliticalRightsViolations #AfricanAmericanDisabledCitizensMatter #MichaelPWilliams #MelissaHarris-Perry #JamesRucker #TriciaRose #CynthiaMcKinney #SylvesterTurner #RachelDolezal
#ADA.gov #ADAAA #CornelWest #MajoraCarter #VanJones #RosaClemente #HenryLouisGatesJr. #MichaelEricDyson #RandallRobinson #CraigWatkins #AlSharpton #JesseJackson #AliceWalker #BoyceWatkins #FarhanaKhera #GabyPacheco #JuanRodriguez #FelipeMatos #CarlosRoa #NewsOne #RolandMartin #OprahWinfreyNetwork #TheAfricanHistoryNetwork #Codeblack Life #Magic102houston #Praise92 #Afro-American Newspapers #HoustonAreaUrbanLeague #NAACP #MinisterLouisFarrahkan #Fox26News #KPRC2 #CW39 #abcnews #FBI

Exhibit 132

Correction of charge

Ellenor
to r wilkerson

Mon, Nov 30, 2015, 8:52 AM

Good morning,

Mr. Wilkerson I noticed the correction was not correct, after I pointed it out to you. You miss typed ADAAA and only typed ADAA. The information must appear just as I submitted it on paper. After a visit to get the correction, I was told you were unavailable and I could schedule a meeting with you.

Please inform me when the correction has been made, I need it asap.

Sincerely,

Ellenor Perkins Ratcliff

Exhibit 133

EEOC Form 161 (11/09)

U.S. EQUAL EMPLOYMENT OPPORTUNITY COMMISSION

DISMISSAL AND NOTICE OF RIGHTS

To: Ellenor Perkins - Ratcliff
Houston, TX 77

From: Houston District Office
Mickey Leland Building
1919 Smith Street, 7th Floor
Houston, TX 77002

[ ] On behalf of person(s) aggrieved whose identity is CONFIDENTIAL (29 CFR §1601.7(a))

EEOC Charge No.	EEOC Representative	Telephone No.
460-2016-00589	Roy Wilkerson, Investigator	(713) 651-4977

THE EEOC IS CLOSING ITS FILE ON THIS CHARGE FOR THE FOLLOWING REASON:

[ ] The facts alleged in the charge fail to state a claim under any of the statutes enforced by the EEOC.

[ ] Your allegations did not involve a disability as defined by the Americans With Disabilities Act.

[ ] The Respondent employs less than the required number of employees or is not otherwise covered by the statutes.

[X] Your charge was not timely filed with EEOC; in other words, you waited too long after the date(s) of the alleged discrimination to file your charge

[ ] The EEOC issues the following determination: Based upon its investigation, the EEOC is unable to conclude that the information obtained establishes violations of the statutes. This does not certify that the respondent is in compliance with the statutes. No finding is made as to any other issues that might be construed as having been raised by this charge.

[ ] The EEOC has adopted the findings of the state or local fair employment practices agency that investigated this charge.

[ ] Other (briefly state)

- NOTICE OF SUIT RIGHTS -
(See the additional information attached to this form.)

Title VII, the Americans with Disabilities Act, the Genetic Information Nondiscrimination Act, or the Age Discrimination in Employment Act: This will be the only notice of dismissal and of your right to sue that we will send you. You may file a lawsuit against the respondent(s) under federal law based on this charge in federal or state court. Your lawsuit **must be filed WITHIN 90 DAYS** of your receipt of this notice; or your right to sue based on this charge will be lost. (The time limit for filing suit based on a claim under state law may be different.)

Equal Pay Act (EPA): EPA suits must be filed in federal or state court within 2 years (3 years for willful violations) of the alleged EPA underpayment. This means that backpay due for any violations that occurred more than 2 years (3 years) before you file suit may not be collectible.

On behalf of the Commission

Rayford O. Irvin,
District Director

DEC 07 2015
(Date Mailed)

Enclosures(s)

cc: Zack Wentz
Human Resources
GENERAL DYNAMICS INFORMATION TECHNOLOGY
3211 Jermantown Rd
Fairfax, VA 22030

Lowell Keig, Executive Director
TWC/Civil Rights Division
101 East 15th Street, Room 144T
Austin, TX 78778

Exhibit 134

```
EQUAL EMPLOYMENT OPPORTUNITY COMMISSION
HOUSTON DISTRICT OFFICE
TOTAL PLAZA
1201 LOUISIANA STREET - 6TH FLOOR
HOUSTON, TX 77002

OFFICIAL BUSINESS
Penalty for Private Use, $300
```

Exhibit 135

Accountability, Reinstate Charge   Inbox x

Ellenor   Tue, Dec 15, 2015, 4:34 AM
to J   Saindon

Ellenor Perkins Ratcliff

Houston, Texas

Radford O. Irvin
Mickey Leland Building
1919 Smith Street, 7th Floor
Houston, Texas 77002

Dear Mr. Irvin,

The Lord instructed me to come to you, in an attempt to reinstate charge and receive due process. The former Director and Jeremy Crosbie obstructed justice. My charge number is #460-2016-00589. From November 19 to December 12, 2015, I visited the EEOC office three times. The Lord instructed me to come to you, in a final attempt before he acts.

Child of the King,

Ellenor Perkins Ratcliff

Exhibit 136

Correction

Ellenor Tue, Dec 15, 2015, 4:50 AM
to E. Henderson

Ellenor Perkins Ratcliff

Houston, Texas

E. Henderson

December 15, 2015

Dear Ms. Henderson

On November 19, I visited the EEOC office. The Investigator who complete the additional information some how made an error. The error on form is ADAA, but it should show ADAAA. The investigator was contacted by email weeks ago and I have received no response. Please instruct your investigator to correct this error. Hopefully, Thursday or Friday of this week we will visit the EEOC.

Sincerely,

Ellenor Perkins Ratcliff

Exhibit 137

RE: Accountability, Reinstate Charge Inbox

Ellenor Dec 15, 2015, 4:56 AM
to me

Mr. Irvin

Your response will be duly noted on 12/24/2015.

Child of the King.

Ellenor Perkins Ratcliff

Exhibit 138

Fwd: Accountability, Reinstate Charge

Ellenor Tue, Dec 15, 2015, 4:59 AM
to E   Henderson@eeoc.gov

Mr. Irvin

Your response will be duly noted on 12/ 24/2015.

Child of the King,

Ellenor Perkins Ratcliff

Exhibit 139

J   SAINDON   SAINDON@eeoc.gov>   Tue, Dec 15, 2015, 10:56 AM
to me

Thank you for your correspondence. I will have your filed pulled and reviewed.

>>   @gmail.com> 12/15/2015 4:34 AM >>>

Exhibit 140

U.S. EQUAL EMPLOYMENT OPPORTUNITY COMMISSION
Houston District Office

Mickey Leland Building
1919 Smith Street, 7th Floor
Houston, TX 77002
Intake Information Group: (800) 669-4000
Intake Information Group TTY: (800) 669-6820
Houston Status Line: (866) 408-8075
Houston Direct Dial: (713) 651-4900
TTY (713) 651-4901
FAX (713) 651-4902
Website: www.eeoc.gov

December 28, 2015

Ms. Ellenor Perkins Ratcliff

Houston, TX 77

Dear Ms. Ratcliff:

This is in response to your letter dated December 15, 2015, concerning your request that the U.S. Equal Employment Opportunity Commission (EEOC) reconsider its final findings on your charge of employment discrimination filed with the EEOC against General Dynamics Information Technology (EEOC Charge No. 460-2016-00589).

The EEOC has no obligation to reconsider the final findings we have issued on a charge. EEOC Directors, therefore, may decline to review a request to reconsider an EEOC final finding unless the Charging Party presents substantial new and relevant evidence, or a persuasive argument that the EEOC's prior decision was contrary to law or the facts.

I have thoroughly reviewed the handling of your charge in light of your expressed concerns and the information that you have submitted. Our records indicate that on March 20, 2014, you filed EEOC Charge No. 460-2014-01770. Because the EEOC was unable to conclude that the information obtained established a violation of the Americans with Disability Act, a Dismissal and Notice of Right to Sue was issued on March 26, 2015. You filed a lawsuit on October 7, 2015 which was dismissed on November 4, 2015.

On November 19, 2015, you insisted in filing Charge No. 460-2016-00589, alleging same or similar allegations that were addressed on Charge No. 460-2014-01770. Because Charge No. 460-2016-00589 was filed beyond the 300-day time limitation for filing a timely charge of employment discrimination, the charge was dismissed and a Dismissal and Notice of Right-to-Sue was issued on December 7, 2015. Based on this information, I have determined that no appropriate evidence was overlooked or misinterpreted in evaluating your charge. Therefore, your request for reconsideration is hereby denied.

It is important to note that a request for reconsideration does not extend or eliminate the statutory 90-day period for pursuing this matter in court. If you still feel you have a case against this employer, <u>it is your responsibility to file in federal court</u>. If a private lawsuit was not filed within 90 days of your receipt of the <u>December 7, 2015</u>, final dismissal notice, the right to sue for the charge was lost and cannot be restored by the EEOC.

I hope this information is helpful to you.

Sincerely,

Rayford O. Irvin
District Director

Exhibit 141

RWJ/T-4

EQUAL EMPLOYMENT OPPORTUNITY COMMISSION
HOUSTON DISTRICT OFFICE
TOTAL PLAZA
1201 LOUISIANA STREET - 6TH FLOOR
HOUSTON, TX 77002

OFFICIAL BUSINESS
Penalty for Private Use, $300

N HOUSTON
TX 773
29 DEC '15
PM 3 L

Ms. Ellenor Perkins Ratcliff

Houston, TX

Exhibit 142

Ellenor
To: @aol.com

Aug 18, 2016 at 10:23 PM

Dear Dr.

Thank you for providing information regarding the Judiciary Committee and it's practices. The information has been very informative. We have seen the recent flood in Louisiana. I hope you are doing well despite the flood. My name is Ellenor and I have quite an experience with judicial injustice. It all began when my past employer violated my rights according to the Americans with Disabilities Act. A case was filed with the U.S. Equal Employment Opportunity Commission and justice was obstructed. Do you have any suggestions for me. I plan to write the House Judiciary Committee regarding a federal judge here in Houston. Below is everyone I contacted regarding my injustice.

March 3, 2014
Mailed letter of resignation to GDIT, due to hostile working environment.

March 20, 2014
Filed claim with EEOC, wasn't contacted until a year later.

March 26, 2015
I was denied due process. The federal investigator did not investigate nor contacted my witnesses.

April 10, 2015
Contacted EEOC for Reconsideration and highlighted facts. Also contacted the President of the United States.

April 29, 2015 I was again denied due ****Process by Martin Ebel of EEOC. Contact was made with CMS, who gave GDIT the Call Center Contract.

May 7, 2015
Contacted attorney for assistance with Workers' Compensation Benefits.

May 11, 2015
Contacted Texas Department of Insurance regarding coverage for GDIT.

July 7, 2015
****Letter from Martin Ebel stated, "This is in response to your April 10, 2015, inquiry to President Obama concerning the charge of employment discrimination... The President has asked this office to respond directly to you." I was denied due process once again.

Exhibit 143

My Copy of Notes 1.26.17

   E
To:

Feb 28 2017 at 6:26 AM

Yahoo/Inbox

January 26, 2017
Dear Mr. President,

Please consider this letter when shifting to make America great again. As a law abiding citizen my rights as well as the rights of others have been grossly violated. My mother taught my siblings and I to work hard in order to accomplish our goals and live a better life than she. Mr. President, there is a grave problem with the operation of U.S. Equal Employment Opportunity Commission, Texas Workforce Commission and U.S. Federal Court here in Houston Texas. My employer General Dynamics Information Technology violated my rights under the Obama Administration. I wrote many for help and I have yet to be relieved by the violation and treatment I faced. During my research I learned thousands, if not millions of people where being illegally denied by U.S. EEOC and were trampled.

During my investigation I learned GDIT is a major government contractor. General Dynamics Information Technology received a call center contract from CMS. GDIT was responsible for signing up citizens for the Affordable Care Act. As a past participant under the Texas Department of Human Resources, I have a great understanding of policy and procedures, due to operating a childcare myself. The State has rules and regulations that were mandatory to operate under, if I made the choice not to operate by rules set forth, my permit would have been placed in jeopardy; therefore I ran my childcare and operated according to state law.

The obstruction of justice I have received has truly hurt my family and I. GDIT developed policy and procedures and I'm sure it signed an agreement to protect all employees under that government contract. GDIT failed to protect me and lied to U.S. Equal Employment Opportunity Commission, Texas Workforce Commission, Centers for Medicaid and Medicare, as well as Broadspire Insurance Company. My employer GDIT allowed employees to actively spray cologne and perfume fragrances at desk and lockers on a call center floor. This behavior caused injury to my lungs and I was later diagnosed with Asthma, brought on by allergic rh. Throughout my 20 plus years of working, I have personally never experienced such behavior on a job. An overwhelming documentation of facts and truth was submitted to U.S. Equal Employment Opportunity Commission, one year later that agency responded and denied my case without investigation. My witnesses were never contacted and justice was obstructed. This situation really broke my heart and love for this country. I graduated from high school, pursued a trade, attended college and worked hard. Never have I been trouble to this government and I have reared my children as such.

Mr. President, I would kindly like to ask for your assistance in the reinstatement of the charges brought against my past employer. Attached is my Journey of Injustice.

Sincerely,

Exhibit 144

1.18.17

1.18.17
This company came to Houston Texas after receiving a government contract from Centers for Medicare and Medicaid. GDIT received tax dollars to run the Affordable Care Act and enroll citizens. This company violated so many with disabilities. I will fight to the death for my rights. This company has no integrity, yet they have a huge amount of government funds to run their organization.

Exhibit 145

President Donald Trump
1600 Pennsylvania Ave NW
Washington, DC 20500

Ellenor Perkins

Cypress, Texas

September 4, 2018

Greetings,

President Trump, I come to you in hope that you would grant my petition, as God has instructed me. You have the power and authority to carry out this request. I have prayed for you since you won the office. My name is Ellenor Perkins Ratcliff and I have been greatly wronged by other government offices such as EEOC and Federal Court. I have fought the good fight since 2013 and on January 21, 2018, God instructed me to write you, at the time I didn't write because I was so consumed by my troubles.

God said to me, "Ask President Trump to rescind the decision made by U.S. EEOC on charge #460-2014-01770 by Martin S. Ebel and charge #460-2016-00589 by Roy Wilkerson. Thank you for your time and I believe God will use you to do great things. I look forward to hearing from you.

Sincerely,

Ellenor P. Ratcliff

Enclosed:
My Journey, 4 page document

Exhibit 146

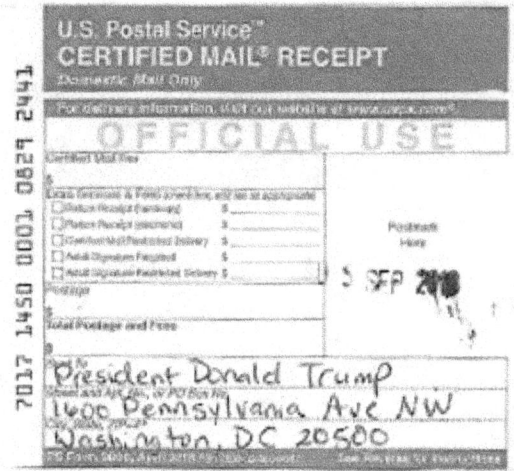

Exhibit 147

THE WHITE HOUSE
WASHINGTON

November 20, 2018

Ms. Ellenor Ratcliff

Cypress, Texas

Dear Ms. Ratcliff,

Thank you for taking the time to write and share your story with President Donald J. Trump. He is honored by the opportunity to serve you and the American people.

White House staff reviewed your correspondence and forwarded it to the appropriate Federal agency for further action. For additional information about the Federal government in the meantime, please visit www.USA.gov or call 1-800-FED-INFO.

Respectfully,

The Office of Presidential Correspondence

Exhibit 148

THE WHITE HOUSE
WASHINGTON, DC 20502

Ms. Ellenor Ratcliff

Cypress, Texas

Exhibit 149

Appendix B

UNITED STATES DISTRICT COURT
SOUTHERN DISTRICT OF TEXAS
Southern DIVISION

Ellenor Perkins Ratcliff §
§
versus § CIVIL ACTION NO. 4:15-CV-03038
§
U.S. Equal Employment Opportunity Commission §
U.S. Attorney General Loretta E. Lynch §
U.S. Attorney Kenneth Magidson §

ORIGINAL COMPLAINT

1. Civil Rights and Political Rights Violation

Discrimination based on color and disability. Politically I was denied natural justice. The suit is brought against Equal Employment Opportunity Commission, Jeremy Crosbie, Martin S. Ebel, U. S. Attorney General Loretta E. Lynch and U. S. Attorney Kenneth Magidson.

2. Southern District of Texas has jurisdiction due to the violation taking place in Harris, Houston, Texas 77002.

3. A charge of discrimination was completed on March 17, 2014 and was brought before the EEOC on March 20, 2014 (Exhibit 1A). After questioning Mr. Crosbie he stated, "I didn't have to file with TWC." The EEOC held my case for an entire year (3/20/14, Exhibit 1A to 3/26/15, Exhibit 4B) and stated, "Based upon its investigation, the EEOC is unable to conclude that the information obtained establishes violations of the statutes." Mr. Crosbie has obstructed justice. Jeremy Crosbie finally contacted me. I asked, "What took so long for your investigation?" Jeremy Crosbie stated, "I sent the charge to the

Ellenor Perkins Ratcliff   V.   U.S. Equal Employment Opportunity Commission
I, Ellenor Perkins Ratcliff, have sent a copy of this document to all parties in Case: 4:15-cv-03038.

Exhibit 150

wrong address for GDIT." (Exhibit 1A page 2, section 2 and Exhibit 4B, Enclosure section for GDIT address). Mr. Crosbie also stated, "GDIT was not obligated to enforce the perfume issue and GDIT gave reasonable accommodations. GDIT asked you for medical documentation (Exhibit 2) and you didn't provide it and they moved you to a different supervisor." April 10, 2015, I requested a substantial weight review (Exhibit 1C). Martin Ebel responded, April 29, 2015 (Exhibit 4C). Mr. Ebel stated, "The EEOC has no obligation to reconsider the final findings we have issued on a charge." I made contact with President Obama in April, regarding the EEOC bias and corruption. July 7, 2015, Mr. Ebel contacted me by letter and stated, "This is in response to your April 10, 2015, inquiry to President Obama concerning the charge of employment discrimination you filed with the EEOC," (Exhibit 4D.) "You were not accorded a substantial weight review, because that process only occurs where a FEPA has made a determination on a charge that was dual filed with both a FEPA and the EEOC. Your charge was not filed with a FEPA, but rather was filed directly with the EEOC, so a substantial weight review is not possible." August 6, 2015, I contacted President Obama (Exhibit 1D) and September 1, 2015, I contacted Attorney General Lynch (Exhibit 1E) regarding the Corruption and bias at the EEOC. Jeremy Crosbie never contacted witnesses; I have spoken with the witnesses. Jeremy Crosbie lied regarding difficulty locating organization GDIT, the address on EEOC Intake Questionnaire dated for 3/17/2015, is the same address on Dismissal and Notice of Rights dated March 26, 2015, addressed to Lesley P. Marlin, Assistant General Counsel of General Dynamics Information Tech. Mr. Ebel also obstructed Justice on July 7, 2015; stating because I didn't dual file, a substantial weight review is not possible. EEOC Printout (Exhibit 3A) dated 3/10/2014 - How to File a Charge of Employment Discrimination states, "According to these agreements, if you file a charge with either EEOC or a FEPA, the charge also will be automatically filed with the other agency. This process, which is defined as dual filing, helps to protect charging party rights under both federal and state or local law;" also TWC Printout (Exhibit 3B) dated 10/2/2015 - How to Submit an Employment Discrimination Complaint states, "When you submit an employment discrimination complaint with the

Ellenor Perkins Ratcliff V. U.S. Equal Employment Opportunity Commission
I, Ellenor Perkins Ratcliff, have sent a copy of this document to all parties in Case: 4:15-cv-03038.

Exhibit 151

Civil Rights Division, it is automatically submitted with EEOC through our Worksharing Agreement. You cannot submit with both the Civil Rights Division and the EEOC."

4. Clearly the EEOC has intentionally discriminated against me as well as obstruct justice in my case by abusing its authority, accepting bribes to throw the investigation of the charge brought against GDIT. I tell you today, "For the Lord is a God of justice." Isaiah 30:18 "Hate evil, love good; maintain justice in the courts." Amos 5:15 "Cursed be anyone who perverts the justice"...in Jesus name, Amen. Deuteronomy 27: 19.

5. The plaintiff requests that the defendant be ordered to reinstate charge of discrimination against GDIT. I pray the court grants me compensatory and punitive damages for the wicked actions of EEOC in the amount of $20,000,000. I have been oppressed; EEOC abused its authority by obstructing justice. Depression and anxiety have filled my life, I have isolated myself, I suffer with insomnia. I sustained injury to my lungs and due to EEOC, I loss the opportunity of claiming workers' compensation from GDIT. EEOC wickedly pretended to help me, but obstructed justice.

X _____

Houston, Texas 77

Ellenor Perkins Ratcliff V. U.S. Equal Employment Opportunity Commission

I, *Ellenor Perkins Ratcliff*, have sent a copy of this document to all parties in Case: 4:15-cv-03038.

Exhibit 152

* AO 187 (Rev. 7/87) Exhibit and Witness List

UNITED STATES DISTRICT COURT

Southern DISTRICT OF Texas

Ellenor Perkins Ratcliff

v.

Equal Employment Opportunity Commission

EXHIBIT AND WITNESS LIST

Case Number: 4:15-CV-03038

PRESIDING JUDGE	PLAINTIFF'S ATTORNEY	DEFENDANT'S ATTORNEY
Lynn N. Hughes		
TRIAL DATE(S)	COURT REPORTER	COURTROOM DEPUTY

PLF. NO.	DEF. NO.	DATE OFFERED	MARKED	ADMITTED	DESCRIPTION OF EXHIBITS* AND WITNESSES	
1A		10/7/15			U.S. EEOC Intake Questionnaire	4 pages
1B		10/7/15			Additional Information Packet also submitted to EEOC	16 pages
3A		10/7/15			U.S. EEOC - How to File a Charge of Employment Discrimination	2 pages
3B		10/7/15			TWC - How to Submit an Employment Discrimination Complaint	2 pages
4A		10/7/15			Form 5, U.S. EEOC Charge of Discrimination	3 pages
4B		10/7/15			Form 161, U.S. EEOC Dismissal and Notice of Rights	4 pages
1C		10/7/15			Letter 04/10/15 - Request Substantial Weight Review	4 pages
4C		10/7/15			Letter 04/29/15 - U.S. EEOC Response	2 pages
4D		10/7/15			Letter 04/07/15 - U.S. EEOC Response to President contact	1 page
1D		10/7/15			Letter 08/06/15 - Plea to President Obama	3 pages
1E		10/7/15			Letter 09/01/15 - Plea to Attorney General Lynch	3 pages
1F		10/7/15			Letter 09/14/15 - President Obama	1 page
1G		10/7/15			Letter 09/14/15 - Attorney General Lynch	1 page
5A		10/7/15			Centers for Medicare & Medicaid Services Response	1 page
1H		10/7/15			Letter 07/30/15 - Response to CMS	1 page
2		10/7/15			Medical Excuses and Dr. Statements	9 pages
A		10/7/15			Vangent Dress Code Standards - Revised 02/01/12	1 page
B		10/7/15			GDIT Dress Code Standards - Revised 06/12/13	1 page
6A		10/7/15			Withdrawal of Representation - Curry 08/21/15	3 pages
6B		10/7/15			Denial - PLLC 08/26/15	1 page
6C		10/7/15			Denial - PLLC 09/08/15	1 page
					Continue to Witness List	

* Include a notation as to the location of any exhibit not held with the case file or not available because of size.

Page 1 of 2 Pages

I, Ellenor Perkins Ratcliff, have sent a copy of this document to all parties in Case: 4:15-cv-03038.

Exhibit 153

- AO 187A (Rev. 7/87)

EXHIBIT AND WITNESS LIST – CONTINUATION

Ellenor Perkins Ratcliff vs. Equal Employment Opportunity
CASE NO. 4:15-CV-03038

PLF. NO.	DEF. NO.	DATE OFFERED	MARKED	ADMITTED	DESCRIPTION OF EXHIBITS AND WITNESSES
W1		10/7/15			Reimer Subpoena to Testify
W2		10/7/15			Bosie - Subpoena to Testify
W3		10/7/15			Clem - Subpoena to Testify
W4		10/7/15			Singletary - Subpoena to Testify
W5		10/7/15			Jeremy Crosbie - Subpoena to Testify
W6		10/7/15			Martin Ebel - Subpoena to Testify
W7		10/7/15			Marlin - Subpoena to Testify
W7		10/7/15			Marlin - Subpoena to Produce
W2		10/7/15			Bosie - Subpoena to Produce

Page 2 of 2 Pages

I, Ellenor Perkins Ratcliff, have sent a copy of this document to all parties in Case: 4:15-cv-03038.

Exhibit 154

GUIDELINES FOR LITIGANTS WITHOUT LAWYERS
SOUTHERN DISTRICT OF TEXAS

1. Introduction

    A. These guidelines are to make persons who represent themselves in lawsuits familiar with some of the rules and procedures which must be followed in the United States District Court for the Southern District of Texas.

    B. Disclaimer. This summary does not take the place of a pro se litigant's responsibility to comply with the Local Rules (L.R.), the Federal Rules of Civil Procedure (Fed.R.Civ.P.) and all other laws. This summary is not legal advice and reliance on it is at your own risk.

2. The Complaint

    A. A civil lawsuit is begun by filing a complaint in the office of the Clerk of the Court. The purpose of the complaint is to give notice to the persons being sued and to the court about the nature of the lawsuit. The complaint must contain:

        1. a caption specifying the court in which the suit is brought and names of the parties;

        2. a short, plain statement of why the court has jurisdiction;

        3. a short, plain statement of the claim that entitles the plaintiff to relief, including a concise statement of the facts;

        4. a statement of the particular relief sought; and

        5. your signature, address and telephone number.

    B. Pleadings should be simple and direct; technical, legal jargon is not required.

    C. Generally, each statement of claim should be made in separately numbered paragraphs, with each paragraph limited as far as possible to a statement of a single set of facts.

    D. If the basis of your suit is employment discrimination, there is a form attached which you may use for filing your complaint. (Appendix A) If your suit has any other nature, the Original Complaint form attached (Appendix B) may be used to get started.

3. Where to File

    A. <u>Clerk</u>. All papers to be filed must be delivered or mailed to the Clerk's Office.

Exhibit 155

Never send papers directly to the judge.

B. Options. Generally, the suit must be filed in the district where the defendant resides or where the claim arose. In suits based on diversity of citizenship (when the plaintiff and defendant are residents of different states), the suit may be brought in the district where the plaintiff resides (28 U.S.C. §1391).

C. Divisions. There are seven divisions of the Southern District of Texas:

1. Brownsville
   a. Mail and Delivery: 600 E. Harrison Street, Room 101, Brownsville, TX 78520
   b. Counties: Cameron and Willacy.

2. Corpus Christi
   a. Mail and Delivery: 1133 North Shoreline Boulevard, Corpus Christi, TX 78401
   b. Counties: Aransas, Bee, Brooks, Duval, Jim Wells, Kenedy, Kleberg, Live Oak, Nueces and San Patricio.

3. Galveston
   a. Mail: P.O. Box 2300, Galveston, TX 77553
   b. Delivery: 601 Rosenberg, Room 411, Galveston, TX 77550
   c. Counties: Brazoria, Chambers, Galveston and Matagorda.

4. Houston
   a. Mail: P.O. Box 61010, Houston, TX 77208
   b. Delivery: 515 Rusk, Room 1217, Houston, TX 77002
   c. Counties: Austin, Brazos, Colorado, Fayette, Fort Bend, Grimes, Harris, Madison, Montgomery, San Jacinto, Walker, Waller and Wharton.

5. Laredo
   a. Mail and Delivery: 1300 Victoria Street, Suite 1131, Laredo, TX 78040
   b. Counties: Jim Hogg, LaSalle, McMullen, Webb and Zapata.

6. McAllen
   a. Mail and Delivery: 1701 West Business Highway 83, Suite 1011, McAllen, TX 78501
   b. Counties: Hidalgo and Starr.

2

Exhibit 156

7. Victoria
   a. Mail: P.O. Box 1638
      Victoria, TX 77902
   b. Delivery: 312 S. Main Street, Room 406
      Victoria, TX 77901
   c. Counties: Calhoun, De Witt, Goliad, Jackson, Lavaca, Refugio and Victoria.

4. Requirements for Filings

   A. The requirements for filing the complaint and all other pleadings are found in LR5 and LR10 as well as Fed.R.Civ.P. 10 and 11. They include

      1. be on 8½" x 11" paper;
      2. be double spaced and paginated;
      3. stapled at the top only;
      4. punched with two holes;
      5. include the plaintiff's address and telephone number; and
      6. be signed by the plaintiff.

   B. Address. Failure of a litigant to keep the Clerk of the Court informed of his current address and telephone number during the pendency of the lawsuit. (LR83.4)

5. Filing Fees

   A. The fee for filing a civil action is $400.00. Filing fees must be paid to the Clerk at the time of filing the complaint, unless the Court grants leave to proceed in forma pauperis.

   B. In Forma Pauperis:

      1. A plaintiff who cannot pay the filing fee and the costs for service may request to proceed in forma pauperis. (Appendix C) The request must be submitted with the complaint and must be accompanied by an affidavit setting forth the plaintiff's financial resources.

      2. If leave to proceed in forma pauperis is granted, the plaintiff's suit will be filed without prepayment of the filing fee.

      3. If leave to proceed in forma pauperis is denied, you must pay the filing fee for your case (suit) to be filed.

6. Judge's Procedural Manual

   A procedure manual containing information about the specific requirements of a

Exhibit 157

Appendix A

UNITED STATES DISTRICT COURT
SOUTHERN DISTRICT OF TEXAS
_____ DIVISION

Ellena Perkins Ratcliff §
§
versus §
General Dynamics Information Technology § CIVIL ACTION NO. _____
Zandra Bosie §
William Reiner (Bill) §
Linda M Bair §

EMPLOYMENT DISCRIMINATION COMPLAINT

1. This action is brought under Title VII of the Civil Rights Act of 1964 for employment discrimination. Jurisdiction is conferred by Title 42 United States Code, Section § 2000e-5.

2. The Plaintiff is: Ellena Perkins Ratcliff
   Address: _____
   Houston Texas 77
   County of Residence: Harris County

3. The defendant is: General Dynamics Information Technology
   Address: 3211 Jermantown Road
   Fairfax, VA 22030

   ☑ Check here if there are additional defendants. List them on a separate sheet of paper with their complete addresses.

4. The plaintiff has attached to this complaint a copy of the charges filed on _____ with the Equal Opportunity Commission.

5. On the date of _____, the plaintiff received a Notice of Right to Sue letter issued by the Equal Employment Opportunity Commission; a copy is attached.

Exhibit 158

6. Because of the plaintiff's:

    (a) ☐ race

    (b) ☒ color

    (c) ☐ sex

    (d) ☐ religion

    (e) ☐ national orgin,

    the defendant has:

    (a) ☐ failed to employ the plaintiff

    (b) ☐ terminated the plaintiff's employment

    (c) ☐ failed to promote the plaintiff

    (d) ☒ other: ~~failed~~ Refused to enforce rules & regulation set forth by FAR.

7. When and how the defendant has discriminated against the plaintiff: From 10/2013 to 02/2014 GDIT refused to enforce Dresscode Standards ~~policy~~ on section 3.2 which states, "Overly strong or offensive odors or scents such as perfumes and cologne...... will not be allowed in the workplace."

8. The plaintiff requests that the defendant be ordered:

    (a) ☐ to stop discriminating against the plaintiff

    (b) ☐ to employ the plaintiff

    (c) ☐ to re-employ the plaintiff

    (d) ☐ to promote the plaintiff

Exhibit 159

AO 440 (Rev. 12/09) Summons in a Civil Action — Appendix D

UNITED STATES DISTRICT COURT
for the
_____ District of _____

Ellenor Perkins Ratcliff)
Plaintiff)
)
v.) Civil Action No. _____
)
General Dynamics Information Technology)
Defendant)

SUMMONS IN A CIVIL ACTION

To: *(Defendant's name and address)*

Lesley Martin
3211 Jermantown Road
Fairfax, VA 22030

A lawsuit has been filed against you.

Within 21 days after service of this summons on you (not counting the day you received it) — or 60 days if you are the United States or a United States agency, or an officer or employee of the United States described in Fed. R. Civ. P. 12 (a)(2) or (3) — you must serve on the plaintiff an answer to the attached complaint or a motion under Rule 12 of the Federal Rules of Civil Procedure. The answer or motion must be served on the plaintiff or plaintiff's attorney, whose name and address are:

If you fail to respond, judgment by default will be entered against you for the relief demanded in the complaint. You also must file your answer or motion with the court.

CLERK OF COURT

Date: _____ _____
Signature of Clerk or Deputy Clerk

Exhibit 161

AO 399 (01/09) Waiver of the Service of Summons

UNITED STATES DISTRICT COURT
for the
Southern District of Texas

Ellenor Perkins Ratcliff	)	
Plaintiff	)	
v.	)	Civil Action No.
U.S. Attorney Kenneth Magidson	)	
Defendant	)	

WAIVER OF THE SERVICE OF SUMMONS

To: Ellenor Perkins Ratcliff
(Name of the plaintiff's attorney or unrepresented plaintiff)

I have received your request to waive service of a summons in this action along with a copy of the complaint, two copies of this waiver form, and a prepaid means of returning one signed copy of the form to you.

I, or the entity I represent, agree to save the expense of serving a summons and complaint in this case.

I understand that I, or the entity I represent, will keep all defenses or objections to the lawsuit, the court's jurisdiction, and the venue of the action, but that I waive any objections to the absence of a summons or of service.

I also understand that I, or the entity I represent, must file and serve an answer or a motion under Rule 12 within 60 days from 10/07/2015, the date when this request was sent (or 90 days if it was sent outside the United States). If I fail to do so, a default judgment will be entered against me or the entity I represent.

Date: _____

_____
Signature of the attorney or unrepresented party

_____
Printed name of party waiving service of summons

_____
Printed name

_____
Address

_____
E-mail address

_____
Telephone number

Duty to Avoid Unnecessary Expenses of Serving a Summons

Rule 4 of the Federal Rules of Civil Procedure requires certain defendants to cooperate in saving unnecessary expenses of serving a summons and complaint. A defendant who is located in the United States and who fails to return a signed waiver of service requested by a plaintiff located in the United States will be required to pay the expenses of service, unless the defendant shows good cause for the failure.

"Good cause" does *not* include a belief that the lawsuit is groundless, or that it has been brought in an improper venue, or that the court has no jurisdiction over this matter or over the defendant or the defendant's property.

If the waiver is signed and returned, you can still make these and all other defenses and objections, but you cannot object to the absence of a summons or of service.

If you waive service, then you must, within the time specified on the waiver form, serve an answer or a motion under Rule 12 on the plaintiff and file a copy with the court. By signing and returning the waiver form, you are allowed more time to respond than if a summons had been served.

Exhibit 165

Ellenor Perkins Ratcliff

Houston, Texas 7709[?]

United States District Court
515 Rusk, Room 1217
Houston, Texas 77002

October 7, 2015

Motion for Court Appointed Attorney

Dear Presiding Judge:

On three occasions I have attempted to obtain legal representation and have either been denied or the attorney withdrew. Therefore, I pray that you would grant my petition for a Court Appointed Attorney. Thank you for any consideration you may give me.

Sincerely,

Ellenor Perkins Ratcliff

Exhibit 166

DC CM/ECF LIVE- US District Court-Texas Southern

U.S. District Court
SOUTHERN DISTRICT OF TEXAS (Houston)
CIVIL DOCKET FOR CASE #: 4:15-mc-02406
Internal Use Only

Ratcliff v. US Equal Employment Opportunity Commission et al   Date Filed: 10/07/2015
Assigned to: Judge Lynn N. Hughes

Plaintiff

Ellenor Perkins Ratcliff   represented by   Ellenor Perkins Ratcliff
                                               PRO SE

V.

Defendant

US Equal Employment Opportunity Commission

Defendant

US Attorney General Loretta E. Lynch

Defendant

US Attorney Kenneth Magidson

Date Filed	#	Docket Text
10/07/2015	1	APPLICATION to Proceed In Forma Pauperis filed by Ellenor Perkins Ratcliff. (Attachments: # 1 Proposed Order, # 2 Complaint, # 3 Exhibit and Witness List, # 4 1A, # 5 1B, # 6 3H, # 7 3B, # 8 4A, # 9 4B, # 10 1C, # 11 4C, # 12 4D, # 13 1D, # 14 1E, # 15 1F, # 16 1G, # 17 5A, # 18 1H, # 19 2, # 20 A, # 21 B, # 22 6A, # 23 6B, # 24 6C, # 25 Motion for Court Appointed Attorney)(rosaldana, 4) (Additional attachment(s) added on 10/7/2015: # 26 Summons, # 27 Summons, # 28 Summons) (rosaldana, 4). (Entered: 10/07/2015)

Exhibit 167

Case 4:15-mc-02406   Document 2   Filed in TXSD on 10/08/15   Page 1 of 1

AO 240A (Rev. 01/09) Order to Proceed Without Prepaying Fees or Costs

UNITED STATES DISTRICT COURT
for the
Southern District of Texas

United States Courts
Southern District of Texas
FILED

OCT 07 2015

David J. Bradley, Clerk of Court

Elienor Perkins Ratcliff	)	Miscellaneous
Plaintiff	)	~~Civil~~ Action No.
v.	)	
EEOC, Lorretta E. Lynch, Kenneth Magidson	)	H-15-2406
Defendant	)	

ORDER TO PROCEED WITHOUT PREPAYING FEES OR COSTS

IT IS ORDERED: The plaintiff's application under 28 U.S.C. § 1915 to proceed without prepaying fees or costs is:

☒ Granted:

The clerk is ordered to file the complaint and issue a summons. The United States marshal is ordered to serve the summons with a copy of the complaint and this order on the defendant(s). The United States will advance the costs of service. Prisoner plaintiffs are responsible for full payment of the filing fee.

☐ Granted Conditionally:

The clerk is ordered to file the complaint. Upon receipt of the completed summons and USM-285 form for each defendant, the clerk will issue a summons. If the completed summons and USM-285 forms are not submitted as directed, the complaint may be dismissed. The United States marshal is ordered to serve the completed summons with a copy of the complaint and this order on the defendant(s). The United States will advance the costs of service. Prisoner plaintiffs are responsible for full payment of the filing fee.

☐ Denied:

This application is denied for these reasons:

The clerk will directly assign this case to Judge Lynn N. Hughes.

Date: ~~10/07/2015~~ October 8, 2015

Judge's signature

Lynn N. Hughes
United States District Judge
Printed name and title

Exhibit 168

UNITED STATES DISTRICT COURT
SOUTHERN DISTRICT OF TEXAS

CLERK OF COURT
P.O. Box 61010
HOUSTON, TEXAS 77208

www.txs.uscourts.gov

Ellenor Perkins Ratcliff

Houston TX US

Case: 4:15-cv-03038   Instrument: 3 (2 pages)   pty
Date: Oct 15, 2015
Control: 15107212
Notice: The attached order has been entered.

Exhibit 169

UNITED STATES DISTRICT COURT   SOUTHERN DISTRICT OF TEXAS

Ellenor Perkins Ratcliff   §
                                    §

versus   §   Civil Action 4:15–cv–03038
                                    §

US Equal Employment Opportunity   §
Commission, et al.

Order for Conference

1. The plaintiff must accomplish service within 60 days.

2. Counsel must appear for an initial pretrial conference on:

   > January 11, 2016, at 11:00 AM
   > before Judge Lynn N. Hughes
   > at 515 Rusk Avenue, Room 11122
   > Houston, Texas.

3. Initial disclosures may not be delayed. Documents and other disclosures must be exchanged, reviewed, and discussed with opposing counsel well before the conference.

4. No interrogatories, requests for admission, or depositions may be done without court approval.

5. A joint discovery plan is not required. Counsel must (a) master the facts, (b) ascertain the discovery needed, (c) discuss it with each other, and (d) be prepared to discuss discovery in a conference so that the court may fashion a brief, effective management plan.

6. The court will schedule additional preparation and may rule on motions pending or made at the conference.

7. To ensure full notice, each party who receives this notice must confirm that every party knows of the setting.

8. Failure to comply with this order may result in sanctions, including dismissal, and prolonged tirades by the court.

Lynn N. Hughes
United States District Judge

Exhibit 170

Judge Lynn N. Hughes

Courtroom 11-C, Eleventh Floor
United States Court House
515 Rusk Avenue, Room 11122
Houston, Texas 77002-2605
(713) 250-5900

Glenda Hassan, Case Manager
United States District Clerk
Post Office Box 61010
Houston, Texas 77208-1010
(713) 250-5516
Glenda_Hassan@txs.uscourts.gov

Procedures. Suggestions for practice before Judge Hughes may be found at www.txs.uscourts.gov. Please read them.

Contact. Make case-related telephone inquiries to the case manager only. Counsel should alert the case manager to matter requiring prompt attention.

Information. Get information about filings, orders, or docket entries from the computer or from the clerk's office at (713) 250-5500 or (800) 745-4459.

Letters. Do not write letters. Put your message in a document with the case style.

Emergencies. Apply for immediate relief through the Intake Section of the Clerk's Office, 515 Rusk Avenue, Houston; (713) 250-5500.

Counsel should send a copy of emergency motions directly to the case manager so that they quickly reach the court's attention. In case of an emergency when the case manager cannot be reached, please call the judge's secretary, Kathy Grant, at (713) 250-5900.

Continuances. Joint motions for continuance do not bind the court. The court will respect counsel's vacations.

Discovery Problems. The court will hear oral motions that affect discovery or scheduling soon as both counsel can appear in person or by telephone.

Exhibit 171

CLERK
UNITED STATES DISTRICT COURT
SOUTHERN DISTRICT OF TEXAS
POST OFFICE BOX 61010
HOUSTON, TEXAS 77208

OFFICIAL BUSINESS

Exhibit 172

UNITED STATES DISTRICT COURT
SOUTHERN DISTRICT OF TEXAS

CLERK OF COURT
P.O. Box 61010
HOUSTON, TEXAS 77208

www.txs.uscourts.gov

Ellenor Perkins Ratcliff

Houston TX US 77096

Case: 4:15-cv-03038 Instrument: 4 (1 pages) pty
Date: Oct 15, 2015
Control: 15107213
Notice: The attached order has been entered.

Forwarded to Marshall Service 10/15/15

Exhibit 173

UNITED STATES DISTRICT COURT
SOUTHERN DISTRICT OF TEXAS

Re: Civil Action 4:15-cv-03038
Ratcliff v. US Equal Employment Opportunity Commission et al

To: Plaintiff

You should have already received a copy of the order granting your application to proceed as a pauper.

Because the court has granted your application, this civil action number has been assigned to your case. All papers about your case must include this number.

If you submitted your complaint with your application, it has been filed in the case with the civil action number. If you did not submit your complaint with your application, you may file it now under the civil action number.

You are responsible for the summons. You must prepare and have one summons issued for each defendant in your complaint pursuant to Fed. R. Civ. P. 4. You are also responsible for service of the summons unless otherwise ordered by the court.

If you do not have summons issued within 120 days of the filing of your complaint, the court may dismiss it, ending your case.

Date: October 15, 2015

David J. Bradley, Clerk

Exhibit 174

```
              CLERK
UNITED STATES DISTRICT COURT
    SOUTHERN DISTRICT OF TEXAS
      POST OFFICE BOX 61010
      HOUSTON, TEXAS 77208
        ─────────────────
          OFFICIAL BUSINESS
```

N HOUSTON
TX 773
15 OCT '15
PM 1 L

U.S. POSTAGE ≫ PITNEY BOWES

ZIP 77002 $ 000.48
02 1W
0001374615 OCT 15 2015

77096250502

Exhibit 175

Selg   Yahoo/Inbox

 E
To: e   Oct 23, 2015 at 4:45 PM

AO088AL.pdf
527.3 KB

Exhibit 176

AO 88 (Rev. 02/14) Subpoena to Appear and Testify at a Hearing or Trial in a Civil Action

UNITED STATES DISTRICT COURT
for the
Southern District of Texas

Ellenor Perkins Ratcliff	)	
Plaintiff	)	
v.	)	Civil Action No. 4:15-cv-03038
U.S. Equal Employment Opportunity Commission	)	
Defendant	)	

SUBPOENA TO APPEAR AND TESTIFY
AT A HEARING OR TRIAL IN A CIVIL ACTION

To: Lesley P. Marlin, 3211 Jermantown Road, Fairfax, VA 22030 (Assistant General Counsel of General Dynamics I.T)

(Name of person to whom this subpoena is directed)

YOU ARE COMMANDED to appear in the United States district court at the time, date, and place set forth below to testify at a hearing or trial in this civil action. When you arrive, you must remain at the court until the judge or a court officer allows you to leave.

Place: Judge Lynn N. Hughes	Courtroom No.:
515 Rusk, Room 11122 Houston, Texas 77002	Date and Time: 01/11/2016 11:00 am

You must also bring with you the following documents, electronically stored information, or objects *(leave blank if not applicable)*:

All communication regarding EEOC Charge No. 460-2014-01770; between GDIT, EEOC Federal Investigator, Jeremy Crosby and Acting District Director, Martin S. Ebel. Information should be dated from 03/20/2014 to 10/29/2015. All employee human resource records for location on Corporate Drive in Houston Texas. The information must be made available before the hearing on 1/11/2016. To give sufficient time, contact Plaintiff Ellenor P. Ratcliff by 11/23/2015.

The following provisions of Fed. R. Civ. P. 45 are attached – Rule 45(c), relating to the place of compliance; Rule 45(d), relating to your protection as a person subject to a subpoena; and Rule 45(e) and (g), relating to your duty to respond to this subpoena and the potential consequences of not doing so.

Date: 10/29/2015

DAVID J. BRADLEY
CLERK OF COURT

Signature of Clerk or Deputy Clerk   OR   *Attorney's signature*

The name, address, e-mail address, and telephone number of the attorney representing *(name of party)* Ellenor P. Ratcliff
_____, who issues or requests this subpoena, are:

Ellenor P. Ratcliff,   Houston, Texas 77

Notice to the person who issues or requests this subpoena

If this subpoena commands the production of documents, electronically stored information, or tangible things before trial, a notice and a copy of the subpoena must be served on each party in this case before it is served on the person to whom it is directed. Fed. R. Civ. P. 45(a)(4).

Exhibit 177

UNITED STATES DISTRICT COURT
SOUTHERN DISTRICT OF TEXAS

CLERK OF COURT
P.O. Box 61010
HOUSTON, TEXAS 77208

www.txs.uscourts.gov

Ellenor Perkins Ratcliff

Houston TX US

Case: 4:15-cv-03038   Instrument: 5   (1 pages)   pty
Date: Nov 4, 2015
Control: 15112509
Notice: The attached order has been entered.

Exhibit 178

Case 4:15-cv-03038   Document 6   Filed in TXSD on 11/03/15   Page 1 of 1

UNITED STATES DISTRICT COURT	SOUTHERN DISTRICT OF TEXAS

United States District Court
Southern District of Texas
ENTERED
November 04, 2015
David J. Bradley, Clerk

Ellenor Ratcliff, §
§
  Plaintiff, §
§
versus § Civil Action H-15-3038
§
U.S. Equal Employment §
Opportunity Commission, et al., §
§
  Defendants. §

Final Dismissal

Ellenor Ratcliff's claims against the United States Equal Employment Opportunity Commission, Loretta Lynch, and Kenneth Magidson are dismissed with prejudice.

Signed on November 3, 2015, at Houston, Texas.

_____
Lynn N. Hughes
United States District Judge

Exhibit 179

UNITED STATES DISTRICT COURT   SOUTHERN DISTRICT OF TEXAS

Ellenor Ratcliff, § § Plaintiff, § § versus § § U.S. Equal Employment § Opportunity Commission, *et al.*, § § Defendants. §	Civil Action H-15-3038

Opinion on Dismissal

Ellenor Ratcliff sued the Equal Employment Opportunity Commission, the United States Attorney General, and the United States Attorney for the Southern District of Texas for civil rights violations. Ratcliff does not describe a transaction that the law recognizes.

On February 17, 2014, Ratcliff resigned from her job. She complained that her employer did not accommodate her disability as required by the Americans with Disabilities Act. Ratcliff filed a complaint with the Equal Employment Opportunity Commission.

The Commission sent Ratcliff a final notice of dismissal on March 26, 2015, informing Ratcliff that she could sue her employer privately within ninety days. Instead, Ratcliff sued the Commission and other parties unrelated to her complaint.

The Commission is authorized to investigate allegations of discrimination and may, at its discretion, bring an enforcement action against an employer. The agency's decision not to bring an enforcement action cannot be challenged by the complainant in a lawsuit.

Ratcliff's complaint will be dismissed with prejudice.

Signed on November 3, 2015, at Houston, Texas.

                                               Lynn N. Hughes
                                               United States District Judge

Exhibit 180

CLERK
UNITED STATES DISTRICT COURT
SOUTHERN DISTRICT OF TEXAS
POST OFFICE BOX 61010
HOUSTON, TEXAS 77208

OFFICIAL BUSINESS

Exhibit 181

Ratcliff v. US Equal Employment Opportunity Commission et al

Justia › Dockets & Filings › Fifth Circuit › Texas › Texas Southern District Court › Ratcliff v. US Equal Employment Opportunity Commission et al

Plaintiff:	Ellenor Perkins Ratcliff
Defendant:	US Equal Employment Opportunity Commission, US Attorney General Loretta E. Lynch and US Attorney Kenneth Magidson
Case Number:	4:2015mc02406
Filed:	October 7, 2015
Court:	Texas Southern District Court
Office:	Houston Office
Presiding Judge:	Lynn N. Hughes
Nature of Suit:	Other

Access additional case information on PACER

Use the links below to access additional information about this case on the US Court's PACER system. A subscription to PACER is required.

Access this case on the Texas Southern District Court's Electronic Court Filings (ECF) System

Exhibit 182

Ogletree Deakins

OGLETREE, DEAKINS, NASH, SMOAK & STEWART, P.C.
Attorneys at Law

Suite 3000
Houston, TX 77002
Telephone: 713/
Facsimile:
www.ogletreedeakins.com

Carolyn Russell

November 17, 2015

Certified Mail 9314 7699 0430 0018 2563 80 RRR
Ellenor Perkins Ratcliff

Houston, Texas

RE: *Civil Action No. 4:15-CV-03038; Ellenor Perkins Ratcliff v. U.S. Equal Employment Opportunity Commission;* in th3e United States District Court, Southern District of Texas, Houston, Division

Dear Ms. Ratcliff:

Attached are Defendant's Non-Party Leslay Marlin's and Non-Party Zandra Bosie's Objections to Subpoena to Appear and Testify at a Hearing or Trial in a Civil Action in the above referenced matter.

Very truly yours,

Carolyn Russell

CR:jlb

Enclosures

Exhibit 183

IN THE UNITED STATES DISTRICT COURT
FOR THE SOUTHERN DISTRICT OF TEXAS
HOUSTON DIVISION

ELLENOR PERKINS RATCLIFF,	§	
Plaintiff,	§ §	
vs.	§ §	C. A. NO.: 4:15-cv-03038
U.S. EQUAL EMPLOYMENT OPPORTUNITY COMMISSION,	§ § §	
Defendant.	§ §	

NON-PARTY ZANDRA BOSIE'S OBJECTIONS TO SUBPOENA TO APPEAR AND TESTIFY AT A HEARING OR TRIAL IN A CIVIL ACTION

Pursuant to Federal Rule of Civil Procedure 45(d)(2)(B), non-party Zandra Bosie serves her Objections to the Subpoena to Appear and Testify at a Hearing or Trial in a Civil Action ("Subpoena") as follows:

RELEVANT FACTS

On November 3, 2015, Plaintiff served a Subpoena on Ms. Bosie, a non-party. The Subpoena commands that Ms. Bosie provide:

> All notes, correspondence, email and electronic communication to all Houston managers, supervisors and CSR's from 10/01/2013 to 10/28/2015. Human Resource file of Ellenor Perkins (W227613). Locker assignment for all employees, located on Corporate Drive.

Id. The Subpoena also commands that "information must be made available before the hearing on 1/11/2016. To give sufficient time, contact Plaintiff Ellenor P. Ratcliff by 11/23/2015." *Id.*

Ms. Bosie objects to the Subpoena in its entirety because it requests documents that are, among other things, irrelevant, harassing, vague, and overly broad, and would impose an undue burden and cost on Ms. Bosie.

Exhibit 184

GENERAL OBJECTIONS

As an initial matter, non-party Ms. Bosie, a Human Resources Generalist at General Dynamics Information Technology ("GDIT"), objects to the Subpoena because it was directed at her, not GDIT.[1] Any responsive documents would be the property of GDIT, not Ms. Bosie. Additionally, the Houston location on Corporate Drive referenced in the Subpoena has closed.

Ms. Bosie objects to all document requests as overly broad, unduly burdensome, harassing, vague, irrelevant to the claims or defenses of the parties to the suit, and not reasonably calculated to lead to the discovery of admissible evidence. The document requests are particularly burdensome given that Ms. Bosie is a non-party to this litigation and is not familiar with the factual and legal disputes of this lawsuit.

Further, Ms. Bosie objects to Plaintiff's document requests to the extent they seek production of documents containing confidential, proprietary, or other information in which Ms. Bosie or other individuals and entities (including non-parties) have an expectation of privacy and confidentiality. Ms. Bosie also objects to Plaintiff's document requests to the extent they seek the production of documents that are subject to the attorney-client, work-product, or other applicable privilege or protection. Ms. Bosie further objects to Plaintiff's document requests because they fail to allow reasonable time for compliance.

SPECIFIC OBJECTIONS

1. **"All notes, correspondence, email and electronic communication to all Houston managers, supervisors and CSR's from 10/01/2013 to 10/28/2015."**

Ms. Bosie objects to this request because it is irrelevant to Plaintiff's claims against the EEOC, vague, harassing, overly broad, and violates the expectation of privacy and

---

[1] Although the Subpoena is directed at Ms. Bosie, Plaintiff attempted to serve her through GDIT's registered agent. Ms. Bosie objects because she was not served with the Subpoena and reserves the right to challenge the Subpoena on this basis.

Exhibit 185

confidentiality of non-parties. Indeed, "[a]ll notes, correspondence, email and electronic communication to all Houston managers, supervisors and CSR's" necessarily entails documents containing confidential, proprietary, and other information in which numerous non-parties (e.g., current and former employees of GDIT) have an expectation of privacy and confidentiality. The request is also unduly burdensome because it is grossly overbroad, seeks the production of voluminous documents irrelevant to Plaintiff's claims against the EEOC, and because the Houston location closed on April 25, 2014. Ms. Bosie further objects to this request to the extent that it seeks the production of documents that are subject to the attorney-client, work-product, or other privileges. Moreover, the requested documents are not likely to lead to the discovery of admissible evidence.

2. **"Human Resource file of Ellenor Perkins (W227613)."**

Ms. Bosie objects to this request because it is irrelevant to Plaintiff's claims against the EEOC, vague, and overly broad. Ms. Bosie also objects to the extent it requests the production of documents or information already in Plaintiff's possession or control, or that is more appropriately discoverable from the EEOC, a party to the litigation. Indeed, GDIT provided responsive documents concerning Plaintiff's employment to the EEOC in connection with its investigation of Charge No. 460-2014-01770. Ms. Bosie objects to making duplicative production of any document produced or to be produced by the EEOC. It is unduly burdensome for Ms. Bosie, or anyone at GDIT, to bear the burden and expense of collecting documents that are in the possession of a party to this litigation. Ms. Bosie further objects because the request is not limited in time or scope. Collecting and searching for documents, without a limitation on time period, is unduly burdensome. To the extent the EEOC is not in possession of Plaintiff's human resources or personnel file, Ms. Bosie suggests that subpoena such an appropriate, narrowly tailored request be directed to GDIT.

Exhibit 186

3. **"Locker assignment for all employees, located on Corporate Drive."**

Ms. Bosie objects to this request because it is irrelevant to Plaintiff's claims against the EEOC, vague, harassing, overly broad, and violates the expectation of privacy and confidentiality of non-parties. Indeed, "[l]ocker assignment[s] for all employees, located on Corporate Drive" is an ambiguous request, and entails documents containing confidential, proprietary, and other information in which numerous non-parties (e.g., current and former employees of GDIT) have an expectation of privacy and confidentiality. Ms. Bosie also objects to this request to the extent that it seeks the production of documents that are subject to the attorney-client, work-product, or other privileges. Moreover, the requested documents are not likely to lead to the discovery of admissible evidence. Ms. Bosie further objects because the request is not limited in time or scope. Collecting and searching for documents, without a limitation on time period, which may or may not even exist at this point relating to locker assignments in the Corporate Drive location, which no longer is in operation, is unduly burdensome.

4. **"The information must be made available before the hearing on 1/11/2016. To give sufficient time, contact Plaintiff Ellenor P. Ratcliff by 11/23/2015."**

Ms. Bosie objects to the request because it fails to allow reasonable time for compliance. Plaintiff served the Subpoena on Ms. Bosie on November 3, 2015, and expects Ms. Bosie to contact Plaintiff twenty (20) days later, and to provide voluminous documents by January 11, 2016. The requests are unduly burdensome, and additional time would be required to produce responsive, non-objectionable documents.

Ms. Bosie reserves the right to amend and/or supplement these objections if and when additional pertinent facts are obtained.

Exhibit 187

Respectfully submitted,

_____
Carolyn Russell
Texas Bar No:
OGLETREE, DEAKINS, NASH, SMOAK
& STEWART, P.C.
One Allen Center
_____ Street, Suite 3000
Houston, Texas 77002
713-___-____

CERTIFICATE OF SERVICE

I hereby certify that a true and correct copy of the foregoing instrument has been sent in accordance with the Federal Rules of Civil Procedure on this 17th day of November, 2015 to:

Ellenor Perkins Ratcliff

Houston, Texas

_____
Carolyn Russell

Exhibit 188

IN THE UNITED STATES DISTRICT COURT
FOR THE SOUTHERN DISTRICT OF TEXAS
HOUSTON DIVISION

ELLENOR PERKINS RATCLIFF,	§ § § §	
Plaintiff,	§	
vs.	§	C. A. NO.: 4:15-cv-03038
U.S. EQUAL EMPLOYMENT OPPORTUNITY COMMISSION,	§ § §	
Defendant.	§ §	

NON-PARTY LESLEY MARLIN'S OBJECTIONS TO SUBPOENA TO APPEAR AND TESTIFY AT A HEARING OR TRIAL IN A CIVIL ACTION

Pursuant to Federal Rule of Civil Procedure 45(d)(2)(B), non-party Lesley Marlin serves her Objections to the Subpoena to Appear and Testify at a Hearing or Trial in a Civil Action ("Subpoena") as follows:

RELEVANT FACTS

On November 3, 2015, Ms. Marlin, a non-party, learned of a Subpoena directed to her in the above matter. The Subpoena commands that Ms. Marlin provide:

> All communication regarding EEOC Charge No. 460-2014-01770; between GDIT, EEOC Federal Investigator, Jeremy Crosby and Acting District Director, Martin S. Ebel. Information should be dated from 03/20/2014 to 10/29/2015. All employee human resource records for location on Corporate Drive in Houston Texas.

Id. The Subpoena also commands that "information must be made available before the hearing on 1/11/2016. To give sufficient time, contact Plaintiff Ellenor P. Ratcliff by 11/23/2015." *Id.*

Ms. Marlin objects to the Subpoena in its entirety because it requests documents that are, among other things, irrelevant, vague, harassing, and overly broad, and would impose an undue burden on Ms. Marlin.

Exhibit 189

GENERAL OBJECTIONS

As an initial matter, non-party Ms. Marlin, Assistant General Counsel for General Dynamics Information Technology ("GDIT"), objects to the Subpoena because it was directed at her, not GDIT.[1] Any responsive documents would be the property of GDIT, not Ms. Marlin.

Ms. Marlin objects to all document requests as overly broad, unduly burdensome, harassing, vague, irrelevant to the claims or defenses of the parties to the suit, and not reasonably calculated to lead to the discovery of admissible evidence. The document requests are particularly burdensome given that Ms. Marlin is a non-party to this litigation and is not familiar with the factual and legal disputes of this lawsuit.

Further, Ms. Marlin objects to Plaintiff's document requests to the extent they seek production of documents containing confidential, proprietary, and/or any other information in which the Ms. Marlin and/or other individuals and entities (including non-parties) have an expectation of privacy and confidentiality. Ms. Marlin also objects to Plaintiff's document requests to the extent they seek the production of documents that are subject to the attorney-client, work-product, or other applicable privilege or protection. Ms. Marlin further objects to Plaintiff's document requests because it fails to allow reasonable time for compliance.

SPECIFIC OBJECTIONS

1. **"All communication regarding EEOC Charge No. 460-2014-01770; between GDIT, EEOC Federal Investigator, Jeremy Crosby and Acting District Director, Martin S. Ebel. Information should be dated from 03/20/2014 to 10/29/2015"**

Ms. Marlin objects to this request because it is vague, harassing, overly broad, and violates the expectation of privacy and confidentiality of non-parties. Ms. Marlin also objects to the extent it requests the production of documents or information already in Plaintiff's

---

[1] Although the Subpoena is directed at Ms. Marlin, Plaintiff attempted to serve her through GDIT's registered agent. Ms. Marlin objects because she was not served with the Subpoena and reserves the right to challenge the Subpoena on this basis.

Exhibit 190

possession or control, or that is more appropriately discoverable from the EEOC, a party to the litigation. Ms. Marlin further objects to the extent the request seeks the production of documents that are subject to the attorney-client, work-product, or other applicable privilege or protection.

Indeed, documents relating to communications between GDIT and the EEOC, if any, would also be in the possession of the EEOC. It is unduly burdensome for Ms. Marlin, or anyone else at GDIT, to bear the burden and expense of collecting documents that are in the possession of a party to this litigation. Likewise, any communications regarding EEOC Charge No. 460-2014-01770 to which Plaintiff is entitled would be already in Plaintiff's possession, custody, or control, or more appropriately discoverable from the EEOC. Ms. Marlin objects to making duplicative production of any document produced or to be produced by the EEOC.

Further, Ms. Marlin objects to the time period, as it calls for production of documents beyond the time frame set forth by the boundaries of relevance or what is reasonably likely to lead to the discovery of admissible evidence.

2. **"All employee human resource records for location on Corporate Drive in Houston Texas."**

Ms. Marlin objects to this request because it is irrelevant to Plaintiff's claims against the EEOC, vague, harassing, overly broad, and violates the expectation of privacy and confidentiality of non-parties. Indeed, a request for "all employee human resource records" necessarily entails documents containing confidential, proprietary, and other information in which numerous non-parties (e.g., current and former employees of GDIT) have an expectation of privacy and confidentiality. Ms. Marlin also objects to this request to the extent that it seeks the production of documents that are subject to the attorney-client, work-product, or other privileges.

Exhibit 191

Ms. Marlin further objects because the requests are not limited in time or scope. Searching and collecting documents, without a limitation on a time period, is unduly burdensome. Moreover, the requested documents are not likely to lead to the discovery of admissible evidence.

3. "**The information must be made available before the hearing on 1/11/2016. To give sufficient time, contact Plaintiff Ellenor P. Ratcliff by 11/23/2015.**"

Ms. Marlin objects to the request because it fails to allow reasonable time for compliance. Plaintiff served the Subpoena on Ms. Marlin on November 3, 2015, and expects Ms. Marlin to contact Plaintiff twenty (20) days later, and to provide voluminous documents by January 11, 2016. The requests are unduly burdensome, and additional time would be required to produce responsive, non-objectionable documents.

Ms. Marlin reserves the right to amend and/or supplement these objections if and when additional pertinent facts are obtained.

Respectfully submitted,

Carolyn Russell
Texas Bar No:
OGLETREE, DEAKINS, NASH, SMOAK
& STEWART, P.C.
One Allen Center
___ _____ ____reet, Suite 3000
Houston, Texas 77002
___-___-____

Exhibit 192

CERTIFICATE OF SERVICE

I hereby certify that a true and correct copy of the foregoing instrument has been sent in accordance with the Federal Rules of Civil Procedure on this 17th day of November, 2015 to:

Ellenor Perkins Ratcliff

Houston, Texas

Carolyn Russell

Exhibit 193

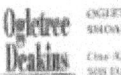

Exhibit 194

February 1, 2016

Mass Corruption within the United States. The Lord is not pleased, because you have intentionally oppressed the children of God. He will no longer stand by, but he will act because EEOC, United States Courts and Officials have broken his laws. You have accepted bribes and exploited the people. **No one will go unpunished.** We have cried out and the Lord has heard us.

Thus say's the LORD of hosts, "Whoever oppresses the poor to increase his own wealth, or gives to the rich, will come to poverty." (Proverbs22:16) The people of the land (Equal Employment Opportunity Commission, United States Courts and all associated with your wickedness) have practiced extortion and committed robbery. You have oppressed the poor and needy and have extorted from the foreigner without justice. (Ezekiel 22:29)

The Spirit of the Lord is upon me, he has anointed me for his good works. By the words of the LORD, he has given me authority to proclaim liberty to the oppressed and to proclaim the year of the LORD's favor.

To every participant whom oppressed, we rebuke you in the name of Jesus and every act that you have delivered upon the children of God shall be rendered unto you hundredfold. For you are cursed and the LORD himself will bring you to poverty, the nations will despise you; your deeds will be known to all the nations in Jesus' name, Amen.

Exhibit 196

SINGLE MOTHER DENIED DUE PROCESS BY FEDERAL GOVERNMENT	DON'T TRUST EEOC! CORRUPT U.S. GOVERNMENT	END GOVERNMENT SYSTEMATIC OPPRESSION NOW!
EEOC CIVIL RIGHTS VIOLATOR	WE DEMAND HOSTILE FREE WORKING ENVIRONMENTS	JUSTICE, WHERE ART THEE?
GDIT Neglected Employees Disabilities	EEOC Denies Claimants Due Process	WHO CAN WE TRUST? OUR GOVERNMENT IS CORRUPT
GDIT+ EEOC + FEDERAL JUDGE = SYSTEMATIC CRIMINAL ACTIVITY	EEOC STOP RACIAL DISCRIMINTION NOW!	MISCONDUCT BY FEDERAL AUTHORITIES

Exhibit 197

313

Exhibit 198

Exhibit 199

U.S. Department of Justice

Civil Rights Division

LJ:tj
3121464, 3115164
170-74-0

Employment Litigation Section - PHB
950 Pennsylvania Ave, NW
Washington DC 20530
www.usdoj.gov/crt/emp

Ellenor Ratcliff

MAR 0 4 2016

Houston, TX 77

Your letter(s) dated September 1 and September 14, 2015, addressed to the Attorney General, has been forwarded to the Employment Litigation Section of the Civil Rights Division of the Department of Justice. Please excuse our delay in responding to your correspondence.

The Employment Litigation Section is one of the federal agencies that enforces laws barring discrimination in employment based on military obligation, race, color, national origin, religion, sex, or retaliation for making a complaint of employment discrimination.

However, the Employment Litigation Section does not take or process individual complaints.

- If you want to file a complaint of employment discrimination based on your race, color, national origin, religion, sex, or retaliation for making such a complaint, you MUST file it with the EQUAL EMPLOYMENT OPPORTUNITY COMMISSION (EEOC). You should contact the EEOC directly. You can find your local office of the EEOC by calling 1-800-669-4000 or at www.eeoc.gov.

- If you want to file a complaint of employment discrimination based on your military service, your employer's failure to reemploy you after your military service, or retaliation for making such a complaint, you should contact the DEPARTMENT OF LABOR (DOL). You should contact DOL directly. You can find your local office of DOL by calling 1-866-487-2365 or at www.dol.gov/vets/aboutvets/contacts/main.htm.

There are STRICT time limits for filing complaints of employment discrimination. If you feel you have been discriminated against in employment, you should contact the correct agency AS SOON AS POSSIBLE. The attached list contains contact information for other federal agencies that may help you.

You may also wish to contact a private attorney to help you. If you cannot afford a private attorney, your local legal services association or the bar association in your state may be able to provide more information.

Exhibit 200

689   536-3 C15996
STATEMENT OF BENEFITS
TEXAS WORKFORCE COMMISSION
PO BOX 370040
EL PASO TX 79937-0040

Statement of Wages and Potential Benefit Amounts
Regular Unemployment Benefits:
Date Mailed: November 16, 2015
(All dates are in month/day/year order)

ELLENOR Y PERKINS RATCLIFF

HOUSTON TX 770

Social Security Number: XXX-XX-

Dear ELLENOR Y PERKINS RATCLIFF

Check your records! TWC has the wages below on file for you for the four quarters of your base period. We use your base period wages to figure out whether you earned enough money to qualify for unemployment insurance benefits and how much you could receive if you are eligible. After TWC looks at whether you earned enough money to qualify, TWC looks at the reason you are no longer working to decide whether you can receive benefits. **Remember, even if you earned enough wages, TWC pays benefits only if you meet the weekly requirements.**

Please check the wage information carefully. If the employer name or the wage amount is incorrect, or if an employer you worked for is missing, please contact a TWC Tele-Center immediately. More information about correcting your wages is on the back of this form.

Based on the wages listed in the box below:

[ ] You earned enough in your base period to receive unemployment benefits, if you are otherwise eligible.

[X] You did not earn enough in your base period to qualify for benefits.

EMPLOYER NAME	ST	YOUR CLAIM IS BASED ON THESE WAGES				TOTALS
		Jul-Sep 2014	Oct-Dec 2014	Jan-Mar 2015	Apr-Jun 2015	
TOTALS		$0.00	$0.00	$0.00	$0.00	$0.00

* You will receive a separate notice explaining why we did not use these wages.

- The maximum weekly benefit amount in Texas this year is $ __479__ . Based on the wages above, your weekly benefit amount is $ __0__ .
- The maximum amount you could receive during your benefit year is $ __0__ .
- Your benefit year is the 52 weeks from __11-08-15__ to __11-05-16__ .
- Keep in mind your benefits may run out before the benefit year ends.

See the back of this page for more information.

Claim ID.:	11-08-15
TWC Telephone No.:	(800)939-6631
FOR HEARING IMPAIRED CLIENTS	
Relay Texas TDD No.:	1-800-735-2989
Voice No.:	1-800-735-2988

BM100E 12/12/07

Exhibit 201

1601   1246-1 C22180
UI Support & Customer Service
TEXAS WORKFORCE COMMISSION
PO BOX 370040
EL PASO TX 79937-0040

DETERMINATION ON PAYMENT OF UNEMPLOYMENT BENEFITS
Date Mailed: November 20, 2015

ELLENOR Y PERKINS RATCLIFF
c
HOUSTON TX 77

Social Security Number: XXX-XX-
Employer: GENERAL DYNAMICS INF
As:
Employer Account No: 07-
All dates are shown in month-day-year order.

Decision

Issue: Alternate Base Period Eligibility
Decision: We cannot use an alternate base period to determine your benefit amounts. We must continue to use your regular base period.
Reason for Decision: The reason you were unable to work during the regular base period of your claim was not a medically verifiable illness or injury.
Law Reference: Subsection 201.011(1)(B) of the Texas Unemployment Compensation Act.

Understanding your Decision
If you receive a decision that says, "we cannot pay you benefits," it means there is a problem with your claim EVEN IF you have received other decisions for the same period that say, "we can pay you benefits." If even one decision for the same period says we cannot pay, you will not receive an unemployment payment for that period.
To resolve issues on decisions you receive:
1. Follow instructions on the notice(s); call the Tele-Center at 800-939-6631 if you have questions;
2. If the instructions tell you to "Report," call the Tele-Center at once;
3. If you disagree with a decision, file an appeal. Appeal each decision separately by the appeal deadline. If you fax your appeal, keep a confirmation sheet.
Your employer can appeal TWC's decision to pay benefits. TWC will notify you of any appeal hearing. If you do not participate, you may lose your benefits and have to repay benefits you received.

Determination of Potential Chargeback for the Employer

If You Disagree with this Decision

If you disagree with this decision, you may appeal. Submit your appeal online, by fax, or by mailing on or before **12-04-15**. TWC will use the postmark date or the date we receive the fax or online form to determine whether your appeal is timely. If you appeal by fax, you should keep your fax confirmation as proof of transmission. Please include a copy of this notice with appeals correspondence. **You must appeal each determination separately.**

Mail the appeal to:

You may appeal by submitting TWC's online appeal form. Go to www.texasworkforce.org

Appeal Tribunal
Texas Workforce Commission
101 E. 15th Street
Austin, TX 78778-0002
Or fax to (512) 475-1135

Case No.: 18
Claim ID.: 11-08-15
Claim Date: 11-08-15
HEARING IMPAIRED CLIENTS
CALL 711 for RELAY TEXAS

Please See Reverse For How To File An Appeal.

BD300E 06/27/2013

Exhibit 202

Texas Workforce Commission
A Member of Texas Workforce Solutions

August 6, 2019

Ellenor Perkins Ratcliff
1
Cypress, TX 774

Date Received: **6/21/2019**
Request No. : 190621-008
Total Charges : $30.90
Balance Due : $30.90

RE: Ellenor Perkins

Dear Ellenor Perkins Ratcliff:

Enclosed please find the information which you requested.

Also enclosed is an invoice for services provided. Please see that this invoice is directed to the proper individual within your organization to ensure prompt payment.

Please reference the Request No. listed above when submitting payment or making inquiry about this request.

If you have any questions regarding the enclosed information, please feel free to contact the UI Ombudsman at 512-475-0435 or 512-463-2999.

Sincerely,

/illarreal
Assistant Disclosure Officer
512-4

Texas Workforce Commission, Open Records Section
• 101 E. 15th Street, Room 266• Austin, Texas 78778-0001 • Tel: (512) 463-2422 • Fax: 512/463-2990 •
• Relay Texas: 800-735-2989 (TDD) 800-735-2988 (Voice) • @twc.state.tx.us • www.twc.state.tx.us •
Equal Opportunity Employer/Services

Exhibit 203

```
14:07:49 Monday, July 29, 2019

  BND42200           Benefits - Non-Monetary Determinations          07-29-19
  BVI             SIDES Employer Response to Ntc of Appl For UI Benefits  14:07:44

  Action: _                                          Updt: 11-25-15 Bro
  SSN:              ELLENOR Y PERKINS RATCLIFF   PGM: REG  Claim Id: 11-08-15
  Claim Dt: 11-08-15  Type: IC  Employer: 07-        GENERAL DYNAMICS INFORMATI


                    Attachment: N
                Amended Response:
         Amended Response Reason: _

                  Notice Sent: 11-16-15
                 Empr Rsp Due: 11-30-15
      Claimant Separation Reason: QT   QUIT
                Empr Responded: 11-25-15
      Employer Separation Reason: QT   Voluntary QT/Separation

                   TMC Action: R    ROUTE ONLY
           Current Investigator:

  F1=Hp      3=Ex 4=Mn 5=NMER                 9=Tg 10=Left  11=Right 12=Pr
  CMD: _____
   SIDES claim response       -0-REG-2015-11-08-2015- displayed successfully
```

Exhibit 204

```
14:07:57 Monday, July 29, 2019

  BND42200           Benefits - Non-Monetary Determinations          07-29-19
  BVI                  SIDES Employment Information                  14:07:56

  Action: _                                          Updt: 11-25-15 Bro
  SSN:              ELLENOR Y PERKINS RATCLIFF   PGM: REG  Claim Id: 11-08-15
  Claim Dt: 11-08-15  Type: IC  Employer: 07-        GENERAL DYNAMICS INFORMATI

  Claimant Information                    Employer Information
  --------------------                    --------------------

  Other SSN:                              Corrected Empr Name:
  Other Name:                             Corrected Empr Acct:
  Was this seasonal employment:           Corrected Empr FEIN:
  First Day of Work: 09-09-13
  Last Day of Work: 02-17-14
  Claimant's average weekly wage: 0.00
  Total Wages Earned: 0.00
  Total Weeks Worked:
  Total Wages Earned After Claim Date: 0.00
  Total Number of Hours Worked After Claim Date:

  F1=Hp      3=Ex 4=Mn 5=NMER                 9=Tg 10=Left  11=Right 12=Pr
  CMD: _____
   Scrolling performed.
```

Exhibit 205

```
14:08:01 Monday, July 29, 2019

   BND42200            Benefits - Non-Monetary Determinations         07-29-19
   BVI                  SIDES General Separation Information          14:07:59

   Action: _                                              Updt: 11-25-15 Bro
   SSN:              ELLENOR Y PERKINS RATCLIFF   PGM: REG  Claim Id: 11-08-15
   Claim Dt: 11-08-15  Type: IC  Employer: 07-       GENERAL DYNAMICS INFORMATI

   Reason for Separation: Voluntary QT/Separation
   Separation Date: 02-17-14                 Strike or Lockout:
   Reasonable assurance of returning to work:    Return to work date:
   If still working, is claimant working all available hours:
   If NO, why isn't claimant working all available hours?

   Additional Information:

   Preparer/Company Name: TALX UCM Services, Inc.                          T
   Preparer/Contact Name: N      Berens
   Title: UCS
   Phone: (800) 829-1510  Ext: 2932      Fax: (888)
   Email:         @equifax.com

   F1=Hp      3=Ex 4=Mn 5=NMER              9=Tg 10=Left  11=Right 12=Pr
   CMD: _____
   Scrolling performed.
```

Exhibit 206

```
14:08:03 Monday, July 29, 2019

   BND42200            Benefits - Non-Monetary Determinations         07-29-19
   BVI                 SIDES Employer Response / Quit Information     14:08:01

   Action: _                                              Updt: 11-25-15 Bro
   SSN:              ELLENOR Y PERKINS RATCLIFF   PGM: REG  Claim Id: 11-08-15
   Claim Dt: 11-08-15  Type: IC  Employer: 07-       GENERAL DYNAMICS INFORMATI

   Separation Information
   Reason for Quitting: Personal Reasons
   Additional Information The claimant voluntarily quit for personal
    reasons.|  Did he/she give a specific reason (other than personal)   _ more

   Was continuing work available?  Y
   Were there changes to the hiring agreement?
   If Yes, what were the changes?


   Did the claimant take actions to avoid quitting?  N
   If yes, what actions?


   F1=Hp      3=Ex 4=Mn 5=NMER              9=Tg 10=Left  11=Right 12=Pr
   CMD: _____
   Scrolling performed.
```

Exhibit 207

```
14:08:13 Monday, July 29, 2019

   BND42200              Benefits - Non-Monetary Determinations        07-29-19
   BVI                   SIDES Employer Response / Quit Information    14:08:01

   Action:   +------------------------------------------------------------+ Bro
   SSN:      |                                      Total Lines: 5        |  __
   Claim Dt  | The claimant voluntarily quit for personal reasons.|  Did  | MATI
             | he/she give a specific reason (other than personal) for    |
   Separati  | resigning (marriage, domestic obligations, school classes, |
   Reason f  | etc.)? No other details are available as the site is now   |
   Addition  | closed.                                                    |
    reasons  |                                                            | ore
             |                                                            |
   Was cont  |                                                            |
   Were the  |                                                            |
   If Yes,   |                                                            |
             |                                                            |
             |         F3=Ex                       7=Up  8=Dn              |
   Did the   +------------------------------------------------------------+
   If yes, what actions?


   F1=Hp          3=Ex 4=Mn 5=NMER                9=Tg 10=Left  11=Right 12=Pr
   CMD: _____
```

Exhibit 208

Exhibit 209

Intake forms › Inbox ×

P Estrada <...@oiec.texas.gov> Tue, Dec 18, 2018, 4:41 PM
to E...   .COM

Please fill out our Intake Packet so the Office of Injured Employee Counsel (OIEC) can help with your workers' compensation dispute
You can find it at http://www.oiec.texas.gov/employee/intakeform.html - it is also attached.
1. Fill out all pages.
2. Print.
3. Sign (three of the pages).
4. Send all pages to OIEC by fax **512-804-4181**
Still have questions? Watch our video about the Intake Packet:
- English: https://www.youtube.com/watch?v=QauzNZIXmL8
- Spanish: https://www.youtube.com/watch?v=YQ0kr3R9ubM&feature=youtu.be

Thank you,

P.
Customer Support Specialist
Office of Injured Employee Counsel
(866) 393-6432

Exhibit 210

Fax Cover Sheet

TO: Office of Injured Employee Counsel
FAX: 512-☐
PHONE: (866) 393-6432 ext.
DATE: 12/20/2018
SUBJECT: Intake Packet

FROM: Ellenor Perkins Ratcliff
FAX: N/A
PHONE: 832-☐
OF PAGES: 26 including Fax Cover

Page 1 Cover

Pages 2-6 Intake Packet

Pages 7-15 Doctor Excuses, Notes and Summary

Pages 16-17 Letter of Constructive Discharge

Pages 18-19 Doctor's Note/ Form H1836-A

Pages 20-24 Emails addressing Job Injury

Pages 25-26 Dress Code Standards Revised 2-1-12 and 6-12-13 (Version 2) Policy/Standards is located in the 3rd paragraph.

Exhibit 211

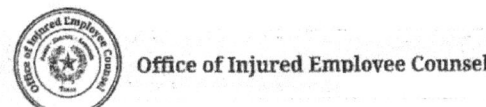
Office of Injured Employee Counsel

7551 Metro Center Drive, Suite 100, Austin, TX 78744
F: (512) 804-4181 | T: (866) 393-6432
@oiec.texas.gov

INTAKE FORM

REQUIRED FORMS

- ☐ OIEC-31, HIPAA Authorization *(Complete, sign, date. It is important that you provide the information for all doctors who have treated you – first and last name, address, and phone and fax number.)*
- ☐ OMB-02, Office of Injured Employee Counsel Assistance Request *(Complete, sign and date.)*

ABOUT YOU

Last name: Perkins Ratcli	First name: Ellenor	Your phone number:
Last 4 social security numbers: XXX-XX- _ _ _ _		Your street address:
Your email address:		Your address - city, state, zip code:

ABOUT YOUR CLAIM

DWC #: 15273437	Date of injury: 10/04/2013
Insurance carrier: Broadspire	Employer at time of injury: General Dynamics
Adjuster's name: S. Fields	Were you working for any other employer when you were injured? ☐ Yes, (employer name) _____ ☒ No
Adjuster's phone number: 214-640-4569	*Attorney's name (If any): *If the claimant is represented, OIEC cannot be involved or assist.
Adjuster's fax number:	*Attorney's phone number (if any):

ABOUT YOUR BENEFITS

Average Weekly Wage:	Treating Doctor:
Are you working? If not, when did you stop? No, 2/17/14	Referral Doctor(s):
Why did you stop working? Due to continued exposer	Treatment(s) Received: ☒ Medication ☐ MRI ☐ Physical Therapy ☐ Injections ☐ Nerve Study (EMG/NCV) ☐ Surgery
Have you been examined by a doctor who assigned an impairment rating? ☒ Yes, (doctor name) Collaco ☐ No	Are you a candidate for surgery? If so what kind? ☐ Yes, (surgery type) _____ ☒ No

OIEC Intake Form (Revised June 2018)

Exhibit 212

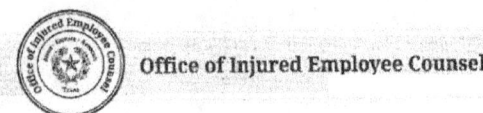

Office of Injured Employee Counsel
7551 Metro Center Drive, Suite 100, Austin, TX 78744
F: (512) 804-4181 | T: (866) 393-6432
r@oiec.texas.gov

DWC # 15273437

ABOUT YOUR INJURY

Tell us how you were injured? Please provide as much information as possible.

While working I informed General Dynamics Information Technology of my injuries. Employees applied perfume and cologne at their lockers on a daily basis, after employees left training classroom for the two weeks. I informed my supervisor and he apologized. I contacted HR and was told, "We can't stop CSR from wearing perfume" per Zandra Bosie. I informed General Dynamics of my injury when I returned to work by providing notification by email, a doctors note and spoke to my superior, Austin Clem and Sherona Johnson. GDIT have a policy in place and refused to enforce policy causing continued injury to my lungs, after I could no longer take it I constructively discharged.

ABOUT YOUR DISPUTE

What type of assistance are you requesting from OIEC?

I pray that Workman's Comp benefits are fully restored and that I am compensated for the pain and suffering caused by the inaction of GDIT and Broadspire. Also, I pray Broadspire and General Dynamics Information Technology is punished to the fullest extent of the law for fraud.

SIGNATURE

The information in this Intake Form is accurate to the best of my knowledge. By signing this form, I authorize the Office of Injured Employee Counsel to submit documents to the Division of Workers' Compensation on my behalf.

[X] I accept and do authorize the Office of Injured Employee Counsel to send text messages to my cell phone.

Cell Phone Number: _____ Cell Phone Provider (AT&T, T-Mobile, Sprint, etc.): Boost

Employee signature: ⇒ _____ Date: 12/20/18

OIEC STAFF ONLY

Reviewed by	CHL	OMB-2	DAL	DCL	DWC32	DWC45	SCN	I12	ADMIN-14

Mail or fax the completed intake form and attached forms to:
Office of Injured Employee Counsel
7551 Metro Center Drive, Suite 100, MS-50, Austin, TX 78744
Fax number (512) 804-4181

OIEC Intake Form (Revised June 2018)

Exhibit 216

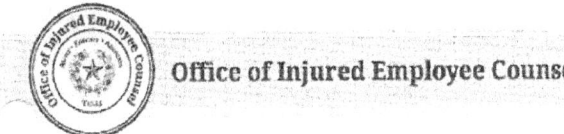

Office of Injured Employee Counsel

"Our mission is to assist, educate, and advocate on behalf of the injured employees of Texas."

oiec.texas.gov | T: 866.393.6432

OFFICE OF INJURED EMPLOYEE COUNSEL ASSISTANCE REQUEST

Name: Ellenor Perkins Ratcliff
DWC#: 15273437
Address: 1
Email address:
City: Cypress, Texas 774
Date of Injury: 10/04/2013
Telephone:

I, Ellenor Perkins Ratc, am requesting the assistance of the Office of Injured Employee Counsel (OIEC). I am not represented by an attorney on the issue for which I am requesting assistance, although I know that I have that right. This document will remain in effect until I terminate it. I may terminate OIEC assistance at any time by notifying the Office of Injured Employee Counsel or by hiring an attorney. If I hire an attorney, I know that my attorney must file his or her contract of employment with the Texas Department of Insurance, Division of Workers' Compensation.

I know and clearly understand that the Ombudsman:

- is an employee of the Office of Injured Employee Counsel.
- is not acting as an attorney nor performing services of an attorney.
- will not be representing me as an attorney or in any other capacity.
- will be assisting me to present my claim for benefits.
- provides assistance at no charge to unrepresented persons requesting assistance.
- cannot and will not provide legal advice.
- cannot and will not make or sign any agreements for me.
- cannot and will not make any decisions for me.

I authorize any OIEC employee to have access to my claim file and other confidential records pertaining to my claim, including medical records.

I understand that any communication made to any OIEC employee is confidential under Texas Labor Code § 404.110 and that the employee cannot generally be compelled to disclose that information on any matter relating to my workers' compensation claim.

I authorize the Ombudsman to sign time-sensitive documents on my behalf that are required to be filed to preserve my rights in the workers' compensation system.

I have read or have had this information read to me by someone of my choice, and I understand and accept these terms.

_____   12/20/2018
Signature of Injured Employee or Beneficiary   Date

NOTE: With few exceptions, upon your request, you are entitled to be informed about the information the Office of Injured Employee Counsel collects about you; receive and review the information (Government Code, §§552.021 and 552.023); and have the Office of Injured Employee Counsel correct information that is incorrect (Government Code, §559.004).

Form OMB-02 (Rev. 03/2017)

Exhibit 219

OFFICE OF INJURED EMPLOYEE COUNSEL
7551 METRO CENTER DR STE 100
AUSTIN TX 78744-1645

RETURN SERVICE REQUESTED

N HOUSTON
TX 77 STATE OF
20 DEC 18

NEOPOST FIRST-CLASS MAIL
12/19/2018
US POSTAGE $000.68

ZIP 77060
041M11276674

ELLENOR PERKINS RATCLIFF

CYPRESS, TX 77433-____

77433-116862

Exhibit 220

Fax Cover Sheet

COMPANY LOGO

TO: OIEC
FAX: 281-
PHONE: (866)
DATE: 1/09/2019
SUBJECT: Updated Medical Providers List and HIPPA Authorization form

FROM: Ellenor Perkins R
FAX: N/A
PHONE: 832-
OF PAGES: 3 including Fax Cover

Page 1 Cover

Page 2 Medical Providers (All providers are still practicing. I have provided an updated list which has all fax numbers).

Page 3 HIPPA Authorization (Please discontinue using the form I signed dated for 12/20/18. I have provided a new form dated for 1/9/2019.

Exhibit 221

OFFICE OF INJURED EMPLOYEE COUNSEL
NORMAN DARWIN, PUBLIC COUNSEL

This was mailed

1/09/2019

Dr.
Harris Health System

Houston, TX 77074

RE: **Claimant:** Ellenor Perkins-Ratcliff
Date of Injury: 10/01/2013
DWC No.: DWC #1
Carrier's Claim No.: 188
Subject: <u>Request for Medical Opinion Regarding Work Injury (Occupational Disease)</u>

Dear Dr.   :

I am the Ombudsman assigned to assist Ellenor Perkins-Ratcliff in the resolution of a dispute regarding the compensability of HIS/HER injury. Your help is requested to provide a professional opinion (within reasonable medical probability) that addresses the following:

1. When did you first examine the claimant for treatment of the Lung injury.
2. What did the claimant tell you regarding how, when, or where she began manifesting symptoms of lung injury. Please describe what she told you about how, when, and where the exposure occurred. Did she indicate how she felt after exposure? If so, please describe. Are you familiar with the substances of perfume and cologne that she described? Are the effects of the exposure consistent with his description?
3. What subjective complaints did the claimant describe to you regarding the Lung Injury
4. Did the claimant manifest any objective signs of a Lung injury on the date of your first examination? If so, please describe them in detail.
5. Did you review any medical records or test results prior to making a diagnosis? If so, please describe them.
6. Did you diagnose a Lung injury on the date of your exam or subsequent thereto, and, if so, what was it?
7. Do you have an opinion as to whether or not the Lung Injury in question was caused by a repetitive trauma (or toxic exposure) to the area of the body where the condition was found? If so, what is your opinion?

350 NORTH SAM HOUSTON PARKWAY EAST, SUITE 140 * HOUSTON, TEXAS 77060
281-260-3035 * FAX:
WWW.OIEC.TEXAS.GOV

Form OIEC-41, Causation Occupational Disease (Revised November 2012)

Exhibit 222

8. How would a repetitive trauma (toxic exposure) cause the Lung injury to occur?
9. What treatment do you recommend for the Lung injury that you have described including the need for any additional testing? (What is the prognosis for the condition caused by the toxic exposure?) [The question of prognosis for a toxic exposure would be in addition to the question of treatment, not instead of.

What is your professional opinion, within reasonable medical probability, that the Claimant's injury of 10/04/2013 is directly related to the inhalation of paint fumes and/or volatile substances at work? If you find that there is a causal connection, what is the nature of the injury and how did it occur in your opinion?

What job duties did the Claimant inform you that HE/SHE is responsible for at HIS/HER place of employment? In your professional opinion, was the Claimant exposed to or contaminated by toxic fumes/substances (chemical, mold, etc.) at work that resulted in any of the Claimant's medical problems? If so, please identify the medical problems that you believe were caused by the exposure.

Are there other possible sources of exposure outside of the Claimant's employment that could cause such medical problems? If so, would you consider that the Claimant's job duties placed HIM/HER at a greater risk of harm than the general public?

What is your understanding of the time proximity of the symptoms and effects (whether immediate or latent) of the toxic exposure that the Claimant started to develop?

In your professional opinion, are the Claimant's medical problems caused by and directly related to HIS/HER ongoing toxic exposure (due to work conditions) OR to a specific incident at work?

How much toxic exposure (type/level of concentration, dosage, duration) was the Claimant subject to at work (either through an incident at work OR over a period of time)?
- What are the detected chemicals (substances or fumes) at the Claimant's place of employment, and is there a clinically significant level of exposure that Claimant sustained at work that the general public would not be exposed to? If Claimant suffered from a harmful exposure to the chemical substances or fumes, how is such exposure distinguishable from the amount and type the general public would ordinarily be exposed to, if at all?
- If this is a one-time incident of toxic exposure, have you previously provided treatment to the Claimant OR are you aware of any prior medical treatment for the symptoms that HE/SHE is currently exhibiting?

If the Claimant had pre-existing medical conditions, did HE/SHE experience a worsening of those conditions from the work incident of DATE OF INJURY OR from the exposure

Exhibit 223

to work environment over a period of time (please give best estimate for length of time that the Claimant was exposed to such toxic fumes or substances)?

If this is a toxic inhalation case and the claimant had a pre-existing condition (e.g. hypersensitive lung reaction), did the exposure to toxic fumes at work cause an increase in HIS/HER symptoms after the exposure?
- Has the Claimant improved somewhat with removal from the work environment as well as medical treatment?
- Can a clinical association be made about the Claimant's medical problems to HIS/HER work environment, with respect to the development of the Claimant's IF APPLICABLE, INSERT THE TYPE OF SYMPTOMATOLOGY, SUCH AS NASAL, ETC symptomatology that is consistent with HIS/HER toxic exposure/fume inhalation and HIS/HER removal from HIS/HER work environment?

Please be as detailed and specific as possible in your response and provide you answer in narrative form. Please also include any diagnostic test results and/or medical reports that support your answers.

Your professional medical opinion addressing the questions above is critical in helping to resolve the current dispute. Thus, your prompt attention and cooperation in this matter are greatly appreciated. Please fax your response to [281-   ] no later than 1/30/19]. **If you have any questions, please feel free to contact me at 866-393-6432 Ext, Thank you for your time and consideration.**

Sincerely,

Ombudsman

cc: Ellenor Perkins Ratcliff

Exhibit 224

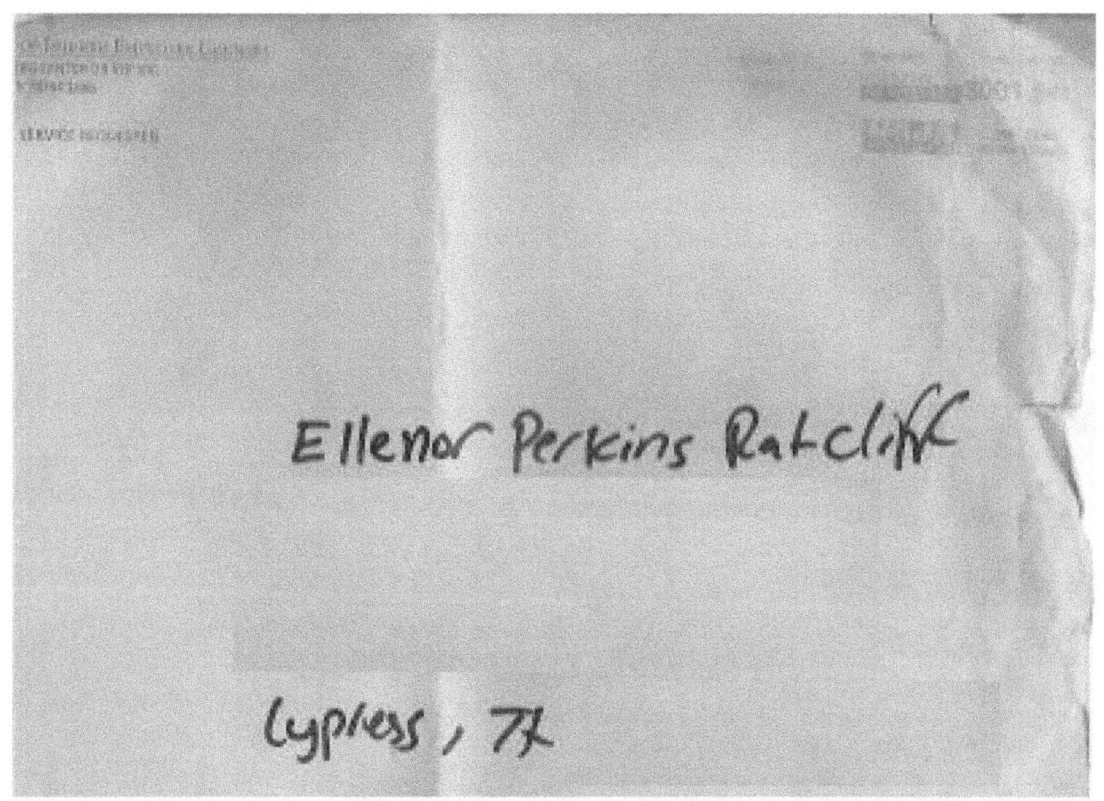

Exhibit 225

 OFFICE OF INJURED EMPLOYEE COUNSEL

03/19/2019

Ellenor Perkins Ratcliff

Cypress, TX 77

RE: Injured Employee Name: Ellenor Perkins Ratcliff
     Date of Injury: 10/04/2013
     DWC Number: 15273437
     Ins. Carrier Claim Number: 188029923001

Dear Ellenor Perkins Ratcliff:

We have been working together on your workers' compensation dispute. We discussed the importance of obtaining the following documents prior to moving forward with your dispute:

1. Letter from your treating doctor specifying the conditions/diagnosis which are related to the mechanism of the injury. (CAUSATION ANALYSIS)

As of today, I have not received these documents. I am going to put your case on hold until I receive these documents OR you contact me to let me know that you would like to move forward with your dispute without these documents.

You can contact me at 1-866-393-6432 EXT: or you can contact customer service should you wish to continue with this dispute. Please fax any documents to 281

Respectfully,

Ombudsman

OIEC-26-Dispute On Hold letter (Revised March 2017)

Exhibit 226

OFFICE OF INJURED EMPLOYEE COUNSEL
7551 METRO CENTER DR STE 100
AUSTIN TX 78744-1645

RETURN SERVICE REQUESTED

N HOUSTON TX
29 MAR '19
PM 2 L

NEOPOST 03-18-2019
US POSTAGE $000.50
ZIP 77080

Ellenor Perkins Ratcliff

Cypress, TX

77433-116962

Exhibit 227

AFTER VISIT SUMMARY

Ellenor Perkins MRN: DoB:
📅 3/28/2019 9:40 AM 📍 Family Practice Valibona 713-272-2600

What's Next
You currently have no upcoming appointments scheduled.

Allergies as of 3/28/2019
Fully Assessed On: 2/19/2015 By:

	Severity	Noted	Reaction Type	Reactions
No Known Drug Allergies	Not Specified	10/06/2009		
No latex allergies	Not Specified	06/24/2014		

Filling your prescription at a Harris Health System Pharmacy?
- Please request your prescription at the pharmacy DROP OFF window
- Want your PRESCRIPTIONS MAILED? Visit myhealth.harrishealth.org

Ellenor Perkins (MRN:) • Printed at 3/28/19 11:16 AM   Page 1 of 2

Exhibit 228

**TEXAS DEPARTMENT OF INSURANCE
DIVISION OF WORKERS' COMPENSATION**

Si prefiere hablar con una persona de habla hispana acerca de esta correspondencia o de su reclamo, sírvase llamar al 1-800-252-7031.

May 15, 2019

ELLENOR PERKINS RATCLIFF

CYPRESS, TX 774

Claim No: 15273437
Docket No: 15273437-01-BR
Carrier No: 188029923001
Employee: ELLENOR PERKINS RATCLIFF
Employer: GENERAL DYNAMICS CORP

Date of
Injury: October 4, 2013

BENEFIT REVIEW CONFERENCE
DATE: June 18, 2019
TIME: 09:15 AM
PLACE: TDI-DIV WORKERS' COMPENSATION

HOUSTON, TX 77060
(800) 2

Description of Issues*
C06 EXISTENCE OF COMPENSABLE INJ

*Additional Issues may be discussed.

THIS CLAIM HAS BEEN SET FOR A BENEFIT REVIEW CONFERENCE

You are required to appear at this conference at the time and location stated above. The parties will attempt to resolve any disputes about this claim. If you are an injured employee and are not represented by an attorney and would like Office of Injured Employee Counsel ombudsman assistance, please contact the field office at the address or phone number shown below.

The Benefit Review Conference is an informal meeting between an injured employee, the employee's designated representative (if any), a sub-claimant (if any), and a representative of the insurance carrier. The employer is also entitled, but not required, to attend the conference. A Benefit Review Officer, who is an impartial Texas Department of Insurance, Division of Workers' Compensation (TDI-DWC) employee, will also be present and will assist the parties in resolving the dispute. No testimony will be taken and no recording will be made.

Not later than 14 days before the conference, you must provide copies of all written information relevant to the disputed issue or issues to all other parties and the TDI-DWC field office handling the claim. If it is not possible to mail the information in time, bring enough copies to the conference to give to all parties.

DR01 (Rev. 02-28-18)

An Equal Opportunity Employer

Exhibit 229

If you wish to cancel or reschedule this conference, you must contact the TDI-DWC field office at the address or telephone number below. A request to cancel or reschedule this conference must be made within 10 days after you receive this notice. A request received after 10 days may not be granted unless the TDI-DWC determines there was good cause for the delay.

You are required to attend this conference. Failure to attend may result in an Administrative Violation and be subject to a penalty up to a maximum of $25,000.

Sincerely,

TDI-DIV WORKERS' COMPENSATION

HOUSTON, TX 77060

THIS LETTER WAS ALSO SENT TO THE FOLLOWING:
NEW HAMPSHIRE INSURANCE CO
PO BOX 25974
OVERLAND PARK, KS 66225-5974

INFORMATION COPIES WERE ALSO SENT TO:
GENERAL DYNAMICS CORP
2941 FAIRVIEW PARK DR
FALLS CHURCH, VA 22042-4522

OMBUDSMAN
HOUSTON, TX 77060

DR01 (Rev. 02-28-18) An Equal Opportunity Employer

Exhibit 230

 **Texas Department of Insurance**
DIVISION OF WORKERS' COMPENSATION
7551 METRO CENTER DR STE 100
AUSTIN TX 78744-1645

RETURN SERVICE REQUESTED

54 DMAGNA8 77433

Exhibit 231

OFFICE OF INJURED EMPLOYEE COUNSEL
350 N. SAM HOUSTON PKWY E #110, HOUSTON, TX 77060
(866) 393-6432
(@oiec.texas.gov
www.oiec.texas.gov

May 16, 2019

ELLENOR PERKINS RATCLIFF
CYPRESS, TX 774

Injured employee:	PERKINS RATCLIFF, ELLENOR
WC #:	15273437-HW
Date of injury:	October 04, 2013
Carrier:	NEW HAMPSHIRE INSURANCE CO
Carrier claim #:	188029923001

Item 1. Type of Appointment	Item 2. Assigned Ombudsman
BENEFIT REVIEW CONFERENCE	ALEXANDER ELIAS
Item 3. Date / Time of Appointment	**Item 4. Location**
May 31, 2019 11:00 AM	HOUSTON

ABOUT YOUR APPOINTMENT WITH YOUR OMBUDSMAN

You have an appointment to meet with your ombudsman at the date and time shown above. This meeting might be in person or by phone. If it is by phone, they will call you.

This appointment is to help you prepare for your dispute resolution proceeding. Your ombudsman can also attend that proceeding with you. Help from your ombudsman is free.

Bring any letters or reports from:
- Division of Workers' Compensation,
- insurance carrier,
- your employer, and
- any doctors you have seen about your workers' compensation injury.

Call us as soon as possible if you need to reschedule your appointment or no longer want help from an ombudsman.

If we do not hear from you, we will expect you to keep the scheduled appointment.

Contact us at c   )oiec.texas.gov or 1-866-393-6432, ext. 441   /ou have questions or need to reschedule.

Sincerely,

Office of Injured Employee Counsel

OIEC-71 (Rev. 8/18)

Exhibit 232

TEXAS DEPARTMENT OF INSURANCE
DIVISION OF WORKERS' COMPENSATION
7551 METRO CENTER DR STE 100
AUSTIN TX 78744-1645

RETURN SERVICE REQUESTED

54 DMIWNAB 77433

Exhibit 233

 OFFICE OF INJURED EMPLOYEE COUNSEL

May 17, 2019

ELLENOR PERKINS RATCLIFF

CYPRESS TX 774

Date of Injury: 10/4/13
DWC Number: 15273437
Ins. Carrier Claim Number: 188029923001

Dear Injured Employee:

Your claim has been referred to an Ombudsman for assistance with your workers' compensation dispute.

We will call you on 6/4/19 at 3:00 to discuss your case further.

Please have anything that may be helpful to your workers' compensation claim available at this appointment.

If you need to reschedule your appointment, please call OIEC at 1-866-393-6432 or email us at @oiec.texas.gov.

Sincerely,

Office of Injured Employee Counsel

350 NORTH SAM HOUSTON PARKWAY EAST, SUITE 110 ★ HOUSTON, TEXAS 77060
281-260-3035 ★ FAX:
WWW.OIEC.TEXAS.GOV

Exhibit 234

OFFICE OF INJURED EMPLOYER COUNSEL
7551 METRO CENTER DR STE 100
AUSTIN TX 78744-1645

RETURN SERVICE REQUESTED

N HOUSTON
TX 77
20 MAY
PM 9 L

NEOPOST
05/17/2019
$000.50

ZIP 77700
041M11276

ELLENOR PERKINS RATCLIFF
CYPRESS   TX

Exhibit 235

Fax Cover Sheet

COMPANY LOGO

TO: MEDICAL RECORDS
FAX: 713-
PHONE: 713-
DATE: 8/20/19
SUBJECT: Intake Packet

FROM: Ellenor Perkins
FAX: N/A
PHONE: 832-
OF PAGES: 2 including Fax Cover

Page 1 Cover

Page 2 HARRIS HEALTH SYSTEM – AUTHORIZATION FORM 284355

Exhibit 236

TRANSMISSION VERIFICATION REPORT

```
                              TIME  : 08/20/2019 09:38
                              NAME  :
                              FAX   :
                              TEL   :
                              SER.# : BROE
```

```
DATE,TIME              08/20  09:36
FAX NO./NAME           713272
DURATION               00:01:07
PAGE(S)                02
RESULT                 OK
MODE                   STANDARD
                       ECM
```

Exhibit 237

TRANSMISSION VERIFICATION REPORT

```
                              TIME  : 08/20/2019 09:38
                              NAME  :
                              FAX   :
                              TEL   :
                              SER.# : BROE
```

```
DATE,TIME              08/20  09:36
FAX NO./NAME           713272
DURATION               00:01:07
PAGE(S)                02
RESULT                 OK
MODE                   STANDARD
                       ECM
```

this fax is proof that I Ellenor Perkins Ratcliff completed the HIPPA Authorization Form for Harris Health System.

Exhibit 238

TRANSMISSION VERIFICATION REPORT

```
                              TIME  : 08/20/2019 09:51
                              NAME  :
                              FAX   :
                              TEL   :
                              SER.# : BROE8
```

```
DATE,TIME              08/20  09:49
FAX NO./NAME           713771
DURATION               00:01:03
PAGE(S)                03
RESULT                 OK
MODE                   STANDARD
```

Exhibit 239

HARRIS HEALTH SYSTEM

PERKINS, ELLENOR YVETTE
MRN:
DOB: , Sex: F
Enc. Date: 01/06/14

Results
XRAY CHEST 2 VIEWS (Order

Result Information

Status	Provider Status
Final result (1/6/2014 10:29 AM)	Reviewed

Result Date - 1/6/2014

Narrative

EXAMINATION: CHEST 2 VIEWS   Jan 06, 2014 08:53:45 AM

CLINICAL INDICATION: 36 y/o female with Asthma

COMPARISON: CXR 01/31/2013

DISCUSSION:
Lines/tubes: None.

Lungs: Mildly increased lung volumes. No evidence of pneumonia or pulmonary edema.

Pleura: No pleural effusion or pneumothorax.

Heart and mediastinum: Prominent cardiomediastinal silhouette, especially the left ventricle on lateral view.

Bones and soft tissues: No acute osseous or soft tissue abnormality.

Impression

IMPRESSION:
1. Mildly increased lung volumes. No focal consolidation.
2. Prominent cardiac silhouette. Recommend correlation with echocardiogram given patient's symptoms.

A "PRELIMINARY" report was made available via EPIC at the time of dictation by the resident indicated below. If the report is described as "FINALIZED" it indicates the attending/staff radiologist below has reviewed the images and agrees with the resident's interpretation.

Resident   Roark
Staff: Lenge

Lab and Collection
XRAY CHEST 2 VIEWS on 1/6/2014

Result History
XRAY CHEST 2 VIEWS on 1/6/2014

Result Notes
Notes Recorded by Simpson-   n 1/16/2014 at 4:45 PM
I have reviewed your labs/exams. There are some abnormalities. Please have patient schedule an

Exhibit 240

Result Information
Status: Final result (4/15/2014 2:16 PM) Provider Status: Reviewed

Result Date - 4/15/2014
Component Results

Component	Value	Ref Range & Units	Status
Vitamin B12	602	211 - 911 pg/mL	Final

Lab and Collection
VITAMIN B12 on 4/15/2014

Result History
VITAMIN B12 on 4/15/2014

Result Notes
Notes Recorded by Truong, DO on 4/15/2014 at 2:20 PM
Please send normal results letter to Pt.

Reviewed by List
Ozaeta, RN on 4/16/2014 4:18 PM
Truong, DO on 4/15/2014 2:20 PM

HARRIS HEALTH SYSTEM

PERKINS, ELLENOR YVETTE
MRN:
DOB: F
Enc. Date: 02/13/14

Location

Name	Address
SMITH CLINIC	2525 HOLLY HALL ST Bldg A Houston TX 77054-4124

Patient and Visit Information
Patient Information

Patient Name	MRN	Sex	DOB	SSN
Perkins, Ellenor		Female		7

Visit Information

	Provider	Department	Encounter #
2/13/2014 8:00 AM	Hanania, MD	Sc Pulmonary Clinic	

Results
IGE TOTAL (0

Result Information
Status: Abnormal Final result (2/13/2014 4:35 PM) Provider Status: Reviewed

Result Date - 2/13/2014
Component Results

Component	Value	Ref Range & Units	Status
IgE, Total	120.0 (H)	0.0 - 100.0 IU/mL	Final

Lab and Collection
IGE, TOTAL on 2/13/2014

Exhibit 241

_____ Never Reviewed

Reason for Visit

Reason for Visit
Breathing Problem

Vitals

Vital Signs - Last Recorded

BP	Pulse	Temp(Src)	Resp	Ht	Wt
113/68 mmHg	64	97.9 °F (36.6 °C) (Oral)	18	5' 6" (1.676 m)	216 lb 9.6 oz (98.249 kg)
BMI	LMP				
34.98 kg/m2	01/31/2014				

Vitals History

Progress Notes

Progress Notes

Author	Status	Last Editor	Updated	Created
Thakur,	Signed	Thakur,	2/19/2014 10:03 AM	2/19/2014 8:45 AM

Patient was engaged in plan of care and encouraged to continue to be actively involved in her own care, therefore, improving safety. AVS given and explained to the patient and advised her to share it with other health care providers. Patient had no questions regarding treatment received, patient instructions and appointments. Patient demonstrated/verbalized understanding of instructions given.

Thakur

Author	Status	Last Editor	Updated	Created
Truong,	Signed		2/19/2014 10:03 AM	2/19/2014 8:22 AM

Chief complaint: Breathing Problem

Ellenor Yvette Perkins is a 36y.o. female who presents for evaluation of Breathing Problem

HPI:
HPI

Pt wants to transfer from MLK to here

1. SOB followed by Pulm-She has had EKG, CXR, PFT. TTE and methacholine challenge appts in future. Pt spoke at length about call center job she started 9/2013 where "people spraying perfume" that causes her sxs, but sxs worsened after quit her job. She has written emails to HR that rule was not enforced and wants to report to CDC also. Had child care at her home prior to last job but was involved

Exhibit 242

in car accident and stopped. She also reports fatigue. Admits to onset of these sxs when exposed to mold which is noted on Pulm notes. Pt says she was told by Pulm she doesn't have asthma. Referred to allergy clinic 12/2013 and appt is pending.

PER LAST PULM VISIT 6 D AGO:
A/P:
Ms. Perkins is a 36 y.o F with PMH of Allergic Rhinitis, GERD, 3 year history of asthma symptoms with SOB, chest tightness, still poorly controlled despite multiple medications.
Asthma:
-currently on: _____ (also atrovent but not using), but still having problems when exposed to triggers at work. Continue current regimen.
-counseled on avoiding triggers, correct usage of inhaler devices.
-Serum IgE
-RAST
-EKG to evaluate chest tightness, given findings on CXR.
-_____ ng for GERD.
-methacholine challenge given normal PFTs
RTC after methacholine challenge.

Past Medical History
Diagnosis   Date
- Allergic rhinitis
   no dm or ht
- Mold suspected exposure
- Gastro-oesophageal reflux disease
- Allergic
- DEPRESSION, MENTAL FUNCTION

Past Surgical History
Procedure   Laterality   Date
- Cesarean delivery only
   C-section, low cervical
- Hx tubal ligation
- Hx dilation and curettage
   2/2 abnl pregnancy
- Hx foot surgery

History
Substance Use Topics
- Smoking status: Never Smoker
- Smokeless tobacco: Never Used
- Alcohol Use: Yes
   social intake

ROS:
Review of Systems
Takes iron daily for anemia
Last pap 2011

PHYSICAL EXAM:
BP 113/68 | Pulse 64 | Temp(Src) 97.9 °F (36.6 °C) (Oral) | Resp 18 | Ht 5' 6" (1.676 m) | Wt 216 lb 9.6 oz (98.249 kg) | BMI 34.98 kg/m2 | LMP 01/31/2014
Normalized stature-for-age data available only for age 0 to 20 years.
Physical Exam
Constitutional: No distress.

Exhibit 243

| Adeyemi, RN | Signed | Adeyemi, RN | 7/25/2014 12:29 PM | 7/25/2014 12:18 PM |

At Approximately 11:25am, patient came out of Dr. Afzalpurkar's room and stated , "I want to go to Administration because I need the paper work filled out and I need to see my own doctor" Patient was overheard telling someone on the phone that she is going to call a news station to make a report. Patient was informed prior to vital signs being taken and prior to seeing the doctor that Dr. Juneja is sick. I told the patient we are sorry for last minute changes. Patient was also informed that the person who notified her of the appointment yesterday probably did not know Dr. Juneja was sick and would not be able to see her today. Patient also had complaint about paper works that she needed filled out. Patient was informed that Dr. Juneja will be back next week and we can contact her if Dr. Juneja decides or does not decide to fill out the paper work. Patient did not want to hear what I had to say and walk off to Administration.

Mrs. Gracie was informed on the situation prior to the patient arriving at administration.

Adeyemi RN

Author	Status	Last Editor	Updated	Created
Yu, F / VN	Signed	Yu, /VN	7/25/2014 12:31 PM	7/25/2014 12:03 PM

Patient left without being properly discharged. Patient wanted a form to be filled out but Dr. Afzalpurkar denied due to the fact that all the results are normal pertaining to condition she claims she has. Patient wanted to speak with administration, left to go to administration and therefore left with no discharge papers.

Yu, LV

Author	Status	Last Editor	Updated	Created
Afzalpurkar, MD	Signed	Afzalpurkar, Rekha, MD	7/25/2014 12:31 PM	7/25/2014 11:13 AM

Ellenor ___ a 37y.o. female is here for a check up.

Chief Complaint
Patient presents with
- Lab Follow-up

1/ Patient states any kind of smell/ odor like perfume, cooking makes her short of breath and so can not work
Needs CT sinus results- not in system- EPIC
States it was done outside
Talked to medical records, they have placed papers fom outside doctor in system

Noted results of methacholine challenge test- are
Spirometry- normal results

Chart and results reviewed and discussed with patient.

Exhibit 244

HARRIS HEALTH SYSTEM

PERKINS, ELLENOR YVETTE
MRN:
DOB: Sex: F
Enc. Date: 08/14/14

Location

Name	Address	Phone
VALLBONA	6630 DE MOSS STREET Houston TX 77074-5004	

Patient and Visit Information

Patient Information

Patient Name	MRN	Sex	DOB	SSN
Perkins, Ellenor		Female		

Visit Information

	Provider	Department	Encounter #
8/14/2014 10:20 AM	Juneja, MD	VI Family Practice	

Allergies

Fully Assessed On: 8/14/2014 By: Schneide

Allergies as of 8/14/2014

Allergen	Noted	Reaction Type	Reactions
No Known Drug Allergies	10/06/2009		(Not Noted)
No latex allergies	06/24/2014		(Not Noted)

Immunizations

Immunizations as of 8/14/2014 — Never Reviewed

Vitamin B12 Cyanocobalamin 1000mcg Inj — 8/14/2014 (37y.o.)

Reason for Visit

Reason for Visit
Follow-up

Vitals

Vital Signs - Last Recorded

BP	Pulse	Temp(Src)	Resp	Ht	Wt
117/75 mmHg	65	98.1 °F (36.7 °C) (Oral)	18	5' 4" (1.626 m)	233 lb 6 oz (105.858 kg)

BMI	LMP
40.04 kg/m2	06/09/2014

Vitals History

Progress Notes

Exhibit 245

Progress Notes

Author	Status	Last Editor	Updated	Created
Adeyemi, RN	Signed	Adeyemi, RN	8/14/2014 2:55 PM	8/14/2014 2:44 PM

At 12:45pm, allergies verified and patient verbally consented to Vitamin B12 injection and consent signed during registration as part of treatment. I administered 1ml of Vitamin B 12 to the patient's left deltoid intramuscularly. Patient Waited 15 minutes after injection patient states she feels fine. Patient tolerated well with no distress noted.

Patient was engaged in plan of care and encouraged to continue to be actively involved in his/her own care, therefore, improving safety. AVS and medication reconciliation sheet given and explained to the patient. Patient had no questions regarding E-prescriptions/prescriptions/medications given, treatment received, patient instructions and appointments. Patient demonstrated/verbalized understanding of instructions given.

Adeyemi RN

Author	Status	Last Editor	Updated	Created
Juneja, MD	Signed	Juneja, MD	8/17/2014 11:09 PM	8/14/2014 11:55 AM

SUBJECTIVE: Ellenor _____ s a 37y.o. female is here today for follow up

Established patient Juneja, _____ MD
Chief complaint registered - patient is here for - Follow-up
HPI:
Patient is here for follow up
Is not having energy to go anything - chief complaint
She was given forms for food stamps few weeks ago where it was mentioned that she can work parttime given that her pulmonary status is not compromised

She admits she is going to change her pcp with her insurance card
She discussed the same forms earlier which were not completed and appears upset about why her first forms were not filled and her last forms showed need to work
I reviewed the records of the outside ent with her which does not have a CT attaached and also the pulmonary record from harris health where her sinus CT was not done
The results of these point toward upper respiratory allergies more than any asthma as underlined by the spirometry tests and we have no imaging to determine how extensiver her allergic sinus problems are.
In light of these exams and procedure there is no evidence of me filling disability for breathing issues
Because of his her forms were not completed till her last visit and we awaited her visit to discuss with her
Patient is informed about this and offered medication help

She is offered vit B injections for her fatigue and we will continue to medically treat her till she finds another provider outside

Exhibit 246

Fax Cover Sheet

COMPANY LOGO

TO: OIEC
FAX: 281-
PHONE: (866) 393-6432
DATE: 9/18/2019
SUBJECT: Updated Medical Providers List

FROM: Elienor Perkins R
FAX: N/A
PHONE: 832-
OF PAGES: 2 Including Fax Cover

Page 1 Cover

Page 2 Medical Provider

please send the Causation document that must be completed to the doctor that has been listed on the Medical Provider form. The doctor has received some of my medical records and we are awaiting for the other records to be received by next week.

Exhibit 247

FLAHIVE, OGDEN & LATSON
ATTORNEYS AT LAW, P.C.

Mailing Address:
Post Office Drawer
Austin, Texas 78721
Main Number: 512

June 12, 2019

BRC EXCHANGE LETTER

TO: DWC – Austin Central – via SFTP

FROM: New Hampshire Insurance Company
       C/O Broadspire Services, Inc.
       P.O. Box 14351
       Lexington, Ky 40512

RE: Benefit Review Conference : 06/18/2019; 9:15AM;
    Claim No.   : 1
    Docket No.   : 1
    DWC No.   : 1
    Claimant   : Ellenor Perkins Ratcliff
    D/O/I   : 10/04/2013
    Employer   : General Dynamics Corp. - Falls Church
    FOL Case No.   : 2

As required by Rule 141.4, attached are copies of all medical records, witness statements and DWC filings currently in our possession.

By copy of this letter, employer presence is not required.

By copy of this letter, we are requesting the Claimant or Claimant's Representative to forward all information required to be exchanged directly with Carrier Representative, Flahive, Ogden and Latson.

Attached is a medical release. Please sign and return it to the adjuster or attorney representing the carrier. We will use the signed medical release to obtain your medical records. A copy of those records will be sent to you. Should you have any questions, please contact the adjuster or the attorney representing the carrier.

Exhibit 248

cc: Ellenor Perkins Ratcliff (Enclosures)

Cypress, TX

cc: Teri Cohen (letter only)
New Hampshire Insurance Company
c/o Broadspire Services, Inc.
P.O. Box 14351
Lexington, KY 40512

Exhibit 251

REFERENCE NUMBER

DWC FORM-001
(Employer's First Report of Injury or Illness)

The employer is required to file an **Employer's First Report of Injury or Illness** [DWC FORM-001 Rev. 10/05] with the injured worker's insurance carrier, and the injured claimant or the claimant's representative within 8 days after the employee's absence from work or receipt of notice of occupational disease.

The **Employer's First Report of Injury or Illness** provides information on the claimant, employer, insurance carrier and medical practitioner necessary to begin the claims process. Details of the claimant's employment and circumstances surrounding the injury or illness are also requested.

Send the specified copies to your **Workers' Compensation Insurance Carrier** and the injured employee. *Employers - Do not send this form to the Texas Department of Insurance, Division of Workers' Compensation, unless the Division specifically requests a direct filing.*

[Workers' Compensation Rule 120.2]

DWC FORM-001 (Rev. 10/05)
WC7631g (10-05) Wolters Kluwer Financial Services | Uniform Forms

DCN - BroadSpire Receive date -5/26/2015 6:00:00 AM ACS process date -5/26/2015 6:00:00 AM

Exhibit 252

REFERENCE NUMBER 719665711

INSTRUCTIONS FOR EMPLOYERS FIRST REPORT OF INJURY OR ILLNESS (DWC FORM-001)

Type (or print in black ink) each item on this form. Failure to complete each item may delay the processing of the injury claim.

Section 409.005, Texas Workers' Compensation Act, requires an Employer's First Report of Injury or Illness (DWC FORM-001 Rev. 10/05) to be filed with the Workers' Compensation Insurance Carrier not later than the eighth day after the receipt of notice of occupational disease, or the employee's first day of absence from work due to injury or death. A copy of this report must be sent to the employee or the employee's representative. For purposes of this section, a report is filed when personally delivered, or postmarked. Send the specified copies to your **Workers' Compensation Insurance Carrier** and the injured employee. ***Employers - Do not send this form to the Texas Department of Insurance, Division of Workers' Compensation, unless the Division specifically requests a direct filing.**

If a report has not been received by the carrier, the employer has the burden of proving that the report was filed within the required time frame. The employer has the burden of proving that good cause existed if the employer failed to file the report on time.

An employer who fails to file the report without good cause may be assessed an administrative penalty. An employer who fails to file the report without good cause waives the right to reimbursement of voluntary benefits even if no administrative penalty is assessed.

Once the employer has completed all information pertaining to the injury the employer should maintain the copy of this report to serve as the Employer's Record of Injury required by Section 409.006. Send the specified copies to your **Workers' Compensation Insurance Carrier** and the injured employee. ***Employers - Do not send this form to the Texas Department of Insurance, Division of Workers' Compensation, unless the Division specifically requests a direct filing.** The Division's Health and Safety will use data from this report for the Job Safety Information System established in Section 411.032 of the Texas Workers' Compensation Act.

This report may not be considered admission or evidence against the employer or the insurance carrier in any proceeding before the Division or a court in which facts set out in the report are contradicted by the employer or insurance carrier.

"SPECIAL INSTRUCTIONS FOR CERTAIN ITEMS"

Items 2, 7, 8:	Section 402.082, Texas Workers' Compensation Act requires the Division to maintain information as to the race, ethnicity and sex on every compensable injury. This information will be maintained for non-discriminatory statistical use.
Item 4:	If no home phone, please provide a phone number where the employee can be reached.
Items 5, 15, 17, 26, 29, 30:	Enter data in month, day, year format. Example: 08-13-54.
Item 18:	List nature of accident or exposure, e.g., fall from scaffold, contact with radiation, etc. If occupational disease, so state.
Item 19:	List specific body part, e.g., chin, right leg, forehead, left upper arm, etc. If more than one body part is affected, list each part.
Item 20:	Describe in detail (1) the events leading up to the injury/illness, (2) the actual injury, e.g., cut left forearm, broken right foot, etc., and (3) the reason(s) why accident/injury occurred. Use an additional sheet of paper if necessary.
Item 22:	State the exact work-site location of the injury, e.g., construction site, office area, storage area, etc.
Item 24:	List object, substance, or exposure that directly inflicted the injury or illness, e.g., floor, hammer, chemicals, etc.
Items 32, 33:	Enter date in month-year format. Example: 02-56.
Item 37:	Enter the number of days or hours that make up a full work week for your employees.
Item 45:	Enter the 6-digit North American Industry Classification System (NAICS) Code of the employer. The primary code is the code which appears in block 5 of Form C-3, "Employer's Quarterly Report" to the Texas Workforce Commission.
Item 46:	For companies with a single NAICS code, the specific code is the same as the primary code. For companies with multiple NAICS codes, enter the code that identifies the specific business, activity, or work-site location the employee was working in at the time of the injury. This may or may not be the same as the primary code.

DWC-FORM-001 (Rev. 10/05)
WC7631g (10-05)

DCN -201505261020050 BroadSpire Receive date -5/26/2015 6:00:00 AM ACS process date -5/26/2015 6:00:00 AM

Exhibit 253

REFERENCE NUMBER 719665

Send the specified copies to your
Workers' Compensation Insurance Carrier
and the injured employee.

*Employers - Do not send this form to the
Texas Department of Insurance, Division of Workers' Compensation,
Unless the Division specifically requests a direct filing.

CLAIM # _____

CARRIER'S CLAIM # _____

EMPLOYERS FIRST REPORT OF INJURY OR ILLNESS

1	Name (Last, First, M.I.)	Perkins Radcliff Ellenor
2	Sex	F
15	Date of Injury (m-d-y)	10/04/2013
16	Time of Injury	
17	Date Lost Time Began (m-d-y)	
3	Social Security Number	***-**-...
4	Home Phone	
5	Date of Birth (m-d-y)	
18	Nature of Injury	Respiratory disorders (gases, fumes, chemicals)
19	Part of Body Injured or Exposed	Trunk: Lungs
6	Does the Employee Speak English?	YES
20	How and Why Injury/Illness Occurred	(s)states having asthma attack due to spraying of perfume
7	Race	(Other checked)
8	Ethnicity Hispanic	Other ✓
21	Was employee doing his regular job?	YES ✓
22	Worksite Location of Injury	Call Center
9	Mailing Address	9C
23	Address Where Injury or Exposure Occurred	5959 Corporate Dr, Houston, TX 77036, Harris
	City	Houston
	State	TX
	Zip Code	77096
	County	Harris
10	Marital Status	Married ✓
24	Cause of Injury	Miscellaneous: Chemical exposure other than asbestos
11	Number of Dependent Children	3
12	Spouse's Name	
13	Doctor's Name	D Juneja
25	List Witnesses	Clem; Reimer Singletary
14	Doctor's Mailing Address	Peoples Clinic; Unknown
26	Return to work date/or expected (m-d-y)	
27	Did employee die?	NO ✓
28	Supervisor's Name	
29	Date Reported (m-d-y)	10/04/2013
30	Date of Hire (m-d-y)	09/09/2013
31	Was employee hired or recruited in Texas?	YES ✓
32	Length of Service in Current Position	Months 04 Years 00
33	Length of Service in Occupation	Months 05 Years 00
34	Employee Payroll Classification Code	
35	Occupation of Injured Worker	Customer Service Representativ
36	Rate of Pay at this Job	$ 13.98 Hourly $ 0.00 Weekly
37	Full Work Week is	8 Hours 5 Days
38	Last Paycheck was	$ for Hours or 0 days
39	Is employee an Owner, Partner, or Corporate Officer?	NO ✓
40	Name and Title of Person Completing Form	Ellenor Perkins Radcliff
41	Name of Business	General Dynamics Information
42	Business Mailing Address and Telephone Number	Telephone (785) 838-2281
43	Business Location (if different from mailing address)	3211 Jermantown Rd, Fairfax, VA 22030
44	Federal Tax Identification Number	
45	Primary North American Industry Classification System Code (6 digit)	
46	Specific NAICS Code (6 digit)	
47	Texas Comptroller Taxpayer No	
48	Workers' Compensation Insurance Company	
49	Policy Number	
50	Did you request accident prevention services in past 12 months?	
51	Signature and Title	X _____ Date _____

DWC FORM-1 (Rev. 10/05)
WC7631g (10-05)

DCN - BroadSpire Receive date -5/26/2015 6:00:00 AM ACS process date -5/26/2015 6:00:00 AM

Exhibit 254

7565573

WORKERS COMPENSATION – FIRST REPORT OF INJURY OR ILLNESS

EMPLOYER (NAME & ADDRESS INCL ZIP)
GENERAL DYNAMICS
GDIT VANGENT, INC.
1515 ALDINE MEADOW RD
HOUSTON, TX 77001

CARRIER/ADMINISTRATOR CLAIM NUMBER: 188029923
JURISDICTION: TX
INSURED REPORT NUMBER:
EMPLOYER'S LOCATION ADDRESS (IF DIFFERENT):
LOCATION #:
PHONE #: (999) 999-9999

INDUSTRY CODE: 3731
EMPLOYER FEIN: 99-9999999

CARRIER/CLAIMS ADMINISTRATOR

CARRIER (NAME, ADDRESS, & PHONE #):
NEW HAMPSHIRE INSURANCE CO C/O
BROADSPIRE A CRAWFORD CO.
P.O. BOX 14351
LEXINGTON, KY 40512
(800) 627-7358

POLICY PERIOD: 07/01/2013 TO 07/01/2014
CHECK IF APPROPRIATE: ☐ SELF INSURANCE

CLAIMS ADMINISTRATOR (NAME, ADDRESS & PHONE NO):
BROADSPIRE A CRAWFORD CO.
P.O. BOX 14351
LEXINGTON, KY 40512
(800) 627-7358

CARRIER FEIN:
POLICY/SELF-INSURED NUMBER:
ADMINISTRATOR FEIN:

EMPLOYEE/WAGE

NAME (LAST, FIRST, MIDDLE): PERKINS RATCLIFF, ELLENOR
DATE OF BIRTH:
SOCIAL SECURITY NUMBER:
DATE HIRED: 09/09/2013
STATE OF HIRE: TX

ADDRESS (INCL ZIP):
HOUSTON, TX 771--
PHONE:

SEX: ☒ FEMALE
MARITAL STATUS: ☒ UNKNOWN
 # OF DEPENDENTS:

OCCUPATION/JOB TITLE: CUSTOMER SERVICE REP
EMPLOYMENT STATUS: FULL-TIME
NCCI CLASS CODE: 8810

RATE PER: $13.88
DAY / WEEK ☒ / MONTH / HOURLY / OTHER:
DAYS WORKED/WEEK: 5
FULL PAY FOR DAY OF INJURY?: YES
DID SALARY CONTINUE?: YES

OCCURRENCE/TREATMENT

TIME EMPLOYEE BEGAN WORK: 09:00 ☒ AM
DATE OF INJURY/ILLNESS: 10/04/2013
TIME OF OCCURRENCE: 12:00 ☒ PM
LAST WORK DATE:
DATE EMPLOYER NOTIFIED: 10/04/2013
DATE DISABILITY BEGAN:

CONTACT NAME/PHONE NUMBER: UNKNOWN UNKNOWN
TYPE OF INJURY/ILLNESS: RESPIRATORY DISEASE, RESPIRATORY SYSTEM
PART OF BODY AFFECTED: UPPER RESPIRATORY SYSTEM

DID INJURY/ILLNESS/EXPOSURE OCCUR ON EMPLOYER'S PREMISES?: ☐ YES ☒ NO
TYPE OF INJURY/ILLNESS CODE: 60
PART OF BODY AFFECTED CODE:

DEPARTMENT OR LOCATION WHERE ACCIDENT OR ILLNESS EXPOSURE OCCURRED: 5959 CORPORATE DR, HOUSTON, TX 77036
ALL EQUIPMENT, MATERIALS, OR CHEMICALS EMPLOYEE WAS USING WHEN ACCIDENT OR ILLNESS EXPOSURE OCCURRED: SPECIFIC INJURY

SPECIFIC ACTIVITY THE EMPLOYEE WAS ENGAGED IN WHEN THE ACCIDENT OR ILLNESS EXPOSURE OCCURRED:
WORK PROCESS THE EMPLOYEE WAS ENGAGED IN WHEN ACCIDENT OR ILLNESS EXPOSURE OCCURRED: AT PROVIDED LOCKER

HOW INJURY OR ILLNESS/ABNORMAL HEALTH CONDITION OCCURRED. DESCRIBE THE SEQUENCE OF EVENTS AND INCLUDE ANY OBJECTS OR SUBSTANCES THAT DIRECTLY INJURED THE EMPLOYEE OR MADE THE EMPLOYEE ILL:
EE WAS AT HER COMPANY PROVIDED LOCKER DURING SCHEDULED BREAK TIME. PEER CSR SPRAYED COLOGNE NEAR EMPLOYEE AT LOCKER BAY INHALATION OF CHEMICAL, RESPIRATORY DISEASE, RESPIRATORY SYSTEM

CAUSE OF INJURY CODE: 80

DATE RETURN(ED) TO WORK:
IF FATAL, GIVE DATE OF DEATH:
WERE SAFEGUARDS OR SAFETY EQUIPMENT PROVIDED?: ☐ YES ☒ NO
WERE THEY USED?: ☐ YES ☐ NO

PHYSICIAN/HEALTH CARE PROVIDER (NAME & ADDRESS):
JUNEJAMD
HOUSTON, TX 77074

HOSPITAL OR OFF SITE TREATMENT (NAME & ADDRESS):

INITIAL TREATMENT:
0 NO MEDICAL TREATMENT
1 MINOR: BY EMPLOYER
☒ MINOR CLINIC/HOSP
3 EMERGENCY CARE
4 HOSPITALIZED > 24 HOURS
5 FUTURE MAJOR MEDICAL/LOST TIME ANTICIPATED

OTHER

WITNESSES (NAME & PHONE #):

DATE ADMINISTRATOR NOTIFIED: 06/08/2015
DATE PREPARED: 06/09/2015
PREPARER'S NAME & TITLE: / UNKNOWN
PHONE NUMBER: (999) 999-9999

FORM IA-1(r 1-1-02)   SEE BACK FOR IMPORTANT INFORMATION   ©IAIABC 2002

Exhibit 255

188029923

EMPLOYER'S INSTRUCTIONS

DO NOT ENTER DATA IN SHADED FIELDS

DATES:
Enter all dates in MM/DD/YY format.

INDUSTRY CODE:
This is the code which represents the nature of the employer's business, which is contained in the Standard Industrial Classification Manual or the North American Industry Classification System, published by the Federal Office of Management and Budget.

CARRIER:
The licensed business entity issuing a contract of insurance and assuming financial responsibility on behalf of the employer of the claimant.

CLAIMS ADMINISTRATOR:
Enter the name of the carrier, third party administrator, state fund, or self-insured responsible for administering the claim.

AGENT NAME & CODE NUMBER:
Enter the name of your insurance agent and his/her code number if known. This information can be found on your insurance policy.

OCCUPATION/JOB TITLE:
This is the primary occupation of the claimant at the time of the accident or exposure.

EMPLOYMENT STATUS:
Indicate the employee's work status. The valid choices are:

Full-Time	On Strike	Unknown	Volunteer
Part-Time	Disabled	Apprenticeship Full-Time	Seasonal
Not Employed	Retired	Apprenticeship Part-Time	Piece Worker

DATE DISABILITY BEGAN:
The first day on which the claimant originally lost time from work due to the occupation injury or disease or as otherwise designated by statute.

CONTACT NAME/PHONE NUMBER:
Enter the name of the individual at the employer's premises to be contacted for additional information.

TYPE OF INJURY/ILLNESS:
Briefly describe the nature of the injury or illness, (eg. Lacerations to the forearm).

PART OF BODY AFFECTED:
Indicate the part of body affected by the injury/illness, (eg. Right forearm, lower back).

DEPARTMENT OR LOCATION WHERE ACCIDENT OR ILLNESS EXPOSURE OCCURRED:
(eg. Maintenance Department or Client's office at 452 Monroe St., Washington, DC 26210)

If the accident or illness exposure did not occur on the employer's premises, enter address or location. Be specific.

FORM IA-1(r 1-1-02) ©IAIABC 2002

Exhibit 256

188029923

EMPLOYER'S INSTRUCTIONS – cont'd

ALL EQUIPMENT, MATERIAL OR CHEMICALS EMPLOYEE WAS USING WHEN ACCIDENT OR ILLNESS EXPOSURE OCCURRED:
(eg. Acetylene cutting torch, metal plate)

List all of the equipment, materials, and/or chemicals the employee was using, applying, handling or operating when the injury or illness occurred. Be specific, for example: decorator's scaffolding, electric sander, paintbrush, and paint.

Enter "NA" for not applicable if no equipment, materials, or chemicals were being used. NOTE: The items listed do not have to be directly involved in the employee's injury or illness.

SPECIFIC ACTIVITY THE EMPLOYEE WAS ENGAGED IN WHEN THE ACCIDENT OR ILLNESS EXPOSURE OCCURRED:
(eg. Cutting metal plate for flooring)

Describe the specific activity the employee was engaged in when the accident or illness exposure occurred, such as sanding ceiling woodwork in preparation for painting.

WORK PROCESS THE EMPLOYEE WAS ENGAGED IN WHEN ACCIDENT OR ILLNESS EXPOSURE OCCURRED:
Describe the work process the employee was engaged in when the accident or illness exposure occurred, such as building maintenance. Enter "NA" for not applicable if employee was not engaged in a work process (eg. walking along a hallway).

HOW INJURY OR ILLNESS/ABNORMAL HEALTH CONDITION OCCURRED. DESCRIBE THE SEQUENCE OF EVENTS AND INCLUDE ANY OBJECTS OR SUBSTANCES THAT DIRECTLY INJURED THE EMPLOYEE OR MADE THE EMPLOYEE ILL:
(Worker stepped back to inspect work and slipped on some scrap metal. As worker fell, worker brushed against the hot metal.)

Describe how the injury or illness/abnormal health condition occurred. Include the sequence of events and name any objects or substance that directly injured the employee or made the employee ill. For example: Worker stepped to the edge of the scaffolding to inspect work, lost balance and fell six feet to the floor. The worker's right wrist was broken in the fall.

DATE RETURN(ED) TO WORK:
Enter the date following to most recent disability period on which the employee returned to work.

FORM IA-1(r 1-1-02) ©IAIABC 2002

Exhibit 257

Exhibit 258

Fax Cover Sheet

TO: OIEC
FAX: 281-
PHONE: (866) 393-6432
DATE: 9/25/2019
SUBJECT: BRC EXCHANGE LETTER

FROM: Ellenor Perkins Ratcliff
DWC: 1
PHONE: 832-
OF PAGES: 14 including Fax Cover

today I received this information in the mail.

Page 1 — Cover
Page 2-3 — Letter
Page 4-5 — HIPPA Authorization for Disclosure of Protected Health Info.
Page 6 — DWC Document Cover
Page 7-9 — DWC FORM-001 (Rev. 10/05) 3 Pages
Page 10 — WC – First Report of Injury or Illness, FORM IA-1 (r 1-1-02)
Page 11-12 — Employer's Instructions FORM IA-1 (r 1-1-02)
Page 13 — Statement Document Cover
Page 14 — Broadspire – 1

Exhibit 259

DWC154

TEXAS DEPARTMENT OF INSURANCE
Division of Workers' Compensation - Compliance & Investigations (MS-8)
7551 Metro Center Drive, Suite 100, Austin, Texas 78744-1645
(512) 804-4000 | F: (512) 490-1030 | (800) 252-7031 | TDI.texas.gov | @TexasTDI

Workers' Compensation Complaint Form

Este formulario está disponible en español en el sitio web de la División en
http://www.tdi.texas.gov/forms/dwc/dwc154compls.pdf.
Para obtener asistencia en español, llame a la División al 800-252-7031.

Complainant Information (Person Filing Complaint)

1. Name* (First, Middle, Last)	2. Date of Complaint (mm/dd/yyyy)	3. Email Address
Ellenor Yvette Perkins - Ratcliff	12/18/2018	
4. Address (Street or P.O. Box, City, State, ZIP Code)		5. Phone Number (832)

*Required under Texas Labor Code §402.023(d)(2)

Injured Employee Information

6. Name (First, Middle, Last)	7. Phone Number
Ellenor Yvette Perkins	(832)
8. Address (Street or P.O. Box, City, State, ZIP Code)	9. DWC Claim # (if known) 1
10. Employer (at time of injury) General Dynamics Information Technology	11. Date of Injury (mm/dd/yyyy) 10/04/2013

Complaint

A *complaint* is a written allegation that a system participant has violated Title 5, Subtitle A, of the Texas Labor Code or Texas Department of Insurance, Division of Workers' Compensation (TDI-DWC) rules. If your issue is a *complaint*, please describe the facts of the alleged violation of workers' compensation laws or rules, including the dates or time period during which the violation occurred, in the space below (attach additional pages if necessary). Also include the following information:

- the nature of the violation, including specific sections of Title 5, Subtitle A, of the Texas Labor Code or TDI-DWC rules alleged to have been violated, if known;
- name and contact information of the subject of or parties to the complaint, if known; and
- name and contact information of witnesses, if known.

Example: By failing to send my impairment income benefit check for the week of December 13th, ABC Insurance Company violated Texas Labor Code section 408.081, which requires weekly payment of income benefits. The insurance adjuster is Mr. Jones and his phone number is (512) 555-1234.

12. Description of Complaint

This complaint is to report insurance fraud on part of Broadspire and Debbie S. Fields against DW#   Debbie Fields deliberately acted in deception to deny my claim of work related injury, which arose out of and in the course and scope of employment with General Dynamic Information Technology from 9/13-2/14 (SEC. 409.001. NOTICE OF INJURY TO EMPLOYER and SEC. 406.031. LIABILITY FOR COMPENSATION). This deception arose out of my right to use Workman's Comp Benefits. I believe fraud has been committed against me. Debbie S. Fields was aggressive with me because I called and questioned her regarding my claim. This has financially damaged my household. GDIT was notified of my injury, there are witnesses to substantiate my claim, as well as documentation filed in the system of human resource department. The claim was filed in a timely fashion, SEC. 409.003. CLAIM FOR COMPENSATION. According to conversations on 12/14, there is no documentation of fact maintained in my file by Broadspire on part of GDIT to substantiate GDIT human resource department claim which lead to a fraudulent denial of benefits.
In accordance to the Texas Workers' Compensation Act (81st Legislature, 2009) Broadspire has committed a number of violations. I will list them below: SEC. 415.002. ADMINISTRATIVE VIOLATION BY INSURANCE CARRIER.
SEC. 415.0036. ADMINISTRATIVE VIOLATION BY PERSON PERFORMING CERTAIN CLAIM SERVICES.
SEC. 415.008. FRAUDULENTLY OBTAINING OR DENYING BENEFITS; ADMINISTRATIVE VIOLATION.
SEC. 415.009. FRIVOLOUS ACTIONS; ADMINSTRATIVE VIOLATION.
Due to the gross fraudulent actions of Broadspire, I'm requesting my denial for benefits be rescinded and properly handled by a private party not connected to General Dynamics Information Technology or Broadspire.

Exhibit 260

DWC154

Frequently Asked Questions

What types of documentation should I submit to support my complaint?

Please submit any supporting documentation with your complaint. Supporting documentation may include:
- medical bills;
- explanations of benefits (EOBs);
- copies of invoices or checks;
- evidence of communications (written correspondence or documentation of conversations) between you and the insurance carrier, attorney, or health care provider, including names, dates, and phone numbers;
- proof of timely submission or filing (for example, certified receipts or fax receipts);
- off-work slips;
- copies of relevant DWC forms;
- photographs, reports, and recordings (video, audio, surveillance) if fraud is alleged; and
- any other documentation to support your complaint.

Where can I find additional information about complaints?
- Texas Labor Code §402.023, Complaint Information, and §402.0235, Priorities for Complaint Investigation;
- 28 Texas Administrative Code §180.2, Filing a Complaint; and
- The "File a Complaint" section of the TDI-DWC website, http://www.tdi.texas.gov/wc/indexwc.html.

Is the information I submit confidential?

The information in TDI-DWC's investigation files is confidential per Texas Labor Code §402.092 and generally may not be disclosed except:
- in a criminal proceeding;
- in a hearing conducted by TDI-DWC;
- on a judicial determination of good cause;
- to a governmental agency, political subdivision, or regulatory body if the disclosure is necessary or proper for the enforcement of the laws of this or another state or of the United States; or
- to an insurance carrier if the investigation file relates directly to a felony regarding workers' compensation or to a claim in which restitution is required to be paid to the insurance carrier.

In addition, TDI-DWC investigation files are not open records for purposes of the Public Information Act, Chapter 552, Government Code.

How do I submit my complaint and supporting documentation to DWC?

E-mail: DWCCOMPLAINTS@tdi.texas.gov
Fax: (512) 490-1030
Mail: Texas Department of Insurance
Division of Workers' Compensation, MS-6
7551 Metro Center Drive, Suite 100
Austin, Texas 78744

For questions or assistance with submitting a workers' compensation complaint, call (800) 252-7031.

Note: With few exceptions, upon your request, you are entitled to be informed about the information TDI-DWC collects about you; get and review the information (Government Code, §§552.021 and 552.023); and have TDI-DWC correct information that is incorrect (Government Code, §559.004). For more information, contact the Agency Counsel Section of TDI's Legal Services Division at AgencyCounsel@tdi.texas.gov or you may refer to the Corrections Procedure section at www.tdi.texas.gov.

Exhibit 261

```
TRANSMISSION VERIFICATION REPORT

                                      TIME  : 12/18/2018 00:49
                                      NAME  :
                                      FAX   :
                                      TEL   :
                                      SER.# : BROE


DATE,TIME              12/18  00:48
FAX NO./NAME           15124901038
DURATION               00:00:41
PAGE(S)                01
RESULT                 OK
MODE                   STANDARD
                       ECM
```

Exhibit 262

DWC154

TEXAS DEPARTMENT OF INSURANCE
Division of Workers' Compensation - Compliance & Investigations (MS-8)
7551 Metro Center Drive, Suite 100, Austin, Texas 78744-1645
(512) 804-4000 | F: (512) 490-1030 | (800) 252-7031 | TDI.texas.gov | @TexasTDI

Workers' Compensation Complaint Form

Este formulario está disponible en español en el sitio web de la División en
http://www.tdi.texas.gov/forms/dwc/dwc154compls.pdf.
Para obtener asistencia en español, llame a la División al 800-252-7031.

Complainant Information (Person Filing Complaint)

1. Name* (First, Middle, Last)	2. Date of Complaint (mm/dd/yyyy)	3. Email Address
Ellenor Yvette Perkins - Ratcliff	12/18/2018	
4. Address (Street or P.O. Box, City, State, ZIP Code)		5. Phone Number (832)

*Required under Texas Labor Code §402.023(d)(2)

Injured Employee Information

6. Name (First, Middle, Last)	7. Phone Number
Ellenor Yvette Perkins	(832)
8. Address (Street or P.O. Box, City, State, ZIP Code)	9. DWC Claim # (if known)
10. Employer (at time of injury)	11. Date of Injury (mm/dd/yyyy)
General Dynamics Information Technology	10/04/2013

Complaint

A *complaint* is a written allegation that a system participant has violated Title 5, Subtitle A, of the Texas Labor Code or Texas Department of Insurance, Division of Workers' Compensation (TDI-DWC) rules. If your issue is a *complaint*, please describe the facts of the alleged violation of workers' compensation laws or rules, including the dates or time period during which the violation occurred, in the space below (attach additional pages if necessary). Also include the following information:
- the nature of the violation, including specific sections of Title 5, Subtitle A, of the Texas Labor Code or TDI-DWC rules alleged to have been violated, if known;
- name and contact information of the subject of or parties to the complaint, if known; and
- name and contact information of witnesses, if known.

Example: By failing to send my impairment income benefit check for the week of December 13th, ABC Insurance Company violated Texas Labor Code section 408.081, which requires weekly payment of income benefits. The insurance adjuster is Mr. Jones and his phone number is (512) 555-1234.

12. Description of Complaint

General Dynamics Information Technology has committed insurance fraud against claim DW#   GDIT deliberately lied to have my claim denied. General Dynamics Information Technology neglected to notify insurance carrier of time off work due to each injury; SEC. 409.005. REPORT OF INJURY; MODIFIED DUTY PROGRAM NOTICE; ADMINISTRATIVE VIOLATION. Zandra Bosie and supervisor received report of injury by company email and multiple notices were received by hand, (SEC. 409.001. NOTICE OF INJURY TO EMPLOYER.) following my difficulty breathing while working on the call center floor of General Dynamic Information Technology from 9/13-2/14. Zandra Bosie and upper management were immediately notified of my injury, which arose out of and in the course and scope of employment; SEC. 406.031. LIABILITY FOR COMPENSATION. General Dynamics Information Technology neglected to maintain record of each employee injury, see SEC. 409.006. RECORD OF INJURIES; ADMINISTRATIVE VIOLATION. GDIT did not provide documentation of facts to substantiate it's statement.

In accordance to the Texas Workers' Compensation Act (81st Legislature, 2009) General Dynamics Information Technology has committed a number of violations. I will list the rest of violations below:
SEC. 409.008. FAILURE TO FILE EMPLOYER REPORT OF INJURY; LIMITATIONS TOLLED.
SEC. 411.103. DUTY OF EMPLOYER TO PROVIDE SAFE WORKPLACE.

DWC154 Rev. 03/16

Exhibit 263

```
              TRANSMISSION VERIFICATION REPORT

                                        TIME  : 12/18/2018 01:53
                                        NAME  :
                                        FAX   :
                                        TEL   :
                                        SER.# : BROE8J1


   DATE,TIME              12/18  01:52
   FAX NO./NAME           15124901030
   DURATION               00:00:39
   PAGE(S)                01
   RESULT                 OK
   MODE                   STANDARD
                          ECM
```

Exhibit 264

TEXAS DEPARTMENT OF INSURANCE
Division of Workers' Compensation - Compliance & Investigations (MS-8)
7551 Metro Center Drive, Suite 100, Austin, Texas 78744-1645
(512) 804-4000 | F: (512) 490-1030 | (800) 252-7031 | TDI.texas.gov | @TexasTDI

January 7, 2019

ELLENOR PERKINS RATCLIFF

CYPRESS TX

PROBLEM REPORT ID: 2
INJURED EMPLOYEE: ELLENOR PERKINS RATCLIFF
EMPLOYER: GENERAL DYNAMICS CORP
INSURANCE CARRIER: NEW HAMPSHIRE INSURANCE CO
DATE OF INJURY: 10-04-2013
DWC CLAIM NUMBER: 1
INS. CAR. NUMBER: 1

RE: ACKNOWLEDGMENT LETTER

Dear Ms. Ratcliff:

The Texas Department of Insurance, Division of Workers' Compensation has received your complaint form, related to the above noted workers' compensation insurance claim.

A specialist will be assigned to review your allegation for resolution or other appropriate action. If additional information is needed, you will be contacted. However, if you obtain newly discovered information relevant to your allegation, please e-mail, fax or mail it to the above noted address, referencing the above problem report ID number assigned to your allegation.

At the conclusion of our review, we will provide you with a written explanation regarding the resolution of this allegation.

Sincerely,

Compliance Review
Telephone: 512-
Email: @tdi.texas.gov

Exhibit 265

TEXAS DEPARTMENT OF INSURANCE
DIVISION OF WORKERS' COMPENSATION
7551 METRO CENTER DR STE 100
AUSTIN, TX 78744-1645

RETURN SERVICE REQUESTED

54 LNJ-NAB 77433

Exhibit 266

TEXAS DEPARTMENT OF INSURANCE
Division of Workers' Compensation - Compliance & Investigations (MS-8)
7551 Metro Center Drive, Suite 100, Austin, Texas 78744-1645
(512) 804-4000 | F: (512) 490-1030 | (800) 252-7031 | TDI.texas.gov | @TexasTDI

January 10, 2019

ELLENOR PERKINS RATCLIFF

CYPRESS TX

PROBLEM REPORT ID:	2
INJURED EMPLOYEE:	ELLENOR PERKINS RATCLIFF
EMPLOYER:	GENERAL DYNAMICS CORP
INSURANCE CARRIER:	NEW HAMPSHIRE INSURANCE CO
DATE OF INJURY:	10-04-2013
DWC CLAIM NUMBER:	1
INS. CAR. NUMBER:	1

RE: CLOSURE LETTER

Dear Ms. Ratcliff:

The Texas Department of Insurance, Division of Workers' Compensation (DWC) has received your correspondence requesting our assistance. As a result of our review we are providing you with the following information:

This complaint involves a dispute regarding **indemnity benefit delivery**. All questions regarding workers' compensation disputes or claims may be directed to the insurance carrier representative or a DWC field office. DWC strives to provide all customers with excellent customer service. Please contact your assigned single point of contact M____ **Dykes** at 1-800-252-7031, extension ____, if you have questions or concerns about your workers' compensation claim.

Any information furnished by you, and any additional information compiled or maintained by DWC regarding this referral, shall remain confidential as allowed by law. Information maintained in a DWC investigation file is confidential per Texas Labor Code (TLC), Section 402.092, and disclosure is not made except when required by TLC, Section 402.092 and 413.0513.

In addition, to resolve a dispute you may request a Benefit Review Conference at the local field office handling the claim. Your point of contact may assist you with filing a request for a Benefit Review Conference.

If a DWC agreement or order is issued that is not complied with, then a complaint may be filed with the DWC Compliance Review Section for review and appropriate handling. A copy of the Benefit Review Conference Agreement, DWC Interlocutory Order, or Contested Case Hearing Officer's decision & order should be included with your complaint letter.

Exhibit 267

Page 2   PROBLEM REPORT ID 2

Thank you for the opportunity to assist you. We hope this information has been helpful. If you experience workers' compensation insurance problems in the future, please feel free to contact us again.

Sincerely,

S   Wright
Compliance Specialist IV
Telephone: 512-
Email: @tdi.texas.gov

Exhibit 268

Texas Department of Insurance
DIVISION OF WORKERS' COMPENSATION
7551 METRO CENTER DR STE 100
AUSTIN, TX 78744-1645

RETURN SERVICE REQUESTED

OFFICIAL BUSINESS
STATE OF TEXAS
PENALTY FOR
PRIVATE USE

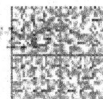

PRESORTED FIRST CLASS

U.S. POSTAGE ≫ PITNEY BOWES
ZIP 78701
02 1R $ 000.40
0001401603 JAN 11 2019

4 LQW-NAB 77433

Exhibit 269

Request Form for Texas Workforce Commission (TWC) Records
Use this optional form to help TWC expedite the handling of your records request

A. Requester Contact Information
Name: Ellenor Perkins Ratcliff	Address:
Company Name: GENERAL DYNAMICS	City, State, Zip:
Telephone Number: 832	Email:

B. Authorization to obtain confidential information:
- [X] I am an INDIVIDUAL requesting records on myself.
  (Include proof of identification – copy of State or Government issued photo ID. NOTE: Individuals may obtain certain information on current UI claims online for free at www.twc.state.tx.us.)
- [ ] I have a SIGNED AUTHORIZATION from the individual or entity to obtain confidential records.
- [ ] I am an ATTORNEY requesting confidential records on my client. [ ] Yes [ ] No?
  If "No", submit either a signed authorization (Complete Section D) from the subject, a court order authorizing TWC to release the specified records to you or an explanation of your authority to obtain the confidential records.
- [ ] I am LAW ENFORCEMENT OR A PUBLIC OFFICIAL with authority to obtain the records.
- [ ] I am an EMPLOYER/BUSINESS requesting records on my business entity.

C. Specify the records you seek:
- [X] I seek records on the following Individual(s): Ellenor Perkins
- [X] I seek records on the following Business Entity(s): General Dynamics

I seek the following type of records regarding the individual/entity:
- [ ] Wage Records. Include processing fee of $10. Enter Social Security Number:
- [ ] Employer Tax Reports. Enter Employer Tax ID Number:
- [ ] Unemployment Insurance (UI). Enter the Appeal Number or Social Security Number:
  - [X] All information on the UI claim filed on: March 20, 2014
  - [ ] All information on all UI claims filed since:
  - [X] The employer response for the UI claim filed on: 03-20-14 and 11-08-15
  - [ ] Determination for UI on or about: 2014-2015
- [ ] Payday Wage Claim. Enter Payday Claim Number or Social Security Number:
- [X] TWC Civil Rights Records (CRD). Enter the EEOC Charge, HUD or TWC CRD Number: 460-2014-01770
- [ ] Hearing Audio Recording. Enter the Appeal Number or Social Security Number:
- [X] Other/Comments. Enter the description of the records you seek and attach additional sheet if necessary:
  The employer response for EEOC Charge 460-2014-01770.

D. Complete if Authorization is given to another person:
I, _____, authorize TWC to release the records specified in Section C to _____ for the following purpose:

E. Cost of Records:
TWC will calculate charges based on 10 cents per page plus staff labor at $3.75 per ¼ hour and $.75 per ¼ hour for overhead unless computer resources, standardized or other charge apply. An invoice will be mailed to you or if the charges are over $40, an estimate will be sent. Upon receipt of payment, TWC will complete the request. Mail payments to TWC Revenue and Trust Management PO Box 877, Austin, TX 78767.

F. Delivery Instructions:
- [X] I would like the records certified. (Note: A charge of $15.00 is required for certified records.)
- [ ] I would like to pick up the records in person. (101 East 15th Street, RM 266, Austin, TX 78778)
- [ ] I would like to review records in person. (101 East 15th Street, RM 266, Austin, TX 78778)
- [ ] I would like to receive the records by private courier service, provide billing account number:

AGREEMENT: I assert that all of the information above is true and correct to the best of my knowledge.

Signature*: _____   Date*: 06/21/2019

Where to mail request: If payment is enclosed, send request, proof of ID and payment to TWC Revenue and Trust Management, PO Box 877, Austin, TX 78767. If no payment is enclosed, send request and proof of ID to: Texas Workforce Commission, ATTN: Open Records, 101 East 15th Street, RM 266, Austin, TX 78778-0001.
Social Security Numbers and About Your Rights: TWC is requesting your Social Security number (SSN) to locate the records pertaining to your request for information. Providing the SSN is voluntary; however, for some records TWC will not be able to locate the records without the SSN. TWC does not disclose SSNs except as permitted by law. For more information see http://www.twc.state.tx.us/racinfo/privacy.html. Individuals may obtain a copy of or review information maintained by TWC about the individual by contacting TWC Open Records at 101 East 15th St., Rm 266, Austin, TX 78778-0001.
Questions: If you have questions about this form or other records-related issues please send an email to openrecords@twc.state.tx.us or call 512-463-2422.
http://www.twc.state.tx.us/recinfo/openrec.html

Last revised September 11, 2013

Exhibit 270

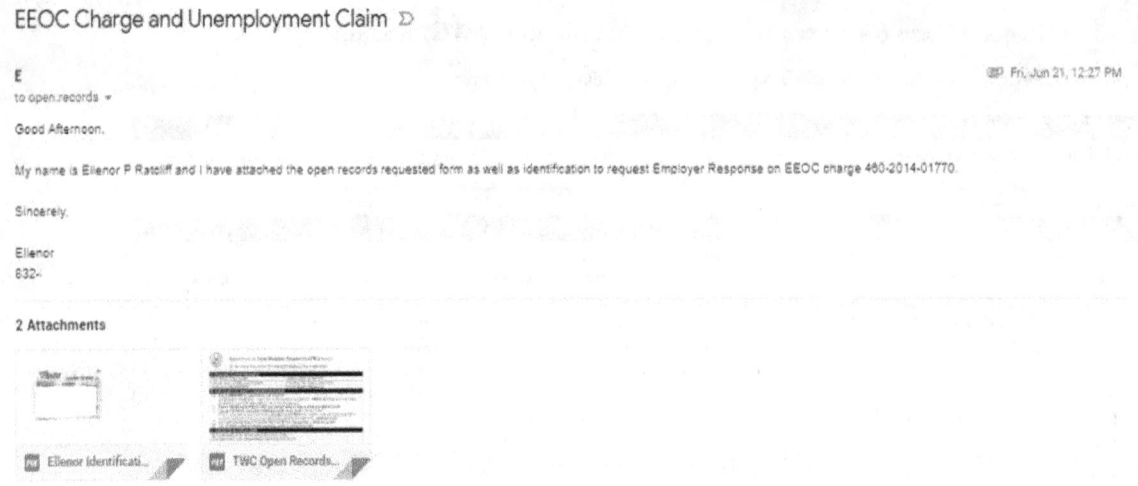

Exhibit 271

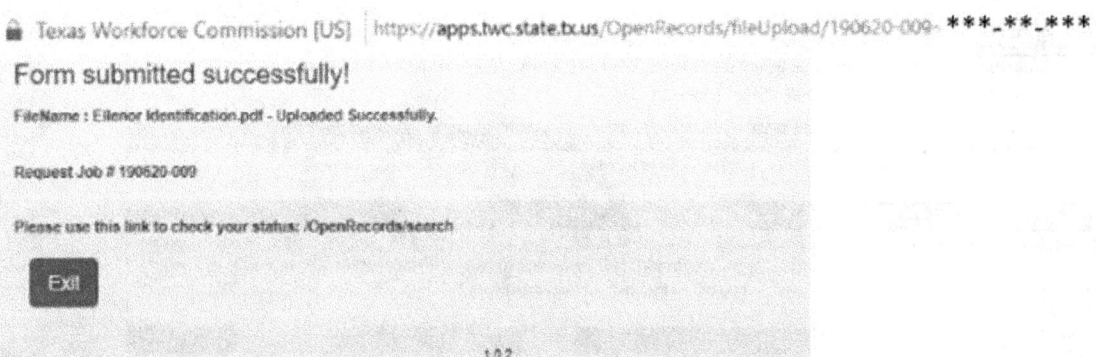

Exhibit 272

Open Records On-line Request # 190620-009 Inbox

Open Records @twc.state.tx.us
to me

Dear Requestor:

The Open Records Department received your Open Records Request. We are unable to process the request until we receive your following information:

- Statement of request – Please clarify what type of records you seek
- Handwritten signature – Electronic signatures are not accepted

You may fax, email or mail the information to our department.

FAX: 512-   / ATN: Open Records
EMAIL: @twc.state.tx.us
MAIL: Texas Workforce Commission
         101 East 15th Street, RM 266
         Austin, TX 78778

Thank you,
Open Records
512-

Exhibit 273

E   Jun 21, 2019, 2:40 PM
to Open

Thank you for your response. I have submitted an email with my identification and the open records request form. It was emailed this morning and the form has my signature on it.

Exhibit 274

Texas Workforce Commission
A Member of Texas Workforce Solutions

Notice of Receipt Letter

June 25, 2019

Ellenor Perkins Ratcliff

RE: Ellenor Perkins
Request Job #: 190621-008

Dear Ellenor Perkins Ratcliff:

The Texas Workforce Commission (TWC) is in receipt of your request for information. The marked paragraphs below apply to your request.

[X] TWC received your Unemployment Insurance (UI) file request and on initial review, the request appears sufficient to process without further information. We anticipate contacting you within 45 business days with one of the following responses: (1) additional clarification is necessary, (2) exceptions to disclosure may apply; (3) acceptance of a cost estimate is needed to process and/or (4) the response to your request.

[ ] Additional information is needed to process your request. Please remit the following items marked to the address at the bottom of the letter. Include the optional form to expedite your request. To verify your identity for purposes of releasing confidential information for which you may have a right of access, and/or to associate the appropriate records with your request, please provide the following:

- [ ] Copy of photo identification (ID) (Driver's license or State issued Identification) required.
  - [ ] The copy you submitted of your proof of ID was not clear. Please resubmit.
- [ ] Complete Social Security Number is needed to locate your records.
- [ ] An original signature is required for copies of information confidential by law.
  - (Electronic signatures are not accepted; faxed or scanned signatures are accepted)
- [ ] Persons other than the subject of the records require proof of authorization or representation. (Third Parties, including attorneys must provide:
  - (1) a signed authorization from the individual/subject of the request;
  - (2) evidence of representation of the person/subject of the requested information or
  - (3) explain the basis in law for accessing the records. Include the form or an explanation in writing signed on your official letterhead.
- [ ] Equal Employment Opportunity Charge Number (EEOC) is required to locate EEOC records.
- [ ] Clarification is required. (Clarify what type of records you seek)
- [ ] Payment required. [ ] Processing fee of $10 required for wage records or [ ] see cost estimate.
- [ ] Complete/current mailing address required.
- [ ] Other: _____

You may check the status of your pending request online at: https://apps.twc.state.tx.us/OpenRecords/search

Thank you
Open Records Section, TWC

Texas Workforce Commission, Open Records Section
● 101 E. 15th Street, Room 266● Austin, TX 78778-0001 ● Payments must be sent to TWC-Revenue & Trust Mngmt at PO Box 877, Austin, TX 78767
Tel: (512) 463-2422 ● Fax: 512/4   ● Relay Texas: 800-735-2989 (TDD) 800-735-2988 (Voice)
● or   ]twc.state.tx.us ● www.twc.state.tx.us ●Equal Opportunity Employer/Services

Exhibit 275

IMPORTANT TWC DOCUMENTS: OPEN IMMEDIATELY

TEXAS WORKFORCE COMMISSION
101 E 15TH ST
AUSTIN TX 78778-0001

OFFICIAL BUSINESS

7743381188 R082

Exhibit 276

Texas Workforce Commission
A Member of Texas Workforce Solutions

Notice of Receipt Letter

June 25, 2019

Ellenor Perkins Ratcliff

RE: Ellenor Perkins
Request Job #: 190621-009

Dear Ellenor Perkins Ratcliff:

The Texas Workforce Commission (TWC) is in receipt of your request for information. The marked paragraphs below apply to your request.

[X] TWC received your Civil Rights Division (CRD) file request and on initial review, the request appears sufficient to process without further information. We anticipate contacting you within 45 business days with one of the following responses: (1) additional clarification is necessary, (2) exceptions to disclosure may apply; (3) acceptance of a cost estimate is needed to process and/or (4) the response to your request.

[ ] Additional information is needed to process your request. Please remit the following items marked to the address at the bottom of the letter. Include the optional form to expedite your request. To verify your identity for purposes of releasing confidential information for which you may have a right of access, and/or to associate the appropriate records with your request, please provide the following:

- [ ] Copy of photo identification (ID) (Driver's license or State issued Identification) required.
    - [ ] The copy you submitted of your proof of ID was not clear. Please resubmit.
- [ ] Complete Social Security Number is needed to locate your records.
- [ ] An original signature is required for copies of information confidential by law.
    (Electronic signatures are not accepted; faxed or scanned signatures are accepted)
- [ ] Persons other than the subject of the records require proof of authorization or representation. (Third Parties, including attorneys must provide:
    (1) a signed authorization from the individual/subject of the request;
    (2) evidence of representation of the person/subject of the requested information or
    (3) explain the basis in law for accessing the records. Include the form or an explanation in writing signed on your official letterhead.
- [ ] Equal Employment Opportunity Charge Number (EEOC) is required to locate EEOC records.
- [ ] Clarification is required. (Clarify what type of records you seek)
- [ ] Payment required. [ ] Processing fee of $10 required for wage records or [ ] see cost estimate.
- [ ] Complete/current mailing address required.
- [ ] Other: _____

You may check the status of your pending request online at: https://apps.twc.state.tx.us/OpenRecords/search

Thank you
Open Records Section, TWC

Texas Workforce Commission, Open Records Section
• 101 E. 15th Street, Room 266• Austin, TX 78778-0001 • Payments must be sent to TWC-Revenue & Trust Mngmt at PO Box 877, Austin, TX 78767
Tel: (512) 463-2422 • Fax: 512/- ▸ Relay Texas: 800-735-2989 (TDD) 800-735-2988 (Voice)
• or ori@twc.state.tx.us • www.twc.state.tx.us •Equal Opportunity Employer/Services

Exhibit 277

```
U-24
IMPORTANT TWC DOCUMENTS: OPEN IMMEDIATELY
TEXAS WORKFORCE COMMISSION
       101 E 15TH ST
   AUSTIN TX  78778-0001
         OFFICIAL BUSINESS
```

$ 000.50

7743331158 R062

Exhibit 278

Texas Workforce Commission
Austin, Texas
Open Records - Invoice

Client Mailing Address:	Invoice Address (if other than client address):
Ellenor Perkins Ratcliff	
TX	

Request Order #:	190621-009	460-2014-01770	
Subject Reference:	Ellenor Perkins	Date Information Released:	
Request Rec'd Date:	6/21/2019	Invoice Date: 7/1/2019	
		Total Charges:	$19.50
		Amount Paid:	$0.00
		Date Paid:	
		Balance Due:	$19.50

Comment

Make Payable To: Texas Workforce Commission
Revenue And Trust Management
P.O. Box 877
Austin, Texas 78767
Questions To: G _   Johnson

TDD 1-800-735-2989
TWC's FEIN: 74-
RTI Code: 191415
Phone #:   512-
Fax #:   512-

Cut here and return bottom portion with payment

Exhibit 279

Itemized Search Items

CRD Employment Discrimination File
staff labor time at $18 plus 10

Pages: 0	@$0.10 /page	$0.00
Units: 0	@$0.00 /Unit	$0.00
Labor Hours: .25	@$18.00/hr	$4.50
	Manually Entered Charges:	$0.00
	Total for Search Item:	$4.50

Certification Charges
Certification Charges

Pages: 0	@$0.00 /page	$0.00
Units: 1	@$15.00 first unit + @$5.00 /add'l Units	$15.00
Labor Hours: 0	@$0.00/hr	$0.00
	Manually Entered Charges:	$0.00
	Total for Search Item:	$15.00

Please mail your payment of the Balance Due Amount to the address listed above. Please reference the TWC Request # listed above on your payment. Failure to properly identify payment will result in delays.

Records will be mailed to the Client Mailing address listed above upon receipt of payment unless you schedule an appointment to pick-up records with the individual listed above. Records will not be released until full payment is received.

Exhibit 280

U-24
IMPORTANT TWO DOCUMENTS: OPEN IMMEDIATELY

TEXAS WORKFORCE COMMISSION
101 E 15TH ST
AUSTIN TX 78778-0001

OFFICIAL BUSINESS

7743931168 R082

Exhibit 281

Texas Workforce Commission
A Member of Texas Workforce Solutions

July 23, 2019

Ellenor Perkins Ratcliff

Cypress, TX 7

                                    Date Received: 6/21/2019
                                    Request No.   : 190621-009
                                    Total Charges : $19.50
                                    Balance Due   : $00.00

RE: Ellenor Perkins
       460-2014-01770

Dear Ellenor Perkins Ratcliff:

Enclosed please find the certified results of our search for records regarding the above-referenced subject.

This letter will also confirm that we have received payment in full for the total charges associated with this request, as listed above.

Should you have any questions regarding the enclosed information, please contact me at the phone number listed below.

Sincerely,

Johnson
Assistant Disclosure Officer
512-

Texas Workforce Commission, Open Records Section
● 101 E. 15th Street, Room 266● Austin, Texas 78778-0001 ● Tel: (512) 463-2422 ● Fax: 512/
● Relay Texas: 800-735-2989 (TDD) 800-735-2988 (Voice) ● @twc.state.tx.us ● www.twc.state.tx.us ●
Equal Opportunity Employer/Services

Exhibit 282

STATE OF TEXAS § § §
COUNTY OF TRAVIS

CERTIFIED COPY OF PUBLIC RECORDS

COMPLAINTANT: Ellenor Perkins
RESPONDENT: General Dynamics Information Technology
CHARGE NO.: 460-2014-01770

I, Gloria Johnson, Assistant Disclosure Officer for the Texas Workforce Commission (Commission), an administrative agency of the State of Texas, hereby certify that the Commission has conducted a diligent search for records regarding the above-referenced Charge Number.

I further certify no records were located as a result of this search.

Witness my hand and the official seal of the Texas Workforce Commission, in Austin, Texas on July 01, 2019.

Gloria Johnson
Assistant Disclosure Officer
Texas Workforce Commission

Exhibit 283

Exhibit 284

open records   Inbox

Mills, C   @twc.state.tx.us   Mon, Aug 5, 12:14 PM
to me

Ms. Perkins,

Thank you for contacting me last week. I spoke to the EEOC about your request. They are not able to provide documents from 2014 if no lawsuit has been filed, but you are welcome to contact the Houston EEOC at 713-209-3377.

I also spoke to open records at my office, and we no longer have a copy of your Charge from 2014. I am sorry for any inconvenience, but we do not keep copies of Charges for 5 years.

Thanks,

C   Mills, Manager
Employment Investigations/ADR
101 E. 15th Street, Guadalupe CRD
Austin, TX 78778
Phone: (512)
Fax: (512)

Exhibit 285

DEPARTMENT OF HEALTH & HUMAN SERVICES
Centers for Medicare & Medicaid Services
7500 Security Boulevard, Mail Stop B3-30-03
Baltimore, Maryland 21244-1850

MAY 1 3 2015

Ms. Ellenor Perkins Ratcliff

Houston, TX

Dear Ms. Ratcliff:

On behalf of the Acting Administrator of the Centers for Medicare & Medicaid Services (CMS), thank you for your letter regarding your concerns with one of CMS's contractors, General Dynamics Information Technology (GDIT).

I am sorry that you experienced difficulties while employed at GDIT under CMS's Call Center Contract. While each government contract is unique to the specific requirement, all contracts are governed by the Federal Acquisition Regulation (FAR). The vision of the FAR is to deliver the best value products and services, while also maintaining the public's trust and fulfilling public policy objectives. Therefore, please be assured that all CMS contractors are made aware of their responsibilities under their government contracts; by signing a contract, they have agreed to abide by all applicable regulations. If a violation of contract terms and conditions is identified, contractors are held accountable, as appropriate.

I want to assure you that CMS takes its responsibility for the appropriate use of Federal funds very seriously and regularly monitors its contractors. If you have any further questions, please feel free to contact the Contracting Officer for this contract, D   Lester. She can be reached at   @cms.hhs.gov.

Sincerely,

D.   Kane
Director

Exhibit 286

DEPARTMENT OF
HEALTH & HUMAN SERVICES
Centers for Medicare & Medicaid Services
7500 Security Boulevard
Baltimore Maryland 21244-1850

Official Business
Penalty for Private Use, $300

Ms. Ellenor Perkins Ratcliff

Houston, TX

Exhibit 287

Ellenor Perkins Ratcliff

Houston, Texas

Department of Health & Human Services
Centers for Medicare & Medicaid Services
7500 Security Boulevard, Mail Stop B3-30-03
Baltimore, Maryland 21244-1850

July 30, 2015

Dear D   Lester:

First I want to thank you for responding on May 13, 2015, regarding my horrible experience while working at GDIT, under CMS's Call Center Contract. During my employment I notified GDIT of the issues I was having, I provided everything that was asked of me. I wanted to allow you some time, for your investigation of the complaint I made against General Dynamics Information Technology.

Can you explain what actions have been taken regarding the treatment I received while working at General Dynamics Information Technology? How will such treatment be eliminated to avoid future injury to others? How will CMS ensure employees rights are protected, who may have the same illness or worst? Contractors should have policy and procedures that are not only written but enforced. Please respond in writing.

Sincerely,

Ellenor Perkins Ratcliff

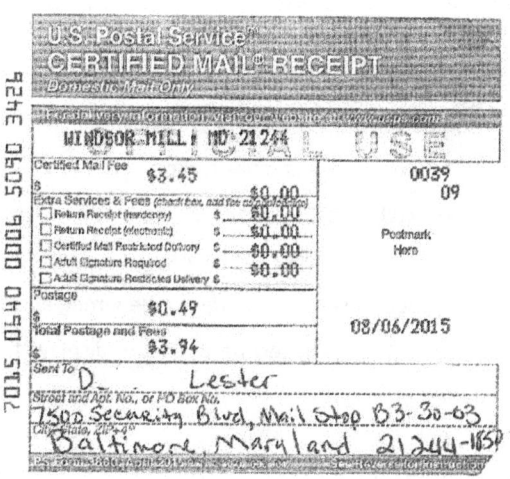

Exhibit 288

Ellenor Perkins Ratcliff

Houston, Texas 77

Federal Bureau of Investigation
1 Justice Park Drive
Houston, Texas 77092

October 22, 2015

Dear Special Agent Perrye K. Turner:

This complaint is in regards to Civil Rights and Political Rights Violations. While employed by General Dynamics Information Technology, discrimination took place from October 2013 to February 17, 2014; As a human, a black woman and an individual with a respiratory disability, discrimination was present. There will also be another issue of discrimination addressed in this letter. A charge was filed with the Equal Employment Opportunity Commission and the case was held for an entire year, before I was informed of any action. Jeremy Crosbie stated, "GDIT was not obligated to enforce policy." The EEOC is bias and corrupt and have systematically discriminated against many employees as well as myself. Enclosed are documents that support the claim presented of discrimination by General Dynamics Information Technology and Equal Employment Opportunity Commission. The information below will explain why discrimination took place.

A charge of discrimination was completed on March 17, 2014 and was brought before the EEOC on March 20, 2014 (Exhibit 1A and 1B). After questioning Mr. Crosbie he stated, "You didn't have to file with TWC." March 27, 2014, letter of assigned investigator was sent (Exhibit 4A). The EEOC held my case for an entire year (3/20/14, Exhibit 1A to 3/26/15, Exhibit 4B) and stated, "Based upon its investigation, the EEOC is unable to conclude that the information obtained establishes violations of the statutes." Mr. Crosbie has obstructed justice. Jeremy Crosbie finally contacted me. I asked, "What took so long for your investigation?" Jeremy Crosbie stated, "I sent the charge to the wrong address for GDIT." (Exhibit 1A page 2, section 2 and Exhibit 4B page 1, section Enclosure displays the same address). Mr. Crosbie also stated,

Exhibit 289

"GDIT was not obligated to enforce the perfume issue and GDIT gave reasonable accommodations. GDIT asked you for medical documentation (Exhibit 2) and you didn't provide it and they moved you to a different supervisor."

April 10, 2015, request for a substantial weight review was mailed (Exhibit 1C). Martin Ebel responded, April 29, 2015 (Exhibit 4C). Mr. Ebel stated, "The EEOC has no obligation to reconsider the final findings we have issued on a charge." Contact was made with President Obama in April, regarding the EEOC bias and corruption. July 7, 2015, Mr. Ebel contacted me by letter and stated, "This is in response to your April 10, 2015, inquiry to President Obama concerning the charge of employment discrimination you filed with the EEOC," (Exhibit 4D.) "You were not accorded a substantial weight review, because that process only occurs where a FEPA has made a determination on a charge that was dual filed with both a FEPA and the EEOC. Your charge was not filed with a FEPA, but rather was filed directly with the EEOC, so a substantial weight review is not possible."

August 6, 2015, contact was made with President Obama (Exhibit 1D) and September 1, 2015, contact was made with Attorney General Lynch (Exhibit 1E) regarding the corruption and bias at the EEOC. Jeremy Crosbie never contacted witnesses; I have spoken with the witnesses. Jeremy Crosbie lied regarding difficulty locating organization GDIT, the address on EEOC Intake Questionnaire dated for 3/17/2015, is the same address on Dismissal and Notice of Rights dated March 26, 2015, addressed to Lesley P. Marlin, Assistant General Counsel of General Dynamics Information Tech.

Mr. Ebel also obstructed Justice on July 7, 2015; Stating because there was no dual filing, a substantial weight review is not possible (Exhibit 4D). EEOC Printout (Exhibit 3A) dated 3/10/2014, How to File a Charge of Employment Discrimination states, "According to these agreements, if you file a charge with either EEOC or a FEPA, the charge also will be automatically filed with the other agency. This process, which is defined as dual filing, helps to protect charging party rights under both federal and state or local law;" also TWC Printout

Exhibit 290

(Exhibit 3B) dated 10/2/2015 How to Submit an Employment Discrimination Complaint states, When you submit an employment discrimination complaint with the Civil Rights Division, it is automatically submitted with EEOC through our Worksharing Agreement. You cannot submit with both the Civil Rights Division and the EEOC." Enclosed are also documents (1F,1G, 5A and 1H) which were submitted to the president and attorney general.

Clearly the EEOC has intentionally discriminated as well as obstruct justice in my case by abusing its authority, accepting bribes to throw the investigation of the charge brought against GDIT. I have been oppressed; EEOC abused its authority by obstructing justice. Depression and anxiety has filled my life, I have isolated myself, and I suffer with insomnia. Injury was sustained to my lungs and due to EEOC, the opportunity to claim workers' compensation from GDIT was lost. EEOC wickedly pretended to help me, but obstructed justice. I pray the FBI will investigate accordingly and bring all parties to justices, whom have cooperated in the obstruction of justice in my case. We are requesting all parties be removed from positions within the EEOC.

Sincerely,

Ellenor Perkins Ratcliff

Exhibit 291

Ellenor P. Ratcliff

Cypress, Texas

NAACP
4805 Mt. Hope Drive
Baltimore MD 21215

December 18, 2018

Dear Staff:

    Due to failed attempts in our fight for justice, we write you on today. We have pleaded with the Baytown Police Department, here in Houston, Texas to correct vital information on crash report. The officer who investigated was biased, due to behavior displayed at the scene of the accident (safety location). The officer allowed the person who caused the accident to leave the scene and then he proceeded to issue a citation to   before   disputed and officer declined to cite. We learned of Officer Martinez police misconduct latter of 2017, after the crash report was released. After the accident of December 10, 2016, the crash report was submitted on or about December 29 of 2016.

    After receiving the report I immediately noticed vital information was omitted and false information was written. An internal investigation was completed and I informed Officer Thompson of the biased behavior as well as information left off our crash report. Our civil rights have been violated as well as an insurance denial of $2,500,000 dollars. If you can assist us it would be greatly appreciated.

Sincerely,

Exhibit 292

Ellenor P. Ratcliff

Cypress, Texas

ACLU
125 Broad Street, 18th Floor
New York NY 10004

December 18, 2018

Dear Staff:

    Due to failed attempts in our fight for justice, we write you on today. We have pleaded with the Baytown Police Department, here in Houston, Texas to correct vital information on crash report. The officer who investigated was biased, due to behavior displayed at the scene of the accident (safety location). The officer allowed the person who caused the accident to leave the scene and then he proceeded to issue a citation to   before   disputed and officer declined to cite. We learned of Officer Martinez police misconduct latter of 2017, after the crash report was released. After the accident of December 10, 2016, the crash report was submitted on or about December 29 of 2016.

    After receiving the report I immediately noticed vital information was omitted and false information was written. An internal investigation was completed and I informed Officer Thompson of the biased behavior as well as information left off our crash report. Our civil rights have been violated as well as an insurance denial of $2,500,000 dollars. If you can assist us it would be greatly appreciated.

Sincerely,

Exhibit 293

Attn: Ellenor
1 message

Staffan De Mistura <C_____@diplomats.com>
To: L_____.com

Mon, Jun 5, 2017 at 6:55 PM

Dear Ellenor,

I trust you and your family are doing great?

Send your bank account details, copies of your identification and a letter indicating who you are and who directed you (Mr Staffan de Mistura) by fax to the UN Humanitarian Council, #3 Whitehall Ct, Westminister, London SW1A 2EL UK.
Tel: +44 20 338 96904 Fax:

Notify me once you fax the details to them.

Remain blessed!

Mr Staffan

Exhibit 294

Attn: Ellenor
2 messages

Staffan De Mistura <_____@diplomats.com>
To: L_____.com

Wed, Jun 7, 2017 at 11:11 PM

Dear Ellenor,

As a matter of urgency our office in London is ready to transfer the total sum of Seven Hundred Thousand United States Dollars to you first and once you receive it they will transfer another until the Two Million Dollars is completetly transferred. This is because according to them the total amount cannot be transferred at one time following the instruction and advice from the US Treasury Department.

But before the transfer takes place, you need to get a Donation Approval from the Buckingham Palace approving the outward remittance to your account following the monetary regulations of UK.

Unfortunately I am still in hospital and therefore won't be able to go to London to represent you and I am sure you too won't be able to go, so if you could allow them to assign a lawyer who would go and get the approval that would be better, but according to them, the Donation Approval and Stamp-Duty would cost One Thousand Seven Hundred Dollars while the Lawyer's fee is Three Hundred and Seventy Dollars. The Total is therefore Two Thousand Seventy Dollars.

You should send this amount to them through Western Union Money Transfer or Moneygram and fax the receipt to them.
The receiver's name is John Howard.

If they receive the fee today the transfer of your donation will commence today.

If you have a relative in London and would want them to handle this on your behalf, that would be perfect.

In Christ,

Sir Staffan.

Exhibit 295

E   com>   Thu, Jun 8, 2017 at 7:50 AM
Draft To: Staffan De Mistura <   @diplomats.com>

Dear Staffan,

Didn't know you were still in hospital. I pray all is well. Unfortunately, I don't have family in London that can assist me with representation and I don't have the funds to hire an attorney to represent me either. I truly thank you for your assistance in helping with my efforts. If it's meant God will make a way.

Sincerely,

Ellenor Ratcliff
[Quoted text hidden]

Exhibit 296

Someone offering aid using, United Nations Humanitarian Council name
1 message

E   .com>   Thu, Jun 8, 2017 at 7:52 AM
To: InfoDesk@ohchr.org

Good Morning,

My name is Ellenor and I have an organization called Lady Justice, in which was founded due to the human rights violations I faced. In my organization I fight for the rights of my people who's human rights have been violated and educate on human rights. Please give this email to the proper authorities. I strongly believe an imposter is portraying to be Staffan de Mistura. This person has offered me financial assistance to further my work and is asking that I provide information to receive help from United Nations Humanitarian Council. I became a little suspicious after he asked me to send money for attorney fees to receive money from London (But before the transfer takes place, you need to get a Donation Approval from the Buckingham Palace approving the outward remittance to your account following the monetary regulations of UK.). Please contact me, I have greater details in regard to the correspondence between the individual and I.

Sincerely,

Ellenor P. Ratcliff
United States Resident of Houston Texas

Exhibit 297

Certified Mail #7017 1450 0001 0829 2434

Ellenor Ratcliff

Houston, Texas

Angela Leticia Gonzalez

Granada Hills, Ca

CC:
K   Edward

Northpoint Asset Management, Inc.

Spring, Tx

February 8, 2018

NOTICE

Regarding Property: , Cypress Tx 77433

Exact letter mailed to Northpoint Asset Management, Inc.

Your ad stated it was move in ready, which was a lie. In good faith we signed the lease on November 27, 2017. We met with you on November 28th at the property to give deposit and first month's rent and to receive the keys. We saw the property was dirty and you began to walk through. Had you walk through the property prior to meeting to receive our deposit and first month rent, you would have known the property was dirty and etc. As a realtor, you should have made sure the plumbing and electrical was in working order. Due to ineffectiveness, there are many issues we have encountered. You delayed our move, pest control, my access to extra help and my husband was forced to take off work without pay.

    a. Electrical has yet to be repaired. It has been 71 days since our move in. Our elderly father has a cord running across the front of his door, which is a tripping hazard. The lights in his room won't stay on unless we plug a cord into the bathroom outlet, which we use for his heart monitor, because the outlets don't work.

    b. Mailbox, we have no access to the mailbox and it has been 71 days since move in.

Exhibit 298

    c. Sinking floor upstairs in bedroom has yet to be repaired and yes, it's been 71 days since move in.

You received notice about all the above issues, as well as all the issues listed below which have finally been repaired. Again, this property was not move in ready!

"Condition of Property prior to move in date 11.29.17, except for 2 conditions noticed after move in and weather change. They are listed at bottom of text.

*Kitchen - Garbage Disposal is not working again.

Vents in ceilings are hanging again downstairs.

Window Latches - * Safety Issue - Window Latches are inoperative in Living Room

* Safety Issue - Window Latches are inoperative in Dining Room

* Safety Issue - Window Latches are inoperative in Kitchen & Breakfast

* Safety Issue - Window Latches are inoperative in Family Room.

* Master Bedroom- Flooring - sinking near closet

* Front/ Back Door –Needs Weather stripping

* Master Bathroom - Sink - Metal Stopper missing

* Bedroom 3 - Door - lock loose at base

Window - water entering at window seal

* Bathroom 2 Upstairs- Lock - loose at base

Sink - missing metal stopper

Tub- Slow draining

Exhaust Fan - inoperative

*Bathroom 3 Downstairs - Lock - inoperative

Sink- missing metal stopper

Tub- Slow draining

Exhibit 299

Toilet - extended flush and water still rises as if it will overflow...I use a thin tissue, so that shouldn't be the issue

* Outlets are inoperative (10 + outlets) in Garage, Outside, Dining Room, Kitchen & Breakfast Area, Family Room and Bathroom 3.

* Outlet cover broken in Livingroom

* Replace bulb outside

* Mailbox Key does not fit

* Backdoor needs adjusting, very difficult to open and close.

* Need Key for Back Door

* Kitchen Cabinets missing handles

* All doors need Door Stops to prevent holes when the door is opened.

****

We have two new issues noticed...

the ac unit does not blow in master bedroom, all vents have been checked, there is no circulation.

Door knob keeps falling off...master bedroom.

Currently, we are dealing with the issue of the stairs, some of the stairs are lose and we have the understanding that this is an issue which occurs due to use. Family trips going up and when coming down, the steps can make us slide down because it lifts up. My children are scared they are going to hurt themselves.

It has taken too long for you to get repairs completed, which should have been rectified before this property was placed online for lease.

Under the Deceptive Trade Practice, we are suing Northpoint Asset Management, Inc and home owner Angela Leticia Gonzalez. You lied about the condition of this property. You received our money and you received it on time, each month with the exception of February, due to the owner texting us in January and demanded we not pay Northpoint, but the new company once contact was made to us. Later this month, after telling owner about the stairs and electrical and etc., did

Exhibit 300

she send another text stating, "Pay Kemeshia and the property will change management for the new month."

As a tenant it's not our concern who burned who, you received our money and we expected everything to be up to par. For the longest my family and I were worried about security because the locks did not work on the windows. We demand half the rent back for each month repairs are not completed, which means November, December, January and February. Should you have all the work completed this month, we will not demand half of March rent. As of today, you owe us $2,376.50. This amount will increase if issues are not rectified. Please do not take us lightly. I told you I was done talking and texting, asking you all to do your job. I don't want any apologies, I want my money. Should this proceed to court our attorney will demand a higher amount. You have ten business days to deliver a check of $2376.50. Since we still don't have access to the mailbox, send it to   , Houston, Texas   .

Regretfully,

_____   _____
Ellenor Ratchff   Date

Exhibit 301

9/11/2018   Print Details

HARRIS COUNTY APPRAISAL DISTRICT
REAL PROPERTY ACCOUNT INFORMATION

Tax Year: 2017

Print

Owner and Property Information

Owner Name & Mailing Address:	GONZALEZ ANGELA LETICIA GRANADA HILLS CA	Legal Description:	LT 22 BLK 3 CYPRESS SPRINGS SEC 4
		Property Address:	CYPRESS TX 77433

State Class Code	Land Use Code	Land Area	Total Living Area	Neighborhood	Neighborhood Group	Map Facet	Key Map®
A1 -- Real, Residential, Single-Family	1001 -- Residential Improved	7,087 SF	2,725 SF	5.04	4153	4562B	406M

Value Status Information

Value Status	Notice Date	Shared CAD
Noticed	03/31/2017	No

Exemptions and Jurisdictions

Exemption Type	Districts	Jurisdictions	Exemption Value	ARB Status	2016 Rate	2017 Rate
None	004	CYPRESS-FAIRBANKS ISD		Certified: 08/11/2017	1.440000	1.440000
	040	HARRIS COUNTY		Certified: 08/11/2017	0.416560	0.418010
	041	HARRIS CO FLOOD CNTRL		Certified: 08/11/2017	0.028290	0.028310
	042	PORT OF HOUSTON AUTHY		Certified: 08/11/2017	0.013340	0.012560
	043	HARRIS CO HOSP DIST		Certified: 08/11/2017	0.171790	0.171100
	044	HARRIS CO EDUC DEPT		Certified: 08/11/2017	0.005200	0.005195
	045	LONE STAR COLLEGE SYS		Certified: 08/11/2017	0.107800	0.107800
	465	HC MUD 165		Certified: 08/11/2017	1.150000	1.100000
	633	HC EMERG SRV DIST 9		Certified: 08/11/2017	0.053310	0.052710

Texas law prohibits us from displaying residential photographs, sketches, floor plans, or information indicating the age of a property owner on our website. You can inspect this information or get a copy at HCAD's information center at 13013 NW Freeway.

Valuations

	Value as of January 1, 2016			Value as of January 1, 2017	
	Market	Appraised		Market	Appraised
Land	20,005		Land	24,123	
Improvement	131,836		Improvement	141,354	
Total	151,841	151,841	Total	165,477	165,477

Exhibit 302

CUSTOMER KEY ORDER REQUEST

CYPRESS POST OFFICE
16835 SPRING CYPRESS RD
CYPRESS TX 77429/77433

DATE: 2/4/15
CLERK: XC

REASON FOR KEY REQUEST:
PREVIOUSLY OWNED HOME NEW RESIDENT: ✓
LOCK MALFUNCTION REPAIR: _____
LOST KEYS: _____

FEE FOR LOST KEYS ONLY (25.00)
CHECK: _____ CASH: _____ CREDIT/DEBIT: _____

CUSTOMER'S NAME: Eleanor Popken
ADDRESS: _____ ZIP CODE: 77433
PHONE #: _____

FOR POSTAL USE ONLY

DATE LOCK CHANGED: 2/26   DATE CONTACTED: 2/26

COMPLETE AFTER CUSTOMER PICK UP KEYS

CUSTOMER SIGNATURE: _____   DATE PICKED UP: 2/28/15

Exhibit 303

3-DAY NOTICE TO PAY RENT OR MOVE OUT

Plaintiff(s): Crown Eagle Realty, Owner(s)

VS.

Defendant(s): _____, Resident

Ellenor Y. Perkins Ratcliff, Resident

_____, Resident

Notice To Pay Rent

To: Ellenor Y. Perkins Ratcliff, Resident(s) AND ALL OTHERS IN POSSESSION. PLEASE TAKE NOTICE that you are justly indebted to the owner of the herein described premises; and notice is hereby given that pursuant to the lease and/or rental agreement under which you hold possession, there is now due, unpaid and delinquent rent in the total sum of One Thousand Five Hundred Fifty Dollars

($1550.00). The total amount owing represents rent due for the following period(s):

$1550.00 Due from March 1, 2018, to March 31, 2018.

$_____ Due from _____, 20___, to _____, 20___

$_____ Due from _____, 20___, to _____, 20___

WITHIN THREE (3) DAYS after service on you of this notice, you are hereby required to pay the amount of the above stated rent in full OR quit the subject premises, move out, and deliver up possession to the owner and/or his authorized agent.

Your payment should be payable to: Crown Eagle Realty and payment shall be delivered to:

Name: Crown Eagle Realty at the following address: _____

Unit #: 108, Houston, TX Zip Code: 77069

and Telephone Number (832) _____ who is usually available on the following

days: Monday thru Saturday and the following hours: 9 AM to 5 PM

PLEASE TAKE FURTHER NOTICE that unless you pay the rent in full OR vacate the premises WITHIN THREE (3) DAYS as required by this notice, that the undersigned does hereby elect to declare a forfeiture of the subject lease and/or rental agreement and will institute legal proceedings for the unlawful detainer against you to recover possession of the premises plus court costs, attorney fees

As required by law, you are hereby notified that a negative credit report reflecting on your credit record may be submitted to a credit reporting agency if you fail to fulfill the terms of your credit obligation.

The premises herein referred to which are now held and/or occupied by you are located in the City of Cypress,

County of Harris, State of TX and commonly known by the street and number of

_____, zip code 77433, apartment or suite number _____

Dated this 5th day of March, 2018

Owner(s): Angela Gonzalez By: Crown Eagle Realty/Aleksander Koronowski Agent

Exhibit 304

Exhibit 305

3-DAY NOTICE TO PAY RENT OR MOVE OUT

Plaintiff(s): Angela Gonzalez, Owner(s)

Defendant(s): _____, Resident
Ellenor Y. Perkins Ratcliff, Resident
_____, Resident

Notice To Pay Rent

To: Ellenor Y. Perkins Ratcliff, Resident(s) AND ALL OTHERS IN POSSESSION. PLEASE TAKE NOTICE that you are justly indebted to the owner of the herein described premises, and notice is hereby given that pursuant to the lease and/or rental agreement under which you hold possession, there is now due, unpaid and delinquent rent in the total sum of One Thousand Five Hundred Fifty Dollars

($1550.00). The total amount owing represents rent due for the following period(s):

$1550.00 Due from August 1, 20 18, to August 31, 20 18.

$ ___ Due from ___, 20 ___, to ___, 20 ___

$ ___ Due from ___, 20 ___, to ___, 20 ___

WITHIN THREE (3) DAYS after service on you of this notice, you are hereby required to pay the amount of the above stated rent in full OR quit the subject premises, move out, and deliver up possession to the owner and/or his authorized agent.

Your payment should be payable to: Crown Eagle Realty and payment shall be delivered to:
Name: Crown Eagle Realty at the following address: _____
Unit #: MAIL ONLY   Zip Code: ___
and Telephone Number (___) ___ who is usually available on the following
days: Monday thru Saturday and the following hours: ___

PLEASE TAKE FURTHER NOTICE that unless you pay the rent in full OR vacate the premises WITHIN THREE (3) DAYS as required by this notice, that the undersigned does hereby elect to declare a forfeiture of the subject lease and/or rental agreement and will institute legal proceedings for the unlawful detainer against you to recover possession of the premises plus court costs, attorney fees

as required by law, you are hereby notified that a negative credit report reflecting on your credit record may be submitted to a credit reporting agency if you fail to fulfill the terms of your credit obligation.

The premises herein referred to which are now held and/or occupied by you are located in the City of Cypress, County of Harris, State of TX and commonly known by the street and number of _____, zip code 77433, apartment or suite number ___.

Dated this 14th day of August, 20 18

Owner(s): Angela Gonzalez   By: Aleksander Koronowski   Agent

Exhibit 306

The Office of Constable Ted Heap
Harris County Precinct 5
Case Information Card

Case #: HC180130385
Title: Terroristic Threat

You have filed a report with law enforcement for the above titled case.
The status of this report is:
Open ○   Closed-Charges Filed ○   Closed-Information Only ○
Referred To: _____

FOR INFORMATION ON OBTAINING COPIES OF REPORTS VISIT:
www.constablepct5.com/openrecords/

Harris County Constable's
Office Precinct 5
17423 Katy Freeway
Houston, TX 77094

Pct. 5 Admin: (832) 927-6700
Pct. 5 Dispatch: (281) 463-6666
Harris County Sheriff: (713) 221-6000
Houston Police Dept: (713) 308-8585

DEPUTY: S. Gregson   UNIT: 85U03

Exhibit 307

Ellenor P. Ratcliff

Cypress Texas

Certified Mail Receipt#
7017 2680 0000 3365 5348

KIM OGG
Harris County District Attorney
500 Jefferson Street
Houston, Texas 77002

December 10, 2018

Notification and Request to Press Charges

On August 14 of 2018 I was assaulted. I called the police immediately after the assault. I explain to the officer what happened. She came back to the door and asked if I would like to file charges. I didn't know what to say. I told the officer let me talk to my husband. I told her I needed to move.

On October 23, I received an email from open records. I made several calls to constable office and told them I wanted to file charges and my calls were never returned. It's horrible enough that I was assaulted and have been dealing with emotional issues due to Aleksander Koronowski actions, and to add insult to injury, I'm told I can't file charges because it would be considered retaliation, yet I was assault.

KIM OGG, I am a victim and I plead for you to press charges against Aleksander Koronowski for assault. It is unknown how many others have suffered at his hands.

Sincerely,

Ellenor Perkins Ratcliff

Exhibit 308

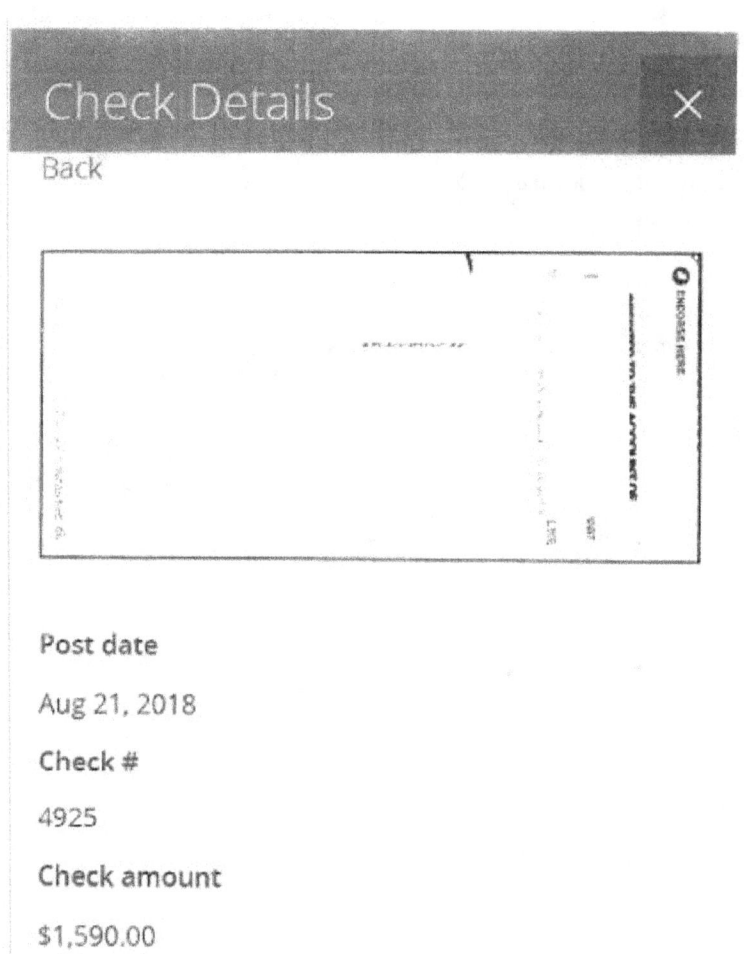

Sent To: KIM OGG
Street: 500 Jefferson Street
City, State: Houston Tx 77002

Exhibit 309

Check Details

Back

Post date

Aug 21, 2018

Check #

4925

Check amount

$1,590.00

403

Exhibit 310

Petition for Eviction from Residential Premises   Case No. _____

Angela Gonzalez Aleksander Koronowski §   IN THE JUSTICE COURT OF
          Landlord (Plaintiff)   §   Harris County, Texas, Precinct __ Place __
VS.   §
_____, Ellenor Y. Perkins Ratcliff   §
          Tenant (Defendant)   §

Name of Landlord (provide full legal name): Angela Leticia Gonzalez, Aleksander Koronowski referred to as "Plaintiff."

Tenants. 1. Name of Tenant (provide full legal name): _____
Defendant may be served at (provide street address and telephone number, if known):
_____, Cypress, TX 77433
All other home and work addresses of this Defendant in Harris County that are known to the Plaintiff are:
_____

☑ Plaintiff knows of no other home or work addresses of this Defendant in Harris County.

2. Name of Tenant (provide full legal name): Ellenor Y. Perkins Ratcliff
Defendant may be served at (provide street address and telephone number, if known):
_____, Cypress, TX 77433
All other home and work addresses of Defendant in Harris County that are known to the Plaintiff are:
_____

☑ Plaintiff knows of no other home or work addresses of this Defendant in Harris County. Tenant(s) are referred to as "Defendant."

Premises. Plaintiff seeks possession of following Premises (describe premises, i.e. house, apartment building, including street address):
Single family home located at _____ Cypress, TX 77433

Grounds for Eviction. Plaintiff seeks to evict Defendant for the following reason:

☑ **Failure to pay rent:**
Residential Lease: ☑ Written ☐ Oral Beginning date of Lease: **November 29, 2017** End date of Lease: **November 30, 2018**
Rent: $ 1550.00   per month   (e.g. month, week) Date of last rental payment: July 6, 2018
Total amount of rent due and unpaid on date of filing: $ 1550.00
Rent subsidized by government: $ 0 paid by _____ ; $ _____ paid by the Defendant.

☐ **Violation of Lease:** Tenant violated Paragraph No. _____ of the Lease by (describe violation): _____

☐ **Holding over after termination of right to possession:** Date of notice of termination: _____

☐ **Foreclosure:** Plaintiff purchased the Premises at foreclosure on _____
☐ Plaintiff intends to live in the Premises as Plaintiff's primary residence.
☐ Defendant is a tenant of the former owner; End date of Lease: _____ Rent: $ _____ per _____

Notice to Vacate: Date Notice to Vacate Delivered: Aug. 14, 2018 Manner of delivery In person

☐ **Attorney Fees:** Plaintiff seeks attorney fees as follows:
Contractual: Lease (written) Paragraph No. _____ Amount of Attorney Fees claimed: $ _____
Statutory: Written demand to vacate sent on: _____ Date received: _____ Attorney Fees claims: $ _____

Plaintiff requests possession of the Premises, past due rent, if applicable, attorney's fees, if applicable, court costs, and such other and further relief to which Plaintiff may be entitl[ed].

Respectfully submitted,

_____   Aleksander Koronowski   Property Manager
Attorney or Authorized Agent   Printed Name   Title

Address: _____
Houston, TX 77069
Daytime Telephone: 832-_____ Fax Number: _____
State Bar No. _____

☐ Plaintiff consents to the e-mail service of the answer and any other motions or pleadings to this e-mail address.
E-Mail Address: _____

THE STATE OF TEXAS §
COUNTY OF HARRIS   §
SWORN TO BEFORE ME on _____, by AUG 2 0 2018 _____, Plaintiff.

Maria Cavazos   Cler____   Notary Public
CLERK OF THE COURT

RECEIVED AUG 2 0 2018 Hon. Jeff Williams JUSTICE OF THE PEACE 5/2

Exhibit 311

Eviction – Judgment/Dismissal Order NonJury

In the Justice Court
Precinct 5, Place 2

Harris County
State of Texas

Case Number: _____

Angela Leticia Gonzalez
Plaintiff
vs.
    Ellenor Y Perkins Ratcliff
Defendant

Represented by:

Represented by:

Leased Premises: Cypress, TX 77433

Plaintiff(s)   ☐ Present   ☐ Not Present at Trial
Defendant(s) ☐ Present   ☐ Not Present at Trial

CORRECTED

On 9/12/2018 the court heard the above-numbered and styled cause.

☐ **DEFAULT JUDGMENT FOR PLAINTIFF**
The Plaintiff, being present, announced ready for trial. The Defendant, although having been duly cited and served with process, said citation with the officer's return thereon having been on file with the clerk of this court, failed to appear or answer in its behalf, and wholly made default. It is therefore decreed that judgment is entered for the Plaintiff for possession of the above described premises, and further, that the Plaintiff have judgment against the Defendant(s) for $_____ as rent owed, plus $_____ as attorney fees, all costs of court, together with post-judgment interest at a rate of 5.00% per annum from the date of judgment until paid, for which let execution issue. No writ of possession will issue before 09/18/18. The Defendant(s) appeal bond is set at: $_____.

☐ **JUDGMENT FOR PLAINTIFF**
The Plaintiff and Defendant, being present, announced ready for trial. The court, having heard the evidence, determined judgment is for the Plaintiff for possession of the above described premises. It is therefore decreed that judgment is entered for the Plaintiff for possession of the above described premises, and further, that the Plaintiff have judgment against the Defendant(s) for $_____ as rent owed, plus $_____ as attorney fees, all costs of court, together with post-judgment interest at a rate of 5.00% per annum from the date of judgment until paid, for which let execution issue. No writ of possession will issue before 09/18/18. The Defendant(s) appeal bond is set at: $_____.

☐ **JUDGMENT FOR DEFENDANT**
The Plaintiff and Defendant, being present, announced ready for trial. The court, having heard the evidence, determined judgment is for the Defendant for possession of the above described premises. It is therefore decreed that the Plaintiff take nothing and that judgment is entered for the Defendant(s) for $_____ as attorney fees, all costs of court, together with post-judgment interest at a rate of 5.00% per annum from the date of judgment until paid, for which let execution issue. The Plaintiff's appeal bond is set at $500.00.

☐ The court ORDERS that this case is DISMISSED:

    ☐ due to lack of jurisdiction.
    ☐ as Plaintiff did not appear.
    ☐ on motion of the   ☐ Plaintiff   ☐ Defendant.
    ☐ by agreement of the parties and that each side bears their cost incurred.

The court denies all other relief not granted above.

Signed: 9/18/2018

                                                          Justice of the Peace Precinct 5, Place 2

Payment of Rent during the Pendency of Any Appeal:

☐ The amount of rent to be paid each rental pay period during the pendency of any appeal is $_____.

☐ A portion of the rent is payable by a government agency, and the amount of rent to be paid each rental pay period during the pendency of any appeal is: $_____ by Defendant and $_____ by government agency.

Exhibit 312

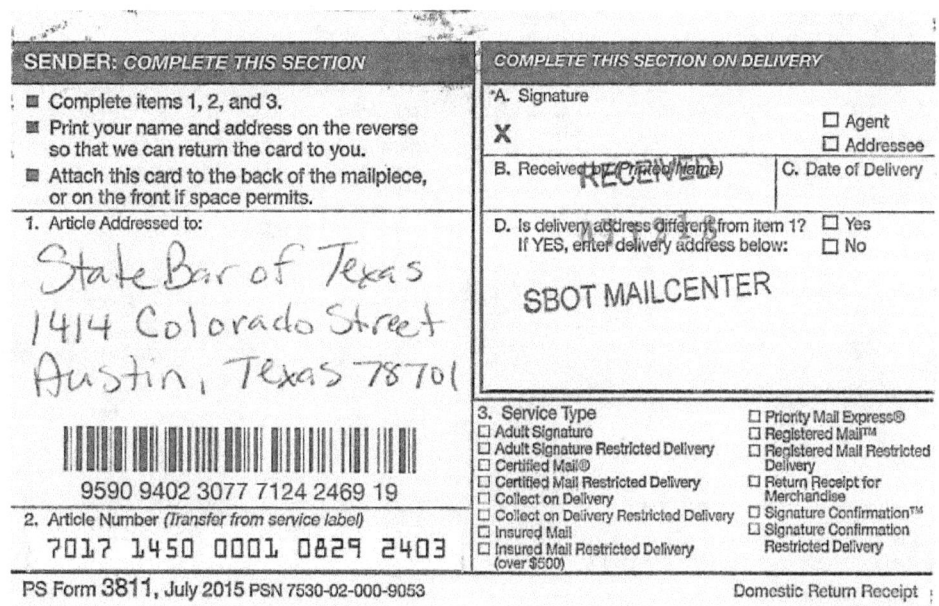

Exhibit 313

Exhibit 314

STATE BAR OF TEXAS

COMPLAINT FORM

ONLY for complaints regarding your experience with the delivery of non-legal services that the State Bar of Texas provides the public and its members. Complaints against an attorney must be made directly to the Office of Chief Disciplinary Counsel. To file a complaint against an attorney please visit cdc.texasbar.com or call 1-800-932-1900. Attorney complaints filed on this form WILL NOT be processed and no response will be received from this site.

POLICY

Pursuant to State Bar Act Section 81.036, the State Bar of Texas maintains a file on the receipt, investigation, resolution, and communications regarding all written complaints, other than a grievance against an attorney, filed with the State Bar. *Please note that anonymous complaints will not be processed.*

COMPLAINT INFORMATION

NAME _____ _____ _____
     (Last)   (First)   (Middle)

BAR MEMBER YES [ ]   NO [✓]   BAR CARD NUMBER _____

MAILING ADDRESS _____ 7 _____ Houston _____ Tx __ 77096 __ US
                 (Street)   (City)   (State) (Zip)   (Country)

EMAIL ADDRESS _____@gmail.com   PHONE ( )

Complaint Details: (*A written complaint must include the facts upon which the complaint is based*)
Attorney-client confidentiality breach/unethical behavior of Tuan Khuu & Associates. View attachments A-1 to A-4 Agreement, B-1/B-2 for Allstate, C-1/D-1 Termination of Representation, D-2/D-3 PIP Forms, E-1 Letter of Representation, F-1/F-2 Claim Processed, G-1 Bodily Injury Claim and H-1 to H-6 Suing Me

If your complaint is related to a State Bar staff member or department, please provide the names of the staff members and departments below.
_____
_____

COMPLAINT SUBMISSION

Please submit written complaints online at texasbar.com/contactus or by mail to:

State Bar of Texas
1414 Colorado Street
Austin, TX 78701

The State Bar will acknowledge receipt of your complaint within 10 working days. A written response will be provided within 60 days of receipt of your complaint.

For any other questions regarding this process please call 800.204.1724

State Bar of Texas

Exhibit 315

STATE BAR OF TEXAS

Office of the Chief Disciplinary Counsel

July 26, 2018

Houston, TX

Re: Correspondence Dated July 12, 2018

Dear M

Please be advised that your recent letter submitted to our office is being returned to you for one (1) or more of the following reasons:

    ____ 1. The Attorney-Client Privilege and Confidentiality Waiver (Part VI) is not signed. Please sign and return with the rest of the information.

    ____ 2. A grievance can only be filed against individual attorneys, not against law firms as a whole. Use a separate form for each attorney about whom you are complaining. Please identify attorney's name and address.

    X 3. The information that you have provided should be submitted on a State Bar grievance form. This form can be submitted via our online website at http://cdc.texasbar.com, or by completing the attached form and returning it to our office by mail or via fax at 512-427-4169.

    ____ 4. The additional information you have provided in support of your grievance was not received within (10) days of submitting your grievance and therefore has not been considered with your pending grievance.

    ____ 5. Your letter is being returned for the following reason:

Please take appropriate action to correct the above referenced items and return all correspondence to the **State Bar of Texas, Office of the Chief Disciplinary Counsel, P.O. Box 13287, Austin, Texas 78711.**

Sincerely,

Office of the Chief Disciplinary Counsel
State Bar of Texas

P. O. Box 12487, Austin, TX 78711, (512) 427-1350, (877) 953-5535, fax: (512) 427-4167

Exhibit 316

THE LAW OFFICES OF
TUAN A. KHUU & ASSOCIATES

3010 N. Classen Blvd, Suite B, Oklahoma City, OK 73106
Phone: (405) 528-1542   Fax: (405) 528-1563

2615 W. Pioneer Pkwy, Suite 103 Grand Prarie, TX 75051
Phone: (817) 583-7911   Fax: (817) 928-1670

9900 Westmark Dr. Suite 188 Houston, TX 77063
Phone: (713) 952-8808   Fax: (713) 952-0303

Attorneys
- Tuan Khuu
- Robert T. Keel
- S. Louis Little
Licensed in Oklahoma

Office Directors
Kim Pham
Trinh Tran
Nancy Estrada
Jannies Nguyen

Of Counsel
David M. Ramsey
Ernie Nalagan

Attorneys
Keith Nguyen •
Licensed in Texas

Office Directors
Lina Do
Vy Nguyen
Kimberly Luong

Of Counsel
Frank B. Daniel
Cindy Purinton
Alan Do

August 2, 2018
L

Houston, TX

RE: Your Personal Injury and Property Damage case

Thank you for allowing us to help with the incident case. Unfortunately, at this time my office is unable to assist you any further. As you have already been informed, you only have until August 2, 2020 to file your lawsuit in the appropriate jurisdiction.

As previously advised, you only have two years from the date of when the accident occurred, more specifically on or before August 2, 2020 to file the lawsuit or your case/claim will be forever barred. If your case is barred, you will forever lose any right to claim any loses and/or injuries associated with the accident you sustained on December 10, 2016

Our office will proceed to close your file as of today and will not be responsible of any statue limitations or other deadlines associated with your personal injury case.

We strongly recommend that you seek legal counsel. A copy of your file has been mailed to the address of record. We appreciate the opportunity and don't hesitate to contact us if you have nay questions or can be of further assistance.

Sincerely,

/s/ Thomas Stephenson

Thomas Stephenson
For the Firm
ATTORNEY LIEN CLAIMED

Web: www.khuulaw.com
Legal Assistants
Maria Guel, Yessica Buenxllo, Veronica Trujillo, Betsy Figueroa, Kimberly Han, Selena Luna, Lupe Zavala, Thao Dang, Jean Williams, Ha Nguyen

E-mail: tuan.khuu@khuulaw.com

Exhibit 317

Fax Cover Sheet

COMPANY LOGO

TO:	Office of the Chief Disciplinary Counsel	FROM:	
FAX:	512-427-4169	FAX:	N/A
PHONE:	713-758-8200	PHONE:	
DATE:	2/14/2019	# OF PAGES:	28 including Fax Cover
SUBJECT:	Grievance against Cindy D Purinton		

Page 1 Cover

Pages 2-5 Copy of Grievance

Pages 6-9 A-1 to A-4 Power of Attorney and Fee Agreement

Pages 10-11 B-1 to B-2 Dated June 22, 2017

Pages 12 C-1 Dated October 31, 2017

Pages 13-15 D-1 to D-3 Dated November 2, 2017 and PIP Claim

Pages 16 E-1 Dated November 10, 2017

Pages 17-18 F-1 to F-2 Dated December 11, 2017

Pages 19 G-1 Dated January 2, 2018

Pages 20-25 H-1 to H-6 Lawsuit Filed against me, served me 3/26/18

Pages 26-27 I-1 and I-2 Dated July 6, 2018

Pages 28 J-1 Dated August 2, 2018

Exhibit 318

TRANSMISSION VERIFICATION REPORT

```
TIME   : 02/14/2019 06:02
NAME   :
FAX    :
TEL    :
SER.#  : BRO
```

```
DATE, TIME       02/14  05:53
FAX NO./NAME     15124274169
DURATION         00:08:30
PAGE(S)          28
RESULT           OK
MODE             STANDARD
```

Exhibit 319

Fax Cover Sheet

 COMPANY LOGO

TO:	Office of the Chief Disciplinary Counsel	**FROM:**	
FAX:	512-427-4169	**FAX:**	N/A
PHONE:	713-758-8200	**PHONE:**	
DATE:	2/14/2019	**# OF PAGES:**	28 including Fax Cover
SUBJECT:	Grievance against Tuan A Khuu		

Page 1 Cover

Pages 2–5 Copy of Grievance

Pages 6-9 A-1 to A-4 Power of Attorney and Fee Agreement

Pages 10-11 B-1 to B-2 Dated June 22, 2017

Pages 12 C-1 Dated October 31, 2017

Pages 13-15 D-1 to D-3 Dated November 2, 2017 and PIP Claim

Pages 16 E-1 Dated November 10, 2017

Pages 17-18 F-1 to F-2 Dated December 11, 2017

Pages 19 G-1 Dated January 2, 2018

Pages 20-25 H-1 to H-6 Lawsuit Filed against me, served me 3/26/18

Pages 26-27 I-1 and I-2 Dated July 6, 2018

Pages 28 J-1 Dated August 2, 2018

Exhibit 320

```
        TRANSMISSION VERIFICATION REPORT

                              TIME   : 02/14/2019 06:02
                              NAME   :
                              FAX    :
                              TEL    :
                              SER.# : BROE8J660422


    DATE,TIME              02/14  05:53
    FAX NO./NAME           15124274169
    DURATION               00:08:30
    PAGE(S)                28
    RESULT                 OK
    MODE                   STANDARD
```

Exhibit 321

Online Grievance Form
Dec 02, 2018 10:27 PM

I. General Information
Have you contacted the Client-Attorney Assistance Program?*
No

II. Information About You
Salutation

First Name
Ellenor

Middle Name

Last Name
Perkins Ratcliff

Address

Cypress, TX

Cell Phone

Email Address

Driver's License Number (if applicable)

Date of Birth

II. Information About You - Additional
Do you understand and write in the English language?
Yes

Are you a Judge?
No

III. Information About Attorney
Attorney Barcard Number

Exhibit 322

Attorney First Name
Cindy

Attorney Middle Name
D.

Attorney Last Name
Purinton

Attorney Address (Please include street, city and zip)
 Dallas, TX 75243

Attorney Work Phone

Attorney Home Phone

Attorney Other Phone

III. Information About Attorney - Grievance Details

Have you or a member of your family filed a grievance about this attorney previously?
No

Have you or a member of your family ever filed an appeal with the Board of Disciplinary Appeals about this attorney?
No

Please select from the following:
This attorney was hired to represent me.

Please give the date the attorney was hired or appointed.
January 6th of 2017

Please state what the attorney was hired or appointed to do.
The attorney was hired to represent myself, Elienor P. Ratcliff and to represent Larry Ratcliff.

What was the fee arrangement with the attorney?
33 1/3%, 40%, 50% or 50% depending on case discriptions

How much did you pay the attorney?
To my knowledge the attorney has received $5,000 in personal injury protecteion, I never signed off for.

III. Information About Attorney - Continued
If you did not hire the attorney, what is your connection with the attorney? Explain briefly

Exhibit 323

Online Grievance Form
Dec 03, 2018 2:52 PM

I. General Information
Have you contacted the Client-Attorney Assistance Program?*
No

II. Information About You
Salutation
Mrs.

First Name
Elienor

Middle Name
Yvette

Last Name
Perkins Ratcliff

Address

Cell Phone

Email Address

Driver's License Number (if applicable)

Date of Birth

II. Information About You - Additional
Do you understand and write in the English language?
Yes

Are you a Judge?
No

III. Information About Attorney
Attorney First Name
Tuan

Attorney Middle Name
A

Attorney Last Name
Khuu

Attorney Address (Please include street, city and zip)
, Oaklahoma City, OK 73106   Houston, Tx 77036

Attorney Work Phone

Attorney Other Phone

Exhibit 324

FAX

To:	Office of the Chief Disciplinary Counsel	From:	Ellenor Perkins Ratcliff
Fax:	512-427-4169	Fax:	
Phone:	713-758-8200	Phone:	
No. Pages:	23 including fax cover	Date:	December 13, 2018
Subject:	Grievance against Tuan A Khuu		

Comments:

Pages 1-2   Cover

Pages 3-6   Copy of Grievance

Pages 7-8   Detail of calls made to Dallas & Houston law office of Tuan Khuu & Associates.

Pages 9-12   Attorney & Client Contract (Provided because law firm would not release my files.) and I signed the same legal and binding documents.

Pages 13-15   Email submission of Crash Report

Pages 16-20   Document dated 6/22/17 emailed to me to sign (Medical detail to be sent to Allstate, Consent to Refer, HIPPA, PIP Application submitted to Amica).

Page 21   Letter of no representation sent to Amica.

Page 22-23   Letter of no representation sent to me from Amica with PIP form attached.

Page 24   Letter of representation sent to Amica.

Pages 25-26   Payment mailed to The Law Offices of Tuan A. Khuu

Pages 27   Letter of intent to pursue uninsured/underinsured motorist bodily injury claim.

Should you have any questions please feel free to contact me at the number provided on the Grievance.

Exhibit 325

FAX

To:	Office of the Chief Disciplinary Counsel	From:	Ellenor Perkins Ratcliff
Fax:	512-427-4169	Fax:	
Phone:	713-758-8200	Phone:	
No. Pages:	23 including fax cover	Date:	December 13, 2018
Subject:	Grievance against Cindy D. Purinton		

Comments:

Pages 1-2   Cover

Pages 3-6   Copy of Grievance

Pages 7-8   Detail of calls made to Dallas & Houston law office of Tuan Khuu & Associates.

Pages 9-12   Attorney & Client Contract (Provided _____ because law firm would not release my files.) _____ and I signed the same legal and binding documents.

Pages 13-15 Email submission of Crash Report

Pages 16-20 Document dated 6/22/17 emailed to me to sign (Medical detail to be sent to Allstate, Consent to Refer, HIPPA, PIP Application submitted to Amica).

Page 21   Letter of no representation sent to Amica.

Page 22-23   Letter of no representation sent to me from Amica with PIP form attached.

Page 24   Letter of representation sent to Amica.

Pages 25-26 Payment mailed to The Law Offices of Tuan A. Khuu

Pages 27   Letter of intent to pursue uninsured/underinsured motorist bodily injury claim.

Should you have any questions please feel free to contact me at the number provided on the Grievance.

Exhibit 326

FAX

To:	Office of the Chief Disciplinary Counsel	From:	Ellenor Perkins Ratcliff
Fax:	512-427-4169	Fax:	
Phone:	713-758-8200	Phone:	
No. Pages:	1 including fax cover	Date:	December 14, 2018
Subject:	Grievance against Tuan A. Khuu		

Comments:

On two separate occasions, after learning the law firm filed on my insurance anyway, I called to verify where the money was and who released my information without my permission. I was given the run around then, I was told,"The person who released your information is no longer with the firm."

Please make note, the phone detail submitted on 12/13/18 is only from 12/14/17 to 2/21/18 and not 12/10/16 – 02/21/18 as mentioned prior.

I would like to also have answers to the following questions.

Why is the Houston law office telephone number no longer in operation?

Why have I not been contacted by email or phone regarding picking up my records?

Please file this with my Grievance.

Exhibit 327

FAX

To:	Office of the Chief Disciplinary Counsel	**From:**	Ellenor Perkins Ratcliff
Fax:	512-427-4169	**Fax:**	
Phone:	713-758-8200	**Phone:**	
No. Pages:	1 including fax cover	**Date:**	December 14, 2018
Subject:	Grievance against Cindy D. Purinton		

Comments:

On two separate occasions, after learning the law firm filed on my insurance anyway, I called to verify where the money was and who released my information without my permission. I was given the run around then, I was told, "The person who released your information is no longer with the firm."

Please make note, the phone detail submitted on 12/13/18 is only from 12/14/17 to 2/21/18 and not 12/10/16 – 02/21/18 as mentioned prior.

I would like to also have answers to the following questions.

Why is the Houston law office telephone number no longer in operation?

Why have I not been contacted by email or phone regarding picking up my records?

Please file this with my Grievance.

Exhibit 328

STATE BAR OF TEXAS

Office of the Chief Disciplinary Counsel

January 2, 2019

Ellenor Yvette Perkins Ratcliff

Cypress, TX

Re: 201807554 - Ellenor Yvette Perkins Ratcliff - Cindy D. Purinton

Dear Ms. Perkins Ratcliff:

The Office of Chief Disciplinary Counsel of the State Bar of Texas has reviewed the above-referenced grievance and determined that the information provided alleges Professional Misconduct or a Disability, or both. The lawyer will be provided a copy of your Complaint, directed to file a response, and provide you a copy of the response within thirty (30) days of receiving notice of the Complaint.

After receipt of the lawyer's written response, the Office of Chief Disciplinary Counsel shall investigate the Complaint to determine whether there is Just Cause to believe that the lawyer has committed Professional Misconduct or suffers from a Disability. During this time it is important that you keep us informed of any changes to your address, telephone number, or employment, and that you cooperate fully with our investigation. You will be notified in writing of further proceedings in this matter.

Please know that the Office of the Chief Disciplinary Counsel maintains confidentiality in the grievance process as directed by the Texas Rules of Disciplinary Procedure.

Sincerely,

Timothy J. Baldwin
Administrative Attorney

TJB/rea

Cc: Ms. Cindy D. Purinton

4801 Woodway Drive, Suite 315-W Houston, Texas 77056
Phone: 713-758-8200 Fax:

Exhibit 329

STATE BAR OF TEXAS
4801 Woodway Drive, Suite 315-W
Houston, Texas 77056

Personal and Confidential

02 JAN '19

US POSTAGE >> PITNEY BOWES
ZIP 77056 $ 000.47
02 4R
0000362357 JAN 02 2019

Ellenor Yvette Perkins Ratcliff

Cypress, TX 77433

Exhibit 330

STATE BAR OF TEXAS

Office of the Chief Disciplinary Counsel

January 2, 2019

Ellenor Yvette Perkins Ratcliff

Cypress, TX

Re: 201807555 - Ellenor Yvette Perkins Ratcliff - Tuan A. Khuu

Dear Ms. Perkins Ratcliff:

The Office of the Chief Disciplinary Counsel of the State Bar of Texas has examined the Grievance concerning the above-referenced individual and determined that this person is not licensed as an attorney in the state of Texas.

Under the Texas Rules of Disciplinary Procedure, we do not have jurisdiction to take action against an individual not licensed to practice law in the state of Texas. Accordingly, this matter has been dismissed as an Inquiry. Please know that the Office of the Chief Disciplinary Counsel maintains confidentiality in the grievance process as directed by the Texas Rules of Disciplinary Procedure. If you have any questions about the dismissal of your grievance, I can be reached at (877) 953-5535.

Sincerely,

E. Hsu
Assistant Disciplinary Counsel

EH/srs

P. O. Box 12487, Austin, TX 78711, (512) 427-1350, (877) 953-5535, fax: (512)

Exhibit 331

STATE BAR OF TEXAS
P.O. Box 12487, Austin, Texas 78711-2487

Personal and Confidential

Exhibit 332

January 29, 2019
State Bar of Texas

Houston, Texas 77056

        In Re: 2018-07554-Ellenor Yvette Perkins Ratcliff

Dear Sir,

My response to the grievance is as follows:

1. I worked in an of counsel capacity for the Khuu Law firm in Grand Prairie, Texas from October 2, 2015 to July 17, 2017 when I resigned to pursue other opportunities. I never officed in Houston, Texas and was only asked to cover two cases during that time period, a divorce and a response to an anti slap motion.

2. I returned to the Khuu Law firm as an independent contractor from November 20, 2017 to help open a new Garland office located on Walnut Street in Garland, Texas and then resigned on April 2, 2018 to pursue other opportunities.

3. I first reviewed the proposed lawsuit on the Ms. Perkins-Ratccliff case on February 15, 2018 as I was told the attorney in the Houston office, Michael Villasana resigned in late 2017 just before I rejoined the firm and the firm asked me to help in the Houston filings until a new Houston attorney could be found. The firm told me that once hired, the new Houston attorney would substitute in. Prior to that time, I had no knowledge Ms. Perkins-Ratcliff was a client of the firm and did not agree to represent Ms. Perkins-Ratcliff and am unaware of any representations and did not approve of any representations made to Ms. Perkins-Ratcliff at the time she signed her contract. I know nothing about any of the events Ms. Perkins-Ratcliff complains of in her grievance and have received none of the notices Ms. Perkins-Ratcliff states she sent to the firm. On November 14, 2018, an amended petition was filed naming Thomas Stephenson of Khuu and Associates as her attorney.

Exhibit 333

State Bar of Texas
January 29, 2019
Page 2

4. I have no knowledge of any of the documents attached to the grievance except that I have reviewed those documents on line in Ms. Perkins-Ratcliff case filed in Harris County, Texas. I did not take part in or have any knowledge of the run around Ms. Perkins-Ratcliff was given regarding correcting the accident report and did not authorize, review or have any knowledge of the letters or documents dated June 22, 2017, October 31, 2017, November 10, 2017 and December 2, 2017 and the September 18, 2017 application for benefits and took no part in nor have any knowledge of releasing any information about Ms. Perkins to any person. Further I have reviewed the contract sent in by Ms. Perkins-Ratcliff and the Contract signed on January 7, 2017 by Mr. Ratcliff was signed by Texas Attorney Adam Chevrier as I recognize his signature.

5. In regards to Ms. Perkins-Ratcliff telephone log, when I returned to the firm November 20, 2017 the Walnut street office did not have telephone service and did not obtain phone service until after I left. Further I received no messages to call Ms. Perkins-Ratcliff.

6. I do not have Ms. Perkins-Ratcliff file or access to it.

7. In addition, I did not receive the check Ms. Perkins-Ratcliff complains about and know nothing about its receipt by the firm.

8. Further I was not working for the firm on on September 18, 2017, October 31, 2017 or November 10, 2017 and was unaware the firm was still placing my name on firm letterhead.

Exhibit 334

State Bar of Texas
January 29, 2019
Page 3

9. I did receive an email from Ms. Perkins-Ratcliff thru the email name Evette Perkins on June 5, 2018 and I responded to Ms Perkins-Ratcliff as indicated in her grievance. Attached as **Exhibit A** are the email from Ms Perkins-Ratcliff, my email response to Ms. Perkins-Ratcliff and my forward of Ms Perkins email to the firm. I never received any further emails from Ms. Perkins-Ratcliff although my email address is the same.

10. Attached hereto as **Exhibit B** are all my emails and the firm's responses to all emails concerning the Perkins-Ratcliff case from February 15, 2018 to the present in chronological order.

Ms. Perkins-Ratcliff is obviously mistaken as to my involvement in her case. I am willing to cooperate with the investigation in any way and would request that this grievance be referred for summary dismissal.

Sincerely,

Cindy D. Purinton

Pc: Ms. Perkins-Ratcliff

Cypress, Texas 77433
CMRRR

Exhibit 335

Exhibit 336

STATE BAR OF TEXAS

Office of the Chief Disciplinary Counsel

January 31, 2019

Ms. Ellenor Yvette Perkins Ratcliff

Cypress, Texas 77-

Re: 201807554 - Ellenor Yvette Perkins Ratcliff - Cindy D. Purinton

Dear Ms. Ratcliff:

The Office of the Chief Disciplinary Counsel has received the written response in the above-referenced complaint. Please notify this office immediately if you have not received a copy of the response.

If you have further documents or information that you want to submit, please do so within ten (10) days.

Sincerely,

P. McPoland
Investigator

JPM/jh

4801 Woodway Drive, Suite 315-W Houston, Texas 77056
Phone: 713-758-8200 Fax:

Exhibit 337

STATE BAR OF TEXAS
4801 Woodway Drive, Suite 315-W
Houston, Texas 77056

N HOUSTON
TX 773
31 JAN '19

Personal and Confidential

Ms. Ellenor Yvette Perkins Ratcliff

Cypress, Texas 77433

77433-116862

Exhibit 338

STATE BAR OF TEXAS

Office of the Chief Disciplinary Counsel

February 20, 2019

Ms. Ellenor Yvette Perkins Ratcliff

Cypress, Texas 77

Re: 201807554 - Ellenor Yvette Perkins Ratcliff - Cindy D. Purinton

Dear Ms. Perkins Ratcliff:

The Office of the Chief Disciplinary Counsel has received the supplemental response in the above-referenced complaint. A copy of the supplemental response has been included for your review.

If you have further documents or information that you want to submit, please do so within ten (10) days.

Sincerely,

P. McPoland
Investigator

JPM/jh

4801 Woodway Drive, Suite 315-W Houston, Texas 77056
Phone: 713-758-8200 Fax:

STATE BAR OF TEXAS

Office of the Chief Disciplinary Counsel

April 3, 2019

Ellenor Yvette Perkins Ratcliff

Cypress, Texas 77

Re: 201807554 - Ellenor Yvette Perkins Ratcliff - Cindy D. Purinton

Dear Ms. Perkins Ratcliff:

Please be advised that an Investigatory Hearing in the above-referenced matter has been scheduled for **June 5, 2019 at 1:00 P.M.** The Hearing will be held at **State Bar of Texas, 4801 Woodway Drive, Suite 315-W, Houston, TX 77056**.

Pursuant to Rule 2.12(F)&(G) of the Texas Rules of Disciplinary Procedure, the Investigatory Panel will take testimony under oath from the Complainant, Respondent and other witnesses, if necessary, in a non-adversarial proceeding in an attempt to resolve this disciplinary matter by agreement. **Your attendance is requested to give testimony and assist the Investigatory Panel with its investigation.** The Investigatory Hearing may result in a dismissal or a negotiated resolution.

Please do not hesitate to contact this office should you have any questions.

Sincerely,

G. Windham
Assistant Disciplinary Counsel
VGW/mal

4801 Woodway Drive, Suite 315-W Houston, Texas 77056
Phone: 713-758-8200 Fax: 713-

Exhibit 341

STATE BAR OF TEXAS

Office of the Chief Disciplinary Counsel

May 29, 2019

Via Email   .com
Via Regular U.S. Mail

Ellenor Yvette Perkins Ratcliff

Cypress, Texas 77

Re: 201807554 - Ellenor Yvette Perkins Ratcliff - Cindy D. Purinton

Dear Ms. Perkins Ratcliff:

Please be advised that V: G. Windham, former Assistant Disciplinary Counsel, was attorney of record and attorney in charge for the CFLD in this matter.

J   S. Brannon, Assistant Disciplinary Counsel, is now the attorney of record and attorney in charge in this action and will have full management and control of this case for the CFLD.

If necessary you may contact J   S. Brannon, Assistant Disciplinary Counsel, State Bar of Texas, 4801 Woodway Drive, Suite 315-W, Houston, Texas, 77056; or by telephone at (713) 758-8200, fax at (713)   , or email at   1@texasbar.com

The State Bar of Texas thanks you for bringing this matter to our attention. If you have any questions or need additional information please do not hesitate to contact me at your earliest convenience.

Sincerely,

   S. Brannon
Assistant Disciplinary Counsel
JSB/cv

4801 Woodway Drive, Suite 315-W Houston, Texas 77056
Phone: 713-758-8200 Fax: 713-

Exhibit 342

STATE BAR OF TEXAS

Office of the Chief Disciplinary Counsel

June 12, 2019

Ellenor Yvette Perkins Ratcliff

Cypress, Texas 77

Re: 201807554 - Ellenor Yvette Perkins Ratcliff - Cindy D. Purinton

Dear Ms. Perkins Ratcliff:

Thank you for bringing this matter to the attention of the State Bar of Texas and thank you for your participation in the Grievance Committee's investigatory hearing. Your participation and testimony was valuable to the investigation of your grievance.

The District Grievance Committee found that there was not enough evidence to continue the investigation. Accordingly, the Chief Disciplinary Counsel's office has closed this investigation, dismissed the grievance and will take no further action.

Also enclosed is a Disciplinary System Questionnaire, which gives us valuable feedback from those involved in the process. We would appreciate your client taking a moment to complete it.

Thank you for bringing this matter to our attention.

Sincerely,

/S. Brannon
Assistant Disciplinary Counsel

JSB/vr

Enclosure:

Exhibit 343

STATE BAR OF TEXAS
4801 Woodway Drive, Suite 315-W
Houston, Texas 77056

Personal and Confidential

U.S. POSTAGE
$ 000.50

Ellenor Yvette Perkins Ratcliff

Cypress, Texas 77433

7743331168 R062

Photograph by Provost Studios

I'm already a Champion because I believe it in my heart and mind. Anything you want to do is first planted in your psyche, and you must bring that dream or goal to manifestation.

ACKNOWLEDGMENTS

Without God pushing me, I would have given up. All praises to **Jehovah-Jireh**, for guidance.

My family, I thank you for standing behind me, even when I couldn't see my way through. To my friends of few, I thank you for your encouragement and your obedience to God concerning me.

Obedient vessels, who came to me during this journey from near and far, I thank you. You gave me words of encouragement from God. I pray you always proper in The Most High God. Stay obedient and I speak blessing over your life.

I benefited greatly from the professional support of Tiff's Editing Café and the amazing artist, Michael LaFrance Lynch, who captured my heart on canvas. I'm truly grateful for the panel who read my book and gave an overall review of the experiences, as well as editing feedback. I also want to thank the literary agent, and Lnoir's Fidelity Publishing for its trust, and confidentiality. It was not easy finding a publisher to publish such controversial work. I take full responsibility for its shortcomings.

PERMISSIONS

Unless otherwise indicated, all Scriptures are taken from Scripture quotations are from the ESV® Bible (The Holy Bible, English Standard Version®), copyright © 2001 by Crossway Bibles, a publishing ministry of Good News Publishers. Used by permission. All rights reserved.

Other versions used:
The King James Version of the Bible (KJV).

The Holy Bible, New Living Translation, copyright ©

Holy Bible, New Living Translation, copyright © 1996, 2004, 2007, 2013, 2015 by Tyndale House Foundation. Used by permission of Tyndale House Publishers Inc., Carol Stream, Illinois 60188. All rights reserved.

Scriptures taken from the Holy Bible, New International Version®, NIV®. Copyright © 1973, 1978, 1984, 2011 by Biblica, Inc.™ Used by permission of Zondervan. All rights reserved worldwide.

Timeline of Events as they unfolded regarding the corruption, collusion and cover-up.

09/05/13 – Email from GDIT system at 7:58 a.m., thanking me.

09/05/13 – Email from GDIT at 2:38 p.m., regarding an employment offer.

09/05/13 – Email from GDIT at 3:37 p.m., to complete employment application within 5 days.

09/06/13 – Email from GDIT at 11:14 p.m., with details regarding training/what I should bring.

09/07/13 – Forwarded new hire orientation email to @wrksolutions.com at 1:03 p.m.

09/09/13 – I officially started working for GDIT

10/03/13 – Urgent visit to clinic 1:45p.m., returned to work 10/04/13.

10/04/13 – Emailed notice, 10/3 All Day (to inform supervisor/ HR I was out all day due to illness).

10/04/13 – Emailed A. Clem, Supervisor regarding notice of breathing issues.

10/04/13 – Emailed Z. Bosie, at 6:03 p.m., regarding restricted breathing/ reasonable accommodations.

10/10/13 – Emailed Notice regarding my absence from 9:30 a.m. – 11:00 a.m.

10/11/13 – Emailed Workforce Solutions counselor at 9:16 a.m. regarding difficulty/ childcare issues.

10/17/13 – Urgent Visit to V Clinic at 8:15 a.m.

10/21/13 – Visit Dr for follow-up from 10/03/2013

10/24/13 – Visit Dr for follow-up from 10/17/2013

10/28/13 – Emailed 10:47 a.m., 10/31 All Day

10/28/13 – Emailed 11:21 a.m., 11/1 Ellenor, doctor appointment and pto, 1:00-6:00.

10/29/13 – Emailed Z. Bosie at 3:24 p.m., regarding CSR's spraying perfume.

10/30/13 – Emailed Z. Bosie at 11:39 a.m., regarding HR Policy.

11/08/13 – Forwarded email to supervisor/Z. Bosie at 10:56 a.m., regarding no response from Z. Bosie.

11/08/13 – Verbal communication between supervisor and I, regarding medical condition.

11/08/13 – Emailed A. Clem/ W. Reimer at 12:25 p.m., regarding moving due to exposure.

11/08/13 – Emailed A. Clem at 12:28 p.m., Z. Bosie didn't respond to email from 10/29.

11/08/13 – Email received from supervisor at 12:45 p.m., regarding virtual position.

11/08/13 – Emailed A. Clem, supervisor at 12:48 p.m.

11/08/13 – Emailed supervisor again at 3:31 p.m., regarding someone spraying perfume.

11/08/13 – Email received from supervisor at 3:32 p.m., apologizing/ adjusting my time card.

11/12/13 – Email received at 6:03 p.m., from A. Clem forwarded by W. Reimer regarding virtual position.

11/13/13 – Email forwarded at 7:38 a.m./10:01a.m., from L. Bair to W Reimer, regarding virtual position.

11/18/13 – Email received at 9:51 a.m. from supervisor A Clem, regarding virtual position.

11/18/13 – My supervisor, A. Clem and I had a verbal conversation about me resigning.

11/19/13 – I begin feeling ill, there was smoking near the building and I departed for clinic at 9:40 a.m.

11/19/13 – Doctor statement from Harris Health System regarding breathing issues and prevention.

11/21/13 – Emailed supervisor at 1:18 p.m. and provided information regarding the doctor statement.

11/22/13 – Emailed supervisor at 1:12 p.m., regarding departure to shelter.

12/25/13 – Emailed another supervisor at 11:40 a.m., regarding departing for shelter at 2:00 p.m.

12/16/13 – Emailed supervisor at 2:01 p.m., regarding shelter issues departed after 2:30 p.m.

12/18/13 – Informed supervisor of 1:38 p.m., doctor appointment.

12/19/13 – Doctor Visit, respiratory system in distress, returned to work 12/20.

12/20/13 – Emailed supervisor, A. Clem at 1:21 p.m. and responded to his verbal warning.

12/27/13 – Emailed supervisor, S Johnson at 12:37 p.m., regarding me feeling ill.

12/30/13 – Purchased more mask from Walgreens at 7:21 a.m.

12/30/13 – Emailed supervisor, A. Clem at 3:38 p.m., regarding forgetting to log into phone.

12/31/13 – Urgent visit to doctor at MLK Clinic, I had hard time breathing/ whizzing.

01/06/14 – Visited MLK clinic for follow-up and doctor released me to return to work 1/7/14.

01/07/14 – Emailed supervisor, took break to speak with HR department and logged in at 12:18 p.m.

01/07/14 – Visited the HR department/ spoke to Z. Bosie again regarding call center floor issues.

02/06/14 – Missed work, couldn't make it to doctor, felt like something was sitting on my chest.

02/07/14 – Urgent visit to Harris Health, doctor examined me/discussed my X-ray results.

02/10/14 – Follow-up doctor visit at 8:17 a.m., was released to return to work same day.

02/13/14 – Visited Harris Health, Pulmonary Clinic at 8:00 a.m. Dr. refused not explaining duration to recovery.

02/13/14 – Gave verbal regarding medical condition, doctor statement dated 2/13/14, to Z. Bosie.

02/17/14 – Emailed letter to supervisor, A. Clem for the notice of constructive discharge.

02/20/14 – 4:29 p.m., I saved a note of the email I submitted to HR and staff on my last day of work.

03/03/14 – A formal resignation letter was sent certified mail **(7013 0600 0002 4184 4828).**

03/10/14 – Printed from EEOC website, "How To File A Charge of Employment Discrimination."

03/17/14 – U.S. EEOC Intake Questionnaire was completed/16 pages of supporting documentation was organized.

03/20/14 – U.S. EEOC Intake Questionnaire was submitted. Charge number # 460-2014-01770.

03/25/14 – Copied OSHA information and made contact for help.

03/27/14 – Mailed or delivered letter to EEOC regarding permanent closure of GDIT.

03/27/14 – J. Crosbie mailed EEOC Houston District Office letterhead and attached business card.

04/24/14 – Harris Health System, finally gave me an official diagnosis of asthma/allergic rhinitis.

06/24/14 – Was scheduled to visit Harris Health System, Smith Clinic at 11 a.m. for CT SCAN.

06/26/14 – Was scheduled for 8:30 a.m., to return to Harris Health, Smith Clinic.

07/01/14 – Was scheduled for 1:40 p.m., to return to Harris Health, Smith Clinic for CT Scan.

07/00/14 – I stop breathing.

07/28/14 – Harris Health doctor completed Texas Health and Human Services form, regarding disability.

08/14/14 – Was scheduled for 10:20 a.m., to visit Harris Health.

11/00/14 – I contacted Disability Rights Texas for help.

03/26/15 – EEOC Martin S. Ebel, Acting District Director sent determination.

04/09/15 – I saved a note at 8:15 a.m., regarding state regulations.

04/10/15 – I submitted a notarized substantial weight review to EEOC for reconsideration.

04/10/15 – I sent a copy of the reconsideration to U.S.HHS by certified mail **(7011 0470 0003 5828 4862)**.

04/10/15 – I sent a copy of the reconsideration to The White House by certified mail **(7011 0470 0003 5828 4879)**.

04/10/15 – I sent a copy of the reconsideration to CMS by certified mail **(7011 0470 0003 5828 4855)**.

04/10/15 – At 8:45 p.m., God gave me a word.

04/29/15 – EEOC Martin Ebel denied me due process for the second time.

05/07/15 – I contacted attorney for assistance with workers' compensation benefits.

05/11/15 – I contacted TDI regarding insurance coverage for Vangent/GDIT.

05/11/15 – 5:47 p.m. I received an email from the attorney office regarding an appointment.

05/13/15 – CMS responded to my complaint regarding CMS's Call Center Contractor, Vangent/GDIT.

05/14/15 – Hired attorney to represent me against Vangent/GDIT.

05/14/15 – I made contact with correct insurance company after researching.

05/20/15 – I received an email at 12:39 p.m., from attorney office to pick up my original documents.

05/20/15 – I responded to attorney email at 5:02 p.m. and asked a question regarding the fee.

05/26/15 – I contacted attorney office at 5:25 p.m. by email regarding my contact with GDIT.

06/02/15 – I contacted attorney office again at 2:24 p.m. regarding fee for representation.

06/02/15 – I received an email from GDIT at 4:56 p.m., regarding my web inquiry for workman's comp.

06/03/15 – I sent an email to Human Resource Department at 4:49 p.m. and CC my attorney.

06/04/15 – I received a response from GDIT HR Manager at 3:54 p.m., regarding worker's compensation claim.

06/04/15 – I contacted attorney at 4:08 p.m. and forwarded email I received from GDIT.

06/05/15 – I contacted GDIT HR Department and CC my attorney at 5:28 p.m., regarding Broadspire conversation.

06/08/15 – I received an email from GDIT HR Department at 10:50 a.m., submission for my claim.

06/09/15 – I sent an email to my attorney at 8:51 a.m., regarding GDIT HR conversation regarding my claim.

06/09/15 – Broadspire A Crawford Company received notice of my on the job injury.

06/10/15 – I contacted GDIT HR Department for a follow-up at 11:07 a.m., regarding 6/8/2015 conversation.

06/10/15 – I forwarded an email to my attorney at 3:00 p.m.

06/10/15 – I received an email from GDIT HR Department at 3:35 p.m., regarding my claim number.

06/10/15 – I forwarded the email from GDIT HR Department at 6:56 p.m., to my attorney.

06/22/15 – I received an email from Disability Rights Texas at 8:45 a.m., including an attachment.

06/22/15 – I sent an email at 2:35 p.m., to Disability Rights Texas.

06/22/15 – I received a response email from Disability Rights Texas at 2:54 p.m.

06/22/15 – I sent Disability Rights Texas an email at 3:00 p.m., regarding the spelling of my name.

06/24/15 – I sent an email to my attorney at 7:36 a.m. regarding treating doctors.

06/24/15 – Completed Broadspire Forms.

06/25/15 – I contacted D. Fields of BROADSPIRE by fax to submit claim.

06/26/15 – I sent an email to Broadspire at 11:25 a.m., with two attachments (GDIT policy and resignation letter).

06/26/15 – At 12:51 p.m., I forwarded the email I sent to Broadspire and sent it to my attorney.

07/07/15 – U.S. EEOC contacted me regarding letter sent to President Obama.

07/09/15 – BROADSPIRE A Crawford Company denied my claim.

07/16/15 – I sent an email to my attorney at 6:54 p.m., regarding a follow-up and delivered additional info.

07/17/15 – I sent an email to Broadspire at 1:03 p.m., regarding the treatment I received and the denial.

07/17/15 – At 1:06 p.m., I forwarded the same email I sent to Broadspire and sent it to my attorney.

07/22/15 – My attorney received an email at 2:03 p.m., regarding the notice I received from Broadspire.

07/22/15 – I sent an email to my attorney at 2:30 p.m., regarding one of the witnesses.

07/23/15 – Broadspire sent an email to my attorney and I at 1:24 p.m., regarding sending out a copy of the denial.

07/23/15 – At 1:25 p.m., Broadspire sent me an email to confirm my address.

07/23/15 – At 3:18 p.m., I emailed Broadspire and noted denial was received.

07/29/15 – At 7:18 a.m., I sent an email to my attorney regarding discrediting Z. Bosie statement.

07/30/15 – I contacted CMS by certified mail **(7015 0640 0006 5090 3426)**.

08/06/15 – I contacted President Obama again by certified mail **(7015 0640 0006 5089 8715)**.

08/21/15 – My attorney presented a WITHDRAWL OF REPRESENTATION for Workers' Compensation Claim .

08/26/15 – I received a letter of rejection by a Florida attorney.

08/26/15 – I wrote a poem called, "Justice Where Art Thee?"

09/01/15 – I contacted U.S. Attorney General Loretta E. Lynch by certified mail **(7015 0920 0002 0409 1466)**.

09/01/15 – At 8:28 p.m., I received a response from Lawyers.com regarding my inquiry for an attorney.

09/01/15 – At 8:39 p.m., I received a transcript of the inquiry I submitted to Lawyers.com.

09/01/15 – At 11:15 p.m., I received a response from an attorney regarding my "civil rights matter."

09/04/15 – At 12:30 p.m., I responded to the attorney request per phone conversation.

09/04/15 – At 2:31p.m., I sent email to attorney secretary with attachments.

09/08/15 – I received a letter of rejection from Houston law firm.

09/11/15 – I contact L. P. Marlin for Vangent/GDIT by certified mail **(7015 0920 0002 0409 1473)**.

09/14/15 – I contacted President Barack Obama for the 3rd time, via certified mail **(7011 0470 0003 5834 9387)**.

09/14/15 – I contacted U.S. Attorney General Loretta E. Lynch via certified mail **(7011 0470 0003 5834 9394)**.

09/25/15 – I received response from Vangent/GDIT, L. Marlin, and was denied per EEOC determination.

10/02/15 – I printed from TWC website, "How to Submit an Employment Discrimination Complaint"

10/07/15 – I filed petition in Federal Court, Southern District of Texas (4:15-cv-03038).

10/07/15 – At 11:04 a.m., I sent an email to my attorney regarding another witness who can discredit Z. Bosie.

10/07/15 – At 11:37 a.m., I received an email from my attorney secretary.

10/07/15 – At 11:58 a.m., I emailed my attorney, God is on my side and more than the EEOC and GDIT against me.

10/08/15 – I received Order to Proceed without prepaying Fees or Cost.

10/14/15 – I completed the Affidavit of Financial Resources/ submitted the document.

10/15/15 – The United States District Court, mailed me the Order for Conference.

10/15/15 – The United States District Court, mailed me Instrument 4 – Instructions.

10/22/15 – I drafted FBI Letter and attached supporting documents concerning public corruption.

10/23/15 – At 4:45 p.m. I sent a note to myself regarding subpoenas for witnesses.

10/26/15 – I contacted the FBI in person.

10/29/15 – I contacted court and submitted subpoenas for (7) witnesses.

11/03/15 – Judge Lynn N. Hughes, signed "Opinion on Dismissal"

11/03/15 – Judge Lynn N. Hughes, signed "Final Dismissal with Prejudice" (H-15-3038).

11/04/15 – Judge Lynn N. Hughes, mailed Final Dismissal.

11/04/15 – Judge Lynn N. Hughes, mailed Opinion on Dismissal.

11/05/15 – I printed EEOC case information from Justia website.

11/08/15 – I filed for unemployment with TWC.

11/16/15 – I was denied unemployment benefits.

11/17/15 – Ogletree Deakins responded to Subpoena to testify and produce.

11/00/15 – One morning I heard, "The Enemy of my enemy is my friend."

11/00/15 – An individual told me what to write on Amendment for EEOC.

11/17/15 – I completed the amendment.

11/19/15 – GOD had me to type certain words on amendment.

11/19/15 – GOD sent me back to U.S. EEOC for a continuance to amend Charge NO 460-2016-00589.

11/20/15 – I made a public post to President Barack Obama and Attorney General L Lynch.

11/20/15 – TWC denied my unemployment for an alternate base period.

11/30/15 – At 8:52 a.m., I emailed EEOC District Director, Roy Wilkerson regarding Correction of charge.

12/00/15 – I received a call from someone who asked, "Is this Ellenor Perkins?"

12/07/15 – I was denied by Roy Wilkerson, Fed Investigator/ Rayford O. Irvin.

12/07/15 – I secured two business names which represent truth.

12/2015 – Why have you allowed all these people to go through this?

12/10/15 – Notes for Gentleman I contacted for help.

12/15/15 – The Lord instructed me to contact Rayford O. Irvin and I did by email.

12/15/15 – 4:34 a.m., I sent an email to Radford O. Irvin regarding God sending me.

12/15/15 – 4:50 a.m., I email the secretary of EEOC regarding the charge that was made and noted errors.

12/15/15 – 4:56 a.m., I made a note to myself.

12/15/15 – 4:59 a.m., I emailed Mr. Irvin and warned him.

12/15/15 – 10:56 a.m., I received a response from J. Saindon regarding my email sent at 4:34 a.m.

12/00/15 – I became upset with God after reading and asked God, "How am I going to make a difference?"

12/28/15 – Rayford O. Irvin EEOC denied me a second time.

01/09/16 – Early in the morning I heard, "This is not the time."

01/19/16 – At 4:04 p.m. I sent an email to my old attorney about action.

02/09/16 – I continued to record my video and created new signs.

02/14/16 – I continued to create and this day I was designing art for my T-shirt.

02/22/16 – I continued to edit video credits/added church victims from the Charleston shooting.

02/01/16 – I wrote a letter that I never sent to EEOC.

02/26/16 – I added Lady Justice Resource Services to Instagram.

03/01/16 – A friend told me, "God said, change is coming."

03/04/16 – The Department of Justice responded.

03/00/16 – I created website, www.ladyjusticetx.org.

03/08/16 – God gave me a dream about a well-known person.

03/15/16 – A friend told me, "I saw you at a podium in my dream."

03/17/16 – I created and release the poem, Diamonds.

03/00/16 – Someone help me transcribe my protest flyer to Spanish.

03/00/16 – A web page was created for prayer in unity before protest.

03/29/16 – Another friend gave me a message from God.

04/00/16 – I came up with the name for Lady Justice Films.

04/03/16 – God gave me a message to post to FB.

04/07/16 – God gave me a message to post on FB.

04/10/16 – 1st day of the protest.

04/11/16 – 2nd day of the protest. Lady Justice and Lady Justice Resource Services have been established.

04/12/16 – 3rd day of the protest. At 6:38 a.m., God gave me a message.

04/13/16 – 4th day of the protest.

04/14/16 – 5th day of the protest.

04/15/16 – 6th day of the protest.

04/16/16 – 7th day of the protest. In the morning I heard, "Get up, get up time for your breakthrough."

06/02/16 – God gave me a revelation.

07/13/16 – I secured two more business names.

08/18/16 – At 10:23 p.m., I emailed a gentleman and thanked him for guidance.

02/22/17 – I posted photos of all who participated in my injustice experience.

02/27/17 – At 4:05 p.m., I received a response from another law firm with the transcript. from www.Findlaw.com.

02/28/17 – At 6:26 a.m., I sent a note to myself for President Trump but never mailed it to the President.

02/28/17 – At 6:32 a.m., I sent a note to myself regarding 1/18/17.

06/00/17 – I contacted the UN Humanitarian Council through their ethernet server.

06/05/17 – At 6:55 p.m., the UN Humanitarian Council contacted me by email.

06/06/17 – At 2:03 p.m., I faxed a letter to the UN Humanitarian Council.

06/07/17 – At 11:11 p.m., the UN Humanitarian Council contacted me by email.

06/08/17 – At 7:50 a.m., I responded to the UN Humanitarian Council by email.

06/08/17 – At 7:52 a.m., I contacted the UN Humanitarian Council by email.

07/21/17 – A wise man said to me, "It don't run in our blood to give up easily."

02/27/18 – I submitted a new inquiry to www.Findlaw.com. A response on February 27, 2018 at 4:05 p.m.

07/07/18 – I heard, "You don't have a choice, it's mandatory. You either fall in line or fall behind."

08/08/18 – God gave me a song.

09/04/18 – I contacted President Donald Trump regarding injustice.

09/12/18 – The White House received my letter.

09/30/18 – God said, "A time for retribution is coming!" spoken at 4:36 p.m.

11/20/18 – The White House contacted me.

12/14/18 – I contacted Texas Department of Insurance – Division of Workers' Compensation.

12/14/18 – Division of Workers' Comp faxed me Broadspire denial.

12/14/18 – I learned adjuster was no longer with Broadspire.

12/16/18 – I completed Workers' Compensation complaint form.

12/17/18 – I left a voice mail message with Broadspire.

12/18/18 – File fraud complaint against Broadspire – New Hampshire Insurance Company on DWC154.

12/18/18 – File Fraud complaint against Vangent/GDIT on DWC154/faxed to TWC.

12/18/18 – I received an email regarding intake packet and instructions.

12/20/18 – Intake packet was mailed from Office of Injured Employee Counsel.

12/20/18 – I faxed completed intake packet and 26 pages to Office of Injured Employee Counsel.

01/02/19 – Case development appointment with OIEC.

01/08/19 – Received notice from TDI – Workers' Comp Division on complaint number 241971 for GDIT.

01/09/19 – I faxed updated Medical Providers List/Hippa Authorization to ombudsman of OIEC.

01/11/19 – I received notice of causation letters mailed to medical Providers.

01/11/19 – Received notice from TDI – Workers' Comp Division on complaint number 241975 for Broadspire.

01/23/19 – I was driving one day/God gave me a vision for Lady Justice Resource Services.

01/30/19 – I faxed Dr. S.A. Husain office regarding completing packet from OIEC.

01/30/19 – I faxed Dr. C. Callaco office regarding completing packet from OIEC.

02/01/19 – I faxed Dr. M. Mussahi office regarding completing packet from OIEC.

02/15/19 – I contacted Harris Health by phone to release my records to OIEC.

02/15/19 – I faxed Harris Health System the HIPPA form and requested my medical records be released to OIEC.

02/21/19 – I received a call from OIEC.

03/19/19 – I contacted TDI at 11:45 a.m., regarding problem report Id: 241971 for GDIT.

03/19/19 – I contacted TDI at 11:48 a.m., regarding problem report Id: 241975 for Broadspire.

03/19/19 – I received a letter from OIEC to place case on hold.

00/00/19 – I contacted Harris Health to get a sooner appointment.

03/28/19 – I visited Harris Health for causation review and she refuse to complete the papers.

04/08/19 – I contacted TDI by phone to follow-up on problem report Id: 241971 for GDIT.

05/15/19 – I received notice of Benefit Review Conference.

05/16/19 – I received notice from OIEC regarding appointment for 5/31/19 at 11:00 a.m.

05/17/19 – I received notice from OIEC regarding appointment for 6/4/19 at 3:00 p.m.

06/04/19 – I received notice from TDI for fraud complaint #241971, against GDIT

06/09/19 – I contacted TDI, Division of Workers' Comp – Compliance & Investigation (MS-8)

06/18/19 – I attended hearing, Benefit Review Conference for Workers' Comp claim.

06/20/19 – I downloaded open records request form.

06/21/19 – I completed TWC open records request.

06/21/19 – I received email confirmation from TWC open records department & responded.

06/25/19 – I contacted TWC – Open Records Department.

06/25/19 – I received a letter from TWC regarding Request Job#: 190621-008 for unemployment insurance claim.

06/25/19 – I received a letter from TWC regarding Request Job#: 190621-009 for Civil Rights Division.

07/01/19 – I received an invoice from TWC regarding Open Records Request.

07/03/19 – I contacted a doctor to get help with Worker's Comp.

07/03/19 – I contacted attorney for help with Worker's Comp.

07/03/19 – I contacted OIEC.

07/05/19 – I contacted OIEC.

07/07/19 – I asked God, What is a good title for my book?

07/08/19 – God answered me with book title.

07/09/19 – I contacted TDI for problem report Id: 241971 for Vangent/GDIT

07/16/19 – I missed call from OIEC.

07/17/19 – I was contacted by Therapy Center.

07/18/19 – I visited the Therapy Center.

07/19/19 – I viewed an interesting post my friend shared regarding, "specialized docket".

07/23/19 – I contacted Therapy Center to give medication list.

07/23/19 – I contacted OIEC.

07/23/19 – I contacted TWC, Open Records Department and received documents.

07/24/19 – I contacted Therapy Center and was given name of insurance adjuster and telephone number.

07/26/19 – I received a copy of request no. 190621-009 for EEOC.

07/26/19 – I contacted Open Records by phone regarding request no. 190621-008 for unemployment.

08/05/19 – I received email from TWC regarding EEOC request.

08/06/19 – I received documents from TWC on the Unemployment request, 190621-008.

08/15/19 – I visited the Therapy Center.

08/20/19 – I contacted the therapy center office to verify if Harris Health System released my records.

08/20/19 – I completed and faxed HIPPA form to Harris Health for the Therapy Center.

08/20/19 – I sent the therapy center a copy of the fax and confirmation sheet.

08/29/19 – I contacted OIEC and left a message.

08/30/19 – I contacted TWC and asked for the Ombudsman of the Civil Rights Department.

09/13/19 – I contacted the Therapy Center to verify medical records was received.

09/16/19 – I visited the Therapy Center.

09/16/19 – God spoke to me.

09/00/19 – I viewed my medical records.

09/18/19 – I faxed OIEC new medical provider.

09/23/19 – I contacted OIEC by phone.

09/25/19 – I received request from Flahive, Ogden & Latson Attorney At Law, P.C.

09/25/19 – I faxed OIEC the request received from Flahive, Ogden & Latson Attorney At Law, P.C.

09/27/19 – I completed Harris Health HIPPA form for all parties and faxed to medical records department.

09/28/19 – God gave me a song.

09/30/19 – I contacted Harris Health to verify fax received.

10/07/19 – I visited the therapy center.

10/09/19 – I visited Harris Health to get a copy of records for myself.

10/13/19 – God gave me a song.

10/17/19 – God gave me a song.

10/30/19 – God spoke to me.

10/30/19 – I visited Harris Health Administration.

11/06/19 – I visited the therapy center.

11/13/19 – I visited the pulmonary specialist I was referred to.

Events Outside of My Journey for Justice
Timeline of Events as they unfolded regarding several circumstances.

09/00/13 – Unforeseen Circumstance #1, Transportation Service Help!

02/15/15 – Unforeseen Circumstance #2, Rear ended by male driver.

00/00/15 – Young Men Experience - Police/Vehicle Profiling

10/29/15 – Unforeseen Circumstance #3, Injured on leasing property

11/09/15 – Emergency Housing Inspection

11/10/15 – 2nd Emergency Housing Inspection

12/10/16 – Unforeseen Circumstance #4, Auto Accident/Baytown, Tx.,

12/14/16 – Contacted Baytown Police Department records department

12/16/16 – Contacted Baytown Police Department to follow-up on crash report

12/28/16 – Contacted Baytown Police Department to follow-up and crash report was still not ready.

01/05/17 – While visiting Ophthalmologists, Medical Assistant introduced to Tuan & Associates.

01/06/17 – Unforeseen Circumstance #5, I visited Tuan & Associates for consultation/emailed paperwork

Elderly Assistance - Help! Contacted by family to assist.

07/18/17 – Contacted Internal Affairs at Baytown Police Department

08/02/17 – Internal Affairs at Baytown Police Department

08/04/17 – Internal Affairs at Baytown Police Department

00/00/00 – Contacted Notified Tuan & Associates and informed the office of the internal investigation

08/30/17 – Contacted Txdot to get a copy of the crash report.

09/13/17 – Sent attorney supplemental crash report/ proof of insurance

10/00/17 – I was deployed to Dallas for Briefing, ,training and Federal Clearance

11/00/17 – Signed lease with Northpoint for home in Cypress, Tx

02/14/18 – Visit Postal Station regarding mail for Cypress, Tx

02/23/18 – Attorney Lindley filed in court

03/00/18 – Crown Eagle Realty took over property/ gave notice to move out

04/26/18 – Unforeseen Circumstance #6, Contacted School Assault/

2016 – 2019 Bully Teacher Cypress Fair District

06/05/18 – Unforeseen Circumstance #7, Medical Malpractice/Dentist

07/05/18 – Helped Navy Veteran complete grievance

07/06/18 – Mailed request for file from Tuan Khuu, Dallas

07/06/18 – Mailed request for file from Tuan Khuu, Houston by Certified Mail 7/10/18

07/12/18 – State Bar received complaint for Navy Veteran

07/27/18 – Navy Veteran received complaint back

08/02/18 – Tuan Khuu and Associates release the Navy Veteran

08/14/18 – Unforeseen Circumstance #8, Crown Eagle Realty 2nd 3 day notice/pay rent or move out.

08/20/18 – Crown Eagle Realty cashed check/ filed wrongful eviction on the same day.

8/21/18 – Phone communication

09/11/18 – Missed the court date

09/11/18 – God lead me to the place in my dreams, we signed lease.

09/12/18 – Agent called, "Can we work something out?"

09/20/18 – Received documents from Court

10/19/18 – Visited Precinct 5

10/22/18 – Visited Precinct 5

11/16/18 – Requested my file for the 3rd time from Tuan Khuu &Associates

11/29/18 – Contacted Allstate

00/00/00 – Contacted Texas Department of Insurance regarding improper denial from Allstate on 12/10/16 accident

12/02/18 – Completed online grievance/ State Bar, against Cindy Purinton

12/03/18 – Completed online grievance/ State Bar, against Tuan Khuu

12/03/18 – Contacted Allstate

12/13/18 – Faxed grievance with documents/ State Bar, against Tuan Khuu

12/13/18 – Faxed grievance with documents/ State Bar, against Cindy Purinton

12/14/18 – Faxed/supporting document to State Bar, against Cindy Purinton

12/14/18 – Faxed/ supporting document to State Bar, against Tuan Khuu

12/18/18 – Contacted NAACP in Baltimore, MD/ Officer misconduct at Baytown

12/18/18 – Contacted ACLU in New York, NY/ Officer misconduct at Baytown

12/18/18 – Contacted State Bar of Texas

12/18/18 – Filed grievance/State Bar, against Tuan Khuu

12/18/18 – Filed grievance/State Bar, against Cindy Purinton

01/02/19 – Received letter/State Bar, Investigator Intro.

01/02/19 – Received letter/State Bar, Tuan Khuu not licensed in Texas

01/29/19 – Cindy Purinton response/ grievance

01/31/19 – Received notice/State Bar, Cindy Purinton response/ grievance.

02/14/19 – Helped Navy Veteran/ documentation

02/20/19 – Received notice/State Bar, supplemental response/Purinton

02/26/19 – Wrote rebuttal for Cindy Purinton response

02/28/19 – Filed my rebuttal for Cindy Purinton response

03/11/19 – Navy Veteran received letter from State Bar

03/14/19 – Navy Veteran received letter/State Bar, Tuan Khuu

04/03/19 – Received State Bar notice of hearing

05/15/19 – Purinton sent the Navy Veteran documents

05/15/19 – Purinton/sent release I filed in court

05/29/19 – Received State Bar notice/change of Assistant Disciplinary Counsel

06/05/19 – Attended State Bar Hearing against Cindy Purinton

06/12/19 – Received State Bar notice/dismissal of grievance filed against CP on 12/13/18.

07/29/19 – Navy Veteran received letter/State Bar, Summary Disposition Panel docket

07/29/19 – Navy Veteran received letter/State Bar, regarding determination

11/08/19 – Visited Attorney

11/08/19 – Phone communication with Precinct 5

11/09/19 – Phone communication with Precinct 5

11/11/19 – Learned devastating news

ABOUT THE AUTHOR

Ellenor P. Ratcliff serves as a Humanitarian (www.ladyjusticetx.org) in Houston, Texas. She mentors' youth and writes poetry and has written three manuscripts for children books.

Stay connected. You will find the author's book tour, poetry release dates, as well as new book releases www.ellenorpratcliffauthor.com.

NOTES